Quantum and Consciousness Revisited

Quantum and Consciousness Revisited

Editors

Menas C. Kafatos
Debashish Banerji
Daniele C. Struppa

Nalanda
Consciousness Network

PRINTWORLD
Publishers of Indian Traditions

Cataloging in Publication Data — DK
[Courtesy: D.K. Agencies (P) Ltd. <docinfo@dkagencies.com>]

Quantum and consciousness revisited / editors, Menas C. Kafatos, Debashish Banerji, Daniele C. Struppa.
pages cm
ISBN 9788124612606 (HB)

1. Consciousness. 2. Quantum theory. 3. Philosophy and science. I. Kafatos, Minas C., editor. II. Banerji, Debashish, editor. III. Struppa, Daniele Carlo, 1955- editor. IV. Nalanda Consciousness Network (Los Angeles, Calif.), publisher.

LCC B105.C477Q36 2024 | DDC 126 23

ISBN 978-81-246-1260-6
First published in India 2024

Editors: Menas C. Kafatos (b.1945); Debashish Banerji (b.1954); Daniele C. Struppa (b.1955)

Published by:
Nalanda Consciousness Network
"Nalanda", 6418, Spring Park Avenue
Los Angeles, CA - 90056 (USA)
Phones: (310)-430-8057

and

D.K. Printworld (P) Ltd.
Regd. Office : "Vedaśrī", F-395, Sudarshan Park
ESI Hospital Metro Station, New Delhi - 110015
Phones : (011) 4172 2626, 98713 94815
e-mail : indology@dkprintworld.com
Web : www.dkprintworld.com

Printed by: D.K. Printworld (P) Ltd., New Delhi

Dedicated to
Those who pioneered the Copenhagen Interpretation
and founded the philosophy of Quantum Physics
and the Role of Mind in it:

Niels H.D. Bohr, Werner K. Heisenberg,
Wolfgang E. Pauli, Erwin R.J.A. Schrödinger,
John von Neumann, Henry P. Stapp.

Contents

Introduction: Open Questions of Quantum Mechanics and Consciousness — 1
— *Debashish Banerji, Menas C. Kafatos, Daniele C. Struppa*

1. Resolving Mysteries of Quantum Mechanics and Consciousness — 15
— *Stanley A. Klein*

2. The Quantum Conception of Man: A Tribute and Short Interview with Henry P. Stapp — 51
— *Christopher Cochran*

3. On the Wave Function Collapse and Mind–Matter Interaction — 61
— *Jose Acacio de Barros*

4. Zeno Goes to Copenhagen: A Dilemma for Measurement-collapse Interpretations of Quantum Mechanics — 83
— *David J. Chalmers, Kelvin J. McQueen*

5. Quantum-like Reality — 113
— *Sudip Patra, Menas C. Kafatos*

6. Bohr, QBism and Beyond — 163
— *Ulrich Mohrhoff*

7. Quantum Paradoxes: To Resolve or To Acquiesce 197
— *Ruth E. Kastner*

8. The Epistemic View of Quantum Reality 217
— *Subhash Kak*

9. Gödel's Incompleteness Theorems, Complementarity and Fundamental Awareness 251
— *Neil D. Theise, Goro C. Kato, Menas C. Kafatos*

10. Complexity Theory and Quantum-like Qualities in Biology 285
— *Neil D. Theise*

11. Biologists Ponder: Omnipresent Consciousness? – Implications for Animal Mind, Human–Animal Relationships and Animal Well-Being 311
— *Carolyn A. Ristau, Eric G. Strauss*

Contributors 357

Index 367

Introduction
Open Questions of Quantum Mechanics and Consciousness

Debashish Banerji, Menas C. Kafatos, Daniele C. Struppa

The Modern Age and Classical Science

If there is one thing by which the age in which we live, the modern age, will be known, it is science. Some may say it is technology, but behind the ubiquity of technology in our times stand science and capital. Technology is the capitalization of science, the expression of the will to power in our times applied to the will to knowledge as science. In stating it like this, it is not the predominance of science as a discipline among other disciplines that is meant but as the mode of our modern existence, the assumptions that frame reality for us theoretically and methodically. In fact, to talk of "disciplines" is already to assume the scientific method, a "disciplined" form of inquiry and a consequent way of "disciplining" the world. But even more central than method is the theoretical foundation of modernity as a mode of knowing, a centring of the subject in the rational ego (cogito) and a separation and objectification of the world under the assumption that universal knowledge is available to the human being due to the rational (causal) constitution of reality. This "separation" of human as subject from nature and all its objects completed the transition from a pre-modern world to a world of humanism, the age of the human, between the sixteenth and seventeenth centuries, in what has been called the Enlightenment. The human, here, was understood as sufficient in its power to know and master Nature, whether inanimate or animate. "Nature", "World", "Self" and "God" were all considered abstract categories, unknowable or non-existent in themselves and conceptualized only in the human mind as the universal totality of their constituents. These constituents were grounded in foundational "entities" conceived analogically on the model of objectifiable sense-reality, ultimate particles, the "dust of substance", or atoms, the building blocks of the material world and thereby of all reality. Actually, atomism goes back to *c*. 5th century BCE to Leucippus and his student Democritus of Abdera. In this philosophical belief system, consciousness was considered, if at all, an epiphenomenon of material atomicity. Such sufficiency had no place for transcendental agency and implied an absolute independence of the individual united with other humans through universal knowledge premised on the fulfilment of rationality, the human mastery of the world and itself. This is the mode of existence of our modern world, centred in the monadic individual ego, seated in the rational omniscience of material knowledge and its application, the ultimate fulfilment of the Enlightenment.

This separation of the subject and its radical pluralization in individuality, from its entanglement with nature and its constituents, leading to the isolated independent individual of our times, occurred through a gradual transition from the fifteenth to eighteenth centuries, in a shift of the dependence of man on God and his authorized spokespersons, the Church, to a properly Godless world explainable by science in itself. If the Church lost its authority over knowledge, those who continued to believe in God, either thought of Him as a non-interfering transcendental clockmaker, who had set the universe into action using rational laws, giving humans the power of reason to understand and perfect its workings, the position of deism;

or, if he did not entirely leave the world to its own devices, God intervened predictably to balance out the anomalies of the clockwork. The latter position was held, for instance, by Sir Isaac Newton, the single greatest representative of what has been called "classical physics". Newton's laws mathematized a predictable cosmos at all known scales, from natural phenomena to astronomical ones. Newton, a religious Christian, could not find it in his conscience to affirm the theological foundations of the Church, yet struggled to affirm God's agency in his predictable cosmos. He hypothesized such invisible agency in gravitational action and surmised the eventual collapse of the celestial system unless reset periodically by God. Gottfried Wilhelm Liebniz, a contemporary of Newton and simultaneous co-founder of calculus as a mathematical tool, though not a contributor to science and more recognized as an Enlightenment philosopher, assumed a stance closer to deism in ridiculing Newton for a God who did not have the power to set up a "perpetual motion" cosmos, needing to intervene periodically in its workings. Many of those on whose shoulders Newton himself had rested (in his own telling), had their own ambivalent dealings with the Church as well as with other spiritual and occult lineages. Newton's investigations into gravity had their roots in the astronomical studies and the heliocentric theories of Copernicus, Galileo and Kepler. All these had their conflicted relations with the Church and with belief in God, who increasingly replaced the image of an inscrutable transcendent being by that of a supreme mathematician, who had made human being in his image by providing him/her with his prime faculty, reason, for fully understanding and appreciating His cosmic design. Likewise, Newton drew on Robert Boyle for his theories on light as well as on aspects of his philosophical vision. Boyle's theories were founded on a braiding of rational science and occult alchemy, influencing Newton to become a serious student of alchemy. Similarly, Copernicus, who was the first of the Renaissance thinkers to replace the geocentric cosmology of the Church with a heliocentric cosmology, relied for his ideas as much on his measurements as on Hermetic philosophy, which was circulating as part of the countercultural knowledge of his times. Boyle was among the early explicit proponents of the "clockwork universe" and Pierre-Simon Laplace (1749–1827) perfected the argument, asserting a primary tenet of the timeless determination of the classical world view that complete knowledge of the present state of the world implied the predictability of its past and future with unlimited precision.

Whatever the remnants of pre-modern understanding, the drive to explain reality in terms of matter subject to rational laws of causation, inevitably removed any necessity for transcendental agency or influence, whether that of the Christian God or any other spiritual or mental origin. Philosophy itself, lost its importance as an inquiry into truth, with the exception of natural philosophy, which, subject to scientific method, renamed itself science, laying total claim to the field of knowledge. The advancement of science and its application as technology had no end, it seemed, through the eighteenth and nineteenth centuries, in laying bare the secrets of nature and turning it to human advantage. But from the mid-nineteenth century, this world view began being questioned, at first in the fields of philosophy and culture, and then in science itself. The scientific challenge to the classical world view was preceded by the development of new tools of investigation as well as shifts and corrections in established theory through the nineteenth century. Thomas Young and Augustin Fresnel were responsible for the replacement of the particle or "corpuscular" theory of light established by Laplace and Newton, by the wave theory. This, combined with the development of thermodynamics, introduced the need for new adjustments to the theories of heat, electromagnetism and energy in general and a shift in method to statistical mathematics and interpretations, as introduced by Ludwig Boltzmann and others. The idea of temporal irreversibility in the Second Law of Thermodynamics, added to Charles Darwin's theory of evolution, shook the certainty of the foundations of the reversible and causally determined world, and statistical methods were increasingly understood to be the adequate means to investigate temporally unpredictable random processes, such as radioactivity and Brownian motion.

Transition to Quantum Mechanics

The period between 1900 and 1925 has been called "Old Quantum Theory". It consisted of the application of statistical methods to interpret atomic structure. It was inaugurated in 1900 by Max Planck's work on black body radiation leading to his quantum hypothesis regarding energy. This was followed by Albert Einstein's proposition of the quantized nature of light in 1905 and its modification to the dual properties of particle and wave in 1909. Niels Bohr's model of the hydrogen atom showing quantized electron orbitals was presented in 1913 and Louis de Broglie's introduction of the wave theory of matter in 1924 is one of the other significant developments in quantum theory during this exciting period of origins of the quantum nature of matter and energy. During this period of the Old Quantum Theory, calculations assuming the quantized nature of energy and subatomic particles such as electrons and photons were seen as adjustments to the classical viewpoint, which continued to assume an overall deterministic objective reality. At the same time, the increasing reliance on statistical methods encouraged a turn towards ontological indeterminacy. The transition from this phase to full-fledged quantum physics can be dated to 1925, when Werner Heisenberg described electron behaviour in terms of emission and absorption of light frequencies using matrices for position and momentum. In 1926, Erwin Schrödinger developed his theory of wave mechanics, at the heart of which was his wave equation. Through the interpretive mediation of Max Born, this equation was shown to be an improvement on Heisenberg's matrices in predicting quantum probabilities of subatomic particles such as photons and electrons, and their behaviour in interactions. In 1927, Heisenberg presented his uncertainty principle which asserted the coupled indeterminacy in the measurement of position and momentum of particles. Combined with quantum wave mechanics, this led to the notion of the probability wave function and heightened the conundrum of the particle–wave duality, in terms of epistemology (a problem of knowledge) and ontology (the nature of reality).

The split between these two views can be compared to the Copernican revolution at the turn of the sixteenth and seventeenth centuries in terms of what it implied for human understanding of reality. In fact, the Copernican revolution can be considered the inauguration of the modern view of reality represented by classical physics, an objective reality determined by cause and effect, that functioned mathematically independent of consciousness, but which consciousness could ultimately understand through the use of reason. In place of this reality, there was now a world of uncertainty, with a parting of the ways between those that felt uncertainty was a function of human ignorance (the epistemological argument) and those who held that reality was marked by uncertainty (the ontological argument) and consciousness played a part in giving it the form in which we experienced it. The gap between these two positions grew increasingly into a gulf. Among the most prominent of those who continued to hold to the independent world of predictable laws was Einstein, who despite playing a major part in the early development of quantum mechanics, insisted that the objective world had no need for subjective factors. He was supported in his realism by Max Planck, de Broglie and Schrödinger. On 4 December 1926, in response to the use of the Schrödinger equation on Heisenberg's findings, Einstein wrote famously to Max Born:

> Quantum mechanics is very impressive. But an inner voice tells me that it is not yet the real thing. The theory produces a

> good deal but hardly brings us closer to the secret of the Old One. I am at all events convinced that He does not play dice.
> – Born and Einstein 2005: 90

The Copenhagen Interpretation

On the other hand, scientists working at Niels Bohr's laboratory at the Institute for Theoretical Physics, the University of Copenhagen, took an ontological view of quantum uncertainty, that has come to be called the Copenhagen Interpretation of Quantum Mechanics. The principal founding figures involved in this interpretation were Niels Bohr and his assistant during the years 1926-27, Werner Heisenberg. Though Bohr and Heisenberg did not follow exactly the same approach in their interpretation of Quantum Theory, they both denied the independent existence of an objective reality. Based on his theory of uncertainty, Heisenberg asserted that the linked fuzziness in the momentum and position of quantum-level entities was not due to the inability or limits of measurement devices but rather due to ontological incertitude. He attributed this stand to Niels Bohr in a note to his article introducing his uncertainty principle in 1927:

> Bohr has brought to my attention [that] the uncertainty in our observation does not arise exclusively from the occurrence of discontinuities, but is tied directly to the demand that we ascribe equal validity to the quite different experiments which show up in the [particulate] theory on one hand and in the wave theory on the other hand. – Heisenberg 1983: 83

This statement was in part aimed at what has been called the EPR Paradox, the proposal by Albert Einstein, Boris Podolsky and Nathan Rosen to argue that quantum particles must have definite position and momentum even without being measured, which means that quantum mechanics was an incomplete theory. The EPR Paradox opened up the search for "hidden-variables" among those who wished to conserve the deterministic model of quantum cosmology. One of the solutions this led to was the non-local hidden variable theory of David Bohm in 1952. Following Heisenberg's announcement of the uncertainty principle, in September 1927, Bohr presented his principle of complementarity, according to which quantum objects have pairs of complementary properties which cannot be observed or measured simultaneously. Position and momentum was one such pair; another was their existence as particles and waves. Bohr's principle asserted that the behaviour of atomic and subatomic objects could not be separated from the measuring instruments that created the context in which these objects operated. As against the classical objective view, this was an acknowledgement of a reality in which subject and object were inseparable. Though there were variations in interpretation regarding what this meant, this inseparability of subject and object came to be known as the Copenhagen Interpretation, after the location of Bohr's laboratory. Along with Heisenberg's uncertainty principle and Bohr's complementarity, the Copenhagen Interpretation included Bohr's Principle of Correspondence, which asserted that quantum behaviour, when observed in the limit of large quantum numbers, corresponded to a classical description of reality.

The proponents of the Copenhagen Interpretation had nuanced differences. Whereas Bohr's statement could be taken as a Kantian acknowledgment of human inability to know "the thing-in-itself", with its corresponding dismissal of a causational model, Heisenberg was more decidedly assertive about an anti-materialist view of the Copenhagen Interpretation. He rejected "an objective real world whose smallest parts exist objectively in the same sense as stones or trees exist, independently of whether or not we observe them". Another adherent of the Copenhagen Interpretation during its founding phase was Max Born, who published his statistical interpretation of wave mechanics in 1926, for which he received the Nobel Prize in 1954. The subjective side of the Copenhagen Interpretation was underlined by John von Neumann who affirmed in 1927 that Bohr's Correspondence Principle implied a state transition from a quantum probability wave to determinate behaviour following a "collapse" of the probability wave, an event that he attributed to the consciousness of the observer by 1932. In a more recent continuation of von Neumann's postulate, in 1962, Eugene Wigner proposed a thought experiment to show that "the mind" was the true agent responsible for "the collapse of the probability wave".

The Return of Realism

By 1935, the classical deterministic view of reality was subordinated by the principal conclusions of the Copenhagen Interpretation, such as the inseparability of subject and object, Heisenberg's quantum indeterminacy and Bohr's correspondence and complementarity principles. This was the result of intense debates between the figures mentioned above, often centred around Einstein and Niels Bohr. One can sense the excitement of these years and the seismic importance attributed to interpretations of reality based on the introduction of Quantum Physics. However, Eugene Wigner notwithstanding, the post-Second World War world was much less interested in the revolutionary views that seemed to shake the understanding of reality from 1920 to 1940. The subjective dimension was underplayed, if not forgotten. Max Born, who may be considered a proponent of the Copenhagen Interpretation in its founding stages, stated in 1949:

> I personally like to regard a probability wave, even in 3N-dimensional space, as a real thing, certainly as more than a tool for mathematical calculation. – Born 1964: 107

Victor S. Weisskopf, in his 1958 review of physics and philosophy, contradicted Heisenberg by writing that atomic reality "is as good as any other concept of reality ... the fact that atomic phenomena are hard to catch and hard to describe does not make them less real". However, neither Born nor Weisskopf rejected the Copenhagen Interpretation; but its speculative and subjective side was replaced by a return of realism. In the 1950s and 1960s, there were also a variety of alternatives proposed to the Copenhagen Interpretation, including:

1. a classical statistical interpretation along the lines suggested by Einstein making it compatible with deterministic behaviour. According to this view, quantum mechanics was incomplete;
2. several "hidden-variables" theories must apply, the best known being that proposed by David Bohm from 1951. While it explains quantum uncertainty and complementarity in an objective fashion, it also assumes non-locality and, in his late work, a conscious universe; and
3. the "many worlds" interpretation of Hugh Everett, proposed in 1957 and supported by Neil Graham and Bryce DeWitt.

Following this phase, there has been an increasing tendency to ignore the fact that Quantum Physics seriously problematizes the post-Enlightenment classical view of the objective material cosmos as the foundation of reality. In 1964, Richard Feynman said in a lecture, "I think I can safely say that nobody understands quantum mechanics". In 1989, N. David Mermin wrote: "If I were forced to sum up in one sentence what the Copenhagen Interpretation says to me, it would be 'Shut up and calculate!' This situation continues into our times." A 2016 survey of physicists, conducted by Sujeevan Sivasundaram and Kristian Hvidtfelt Nielsen at Aarhus University in Denmark, shows that a small number of physicists understand the foundational concepts of quantum mechanics – such as a reality in which a particle's position is undetermined until measured, as described by the wave function; and only a minority of respondents had an understanding of the measurement problem that launched the field.

Metaphysical Frameworks

Among the principal reasons for the reluctance of post-1950s physicists to conjecture philosophical explanations for the original quantum mechanics is the subjective implications of the theory. It is interesting to note, in this regard, how deeply invested in philosophy the founding figures of the quantum revolution were. Distanced from Christian theology but also from the deterministic objective materialism of the classical model, several of these figures looked to Eastern philosophies for explanations. Both subjectivity and consciousness found a central place in these views, though the origin and scope of consciousness differed from version to version. Heisenberg is known to have said that Bohr was more of a philosopher than a physicist and it has been noted that Bohr was strongly influenced in his views by Søren Kierkegaard and William James. He also acknowledged the influence of Daoism, adopting the Yin–Yang diagram of Daoism in his coat of arms after he was knighted, a model that was obviously related to his Complementarity Principle. Heisenberg, Wolfgang Ernst Pauli, Schrödinger and Bohm were all deeply interested in Vedāntic thought, which posited a non-dual consciousness at the foundation of reality, whether objective or subjective. Pauli introduced important consequences of quantum mechanics related to chemistry and other aspects that led to the development of the atomic bomb. Troubled by these developments, he conducted important discussions with psychiatrist Carl Gustav Jung that led beyond interpretations of quantum mechanics to questions about human nature itself. This search for meaning beyond both Church and clockwork seems to have stagnated in our times. Yet, recent advances in physics and the reinterpretation of historic experiments have given us a new way to understand and ask fundamental questions about meaning.

Revisiting Consciousness and Meaning

In October 2019, Chapman University honoured Dr Henry P. Stapp for his outstanding contribution to the field of quantum physics and his courage to continue probing the dimension of meaning in quantum physics, invoking consciousness and a Cosmic Mind in accounting for consequences of the Copenhagen Interpretation. At this conference, several other theoretical physicists, representing different philosophical approaches to understanding the paradoxes uncovered by the revolution of quantum mechanics, came together to present their views. These views included further considerations of the Copenhagen Interpretation, the Transactional Interpretation of John G. Cramer and Ruth Krastner, Quantum Bayesianism (QBism) of Fuchs, Schack and David Mermin, and topics including the meaning of observation and measurement; the Orthodox view of quantum mechanics; some discussions about the role of gravity; collapse of the wave function, and time and quantum field theory. The Chapman conference was followed by one at the Loyola Marymount University which focused on the larger implications of quantum physics for philosophy, biology and global understanding. The present volume collects a number of these papers, along with others which all reopen the questions of consciousness and meaning which occupied the minds of the early thinkers of quantum physics. The editors of this volume, who were also co-organizers of both conferences, were inspired by the high excitement of these revaluations of meaning and felt the time was opportune for reinitiating thought about the founding implications of quantum mechanics. The product of this inspiration is this collection of eleven essays on re-evaluating the Copenhagen Interpretation philosophically as well as adding new interpretive views to the quantum phenomenon and extending these philosophical implications to wider fields such as consciousness studies, mathematics and biology.

Since the idea of the volume arose from the event felicitating Henry Stapp, a "chip of the old block", who has continued his work from the 1950s with Wolfgang Pauli, Werner Heisenberg and John Archibald Wheeler, to think about the consciousness implications of quantum mechanics and any further quantum developments in physics, we begin the collection with an essay by Stanley Klein summarizing the remarkable aspects of quantum physics and their implications for consciousness and thereby highlighting the contributions of Stapp. This is followed by an interview with Stapp conducted by Christopher Cochran. After this, there is an article by Jose Acacio de Barros which investigates, through a thought experiment, the "observer causes collapse" hypothesis of John von Neumann and Eugene Wigner, as extended by Stapp. This is followed by another investigation into the measurement-collapse of the Copenhagen Interpretation by David Chalmers and Kelvin McQueen. This consideration of quantum interpretations of reality is continued by the consideration of cognitive conformism, setting the ground for further views of the universe in its foundation as being quantum-like, by Sudip Patra and Menas Kafatos. This is followed by Ulrich Mohrhoff's hearkening to the origins of the Copenhagen view in Niels Bohr in comparison with the views of Erwin Schrödinger and contemporary QBism. An alternative to the Copenhagen Interpretation, that of the Transactional Interpretation, follows in a chapter by Ruth Kastner. These direct considerations of the interpretations of quantum mechanics are followed by its wider implications, such as an information theoretic consideration of the symbolic logic of quantum reality by Subhash Kak. After this is a chapter by Neil Theise, Goro Kato and Menas Kafatos on the implications of complementarity as proposed by Niels Bohr in relation to Gödel's mathematical Incompleteness Theorems. This is followed by Neil Theise's consideration of quantum-like processes in biology; and the volume concludes with Carolyn Ristau's and Eric Strauss' chapter on the consciousness implications of quantum mechanics as applied to animal consciousness and human–animal relations, setting perhaps the ground for even more general future implications between the human quantum system interactions.

References

Born, M., 1964, *Natural Philosophy of Cause and Chance*, Dover.

Born, M. and A. Einstein, 2005, *Born-Einstein Letters, 1916-1955: Friendship, Politics and Physics in Uncertain Times*, London: Macmillan Science.

Heisenberg, W., 1983, "The Physical Contents of Quantum Kinematics and Mechanics", in *Quantum Theory and Measurement*, ed. J.A. Wheeler and W.H. Zurek, Princeton, NJ: Princeton University Press.

1

Resolving Mysteries of Quantum Mechanics and Consciousness

Stanley A. Klein

Abstract: This chapter will focus on three of the deepest mysteries facing science:

a. What causes the collapse of the quantum wave function to go from amplitudes to probabilities and then to actualities?

b. How can science explain the subjective aspects of consciousness (qualia)? One possibility generated by Henry Stapp is that there is a special realm for subjectivity that is beyond quantum mechanics.

c. How might scientists respond to data about claims of paranormal (psychic) phenomena that many people believe in, even though it violates present science, somewhat similar to a belief in a powerful God.

These three mysteries will be called three realms. Stapp has played an important role in advancing all three of these mysteries. The final paragraph before the conclusion has the following important comment about the above three realms: "Thus before saying the other side is wrong it makes sense to work together".

Keywords: Quantum mechanics, collapse mechanisms, qualia/subjectivity, psychic phenomena.

1. Introduction

This chapter has five sections and three realms. The three realms are the following: Realm 1 is standard quantum mechanics (QM) going from amplitudes to probabilities and leads to standard science. Realm 2 goes beyond standard QM to possibly account for subjectivity without violating Realm 1. Realm 3 introduces approaches such as a powerful God or predicting the future that is forbidden by Realm 1. The five sections are the following. Section 1 will briefly introduce the three realms and then will discuss my interaction with Henry Stapp who will be featured especially in the last two sections. Section 2 will introduce the three realms and QM. Since dealing with complex quantum amplitudes requires a physics PhD, we will be quite brief in this section. Section 3 has an emphasis on going from probabilities to actualities, a most important section of this paper. Section 4 provides details for how Realm 1 might connect to Realm 2. Section 5 will focus on paranormal phenomena that will require Realm 3 to go beyond what science can handle.

To give a flavour of what to anticipate, it is useful to point out one of the strangest aspects of QM, i.e. Bell's theorem, showing that particles that are millions of miles apart can influence each other at infinite speed. Kafatos and Nadeau (1990) made the following awesome comment:

> As Henry Stapp puts it, non-locality could be the "most profound discovery in all of sciences".

An important aspect of this paper is to feature Stapp's contributions to physics. A powerful introduction to Stapp's writing skills is shown in his far-reaching article "Whitehead, James and the Ontology of Quantum Theory (2007)" in the journal *Mind and Matter*, available at https://www-physics.lbl.gov/~stapp/WJQO.pdf.

The present chapter will consider Stapp's contribution to three major mysteries facing science. It is because of his strong influence on me that he has a special role in this chapter. It is useful to subdivide the three mysteries into the following three realms.

REALM 1

This realm assumes that everything on earth, including humans and subjectivity, can be explained by six simple wavicles: electron, two quarks, gluon, photon and graviton. Beyond earth neutrinos and Z&W weak bosons are needed, as will be discussed in Sections 2 and 3. That list of six wavicles is much fewer than the eighteen wavicles that have been discovered. As will be discussed, the graviton is presently separated from the other wavicles.

Note that I have replaced the familiar word "particle" with "wavicle" that is actually more appropriate since each entity of QM can act as a particle under some given experimental conditions and as a wave under different conditions.

Section 2 discusses how of the eighteen known wavicles only the above six seem to be needed for life on earth. The theme of Section 3 is to explore the more than 20 different interpretations of QM, all of which surprisingly have identical predictions of experimental outcomes.

REALM 2

This option claims that something beyond quantum mechanics is needed to account for subjectivity (qualia). Stapp calls this realm "Cosmic Mind" as will be discussed in Section 4. This additional realm goes beyond adding extra wavicles to the present eighteen. Nature's Realm 2 does not violate Realm 1, it adds extra capabilities, including a science-compatible version of God.

REALM 3

This realm, to be discussed in Section 5, includes "miracles" that are not compatible with present classical physics. The focus is on the precognition (predicting the future) aspect of psychic phenomena that violates quantum mechanics. I very strongly recommend reading: https://en.wikipedia.org/wiki/Parapsychology for a powerful list of arguments pointing out the many flaws of psi. How to deal with various kinds of psychic phenomena, all of which violate present QM, will be discussed in Section 5. I agree with Stapp that psychic phenomena are likely to not be replicable, so careful experiments need to be done.

The rest of Section 1 will focus on Stapp's impact on me that is largely responsible for this article. It started with my physics PhD that was connected to understanding all the new wavicles being discovered at the Lawrence Berkeley Lab (where Stapp worked). The novel theories were either based on quarks following Gell-Mann (based at Caltech) or based on bootstraps following G. Chew and Stapp (based at Berkeley) with all the wavicles being made (bootstrapped) from each other! My PhD was on the Berkeley bootstrap approach. It was called a "bootstrap" because wavicles that are made out of each other is like being able to fly by pulling up on one's bootstraps. So my PhD experience got me to be open to Stapp's approach to quantum mechanics. The bootstrap lost out to the quarks in the mid-1970s. On the topic of influences on me, it is worth mentioning that in addition to Stapp the other great influence on me was Feynman. His strong influence on me started when I got a summer job in my Junior year at Caltech in Max Delbruck's lab. That summer Feynman spent one day a week in the same room I was in. I was totally lucky to be included as an author together with Feynman in a fancy biology paper (Edgar et al. 1962) due to my summer job. The two individuals who have had the greatest influence on me were Feynman and Stapp.

Stapp's influence on me has been continuous, going from

the mid-1960s, when I was working on the Berkeley bootstrap at Brandeis University. After my PhD, I spent the summers from 1968 to 1972 at the Lawrence Berkeley Lab that got me connected to Stapp (I'll use his first name for this section). However, string theory rapidly became too mathematically challenging for me, so I luckily switched to research in visual psychophysics. I was able to use my math skills in connecting perception to neural activity. However, I could never let go of my deep interest in the strange world of quantum physics, spending ten days at Esalen in 1976 with the "Hippies Who Saved Physics" (Kaiser 2011). Henry was the senior organizer. Although the hippies may not have saved physics, they influenced me to get the California DUALITY license plates for my cars since 1976. It is important to point out that a good fraction of the Esalen participants were believers in psychic phenomena, the topic of Section 5.

I joined the UC Berkeley Vision Science/Optometry faculty in 1987 and my interactions with Henry substantially increased. When I moved to Berkeley, in the daytime I did psychophysics (perception) and many nights I did psychophysics (Henry's version of the quantum collapse that included mind). My interactions with Henry resulted in my writing a book chapter titled "The Duality of Psycho-Physics" (Klein 1991).

A powerful indication that Henry believes that mind has an important connection to quantum mechanics can be seen in the titles of his three books: *Mind, Matter and Quantum Mechanics* (2009); *Mindful Universe: Quantum Mechanics and the Participating Observer* (2011) and *Quantum Theory and Free Will* (2017). It is clear from all three titles that Henry is fundamentally wanting to connect the two main mysteries of science: QM and mind. The importance of mind is exhibited by Henry's desire to refer to Nature as Cosmic Mind that is able to do more than standard quantum mechanics, as will be discussed in Section 4.

2. A Broad Overview of Realm 1 with an Introduction to Realms 2 and 3

REALM 1

At present, seven types of QM "wavicles" have been discovered (Table 1.1). For understandable details I highly recommend looking at: https://en.wikipedia.org/wiki/Particle_physics. That website provides lots of details of the standard wavicles.

The gluon, photon and graviton are all massless and are critical for holding the other wavicles together. The 7th wavicle is the graviton that is governed by Einstein's general relativity rather than quantum mechanics.

Table 1.1: The Seven Wavicle Categories

Wavicles	*Spin*	*Electric Charge*
1. Six leptons, with three like electrons with neutrino partners, are electron, muon, tau. Charge = 0 are the three neutrinos. The electron and may be its neutrino are probably sufficient for what is needed on earth	½	– 1 and 0 Charge = 1
2. Six quarks and only two are probably needed	½	⅔ and – ⅓
3. The gluon that holds the quarks together	1	0
4. Z and W weak bosons. They may not be needed on Earth!	1	0 For Z boson and -1 for W boson
5. The Higgs boson (gives above wavicles mass after Big Bang)	0	0 Also gives itself lots of mass
6. The photon (also produces electricity and magnetism!)	1	0
7. The graviton is stranger than all the others	2	0 Einstein's 1915 paper was awesome

It is strongly hoped that quantum mechanics and gravity will soon become connected. At present, the graviton is in a totally separate realm. At the Big Bang all the wavicles had mass = 0. Within less than a nanosecond after the Big Bang the Higgs wavicle gave massive particles their mass. The Higgs was finally discovered in 1964 after a forty-eight year search.

The proton and neutron are made by 3 quarks with electric charges of (⅔ , ⅔ , – ⅓) and (⅔ , – ⅓ , – ⅓) respectively. Incidentally, most physicists believe that life in our universe could have developed even if the electrons/neutrinos and quarks were reduced from triplets to singlets, giving a total of just 18 – 2 x 4 = 10 wavicles that could account for a universe with sentient creatures. In addition, I suspect that may be the two weak bosons, *Z* and *W*, and the electron's neutrino also are not needed for intelligent life on earth. Thus, for most of measurable things happening on earth, only six wavicles are needed: two quarks, gluon, electron, photon and graviton. I am omitting the Higgs by simply assuming that the quarks and electron have masses given to them at the Big Bang by the Higgs. The gluon is needed to hold three quarks together to produce the proton and neutron that are needed to make atoms!

A major assumption for Realm 1 is that our brains can produce qualia (subjectivity). I strongly recommend going to https://en.wikipedia.org/wiki/Qualia for details. At present, it is not clear how brains produce subjectivity. I believe that within the next 100 years it will be figured out. Another possibility is that a 19th wavicle (maybe to be named "psychon") will be discovered to do the job. How to bring the subjective realm to standard science is a lofty goal.

Realm 1 of standard science has the good news that major progress is being made on human and animal brains. Future technologies of safely stimulating human brains may enable science to learn how brains produce subjective states. It should be pointed out that Realm 1 is quite crazy as shown by the double-slit experiment with one slit being closed *AFTER* a photon or electron goes through it. Shockingly, the interference pattern is killed even though the particle is well beyond the slits when one slit is closed. Feynman would often point to this finding as one of the most crazy or unconventional aspects of quantum mechanics (recall the slit is closed *after* the photon passes the slits). Bell's Theorem (1964) provides a dramatically stronger craziness to QM, with the case of two entangled photons that are millions of miles apart. When the spin of one is measured, then at infinite speed the other one is modified according to the spin of the first one. How can that be? Luckily there is no way that one can use that infinite speed property to send information faster than the speed of light. This infinite speed collapse is one of the strangest aspects of QM.

It is important to point out that Realm 1 includes not only QM but also the rest of physics, chemistry, biology, neuroscience, psychology and pretty much the rest of what is taught at colleges and universities. The previous part of this section only dealt with a tiny overview of the quantum physics that goes from amplitudes to probabilities. We are not going further into the incredible complex QM of how the six wavicles discussed above interact. To go into the modern complexity of QM requires a PhD in physics. I did get a PhD in theoretical particle physics but string theory and the complex details of all the awesome interactions went over my head. The challenges of modern QM got me to switch from physics to vision science and neuroscience. What a lucky decision I made!

REALM 2

Although Stapp is open to the possibility of standard QM being responsible for subjectivity (Realm 1), he is also fully open to the possibility that subjectivity is outside of QM. The idea here is that there is a realm that is a totally separate realm with details to be discussed in Section 4. Stapp's Cosmic Mind, in Realm

2, assumes that subjectivity is not reducible to the underlying wavicles even if they get expanded beyond the present eighteen. Thus, for Stapp and for many religious folks, subjectivity needs to be a realm that is not a part of standard quantum mechanics. Section 4 will point out that Stapp's Cosmic Mind has strong similarities to the theology of John Cobb, a process theologian. It is amazing that Cobb's version of a compatibilist God is very similar to Stapp's version of Cosmic Mind. It is unfortunate that few people are aware that science and religion can be compatible, although in Eastern thought such as Buddhism, that is much more acceptable. Another example of compatibility is Francis Collins, the head of NIH, who is open to a separate realm that he refers to as God. I strongly recommend looking at his recent talk given in accepting the 2020 Templeton Prize (https://www.youtube.com/watch?v=hL6Ua8nXR7Y). Collins is a top scientist and deeply religious. It is because of these individuals who are connecting science and religion that Realm 2 has deep richness.

REALM 3

This is an extension of Cosmic Mind to a more powerful entity that many refer to as a form of God that can produce miracles. A very large fraction of the population of USA and the world belongs to this realm. There is a great diversity of traditions in the world that goes beyond science. There are some religions, or philosophies such as Buddhism, that have a version of God that is science compatible and would belong to Realms 1 and 2. Realm 3 opens up much richer possibilities for special miracles to take place. Our present world is so amazing that it is reasonable to act as though it was indeed a product of God. Most of the world's religious systems are based on the notion that a moral agent created the world. That attitude might help us be nicer about how we treat the planet and the creatures that inhabit it. Realm 3 involves a god who can do miracles of any sort, able to go far beyond the limits of Realms 1 and 2. We will come back to Realm 3 in our Section 5 discussion of precognition, the type of psychic phenomena that violate the laws of quantum mechanics.

In addition to introducing the three realms, the first part of Section 2 focused on Realm 1 going from quantum amplitudes to probabilities. It was a short introduction with only a brief comment on the eighteen wavicles with only six wavicles needed for life on earth: two quarks, gluon, electron, photon and graviton. Before departing from Section 2 it is very important to point out that other than listing the eighteen wavicles in Realm 1, there was close to zero mention of how those wavicles interact. It is important to at least mention that present physics has made great progress in developing very complex formalisms for explaining "almost" all of the phenomena taking place in our universe. The "almost" is due to data like dark matter, dark energy and subjectivity for which there is an over-abundance of theories on which progress is being made. Subjectivity will be discussed in Section 4. The wonderful Feynman diagrams work wonders for the weak interactions that involve photons, but for strong interactions Feynman diagrams are of minimal help, with much fancier approaches being needed. The next section discusses the strange mysteries of going from the probabilities to actualities, a much simpler, but quite crazy topic.

3. The Quantum Mystery of Going from Probabilities to Actualities

Before getting into the details of Section 3, it is important to point out that Section 2 was about going from amplitudes to *almost* probabilities. The reason that amplitudes cannot be probabilities is because amplitudes are complex numbers, whereas probabilities are real numbers. The "almost" is underlined because it is a major challenge to get to true probabilities, as will be mentioned in this section. It is important to distinguish a true probability from an almost probability.

This section is about why there are more than twenty

quite different interpretations of QM that all produce the exact same predictions (probabilities) for laboratory results. We will explore the multiple interpretations of QM starting with the impressive Wikipedia site: https://en.wikipedia.org/wiki/Interpretations_of_quantum_mechanics. The table at that website has fourteen rows of different interpretations of QM in chronological order and nine columns of different aspects of QM. The nine columns are: Deterministic, Wavefunction Real, Unique History, Hidden Variables, Collapsing Wavefunctions, Observer Role, Local Dynamics, Counterfactual Definiteness and Universal Wavefunction Exists. With only a few exceptions (such as a "maybe") the 14 x 9 entries are either "yes" or "no". No two rows have the same yes/no (or maybe) responses. It is important to emphasize that the Wikipedia site mentioned above not only has rich details of all the differences between the fourteen multiple interpretations, it also has comments on other interesting issues. For example, there is a section on Einstein's issues with QM and there is alink to "Minority Interpretations" that includes the following relevant comment: "These range from proposals by mainstream physicists to the more occult ideas of quantum mysticism". An article by Cochran and Klein (2017) presented an updated version of the above Wikipedia table and it is available at https://www.cosmosandhistory.org/index.php/journal/article/viewFile/596/1019.

Cochran and Klein (2017) paper has a critique of the Wikipedia overview that was presented in the preceding paragraph. The argument of our paper was that the multiple interpretations of quantum mechanics provide a good place to begin a science–religion dialogue. The present paper has a similar theme since it is about connecting science to mysteries such as qualia/subjectivity (Section 4) and paranormal phenomena (Section 5).

The many interpretations of quantum mechanics involve disagreements over the meanings of concepts between interpreters. Cochran contacted ten of the cited individuals and we learned that several of them disagreed with the entries made in their own columns for the yes's and no's of the Wiki Table. Cochran and Klein (2017) version of the table has thirteen rows, but with some differences in yes/no entries based on the communication with several of the cited individuals. In addition, Born was removed since he did not really have a full interpretation. In our paper we organized the rows into four meaningful groups, with the top five rows being Epistemic and the other eight being Ontic. The Ontic group was split into subgroups.

Table 1.2 (the updated Table 1.1) Cochran and Klein version has only seven rows and only six columns. A Y in a box indicates a Yes. A blank indicates either a No or an ambiguity.

Table 1.2: Updated Table 1.1 in Klein and Cochran

	Wave function Not Real	*Conscious-ness Causes Collapse*	*Deter-minism*	*Many Worlds & Minds*	*Longer Times for Special Probabilities*	*Beyond Standard QM*
Epistemic *Copenhagen (Bohr/Pauli/ Heisenberg), *von Neumann, *Rovelli, *Fuchs, *Stapp, *Kafatos, *Birkhoff, *Nelson, *Griffiths	Y					
Ontic						
*Bohm 1952/Sutherland/de Broglie						
*Cramer/Kastner, *Aharonov/ Watanabe/de Beauregard			Y			
*von Neumann, *Heisenberg						
*Everett, *Zeh				Y		
*Penrose, *GRW, *Einstein						
Ontic with Consciousness Collapse *Stapp, *Kafatos		Y				Y
Ontic with Special Probabilities for Sentience *Klein/Cochran					Y	

It is important to point out that the previous categories of "Collapsing Wave Function" and "Observer Role" are combined to the new category "Consciousness Causes Collapse". That is why none of the previous listed physicists was included as will be discussed below. To my knowledge, only Stapp and Kafatos would qualify as will be discussed. For simplicity we have grouped several interpretations into a single horizontal group. There are nine "epistemic", thirteen "ontic" (count the asterisks *), two "consciousness based interpretations" and one "special probabilities for sentience". Each separate interpretation is indicated by *. Table 1.2 specifies the interpretation by the author's name. The following is the title of each group:

Epistemic: Birkhoff – Quantum Logic, Nelson – Stochastic, Griffiths – Consistent Histories, Bohr, Pauli, Heisenberg – Copenhagen, Rovelli – Relational, Fuchs – Quantum Bayesian.

It turns out that Copenhagen, Rovelli and Fuchs have a Y for observer in the Wikipedia article's table. However, our new column title is "Consciousness Causes Collapse". These three entries are an N (a blank) because they do not claim that consciousness plays a special role in the collapse mechanism.

Ontic: Bohm and Sutherland & de Broglie – Deterministic; Cramer & Kastner – Transactional, Everett – Many Worlds; Zeh – Many Minds; Einstein, Penrose & GRW – New predictions including gravity; Aharonov / Watanabe / de Beauregard – Time Symmetric

Ontic with Consciousness Collapse: Stapp – Cosmic Mind, Kafatos – Non-local Consciousness, Possibility of Universal Observer. Neither of whom was included in previous articles on this topic.

Ontic with Special Probabilities for Sentience: Klein and Cochran – Life lengthens collapse delay.

Sutherland, Stapp, Einstein, Fuchs, Klein and Cochran were not included in the Cochran/Klein article. The rest of this section will explain the entries for the six columns.

The first column "Wave function Not Real" distinguishes between the wave function being ontic or epistemic. By definition the ontics have real/physical wave function. A limitation of human knowledge is why the epistemics do not believe in a real wave function. I chose to say "Not Real" rather than "Real" to reduce the number of Ys. There is more than one way to define the difference between ontological and epistemological interpretations. Thus, it is not at all surprising that Stapp is a fan of both the Copenhagen epistemic interpretation almost as much as being a fan of the von Neumann ontic approach. Copenhagen has a diversity of approaches as noted in the above Table 1.2 well-known scientists (Bohr, Pauli, Heisenberg). It is worth noting that Copenhagen is the most popular interpretation maybe due to its flexibility in accounting self-consistently for observational results. For people interested in the interpretations of QM we strongly recommend doing a Google search to get a feeling of the many controversies about whether Copenhagen deserved being the most popular interpretation.

The "Consciousness Causes Collapse" column is a most important column for the purpose of this article. We will argue at the end of this Section and in Section 4 that the only QM interpretations that deserve a Y for this column are those proposed by Stapp and Kafatos. However, if one goes to the Table seen by googling "Interpretations of Quantum Mechanics", one sees that Copenhagen, von Neumann, Rovelli and Fuchs are also present on the "observer role" in addition to the two just mentioned. The question remains whether all observers are aspects of one universal consciousness as both Stapp (Cosmic Mind) and Kafatos (Universal Observer) imply. Many observers received a "yes" in the original Wikipedia article because in those interpretations the role of the "observer" involves the epistemological considerations of the experimenters doing experiments. But for the present column, the collapse is done by the subjective aspects of consciousness. For Kafatos, the collapse is related to the observer's information and is not caused by individual measurements. Further details on "consciousness causes collapse" will be discussed in Section 4.

When one goes to the table in https://en.wikipedia.org/wiki/Interpretations_of_quantum_mechanics, one discovers that the "consciousness causes collapse" interpretation is given to von Neumann, Wigner and Stapp. However, when one looks closely at von Neumann's 1932 famous book, *Mathematical Foundations of Quantum Mechanics* one discovers on p. 419 that in addition to the collapse being done by animal sentience, von Neumann claims it could also be done by a thermometer! Wigner held a belief in the sentient collapse model for only a brief two years and then abandoned it. Stapp was consistent in his support for a sentient observer doing the collapse. Given von Neumann's and Wigner's minimal loyalty to consciousness being the collapse mechanism, Stapp is the person truly deserving of that honour, with Kafatos also becoming a major foundational proponent of that approach. That is, the collapse is related to information from the observer and not collapse caused by individual measurements. This is an important topic and as mentioned above it will be revisited in Section 4.

For the "Determinism" column we contacted Sutherland, who is now the main follower of Bohm. He said a Y would be appropriate to indicate that Bohm is a deterministic interpretation. Sutherland's important contribution is that he reduced the number of dimensions needed from Bohm's 10^80 dimensions in the universe down to our familiar four dimensions! The Bohm/Sutherland hypothesis is very special because of its deterministic similarity to classical physics. The way the determinism works is that each particle is guided by a wave as in Bohm (1952)! Cramer/Kastner/Aharonov/Watanabe/de Beauregard have a Y due to their time-symmetric aspect that has some similarity to determinism. So those latter five are in that column for a somewhat looser definition of determinism.

We have added a column titled "Many Worlds and Many Minds" to emphasize its special role. It is for Everett and Zeh. This column is very unique in never really having a probability. It goes straight from amplitude to most all probabilities becoming immediately actualized. Each of the possible probabilities goes into a separate universe. The Everett approach with multiple universes replaces the standard QM approach of probabilities. It is quite surprising to me that top physicists such as Sean Carroll are in favour of it. I strongly recommend googling "Sean Carroll Many Worlds" to see multiple talks and papers on this topic. It is surprisingly elegant.

The "Beyond Standard QM" column is of interest because it provides examples for future changes to QM. The Penrose hypothesis is special because of concrete predictions that seemed to be different from standard QM and there are plans to send up a satellite in the next few years to test his hypothesis. We recently learned that Penrose's new predictions that involve quantum gravity may not really differ from other interpretations. Nobody other than Penrose had thought about the possibility of doing that experiment with single gravitons to see whether the effect would be compatible with general relativity. In any case, connecting quantum mechanics to general relativity is surely important and that is Penrose's goal. Making that connection is probably the top mystery of present QM. Penrose could get a second Nobel Prize if he somehow connects gravity to the other seventeen wavicles. Einstein is in this "Beyond" category for a reason similar to Penrose, viz. Einstein's general relativity is not compatible with QM. He spent the last thirty years of his life trying to solve this deep mystery. The Ghirardi, Rimini and Weber (GRW) interpretation has testable different predictions from standard QM. GRW can be thought of as the most sophisticated of the many dozens of "crazy" ideas that people dream up. The word "crazy" does not negate validity since as Feynman often pointed out, much of quantum mechanics disobeys standard logic and is thereby crazy. We also added Stapp and Kafatos to this column due to the role of Cosmic Mind in those interpretations. It should be noted that the sense in which these interpretations go beyond standard quantum mechanics is different from Penrose and GRW that are materialist interpretations, whereas Stapp and Kafatos use idealist interpretations to understand Cosmic Mind. We will discuss Cosmic Mind in more detail in Section 4.

The "Longer Times for Special Probabilities" column has a novel approach to the probability stage of QM. My colleague Chris Cantor and I came up with this approach that includes how evolution might work in a manner that is special in having a special role for animal minds. We speculate that it is useful to divide the history of life on Earth into three parts: (a) pre-life, (b) early intelligent life, and (c) intelligent life.

a. For the first 8 billion years of our universe there was no earth and it took about a billion years for the beginnings of life on earth. Before the presence of life it makes sense that quantum collapses take place like all the other approaches (except for Many Worlds with no collapses). It is our hypothesis that when life gets started (maybe with bacteria) something new takes place, as discussed next.

b. Instead of the bacteria being immediately actualized, once it hits the probability stage they stay as probabilities for a slightly longer time than non-life due to the rudimentary awareness. As life evolves into higher and higher sentience, the duration before the collapse would gradually become longer until advanced creatures like birds and mammals arrive, at which point the growing duration becomes fixed.

c. At that point, full consciousness takes place with around ten collapses taking place per second rather than a million per second at non-neural locations. The idea is that by having more available time for sentience, in the probability stage it is possible that much greater calculation power is possible as opposed to the much more rapid collapses.

For a final comment on Section 3, it is important to point out that there is great ambiguity for what the above Table 1.2 could have been. If one looks at the two tables discussed above you will see several yes/no switches. The definitions are ambiguous and the individuals have been known to change their beliefs. It was for that reason that I included the bottom row for something new. Present quantum mechanics allows for that flexibility. Rather than fighting with each other about whose theory is best or most elegant, it is best to be friendly with each other. The amazing thing is to appreciate that the many seemingly different interpretations of QM, all give similar predictions.

4. Going Beyond Mainstream Physics with a Realm 2 Science-compatible God

Section 3 explored Realm 1 with standard measurable physics that does not worry about subjectivity. This section will explore Realm 2, centred on Whitehead's and Stapp's approach to how the world works with inclusion of subjectivity and with Cobb being the living carrier of Whitehead's approach. We will start with Whitehead, but we will let Stapp do the introduction. The first sentence of Stapp's article titled "Whiteheadian Quantum Ontology" was:

> Upon completing my article "The Copenhagen Interpretation", which stressed the pragmatic character of that interpretation, I sent the manuscript to Heisenberg for his approval or reaction.

I mention that sentence because Section 4 will include what Stapp was discussing in his article about Whitehead. For example, a few paragraphs later Stapp wrote:

> We need a fundamentally non-anthropocentric ontology

> within which the anthropocentric pragmatic theory is naturally imbedded. That is a big order! Fortunately, however, there already exists an ontology that provides a good starting point. It is the ontology proposed by Alfred North Whitehead. I shall describe here the fusion, as I conceive it, of relativistic quantum field theory with what I take to be the key ideas of Whitehead.

I mention this item since Stapp will be featured in the second half of this section and it is useful to mention him at the beginning.

This section covers some of the important mysteries that go beyond present science. In particular, it is about Realm 2 that goes beyond standard physics, but does not violate it. These are the mysteries associated with subjectivity, mind, consciousness and religion. In a deep sense, this section was born around 1925 when the non-classical new insights into quantum mechanics were born. The physicists began to realize that their new theory of quantum physics totally changed their understanding of the fundamental laws of nature. Although the new QM laws made no logical sense and that is still true today, the new laws can provide a home for subjectivity and religion, the topic of the current section.

Whitehead was one of the deep thinkers of that time. From 1910-13, he and Bertrand Russell produced their revolutionary three-volume book *Principia Mathematica* that changed the way people thought about the depth of mathematics. Then, in 1927-28, at the same time as the birth of QM, Whitehead gave his series of Gifford Lectures giving a very different view of the new quantum physics. The title of the Gifford Lectures was "Process and Reality" that got converted into a book. In the hands of Charles Hartshorne and John Cobb, it became a powerful tool for connecting science and religion. So when you see the word "Whitehead" you can think of "Cobb".

An optimal introduction to modernized Whitehead can be found in the wisdom of two books by Robert Mesle on

Whitehead's process approach. Mesle's first book *Process Theology* (1993) has many hundreds of times that "God" is used to give power to the items being discussed. Mesle is very comfortable with God language, yet he turns out to be a Naturalist as he makes clear in his book's next to last chapter. He is very God friendly as long as the powerful God does not violate the laws of Nature. The final chapter, by John Cobb, emphasizes the similarity of their two approaches, with science-compatible God miracles needed for dealing with special items as will be discussed in the section about Cobb. Mesle's second book, titled *Process-Relational Philosophy: An Introduction to Alfred North Whitehead* (2008) includes more details about process thought. The Appendix of that book begins with the following:

> I have generally avoided using Whitehead's technical language since it is one of the main reasons why process-relational philosophy has not been more widely read.

That Appendix is an eighteen-page dictionary for understanding Whitehead's book *Process and Reality* (1978) that was written at about the same time that the Copenhagen revolution to QM took place.

I will now focus on two novel approaches for implementing Whitehead's insight. The first will be that of John Cobb, who is a direct descendant of Whitehead and Hartshorne. The second will be Henry Stapp's Cosmic Mind approach to quantum mechanics. We will argue that Stapp's "Cosmic Mind" and Cobb's "God" have deep similarity.

Before getting to Cobb, it will be useful to clarify how I first got connected to him. I taught physics at the Claremont Colleges from 1967 to 1981. My office was three short blocks from the Claremont School of Theology that included John Cobb's Center for Process Studies. I mention this because in 1973 I took a year sabbatical at Stanford to switch fields from physics to psychophysics (how does the brain work). I also became very interested in "far out" things, including psychic phenomena. I made a connection between psychic phenomena and God phenomena. Thus after the sabbatical I would attend talks at Cobb's Center for Process Studies. I strongly recommend watching this awesome video of John Cobb interviewing David Bohm (https://www.youtube.com/watch?v=l7VKGcmWVCw). It is a wonderful way to get to know Bohm and Cobb. Another unforgettable memory is my participation in the amazing 1998 Claremont conference that Cobb helped organize. Anyone interested in Whitehead's contribution to physics should have a look at the awesome book from the conference, titled *Physics and Whitehead* edited by Eastman and Keeton (2003). The book included a large amount of wonderful discussions among participants. It is by far the best publication I know of showing the connection of process thought to physics and to science in general. Stapp's presence was also clearly featured in the book.

In order to provide insight into Cobb's approach to the topic of this article, two books by Cobb stand out. The first book coauthored with David Ray Griffin is titled *Process Theology*. Mesle used Cobb's book's title for Mesle's book as a tribute to Cobb. It is my strong opinion that for anyone to understand Whitehead's *Process and Reality* Cobb's book needs to be consulted. It is important to point out that Whitehead's *Process and Reality – Corrected Edition* that was published in 1978 had the same Griffin as one of the two editors that made *Process and Reality* much more understandable and popular. Another of Cobb's books that is quite special is the 482 page book with Herman E. Daly *For the Common Good: Redirecting the Economy Toward Community, the Environment and a Sustainable Future* (1980). It is an awesome, very important book with Daly. Two quite well-known individuals gave the following comments: Kenneth Boulding said:

> If this book were required reading for every graduate student in economics, economics could hardly avoid being much

> improved. Its critique of "standard" economic doctrine is shattering.

Paul Ehrlich's comment was:

> A brilliant book by one of the world's most knowledgeable economists, Herman Daly and a fine philosopher, John B. Cobb. No one who is concerned with solving the human predicament can afford to be without this book.

Finally, to get a detailed glimpse into the wide variety of Cobb's present activities, I strongly recommend looking at: https://cobb.institute/. I am presently active in Zoom discussions at the Cobb Institute.

We now shift to Stapp. There actually is not a need for me to say much, given the details in Sections 1 to 3. Section 1 discussed my long association with Stapp. Section 2 introduced Stapp's view on Cosmic Mind. Section 3 discussed his special role in a unique interpretation of QM (consciousness causes collapse) and some more will be coming in Section 5 regarding his friendly, but sceptical, interest in psi. This section will briefly point out his use of "Cosmic Mind" language for important aspects of Nature that includes our subjectivity and Mind. By "Mind" with a capital M one has a realm that goes beyond the brain. As introduced in Section 2, there are three realms for dealing with these issues, with Stapp and Cobb as bridge builders in the middle realm.

The first broad realm is that of standard science. As was discussed in Sections 2 and 3, most scientists think brains can handle subjectivity with mind (lower case M) being part of being an aspect of brain function. However, there is a major problem: most physicists who think about these issues say that although we do not yet understand the mechanisms, hopefully within another 100 years, mind will become part of science. There are also physicists (and others) who believe that this issue may never be solved and actually belong to the third realm.

The third broad realm has powerful capabilities, often called "God", outside of present science. It is my understanding that a large fraction of the world's population (probably a majority in USA) believes that there are many aspects of our world that go far beyond science.

Stapp and Cobb belong to the middle realm between Realms 1 and 3. This Realm 2 will be the theme of the rest of Section 4. The critical item in Stapp's Cosmic Mind is that it goes beyond the eighteen wavicles. However, Stapp does not simply add more wavicles. His Cosmic Mind is a separate realm that goes beyond quantum mechanics and thus beyond the brain.

Given that this article is in the book that Kafatos has put together, it is useful to also include his views on this topic. Note that the Stapp and Kafatos views in this section are both in Realm 2 and are very similar with a subtle difference: In Kafatos' view, the act of measurement causing collapse is a special case of a more general presence of *information* beyond space–time. To be specific, as Kafatos and Narasimhan (2019) point out, the results of a class of quantum eraser experiments carried out in the laboratory, can be interpreted as indicating that the collapse of the wave function may not necessarily involve choices by (distinct) observers in space–time. Rather, it is the *access to information* itself and any interpretation of such information, outside of space and time, which may be involved. Although this view is not contradicting the standard orthodox interpretation, Kafatos believes it extends and enriches it. As such, the interpretation is consistent with the presence of a universal observer, similar to God, in the quantum universe of many possibilities. Kafatos for a long time has advocated that the entire universe may be conscious, coining the term "the Conscious Universe". The views of Stapp and Kafatos converge in that they both take Cosmic Mind/Universal Consciousness as the primal existence of the universe, with the additional clarification as outlined here that information is beyond space–time.

Stapp and Kafatos, are special because of their being the only Y (yes) in the "Consciousness Causes Collapse" column of Table 1.2. As mentioned before, one of the greatest mysteries facing present physics is what produces the subjective aspects of consciousness (qualia). All the other approaches have collapses from probability to actuality happening all the time, starting with the creation of our universe. Stapp wants the quantum collapse to be connected to subjectivity, so the collapse would need to wait for subjectivity to take place. Thus, even though earth is about 4.5 billion years old, the arrival of sentience would have quantum collapses taking place only 1 billion years ago.

Stapp believes that there is a clear distinction between the objective realm and the totally separate subjective realm that still needs to be explained. When one says "subjectivity" one should be aware that there are aspects to subjectivity that can connect to objectivity. Consider touching a burning flame. There will be a subjective pain as well as an automatic objective reflex. The objective aspect is achieved by the eighteen (or six) wavicles discussed in Section 2. The subjective aspect of qualia was the topic of this section, with Stapp's Cosmic Mind being a clean approach for what is needed and it will be helped by connecting to Cobb.

In order to connect Stapp's Cosmic Mind to Cobb's Connecting to God, it is useful to look at the table of contents of Mesle's *Process Theology*. Most of the following chapter headings in Mesle's book give a strong reminder of the many things that are natural for Realm 2, but not commonly part of Realm 1.

Process Theology: Robert Mesle

1. Love, Power and Worship
2. God's Love and Our Suffering
3. Love, Power and Relatedness
4. Freedom, Time and God's Power
5. Time
6. A World of Experience
12. Ethics and Global Community
13. Religious Pluralism

7. How God Acts in the World
8. How Religion Becomes Oppressive
9. Process Theology of Liberation
10. Women's Experience
11. Revelation and Liberation
14. Jesus
15. Prayer, Liberation and Healing
16. Miracles
17. Process Naturalism
18. Process Theism – by John Cobb

Although God language is used throughout the book, it is a God language the Process God has that is helpful for societies to function well. Recall that Mesle is not a theist.

A large number of thoughtful people think that mind is so different from matter that it is unlikely that brains can do it all. For example, Stapp's Cosmic Mind includes a realm that goes beyond QM. That is the same opinion that Cobb had in his "Process Theism" chapter 18 (Mesle 1993). As a summary of Section 4 it is worth pointing out that for several years I have been deeply concerned about how our universe has such wonderfully optimal properties. I can think of three possibilities for how our universe was so "lucky":

1. String theory explains it with 10^500 possible ways for strings in ten dimensions to produce all sorts of universes. In that theory, our universe is one of the special ones out of the incredibly large number of universes, our universe happens to have wavicles that can make living creatures.
2. There is a deep and as yet unknown reason that our universe is the way it is and it will someday be understood.
3. There is some sort of higher power that Cobb would call God and Stapp would call Cosmic Mind.

I find it exciting that the world views of Cobb and Stapp are sufficiently compatible that they can work together in having healthy societies. Maybe in addition to having healthy societies their approach might also be going in the right direction for how

Nature actually works. I lean towards option 1 of mainstream physics, but any of the three seems fine! Keep in mind in terms of the three realms of Section 2 possibilities 1 and 2 are aspects of Realm 1 and possibility 3 is Realm 2. The next section discusses what could be an aspect of Realm 3 that violates present science.

5. Psychic Phenomena

Some readers of this paper will be disappointed that I will be treating *psychic phenomena* (psi) seriously in this section. Others will be disappointed that I am a psi sceptic. There are three reasons for including psi as a topic:

1. Most of the papers that Stapp and Klein have independently authored in the past few years have included psychic phenomena.
2. Between 50 to 75 per cent of the population of USA (and probably the world) believe in at least one type of psi.
3. Psi might really exist!

There are four different types of psi: telepathy, clairvoyance, psychokinesis and precognition. Telepathy is the simplest to understand. It is like communicating with someone on the telephone but without the telephone. Clairvoyance is the ability to "see" an object with eyes closed or the object covered. One type of clairvoyance is called out of body experience (OBE). Psychokinesis is moving physical objects by mind without use of physical means. Precognition is supernormal knowledge of future events. Although all four types of psi violate present quantum mechanics, by adding some extra particles in addition to the present eighteen it could be possible to enable the types of psi other than precognition. In terms of our three realms of Section 2, as will be discussed, telepathy, clairvoyance and psychokinesis can be either Realms 1 or 2 and precognition is definitely Realm 3.

It is useful to now consider the most famous recent psi

experiment that at first sounds like precognition. It was Daryl Bem's 2011 paper, published in a top journal. We will go into many details of one of the Bem experiments that will be referred to as Expt 1. The main part of Section 5 will be based on three articles on Bem's findings: two by Stapp and one by Klein and Cochran. Expt 1 had two steps for each trial. On step 1 the subject chooses one of two monitors to look at. After fixating on one of the monitors a computer randomly chooses one for the display. The critical discovery was that across many subjects slightly more than 53 per cent of the time the subject chose the correct monitor. When all nine types of Bem's experiments were put together the results showed a probability of less than 10^–5 of it having happened by chance. That 10^–5 value is the criterion for having made an important discovery! One is tempted to say this is evidence for precognition, but that is not the case, as will now be discussed.

It turns out the mechanism for success in the task, depending on the type of random number generator (RNG) that was used for choosing the monitor. Bem used both a standard RNG (SRNG) and a quantum RNG (QRNG). A SRNG is present in most all computers and a QRNG is easy to purchase. If a SRNG was used, then clairvoyance could do the job by "zooming" inside the RNG to see what the next outcome would be. That is possible since the SRND is deterministic. That information would then somehow be communicated to Alice's brain so that she would look at the appropriate monitor. If, however, a fancy quantum QRNG is used, then based on Alice's choice, psychokinesis could be used to zoom inside the QRNG to influence the quantum mechanical outcome. It may not be easily done, but it would not be impossible. In any case, the present eighteen wavicles do not have the needed properties to implement these complex procedures. But maybe awesome new wavicles could do it.

The above paragraph points out the severe difficulty of

obtaining Bem's results. Another possibility is that precognition does the job. But as discussed above, precognition violates all versions of Realms 1 and 2 physics discussed previously. A much simpler explanation is that Bem's results were due to sloppiness in the methodology. For example, there was criticism that positive preliminary data was included in Bem's data. That use of preliminary data was okay in 2011 and was quite common. However, several articles in 2011-12 were strongly critical of Bem's use of preliminary data. The good news is that these articles inspired science publications to not allow including preliminary data. So that was a nice outcome of Bem's data.

The rest of this book chapter will consider three articles on Bem's experiments, two by Stapp and one by Klein and Cochran. The similarity of our views can be seen in Appendix D of Stapp's recent book *Quantum Theory and Free Will*. The Appendix D title is: "The Paranormal and the Principle of Sufficient Reason". Stapp had a detailed discussion of all nine of Bem's psi experiments and he said:

> I make no judgement regarding the technical correctness of the purported evidence for the existence of the reported retrocausal phenomena.

We have a similar attitude. There is so much data supporting psi that open-mindedness, rather than blind rejection, is called for. However, we are sceptical for three reasons. First, psi violates our present understanding of quantum mechanics that accounts for almost all measurable events other than psi (dark matter is beginning to be understood). Second, it has been pointed out that many results, such as those of Bem, have had sloppy aspects like not throwing out preliminary data when exploring optimal conditions. Third and most important, we are shocked that *zero* psi experiments with positive results have been done with involvement of a friendly non-believer. A non-believer is needed to minimize the sloppiness that is fairly common in standard science experiments that deal with human subjects.

I will now focus briefly on a pair of articles, another one by Stapp and one that Klein and Cochran that were both presented at the 2016 Quantum Retrocausation III Conference, published in 2017. It was published by the American Institute of Physics (AIP), a leading national organization of physicists. About half of the articles were favouring psi. The full free proceedings are available at: https://carlossalvarado.wordpress.com/2017/06/06/quantum-retrocausation/. It is important to point out that there are two very different meanings of the word "retrocausation". One definition is the same as precognition, which involves sending information backwards in time (impossible according to mainstream science). The second definition is specific to the collapse mechanism of entangled wavicles that could be light years apart and involves going backwards in time to when the wavicles become entangled and then forwards in time to the partner wavicle. Although it sounds crazy, it is fully compatible with quantum mechanics. We are mainly concerned with the first definition that violates present quantum mechanics. When I attended the 2016 Retrocausation conference, I was amazed that nobody raised that issue of the two very different definitions.

Stapp in the Retrocausation III (2017) proceedings gives the general background for the Bem experiments discussed earlier. The background is followed by a section titled "Orthodox Quantum Description of the Bem Experiment". I cannot think of a better summary of Stapp's approach to QM than that section of less than one page. He starts by comparing the Dirac approach of "*choice on the part of Nature*" (the italics are Stapp's exact wording) vs Heisenberg's approach of the "observer constructing the measuring instruments and reading their recordings". Then Stapp says:

> John Archibald Wheeler showed how these two views could be accommodated simultaneously by likening the process of observation to the parlor game of "twenty questions", in which the interlocutors (in the quantum case the conscious observers)

poses yes/no questions to which "Nature" responds "Yes" or "No".

Stapp then provides an elegant overview of von Neumann's "orthodox quantum mechanics" where in Process 1 there is question asking and Nature's "Yes" or "No" psychophysical response (Stapp's language). That was the basis for Wheeler's approach. I kept the summary of Stapp's article short since his views were discussed earlier.

By a very nice coincidence, the article directly following Stapp's article was by Klein and Cochran and titled "Physics and the Role of Mind". The article covers some of the same issues as the present paper, but with minimal overlap of the details. It provides a nice summary of some important topics. The article's introduction begins with the following four mysteries that are part of present science.

1. *The mystery of retrocausation.* We thoroughly discussed the two very different definitions of retrocausation that had been previously ignored! One type of retrocausation would require precognition that violates QM.
2. *Signal vs influence.* A *signal* involves sending data, for instance, whether the stock market is going up or down, and requires the transfer of energy. An *influence,* on the other hand, involves a pair of entangled particles and no energy transfer! An influence occurs when measurement of a property (e.g. spin) of one particle determines the outcome of the other entangled particle. It turns out that a large fraction of the attendees of the 2016 conference (mentioned above) were not aware of the distinction between a signal and an influence. A financial tip: one can get rich from a signal but not from an influence.
3. *The collapse is moveable.* In Section 3, we pointed out that there were many different approaches to the quantum collapse mechanism. In his book *Mathematical Foundations*

of Quantum Mechanics (1932/55), von Neumann gave a proof that the collapse is movable. He showed it is possible to have a late (high) placement, such as the mind of a sentient observer and on p. 419 he pointed out that the collapse could be done by a thermometer (or almost anything).

4. *Precognition.* One of the most interesting aspects of my 2017 paper was the introduction of Charlie as a participant in the Bem experiments that use a quantum random number generator, QRNG, for determining the experimental outcome. Charlie is a lab assistant whose role is to look at the QRNG 50 per cent of the time before Alice has a chance to see the target. This manipulation can strongly influence the experimental outcome. Given that full access to the article "Physics and the Role of Mind" (in addition to the entire book for free) is given in the References so there is no need to fill in the details here. It turns out Charlie can have a strong influence on the outcome. I am leaving out some very interesting details to encourage interested readers to click on the link in the References (and Stapp's paper is right before mine).

The final, brief section of the paper was titled "Collaboration vs Conflict: How to Convince Mainstream Science to Address Psi". The theme of that section was simple. Rather than fighting with each other, this final section of the paper suggests that the two sides should get together and carefully design and carry out some psi experiments that would clarify the issue. Stapp's "Cosmic Mind" that was discussed in Section 4 could also play a role since it is possible that the minds of believers are different from the minds of sceptics.

Thus, before saying the other side is wrong, it makes sense to work together. I think that either outcome of the proposed experiments would have a major impact on science, with both possible outcomes being wonderful. If the psi results are negative, then many more people would respect science! If the results are positive, then science would take a major new step forward! It is a win-win situation.

In conclusion, I shall summarize Sections 1 to 5. Section 1 began with an Introduction and then aspects of my connection to Henry Stapp. It is worth repeating the following item from Section 1:

> Stapp's influence on me has been continuous, going from the mid-1960s, when I was working on the Berkeley bootstrap at Brandeis University. After my PhD I spent the summers from 1968-72 at the Lawrence Berkeley Lab that got me connected to Stapp.

It is worth pointing out that I have been strongly influenced by my friend Henry Stapp starting about fifty-five years ago!

Section 2 started with an overview of QM that was relevant to what is going on before the QM amplitudes become probabilities. The rest of that section was about the distinction of the three realms. Realm 1 is the realm of standard science based on the presently known eighteen wavicles. Realm 2 is a potential realm with additional aspects of nature that go beyond QM. Stapp introduced Cosmic Mind and Kafatos introduced Non-local Consciousness. This realm enables special outcomes without violating present QM. It may be similar to how the graviton is presently in a realm apart from QM. Realm 3 is a realm that enables miracles such as is found in some religions and is found in psychic phenomena. My own belief is that I favour Realm 1 which is present science. Right before this conclusion, I said that any of these outcomes would be a win-win situation, however, the data supporting Realm 2 or 3 would require supervised replication.

Section 3 was probably the most important section. Table 1.1 had many very different approaches for how probabilities can become actualized. There were twenty-six individuals in the list associated with the Table 1.2. Several individuals were grouped together if their approaches were similar. A surprising aspect of Table 1.2 is that there were important differences from the highly visited article with a somewhat similar Table at: "en_wikipedia. org/wiki/Interpretations_of_quantum_mechanics". We were surprised that when we contacted ten of the people in the Wikipedia article we discovered that they disagreed with what was claimed in the Wikipedia paper. An amazing aspect of these tables is that one might think that all "yes"/"no" differences in many categories would produce differences in predicted outcomes. However, amazingly all the predictions are the same.

Section 4 was on the topic of Realm 2 that is different from the QM realm but is compatible with QM. It started out as the connection between the physics of Henry Stapp and that of Alfred North Whitehead. The idea was that the human mind can do things not available to our present knowledge about what QM can do. I pointed out that I had many interactions with Whitehead's disciple John Cobb. It turns out that Cobb's office and his Center for Process Studies was a short 10 minute walk from my office at the Claremont Colleges. So after I switched from physics research to the type of research this article is about, starting in 1974, I would often attend talks at Cobb's Center for Process Studies. A very important item in Section 4 was the discussion on how Stapp and Kafatos were the only two physicists I am aware of who not only believed in consciousness causing collapse but were open to Realm 2 that goes beyond standard QM. It is worth repeating the comment I made in Section 4:

> The views of Stapp and Kafatos converge in that they both take Cosmic Mind/Universal Consciousness as the primal existence of the universe.

So Stapp and Kafatos both have similar approaches that go beyond current mainstream physics. Although they are in the minority of physicists on this topic they provide an interesting approach for the presently unsolved mystery of subjectivity.

It is also important to point to the eighteen chapters in Mesle's *Process Theology* book that I listed near the end of Section 4. Those brief eighteen chapters gave an excellent representation of Cobb's religious beliefs. Chapter 18, titled "Process Theism" was written by Cobb with an excellent overview of what Section 4 was about.

Section 5 focused on psychic phenomena. It is an unusual topic since psi violates the presently known laws of nature. I began by pointing out that by using clairvoyance or psychokinesis it would be not impossible to account for Daryl Bem's awesome experiments that validated psi in a manner that would be compatible with the approaches of Stapp and Kafatos using Realm 2 type approaches. It was pointed out, however, that it would not be feasible with present technology, but possible with potentially future technology. It was pointed out that precognition, which involves predicting the future, would belong to Realm 3, that is in violation of present science. Bem's experiments were designed in a manner that could be done without precognition. However, I pointed out that the most likely explanation of Bem's results were standard sloppiness where it was common to use preliminary data before deciding on the details of experimental design. After Bem's article in 2011, there was a major commotion that ended up with forbidding use of preliminary experiments. The last part of Section 5 discussed articles focused on Bem by Stapp, and Klein and Cochran in a book titled *Quantum Retrocausation*. I pointed out in Section 5 that it is possible to get the book free of charge as mentioned in the very first item of the References that is next (incidentally following those two articles is an interesting article by Kafatos)!

References

AIP Conference Proceedings on Quantum Retrocausation, 2017. [Amazingly all eleven articles are available for free!].

Bell, J.S., 1964, "On the Einstein–Podolsky–Rosen Paradox", *Physics Physique*, 1: 195-200. Update version in 2004.

Bem, D., 2011, "Feeling the Future: Experimental Evidence for Anomalous Retroactive Influences on Cognition and Affect", *Journal of Personality and Social Psychology*, 100: 407-25.

Bem, D., P. Tressoldi, T. Rabeyron and M. Duggan, 2017, "Feeling the Future: A Metaanalysis of 90 Experiments on the Anomalous Anticipation of Random Future Event", *F1000 Research*.

Cobb, J.B., 1993, "Process Theism", in R. Mesle, *Process Theology: A Basic Introduction*, pp. 134-47, Saint Louis, MO: Chalice Press.

Cochran, C. and S.A. Klein, 2017, "Quantum Interpretations for Building Science/Religion Bridges", *Cosmos and History*, 13(1), https://www.cosmosandhistory.org/index.php/journal/article/viewFile/596/1019.

Daly, Herman E., 1980, *For the Common Good: Redirecting the Economy Toward Community, the Environment and a Sustainable Future* Boston, MA: Beacon Press.

Eastman, Timothy and Hank Keeton (eds), 2003, *Physics and Whitehead: Quantum, Process, and Experience*, Albany, NY: SUNY Press.

Edgar S., R.P. Feynman, S.A. Klein, I. Lielausis and C.M. Steinberg, 1962, "Mapping Experiments with R Mutants of Bacteriophage T4", *Genetics*, 47(2): 179-86.

Kafatos, M. and R. Nadeau, 1990, *The Conscious Universe, Part and Whole in Modern Physical Theory*, New York: Springer-Verlag.

Kafatos, M.C. and A. Narasimhan, 2019, "The Observer and Access to Information in the Quantum Universe", invited chapter in *Quanta and Mind: Essays on the Connection between Quantum Mechanics and Consciousness*, ed. Jose Acacio De Barros and Carlos Montemayor Synthese, Library https://www.springer.com/gp/book/9783030219079.

Kaiser, D., 2011, *How the Hippies Saved Physics*, New York: W. Norton.

Klein, S.A., 1991, "The Duality of Psycho-Physics", *Representations of Vision: Trends and Tacit Assumptions in Vision Search*, ed. A. Gorea, pp. 231-49, New York: Cambridge University Press.

———, 2017, "Using Psychic Phenomena to Connect Mind to Brain and to Revise Quantum Mechanics," *Cosmos and History*, 13(2): 34-46, https://www.cosmosandhistory.org/index.php/journal/article/viewFile/603/1045

———, 2018, "A New Approach to the Measurement Problem of Quantum Mechanics", *Cosmos and History*, 14(1): 83-90, https://www.cosmosandhistory.org/index.php/journal/article/viewFile/685/1135.

Klein, S.A. and C. Cochran, 2017, "Physics and the Role of Mind", in *Quantum Retrocausation III*, ed. D.P. Sheehan, AIP Conf. Proc. 1841, 04002 (see AIP link above), or https://aip.scitation.org/doi/abs/10.1063/1.4982778.

Mesle, C.R., 1993, *Process Theology*, Saint Louis, MO: Chalice Press.

———, 2008, *Process-Relational Philosophy: An Introduction to Alfred North Whitehead*, Pennsylvania: Templeton Foundation Press.

von Neumann, John, 1932 (German)/1955, *Mathematical Foundations of Quantum Mechanics*, Princeton: Princeton University Press.

Stapp, H.P., 2009, *Mind, Matter and Quantum Mechanics*, New York: Springer.

———, 2011, *Mindful Universe: Quantum Mechanics and the Participating Observer*, New York: Springer Science & Business Media.

———, 2017a, *Quantum Theory and Free Will: How Mental Intentions Translate into Bodily Actions*, New York: Springer.

———, 2017b, "Retrocausation in Quantum Mechanics and the Effects of Minds on the Creation of Physical Reality", *Quantum Retrocausation III*, ed. D.P. Sheehan, AIP Conf. Proc. 1841, 04001 (see AIP link above). Or https://aip.scitation.org/doi/abs/10.1063/1.4982777.

Wolchover, N., http://www.quantamagazine.org/why-is-m-theory-the-leading-candidate-for-theory-of-everything-20171218/

Whitehead, Alfred North, 1929, *Process and Reality: An Essay in Cosmology*, New York: Macmillan.

2

The Quantum Conception of Man
A Tribute and Short Interview with Henry P. Stapp

Christopher Cochran

Keywords: Stapp, quantum conception of man, humanism, orthodox interpretation.

Henry P. Stapp has dedicated a life of research to working out the implications of quantum mechanics. Stapp's scholarly work and generous dialogue with colleagues admirably demonstrate his humanistic attitude towards scientific knowledge. His three published books (Stapp 1993; 2007, 2017) and many essays weave science, philosophy and history into a quest for a unified theory of the cosmos and our place in it. Stapp argues that the quantum revolution of the twentieth century has provided human consciousness with a relational or participatory position in a "mindful universe". Stapp shows how he has called the "quantum conception of man" is an improvement over the classical or dualistic vision of mankind provided by classical physics, the latter having no obvious place or role for consciousness.

Henry Stapp is a humanist in the classical sense; he is one who seeks to find values and meaning for mankind through his studies of natural philosophy and science. He is also historical thinker who is concerned with how the historical revolutions of scientific knowledge can influence how we understand ourselves individually and socially. Here, three important themes that have remained consistent throughout Stapp's career are reviewed. The first is Stapp's contributions to the interpretation of quantum mechanics. Stapp is widely known for his elaboration of the John von Neumann "orthodox" interpretation of quantum mechanics. The second theme is Stapp's creative contributions to the scientific community at large, in the form of his persistent calls for a future science of mind that would fit neuroscience within the philosophical foundations of quantum physics, as interpreted in the orthodox interpretation. This would follow the tradition laid down by the founders of quantum mechanics in the twentieth century. Finally, Stapp has been an influential figure in humanistic dialogues on the implications of quantum mechanics for our present understanding of human values and meaning. An appreciation of all three themes together can help us understand the holism of Stapp's thinking and the larger vision that is the basis for his intellectual life.

Stapp often begins his discussions of how to interpret quantum mechanics by making an appeal to the importance of the project of interpretation in the first place. This is because many physicists doubt the importance of quantum interpretation, seeing it as "mere philosophy". To Stapp, this is misguided. Doing away with the project of interpretation of quantum physics is tantamount to abandoning the more noble dimensions of science: the quest to understand the universe (cf. Stapp 1993: 50; 2017: 5-6). In Stapp's reading, many of those physicists who champion the so-called "Copenhagen Interpretation" of quantum mechanics have seen in quantum mechanics a reason to give up on the idea that physics refers to natural phenomena; instead these physicists tend to insist that physics refers to human knowledge of natural phenomena. Stapp has insisted that his reading of von Neumann's "orthodox" interpretation of quantum mechanics is intended to re-establish the physicists' ability to claim that physics refers to nature herself and not only human knowledge of nature. And the most essential thing to understand about the orthodox interpretation is that if physics should refer to nature herself, then the implication of this is that nature is mind-like.

In Stapp's account, to establish an ontological interpretation of quantum mechanics, requires an account of the dynamics between human knowledge and nature. Hence the issue is not to deny the role of human knowledge in the physical process, but to take this role to its fullest conclusion. Stapp places himself within the tradition of the founders of quantum mechanics who emphasized the essential role of mind in the full description of nature, including Niels Bohr, Werner Heisenberg, Wolfgang Pauli and John von Neumann. John von Neumann famously enumerated two distinct portions of the quantum mechanical process as Process 1 and Process 2. Process 1 corresponds to the selection by a mind of a question that can be posed by an action on a physical system that evolves according to Process 2. Many physicists and philosophers have attempted to interpret Process 2 as an underlying physical reality that somehow gives rise to the phenomenal world of Process 1. However, following von Neumann as well as Bohr and Heisenberg, Stapp has emphasized that Process 1 (the phenomenal world in which the scientist operates and experiments) is not an epiphenomenon in relation to Process 2 (the world of potentialities that quantum mechanics describes). Instead, Process 1 and Process 2 exist in a mutual interdependence, but with the acquisition of knowledge (Process 1) always being logically prioritized (Stapp 2007: 24). This implication of this argument is substantial because it implies that the task of quantum interpretation is not one of understanding the "emergence" of classical objects from quantum potentialities. Indeed, classical objects are recast in

Stapp's interpretation as part of human experience. A theory of decoherence, for example, is therefore not sufficient to (fully) account for the relationship between the atomic and human scales. As Stapp explains it in his most recent book,

> the purely atomic-physics-based dynamical process (Process 2) does not fail because the system is "big". It fails because the atomic-based aspects of the dynamics are *only part of the causal story*.
>
> – Stapp 2017: 26

The evolution of Process 2 is not self-contained but depends upon the intervention of Process 1, which involves an experiential and not a physical description. Thus, Stapp concludes, the "materialist" doctrine of a self-contained physical description of nature has been upended by quantum mechanics.

Stapp has been persistent in clarifying these points regarding quantum interpretation for physicists and philosophers, including advocates of other interpretations. His many books and articles provide examples of his advocacy of the "orthodox von Neumann" interpretation of quantum mechanics against the alternative interpretations of Many Worlds, Hidden Variables and Objective Collapse theories, to name a few (cf. Stapp 1993: chap. 3 and 2007: chaps 2 and 9-11). Against the common but loosely defined "pragmatic" version of the Copenhagen Interpretation, which vaguely follows Bohr, Stapp has insisted that the lesson of quantum mechanics be read not pragmatically or epistemologically but as ontology: quantum interpretation should be a demonstration of the fundamental and irreplaceable role of mind in the complete description of nature. Stapp challenges others with what he calls the "basis problem", which emerges when attempting to account for the dynamics of Process 2 without reference to Process 1 (Stapp 2007: chap. 11). The basis problem is a key contribution to scholarship on quantum interpretation and is a serious challenge to any interpretation that prioritizes Process 2 as a stand-alone ground for ontology, as occurs in Many Worlds or Bohmian interpretations.

Beyond his long-time and impressive resume of discussion with other major figures in quantum interpretation (such as Heisenberg, Pauli, Wheeler, Bohm, Hiley, Zeh and more), Stapp has played a prominent role in academic discussions around the science of consciousness and the brain. Notable are his contributions to scholarly discussions of William James and Alfred North Whitehead (see Stapp 2007). His publications have extended beyond physics journals into philosophy and humanities journals and he is well known in academic circles concerned with questions of consciousness, brain and mind (cf. Stapp 1999, 2006, 2007). Stapp's popularity among scholars of consciousness is a good sign that his message of the relevance of quantum physics interpretation to the so-called "mind–matter problem" and science of consciousness has been heard well beyond the physics community. Stapp has proposed several models to encourage neuroscientists and cognitive scientists to creatively think about how minds work within a quantum paradigm rather than a classical one (Schwartz and Stapp 2005; Stapp 2007). His work on the topic of mind and brain has been an important part of the development of emerging fields and research programmes that have attempted to use methods and concepts of quantum theory to explain biological and psychological processes (some examples of that work include contributions from de Barros et al. 2019; Freeman and Vitiello 2011; Hameroff 1998; Schwartz and Stapp 2005; Theise and Kafatos 2006;).

Finally, Henry Stapp has made contributions to the history and philosophy of science, particularly in relation to the role of the historical event of the quantum revolution. Stapp has encouraged his colleagues and peers to think bravely about their own role in history. He reminds us that each one of us is part of a larger story in which the "Newtonian world view" is displaced by the "Quantum Conception of Man" (for example, see Stapp 1993: chap. 10; 2017: chap. 1). Scientific discoveries have important social ramifications, Stapp says, because the authority of the scientific world view helps shape how humans view themselves and how they behave towards others as well. Happily, Stapp believes that quantum mechanics provides a superior picture of nature and the place of humankind within it in comparison to the Newtonian world view of classical physics. The classical or Newtonian world view left no causal role for mind, including the human mind, giving rise to a "mind–matter problem" that asks how consciousness can arise from a material brain. However, as can be seen from Stapp's discussions of quantum interpretation as well as his visions of a quantum-based neuroscience, quantum mechanics rearranges the fundamental cosmological assumptions underlying the science of physics. The result is that the "mind–matter problem" is transformed in a way that gives mind a fundamental rather than epiphenomenal role in nature. The urgency of this recognition is not only scientific, but also political and social, says Stapp (2007). If the scientific world view gives no reality to mind, especially the human mind, people will either tend to distrust science or distrust the importance of mind. Either result is not a positive one. In Stapp's assessment, this has been the result of the Newtonian world view: a bifurcation of mind from science, culminating in a belief among some that science is inherently nihilistic. The central role of mind in the orthodox interpretation of quantum mechanics is an antidote to this state of affairs. By placing mind at the centre of the cosmological story, it becomes possible to imagine how values can be a part of nature, rather than foreign to it.

Henry Stapp's contributions have inspired many scholars and scientists. His books and lectures have also had an important impact for members of the community outside of academia who have taken interest in the themes of his work. He has been especially influential for individuals seeking a bridge between science and spirituality. He has been an intellectually generous and humble interlocutor to many. We are inspired by his mission of promoting human values that can exist in conjunction with scientific objectivity, his books and articles that provide a diverse toolkit for thinking about the technical problems of quantum interpretation, imagining future research programmes and finally for providing suggestions for a holistic world view and philosophy.

Interview with Henry P. Stapp

These questions were posed to Henry P. Stapp by Stanley Klein, Menas Kafatos and Christopher Cochran. Stapp gave his answers in writing.

Question: Do you see your interpretation of QM, following von Neumann and Heisenberg, as the standard interpretation of quantum mechanics by which alternatives should live up to and do at least as well?

Henry P. Stapp: I have described many interpretations. However, my "orthodox" interpretation is that of the founders! I base that claim upon extensive one-on-one personal conversations with Heisenberg, Pauli and Wheeler. In all three cases I spent at least three months in daily discussions about the subtleties of quantum physics. I later realized the need to explicitly add Mind and many quantum physicists have realized its role and other scientists need to do the same.

Question: Why do people continue to seek alternatives to the basic views of Copenhagen and von Neumann?

Henry P. Stapp: The founders viewed the theory as basically a *practical tool* for making precise predictions about observations, whereas others (including myself) often sought a description of an underlying reality whose properties would lead to a natural explanation of the practical tools.

Question: How do you define Mind (which you tend to capitalize and sometimes also refer to as Cosmic Mind) and how does it connect to the eighteen wavicles of present physics?

Henry P. Stapp: Cosmic Mind is a conscious entity engaged in the temporal unfolding of the physical universe!

Question: That is a great response. In the past you have referred to nature. In a very deep sense, nature is totally aware of what is going on in the universe. She needs a name that is more powerful than "Nature". "Cosmic Mind" has a strong power. How has your understanding of Nature or Cosmic Mind changed over the years?

Henry P. Stapp: The most significant shift has been the elevation of conscious Mind from a by-product of brain activity to the Primary Reality of Nature!

Question: You often say that a QM interpretation should be rational and coherent. Can you say more about what makes an interpretation rational and coherent?

Henry P. Stapp: "Rational" means devoid of contradictions. "Coherent" means "having parts that are smoothly tied together".

Question: Have you noticed any changes over the decades in how physicists discuss QM interpretation? Is there anything we can learn from that history?

Henry P. Stapp: The theories have become more complex.

Question: Which of your contributions to physics are you most proud of?

Henry P. Stapp: Development of the idea that the primary reality is Cosmic Mind!

Question: You have argued that the "Newtonian world view" is lacking a place for human values. Did you ever have a "Newtonian world view", perhaps as a teenager or before you learned about QM? Can you tell us about the relationship between human values and your interpretation of QM?

Henry P. Stapp: In High School I held a Newtonian world view that did not support human values. But later I learned how QM allows our actions to be positively influenced by our mental intentions.

Question: Are there aspects of quantum mechanics that are still a deep mystery?

Henry P. Stapp: None that I know of!

References

de Barros, Jose Acacio, Carlos Montemayor, Stanley Klein and Christopher Cochran, 2019, "Henry Stapp and the Orthodox Interpretation", *Activitas Nervosa Superior*, 61: 1-5.

Freeman, W.J. and Giuseppe Vitiello, 2011, "The Dissipative Brain and Non-Equilibrium Thermodynamics", *Journal of Cosmology*, 14.

Hameroff, Stuart, 1998, "Quantum Computation in Brain Microtubules?: The Penrose–Hameroff 'Orch OR' Model of Consciousness", *Philosophical Transactions of the Royal Society of London A*, 356: 1869-96.

Schwartz, Jeffrey, Henry Stapp and Mario Beauregard, 2005, "Quantum Physics in Neuroscience and Psychology: A Neurophysical Model of Mind–Brain Interaction", *Philosophical Transactions of the Royal Society B, Biological Sciences*, 360(1458): 1309-27.

Stapp, Henry, 1993, *Mind, Matter and Quantum Mechanics*, Berlin: Springer-Verlag.

———, 1999, "Attention, Intention and Will in Quantum Physics", *Journal of Consciousness Studies*, 6(8-9): 143-64.

———, 2006, "Quantum Interactive Dualism: An Alternative to Materialism", *Zygon: The Journal of Religion and Science*, 41(3): 599-616.

———, 2007, *Mindful Universe: Quantum Mechanics and the Participating Observer*, Berlin: Springer-Verlag.

———, 2017, *Quantum Theory and Free Will: How Mental Intentions Translate into Bodily Actions*, Berlin: Springer-Verlag.

Theise and Kafatos, 2013, "Complementarity in Biological Systems: A Complexity View", *Complexity*, 18(6): 11-20.

3

On the Wave Function Collapse and Mind–Matter Interaction

Jose Acacio de Barros

Abstract: In this paper, we examine the use of the "consciousness causes collapse hypothesis" as a mechanism for mind–matter interaction. Here we focus on a model proposed by Henry Stapp, where he uses the Inverted Quantum Zeno Effect (IQZE). In his model, a conscious mind's decision to observe an oscillator leads to physical changes in oscillation amplitude through the IQZE. As we discussed in other papers (de Barros and Oas 2015b; 2017; de Barros and Montemayor 2019a), Stapp's model requires specific types of structures in the brain. Those structures would be the site for the interaction between mind and matter. Here we extend some of the arguments in (de Barros and Montemayor 2019a) and point out additional issues and difficulties that originated from this theory. In particular, we revisit the discussion of Wigner's friend, assuming this time that Wigner is equipped with different ways of observations. Our goal is not to defend or criticize the "consciousness causes collapse" interpretation or Stapp's mechanism but to investigate its consequences.

Keywords: Quantum collapse, mental causality, consciousness, Wigner's friend, mind–matter interaction.

1. Introduction

René Descartes (1596–1650) clearly articulated that the mind seemed to have a different nature from the body. In his *Meditations*, Descartes argued that mind, which he called *res cogitans* (mental substance), is of another character from matter, or *res extensa* (extended substance). *Res cogitans* is non-physical and not localized, contrary to ordinary matter, or *res extensa*, which is localized and belonging to the physical realm. As such, he put forth the idea that we humans are composed not just of our bodies (*res extensa*) but also of our minds (*res cogitans*).

The Cartesian theory of mind and body has a problem with mental causation: how can a non-physical substance affect the physical world? Descartes already knew this problem, as documented from his correspondence with Princess Elisabeth of Bohemia. In a letter from 1643, she wrote:

> How the human soul can determine the movement of the animal spirits in the body so as to perform voluntary acts – being as it is merely a conscious substance. For the determination of movement seems always to come about from the moving body's being propelled – to depend on the kind of impulse it gets from what sets it in motion, or again, on the nature and shape of this latter thing's surface. Now the first two conditions involve contact and the third involves that the impelling thing has extension; but you utterly exclude extension from your notion of soul and contact seems to me incompatible with a thing's being immaterial.
>
> – Anscombe and Geach 1954: 274-275,
> as cited in Robb and Heil (2021)

His response to Princess Elisabeth was unsatisfactory. This problem has remained a core issue for dualists, perhaps being one of the reasons why dualism has lost its appeal to many.

The dualist view gained new support from an unlikely place: quantum physics. In 1932, in his famous book entitled *Mathematical Foundations of Quantum Mechanics*, John von

Neumann (1983) discussed the renowned measurement problem in a way that suggested that the collapse of the wave function happened with the interaction of the observer's mind. In this book, after discussing the measurement problem and arguing that quantum mechanics (QM) never yields a single outcome for a measurement, von Neumann states:

> But in any case, no matter how far we calculate – to the [measurement apparatus as the] mercury vessel, to the scale of the thermometer, to the retina, or into the brain, at some time we must say: and this is perceived by the observer.
>
> – 1932: 419-20

Though it was implicit in von Neumann's words that the observer had a different character from matter, the step to explicitly articulate that the mind was non-physical was taken later by Fritz London and Edmond Bauer (1939) and, more famously, by Eugene Wigner (1961). For instance, according to Wigner:

> Until not many years ago, the "existence" of a mind or soul would have been passionately denied by most physical scientists. The brilliant successes of mechanistic and, more generally, macroscopic physics and of chemistry overshadowed the obvious fact that thoughts, desires and emotions are not made of matter and it was nearly universally accepted among physical scientists that there is nothing besides matter. The epitome of this belief was the conviction that, if we knew the positions and velocities of all atoms at one instant of time, we could compute the fate of the universe for all future.
>
> – 1961: 171

Wigner then argues that QM almost required the mind to remain consistent (see our quick discussion in Section 5 for more on this). He then asks the critical question of whether the consciousness causes collapse hypothesis (CCCH), i.e. the hypothesis that the interaction of a conscious observer with a measurement apparatus changes the deterministic dynamic of QM to a probabilistic and non-unitary one, could ever be verified experimentally:

> It follows that there are only two avenues through which experimentation can proceed to obtain information about our first thesis [that consciousness causes collapse of the wave function]: observation of infants where we may be able to sense the progress of the awakening of consciousness and by discovering phenomena postulated by the second thesis, in which the consciousness modifies the usual laws of physics.
>
> – Wigner 1961: 182

We have argued elsewhere that Wigner's proposal, in fact any attempt to verify the CCCH experimentally, is doomed, as CCCH is not falsifiable (de Barros and Oas 2017).

However, not all is hopeless for a science of consciousness involving QM and CCCH. Though we cannot falsify CCCH, models relating CCCH with mental causation may be falsifiable. One such model is that of Henry Stapp (2004). Stapp ingeniously uses the inverse Quantum Zeno Effect in his model to show that, if we accept the CCCH, a mind observing a measurement apparatus can change its physical state. This paper will examine Stapp's model and discuss some possible consequences. In particular, we argue that certain types of structures should be available in the brain if Stapp's theory is correct. We hope this paper provides some suggestions on which research areas are helpful to the neuroscientist or physicist interested in falsifying the CCCH.

This paper is structured as follows: First, in Section 2, we discuss the measurement problem and von Neumann's argument that leads to his comments above. Then, in Section 3, we show Stapp's interaction model between mind and matter via the inverse Quantum Zeno Effect. In Section 4, we use Stapp's model to argue that some brain structures need to exist to allow for the interaction of mind and matter through Stapp's model. Finally, Section 5 discusses further theoretical problems for Stapp's model based on a Wigner-friend-type argument. We end this paper with some comments.

2. The Problem with Measurements

Quantum systems evolve according to a Schrödinger-type equation, described as a unitary operator in a Hilbert space. But the interaction of a physical system with a measurement apparatus changes the dynamic in a non-trivial way. When a measurement is performed, the dynamic is no longer deterministic, but stochastic. These dual dynamics suggest that somewhere in the measurement, new phenomena come about. Thus, the question is, how are measurements different from other interactions with non-measurement apparatuses?

One could argue that it is not the size of the measurement apparatus itself. Imagine the following situation. Let us prepare a quantum superposition of photons in the following state:

$$|\psi\rangle = c_1 |1\rangle + c_2 |2\rangle,$$

where $|1\rangle$ and $|2\rangle$ are Fock states with one or two photons, respectively. Imagine an atom on the ground state (we can think of it as a measurement apparatus). Imagine further that this atom's energy levels are such that they would not absorb a single photon from $|\psi\rangle$, whose energy is, say, $\hbar\omega$, but could absorb two photons, whose energy is $2\hbar\omega$, impinging on it. After the absorption, the atom decays and emits a single photon with energy $2\hbar\omega$. This single atom acts as a detector, as it provides a preferred basis for observation of the two photons. Furthermore, the probability of a person looking at this "measurement" apparatus and seeing a photon is given by $|c_2|^2$, assuming that we select ω such that it is not in the visible spectrum and 2ω is. So, whenever a person looking at this "measurement" apparatus sees a photon, he/she would interpret it as a collapse of the wave function from $c_1|1\rangle + c_2|2\rangle$ into $|2\rangle$ in a probabilistic way.

So, what makes a measurement different? There are several proposals, each carrying distinct ontological baggage. Bohm's theory, for example, requires a different space–time structure from special relativity and it also provides challenges to the idea of causal relations, as it requires instantaneous interactions between spacelike separated measuring events. On the other hand, Everett's interpretation posits that, at each measurement, the universe splits into several universes, each for every possible outcome. This disturbing interpretation has profound ontological consequences to the meaning of self, but a significant number of physicists accept it.

In his influential book, von Neumann (1983) proposed a curious solution to the measurement problem. Let us think about the atom as a measurement apparatus. We can write down its interaction with the photon superposition state and this system would evolve unitarily, with no stochastic dynamic. We could expand our analysis and think of the observer's eyes as a detector themselves. We could then model its interaction with the system "photon superposition plus atom". This system would also evolve unitarily. We could continue until we exhaust all matter that makes up the observer and we still would get no stochastic dynamic. So, von Neumann suggested that what we are left with is the observer's mind. The interaction of the observer's mind leads to this stochastic dynamic and the collapse of the wave function.[1] Now, what is this mind? In his discussion, von Neumann seems to suggest that this would be a mind not subject to the unitary evolution of Schrödinger's equation. London and Bauer (1939), followed by Wigner (1961) and then by Stapp (2004), explicitly advocate the idea of the mind being non-physical.

---

1 The discussion above may oversimplify von Neumann's views and may be more correctly attributable to London and Bauer's work and, later, to Wigner's. For an account of this, see Bueno (2019).

Let us first start with von Neumann's interpretation. In his seminal book (1983), von Neumann discussed what came to be known as the measurement problem. Let us start with a quantum system described by a two-dimensional Hilbert space C^2, for example, a particle with spin ½. Take the basis where there are two vectors which are eigenvectors of the spin in the z-direction,[2] i.e. $\hat{\sigma}_z|\pm\rangle = \pm|\pm\rangle$. Let us focus on the measurement of spin in the z-direction only. For such measurements, there are two separate cases we need to examine: the state of the system before the measurement is an eigenstate of $\hat{\sigma}_z$, i.e. either $|+\rangle$ or $|-\rangle$; or the state of the system before the measurement is not an eigenstate of $\hat{\sigma}_z$, i.e. the state is a linear combination of $|+\rangle$ or $|-\rangle$ such as $c_+|+\rangle + c_-|-\rangle$, where c_+ and c_- are non-zero complex numbers.

For eigenvectors, the situation is straightforward. If we measure $\hat{\sigma}_z$ for a system in states $|\pm\rangle$, the outcome is always ± 1, the eigenvalue corresponding to the eigenstate. Furthermore, if we repeat the measurement, the result is the same. This repetition of results implies that the state is the same after such measurement. For example, if the system is in state $|+\rangle$; measuring $\hat{\sigma}_z$ will result in the value +1 and a post-measurement state $|+\rangle$.

For linear combinations, the situation is different. First, a measurement's outcome is not always the same: it is either +1 or −1. The system's state determines the relative frequencies we expect for each measurement. If we normalize the coefficients c_+ and c_- such that $|c_+|^2 + |c_-|^2 = 1$, then the probability of +1 is $|c_+|^2$ and the probability of −1 is $|c_-|^2$. Second, the final state is not the same, but either $|+\rangle$ or $|-\rangle$. The dynamic determining the final state is probabilistic.

This probabilistic dynamic of measurement is puzzling. Schrödinger's equation determines the evolution of quantum systems when no measurement is performed. Since Schrödinger's

---

2 We use units where $\hbar/2 = 1$.

equation is deterministic, if the initial state of a system is known, then the state at any other time is determined. There are no probabilistic dynamics in this evolution. So, does that mean that measurements, as it seems, do not follow Schrödinger's equation?

To answer the above question, von Neumann (1983) started with the assumption that a vector can describe the state of any physical system in a Hilbert space and its evolution governed by a unitary and linear Schrödinger-like equation in this space. In other words, he assumed that the quantum formalism and its corresponding dynamic could be universally applied to any physical system, including a measurement apparatus. He then used this assumption to model the interaction of a system to be measured and a measurement apparatus. Because of the linearity of Schrödinger's evolution, the interaction of a measurement device with a system initially in a superposition of states does not lead to a definite outcome but a superposition of the measurement apparatus and system. More importantly, after the interaction, neither the measurement apparatus nor the measured system is in an eigenstate of the measurement.

We could take the above example further. Instead of modelling just the interaction of the measurement apparatus and system, von Neumann argued that we could include in it also our eyes, thinking of themselves as another measuring device. Because of the linearity, we still get a superposition. We could keep on going, including the optical nerve, the visual cortex and the whole brain; we still get a superposition. We could include all matter and we still have a superposition. However, when we observe a system and measurement apparatus, we never see a superposition: we always observe one of the possible measurement outcomes. So, von Neumann argued that what caused the end of the superposition, i.e. the collapse of the wave function, was the observer. Though he did not say this, the implied conclusion, explicitly stated by London and Bauer

(1939), is that a non-physical observer's mind is responsible for the collapse of the wave function.

To summarize, if we take Schrödinger's quantum evolution to heart, we bump into the measurement problem: the interaction of a measurement device and a physical system does not explain how we get a particular outcome of a measurement. Instead, we end up with a superposition of possible outcomes if the system starts in a superposition state. To solve this problem, one may bring the observer's mind into play, which interacts with the measurement device and system, and causes a wave function collapse. In the next section, we will see how Henry Stapp used this idea to show how a non-physical mind could interact with a physical system in a way that goes beyond the collapse of the wave function.

3. Stapp's Quantum Zeno Model

Stapp showed that if we accept the mind as causing the collapse of the wave function, then there are cases where an observation could cause changes in the *macroscopic* state of the matter. To do so, Stapp uses the inverse quantum zeno effect (IQZE) [2014]. To describe Stapp's idea, we start with the IQZE and show that if Stapp's assumptions are correct, the observer's mind can increase a harmonic oscillator's physical amplitude. In other words, Stapp argues that collapse allows for a non-physical mind to affect the state of matter measurably.

Let us start with the coherent state for the harmonic oscillator, given by

$$\left|\alpha\right\rangle = e^{-|\alpha|^2/2} \sum \frac{\alpha^n}{\sqrt{n!}} \left|n\right\rangle, \tag{1}$$

where $|n\rangle$ is an energy eigenstate, $n = 0, 1, 2, \ldots, \infty$. The coherent state can be interpreted as a quasi-classical oscillator with amplitude α (Cohen-Tannoudji et al. 1977). Now, consider the following projection operator:

$$P_\beta = |\beta\rangle \langle\beta|. \tag{2}$$

This projector corresponds to an amplitude measurement: does the state have amplitude β? If so, P_β has eigenvalue 1; otherwise, its eigenvalue is 0.

Stapp's ingenious idea was to apply amplitude measurements, represented by operators of the type (2), in a way similar to the quantum zeno effect (QZE), but with a twist. In the QZE, a quantum system whose time evolution may change its state (with non-zero probability) is kept unchanged when continuously observed. In the IQZE, the opposite happens: a quantum system whose state is stationary is affected by continuous observation.

To see how the IQZE works, consider a harmonic oscillator in a coherent state $|\alpha\rangle$, as given in eq. (1). Suppose we measure this state $|\alpha\rangle$ using the following projection operator

$$P_{\alpha+\in} = |\alpha + \in\rangle \langle \alpha + \in|,$$

which corresponds to the measurement "is the amplitude $\alpha + \in$?" After such a measurement, the system ends in the state $|\alpha + 2\in\rangle$ with probability $1 - \in^2$. If we now take the state $|\alpha + \in\rangle$ and measure

$$P_{\alpha+2\in} = |\alpha + \in\rangle \langle \alpha + \in|$$

once again, with probability $1 - \in^2$, the outcome is the state $|\alpha + 2\in\rangle$. It is clear that the state is increasing its amplitude with every new measurement, albeit in small increments. Let us make N measurements such as those two above to produce large increments in amplitude. In particular, take the following N projection operators: $P_{\alpha+\in}, P_{\alpha+2\in}, P_{\alpha+3\in}, \ldots P_{\alpha+N\in}$. Since the wave function collapses for each observation, after these N measurements, the system will end in the state $|\alpha + N\in\rangle$ with probability $(1-\in^2)^N = 1 - N\in^2 + O(\in^4)$, for $\in \ll 1$. If we take the limit $\in \to 0$ and $N \to \infty$, with $N\in = \beta$, constant, the system's final state is $|\alpha + \beta\rangle$ with probability *one*. This increase in amplitude with probability one is the IQZE: the continuous measurement of an oscillator changes its amplitude.

Here, we emphasize the role of measurement in the change of the amplitude. Without measurement, it would not change, as the system would be in a superposition state. It is only after a measurement that an actual amplitude state is created. As discussed in Section 2, for Stapp (2009), following von Neumann (1983) and Wigner (1961), a measurement occurs when a physical system interacts with the observer's mind.[3] This interaction changes the dynamic from the unitary and deterministic evolution dictated by Schrödinger's equation to a probabilistic and non-unitary one given by Born's rule. In this view, if there is no observer's mind, there is no collapse and the amplitude does not increase (at least not with probability one).

If we assume that the observer's mind collapses the wave function, then a fascinating possibility arises. For instance, Stapp proposed that neural oscillators in the cortex could interact with a mind through the IQZE. The mind could force the oscillator to jump from its original amplitude to a much larger one by choosing to observe or not. If correct, Stapp provides a long-sought mechanism for the interaction of mind and matter.

The hypothesis that the wave function collapses when a physical system interacts with an observer's mind is dubbed the CCCH. The CCCH is one of many possible interpretations of what happens in a quantum measurement. Other interpretations exist that carry their own ontological baggage (de Barros et al. 2019). For example, the many worlds interpretation posits splitting the universe into as many experimental outcomes as possible. The choice of which interpretation to use is, ultimately, philosophical. Here we point out that, as far as we know, the CCCH cannot be discarded purely on empirical grounds (de Barros and Oas 2017). However, perhaps we can inspect the

---

3 This is a controversial assumption that is not popular among the physics community (Schlosshauer et al. 2013). For discussions for and against the rule of the observer's mind in quantum physics, see (de Barros and Montemayor 2019b).

consequences of the CCCH and use such results to inform our philosophical choices. To do so, in the following sections, we will explore some of the consequences of Stapp's model.

4. Constraints on Matter from Mind–Matter Model

Let us assume that Stapp's idea is correct, viz. that our brain has neural oscillators that, through a collapse of the wave function, have their amplitude increased by the mind. What are the consequences of such an assumption? In this and the next section, we will examine some of those consequences and possible further lines of inquiry.

Let us start with some physiological consequences. In Stapp's model, the interaction between mind and matter happens with the increase in the amplitude of a group of neural oscillators assumed to be a neuropil in the neocortex (Stapp 2009). Stapp then claims that the mind chooses to observe the amplitude using a projection operator such as $|\alpha\rangle\langle\alpha|$, as shown above. However, Stapp does not go into the details of how such a measurement is performed, simply saying that the mind chooses to do so.

In the previous work, we showed that we must posit further structures to perform such measurements (de Barros and Oas 2015; de Barros and Montemayor 2019a; de Barros 2016). For instance, let us consider what is necessary to have a measurement. First, we need to have a quantum system being observed. This system can be quite general and pretty much anything would satisfy this criterion. Then, we need to have a measurement apparatus. The requirement for a measurement apparatus is not trivial: the measurement device provides the preferred basis for the measurement (Schlosshauer 2005).

Let us consider the following experiment with a Stern-Gerlach (SG) apparatus. A beam of electrons prepared in the state $|+\rangle_x$ impinges on an SG apparatus with a magnetic field gradient in the z-direction. The interaction between spin and field gradient causes the beam to split into two, one with particles in $|+\rangle_z$ and another with particles in $|-\rangle_z$. However, this splitting does not tell the whole story. If the two beams were to be rejoined somehow before an observer interacted with them and extracted information about each particle's trajectory, the final state would be the original one, viz. $|+\rangle_x$. However, if an observer interacted with the beams in the path in a way that they could infer which path (and consequently the value of spin in *z*), the final recombined beam would not be $|+\rangle_x$, but instead a proper mixture of $|+\rangle_x$ and $|-\rangle_x$, viz. $\rho = {}^1\!/\!{}_2(|+\rangle_x\langle+|_x + |-\rangle_x\langle-|_x)$. At first, it may seem that the reason for having the mixture ρ instead of the pure state $|+\rangle_x$ was the observation. But if SG were not there, the observation would not transform $|+\rangle_x$ into the mixture. This transformation occurred because there was a measurement apparatus that interacted with the particle in a certain way as to change the state of the particle. Furthermore, the which-path information that leads to the inevitable transition between a pure state and a proper mixture is not included in the SG with the magnetic field. One needs to imagine another device that provides such information, e.g. perhaps a photon that would interact with the electron (Scully and Druhl 1982).

In other words, just observing a particle is not enough. The experimental apparatus is what determines *what* is observed. To have a measurement, in addition to the collapse of the wave function provided by the observer's mind (according to Stapp), we need to have a measurement apparatus. The mind provides the collapse, whereas the measurement apparatus provides the preferred basis (Schlosshauer 2005).

What is the consequence of the previous discussion on Stapp's model? The immediate one is that Stapp's view that the observer chooses to observe is insufficient. One needs to provide a measurement device that the mind can use to collapse the wave function on the appropriate measurement basis. However, the mind cannot just choose which measurement device to use: it can only choose to observe or not whatever measurement devices are there. The most obvious solution to this problem is having a measurement device with some periodicity in its measurements. For example, a possible model could be a measurement device that, when interacting with the micropil, leads to a measurement of the form

$$P_{F(t)} = |F(t)\rangle\langle F(t)|,$$

where $F(t)$ is a function that is smooth and periodic. The periodicity of $F(t)$ is necessary as the mind needs to have some predictability of F's behaviour to decide when to "observe" and when to "not observe", thus causing the desired physical results.

So, to summarize our argument in this section, Stapp's model seems to require the existence of several structures on the brain. First, neural oscillators in the micropil, which to Stapp could translate into the movement of a limb or the turning of an eye. Second, the measurement apparatus provides the preferred basis for $P_{F(t)}$. This measurement apparatus must also be oscillatory since it must be periodic. More importantly, because the measurements are of amplitude, the periodicity may not be faster than that of the oscillators in the neuropil. Because oscillators in the neuropil have typical frequencies in the hundreds of Hertz, the periodicity of $F(t)$ must be in the tens of Hertz to increase the amplitude by a small amount. This slow frequency means that such a slight amplitude increase may not be sufficient and we should probably expect other neural machinery that would amplify specific processes. In other words, for the researcher trying to validate Stapp's hypothesis, there is fertile ground to look for certain types of structures in the brain. These additional structures suggest that Stapp's mind–matter QZE interaction hypothesis requires ancillary concepts that could be falsified in principle.

5. Wigner's Friend Redux

The previous section discussed some consequences from Stapp's proposal that the QZE could explain how the mind interacts with the brain. This section aims to consider the outcomes of the mind–matter interaction by modifying a thought experiment first proposed by Wigner. We will assume that Stapp's model is correct and seek additional consequences resulting from it.

Let us start with a reminder of the Wigner's friend thought experiment (1961). In this experiment, Wigner imagines a friend who, locked inside a laboratory, performs a measurement on a quantum system. Wigner then observes his friend's laboratory (with his friend inside) and describes them with the formalism of quantum mechanics, treating it as a quantum system. Wigner points out that he, modelling his friend's lab as an external observer, reaches a different conclusion from his friend. These different conclusions seem to constitute an inconsistency in the two views about the same actual experiment.

Wigner's friend Gedankenexperiment gained new traction recently with the publication of a paper by Frauchiger and Renner (2018). Their article changes Wigner's argument to present a no-go theorem. Their theorem starts with the following three assumptions:

(a) Quantum mechanical predictions are consistent;

(b) quantum mechanics is universally valid; and

(c) experiments yield only one outcome.

Assumption (a) means that we cannot predict outcomes of experiments that will lead to a contradiction. It is important to emphasize that they are not talking about Kochen–Specker-type contradictions. Instead, (a) relies on actual contradictions that could be reached experimentally without counterfactual reasoning. The universal validity assumed in (b) is that quantum mechanics applies to everything, including the observer. The role of the observer was at the core of Wigner's paper and he wanted to show that by not including the observer as "outside" of the quantum realm, we were led to disparate descriptions of the same situation. We should point out that (b) is effectively violated by Copenhagen's interpretation, where the experimental apparatus is seen as different from the measuring system because it imposes a non-unitary dynamic via a collapse of the wave function. Finally, (c) is the idea that one always sees only one outcome of an experiment. For example, in the case of Schrödinger's cat, we either observe the cat dead or alive. We notice that (c) is violated by the many worlds interpretation of quantum mechanics, as in this interpretation, all possible outcomes of an experiment are realized, albeit in different worlds (Everett 1957). Frauchiger and Renner's no-go theorem was to show that (a), (b) and (c) led to inconsistencies such that one of them needed to be discarded. As we saw above, in Stapp's (and Wigner's) view, we reject the universality of quantum mechanics: the mind is not subject to the same laws as ordinary matter, the latter described by unitary evolutions via a Schrödinger equation. On the other hand, if one has the proclivities of science fiction writers and prefers to violate (c), one may choose the many worlds interpretation. Of course, one could always take the easy way out: declare that quantum mechanics is all about what we know and not about what nature is, as the proponents of QBism advocate (Ladyman et al. 2007).

Here we are not concerned with possible epistemic or ontic contradictions that may come out of Wigner's thought experiment. Instead, we want to propose a change in the scenario. Imagine that Wigner's consciousness interacts with matter, as Stapp proposes. What are the consequences of Wigner's friend observing him? In other words, what happens to Wigner when his friend (possibly a neurosurgeon) decides to not only watch her friend but also prod inside his brain? More importantly, what possible information may this friend gain about the structures in Wigner's brain that interact with his mind?

We conduct this Gedankenexperiment in two different scenarios to answer the above questions. Scenario 1 is with

Wigner fully conscious. Scenario 2 is with Wigner wholly unconscious, such as under anesthesia, sleeping, or perhaps dreaming.

Let us start with Scenario 1. In this scenario, since Wigner is conscious, his mind interacts with matter by observing it (according to Stapp's model from Section 3). This observation is directed towards some oscillating measurement devices constrained, as described in Section 4. For example, if Wigner wishes to move his arm up, his mind would (perhaps even unconsciously?) direct its "wave collapsing observational powers" to the measurement apparatus whose measurement under observation would cause an increase in neuronal activity in the regions of the motor cortex associated with a contraction of the relevant muscles. Because an observation causes a muscle contraction, this opens up the question of whether Wigner's friend could observe Wigner, thus causing the muscle to contract.

The existence of Wigner's friend causes some difficulties with this model. The brain is a wet and hot environment. As such, the degrees of freedom of the measurement apparatus, modelled by neural oscillators, entangle with that of other parts of Wigner's body through a process known as environmental decoherence (Schlosshauer 2005). Consequently, the simple presence of Wigner's friend observing would cause a collapse of the wave function of the system Wigner's neural oscillators plus body plus local environment, which would be entangled. This collapse would be the same as Wigner observing his neural oscillators. Thus, the simple presence of his friend would cause his arm to move through the contraction of his muscle. If we take Stapp's model to heart and assume that all voluntary muscles in Wigner's body are contracted via the mind's decision to observe an oscillator, Wigner, in the presence of his friend (or any other conscious being) would be left in a state of paralysis as if he were having an overdose of ecstasy or some other drug that causes indiscriminate muscle contraction. To avoid such horrible fate to Wigner, one would have to assume some sort of protective mechanism that prevents the degrees of freedom of the neural oscillators from entangling with those of its surrounding.

It is enough to say that preventing decoherence is an important research topic in quantum computation. Furthermore, quantum computers are usually isolated from the environment and kept at very low temperatures to avert couplings with the thermal bath. Protective mechanisms that work at room temperature are unknown. If this happens in our brain, it will present some interesting new physics.

Let us assume that an unlikely mechanism protects the neural oscillators from decoherence and keeps quantum superpositions when Wigner's mind is not observing it. Even in this case, Wigner's friend, a renowned neurosurgeon, may be able to watch such oscillators herself. The consequence will be the involuntary motion of Wigner's arms, for example, because his friend observed the measurement oscillators.

Now let us examine Scenario 2 when Wigner is unconscious. The same problems that occur with Scenario 1, where Wigner's friend would cause the collapse of the wave function and lead to activations of all muscles. Thus, the same conclusions about the need for a protected environment occur again. Similarly, Wigner's neurosurgeon friend could access the protected neural oscillators and cause their collapse. So, what distinguishes sleep or unconscious states from conscious states? Why do we not see the same neural activities in unconscious states as in conscious states? It could be that the measurement and neuropil oscillators are simply deactivated and would start oscillating again once Wigner becomes conscious.

6. Final Remarks

This paper examined some of the consequences of Stapp's model of interaction between mind and brain using the QZE. If Stapp's model is correct, we saw that some physiological structures should be observed in the brain. These new structures present a possible way to falsify or corroborate Stapp's model.

However, in examining a new version of Wigner's friends, we saw that Stapp's model has some further complications. The existence of neural oscillators that interact with the local measurement apparatus responsible for the interaction between mind and matter cannot have their degrees of freedom entangled with the environment. If such entanglement occurs, a friend observing Wigner will cause observable effects in Wigner's body movement and Wigner's body would not be under his control but under his friend's control. We are left with only one possibility: that the structures in the brain somehow protect those neuropil oscillators plus measurement oscillators from environmental decoherence. Such a prospect is unlikely but, if it existed, would present some interesting new physics with perhaps far-reaching consequences to quantum computation.

We end with a comment on protected environments. Penrose and Hameroff's orchestrated reduction model assumes that conscious interactions happen within microtubules in the brain's neurons (Hameroff and Penrose 1996). For Penrose and Hameroff's model to work, quantum coherence must be maintained at least for some milliseconds. However, estimations of the decoherence time for those systems seem to be far smaller than what is required (Tegmark 2000). We emphasize that microtubules are several orders of magnitude smaller than neuropil oscillators and the decoherence time for those is significantly faster.

References

de Barros, J. Acacio and Carlos Montemayor (eds), 2019, *Quanta and Mind: Essays on the Connection between Quantum Mechanics and Consciousness*, Synthese Library 414, New York: Springer Cham.

de Barros, J. Acacio and Carlos Montemayor, 2019, "Where Does Quanta Meet Mind?", in *Quanta and Mind: Essays on the*

Connections between Quantum Mechanics and Consciousness, Synthese Library 414, pp. 55-66, New York: Springer Cham.

de Barros, J. Acacio and Gary Oas, 2015a, "Quantum Cognition, Neural Oscillators and Negative Probabilities", in *The Palgrave Handbook of Quantum Models in Social Science: Applications and Grand Challenges*, ed. Emmanuel Haven and Andrei Khrennikov, Leicester, UK: Palgrave Macmillan.

———, 2015b, "Quantum Mechanics and the Brain and Some of Its Consequences", *Cosmos and History: The Journal of Natural and Social Philosophy*, 11(2): 146-53.

———, 2017, "Can We Falsify the Consciousness-Causes-Collapse Hypothesis in Quantum Mechanics?", *Foundations of Physics*, 47(10): 1294-1308.

de Barros, J. Acacio et al., 2019, "Henry Stapp and the Orthodox Interpretation", *Activitas Nervosa Superior*, 61(1): 1-5.

de Barros, J. Acacio, 2016, "On a Model of Quantum Mechanics and the Mind", in *Dualism, Platonism and Voluntarism: Explorations at the Quantum, Microscopic, Mesoscopic and Symbolic Neural Levels*, ed. Sean O'Nuallain, pp. 165-77, Berkeley, CA: Cambridge Scholars Publishing.

Bueno, Otávio, 2019, "Is There a Place for Consciousness in Quantum Mechanics?", in *Quanta and Mind: Essays on the Connection between Quantum Theories and Consciousness*, ed. J. Acacio de Barros and Carlos Montemayor, Synthese Library, New York: Springer Cham.

Cohen-Tannoudji, Claude, Bernard Diu and Franck Laloë, 1977, *Quantum Mechanics*, vol. 1, New York: John Wiley & Sons.

Everett, H., 1957, "Relative State Formulation of Quantum Mechanics", *Reviews of Modern Physics*, 29(3): 454-62.

Frauchiger, Daniela and Renato Renner, 2018, "Quantum Theory Cannot Consistently Describe the Use of Itself", *Nature Communications*, 9(1): 3711.

Hameroff, Stuart and Roger Penrose, 1996, "Orchestrated Reduction of Quantum Coherence in Brain Microtubules: A Model for

Consciousness", *Mathematics and Computers in Simulation*, 40(3-4): 453-80.

Ladyman, James et al., 2007, *Every Thing Must Go: Metaphysics Naturalized*, Oxford: Clarendon Press.

London, Fritz and Edmond Bauer, 1939, *La théorie de l'observation en mécanique quantique*", Paris: Hermann & Cie.

von Neuman, John, 1932/1983, *Mathematical Foundations of Quantum Mechanics*, Princeton, NJ: Princeton University Press.

Robb, David and John Heil, 2021, "Mental Causation", in *The Stanford Encyclopedia of Philosophy*, ed. Edward N. Zalta, Spring, Metaphysics Research Lab, Stanford University, https://plato.stanford.edu/archives/spr2021/entries/mental-causation/ (visited on 5 April 2021).

Schlosshauer, Maximilian, 2005, "Decoherence, the Measurement Problem, and Interpretations of Quantum Mechanics", *Reviews of Modern Physics*, 76(4): 1267-1305. doi: 10.1103/RevModPhys.76.1267.

Schlosshauer, Maximilian et al., 2013, "A Snapshot of Foundational Attitudes toward Quantum Mechanics", *Studies in History and Philosophy of Science, Studies in History and Philosophy of Modern Physics*, 44(3): 222-30.

Scully, Marlan O. and Kai Druhl, 1982, "Quantum Eraser: A Proposed Photon Correlation Experiment Concerning Observation and 'Delayed Choice' in Quantum Mechanics", *Physical Review A*, 25(4): 2208-13.

Stapp, Henry P., 2004, "Mind, Matter and Quantum Mechanics", in *Mind, Matter and Quantum Mechanics*, ed. Henry P. Stapp, pp. 81-118, The Frontiers Collection, Berlin/Heidelberg: Springer-Verlag.

———, 2014, "Mind, Brain and Neuroscience", *Cosmos and History*, 10(1): 227-31.

Tegmark, Max, 2000, "Importance of Quantum Decoherence in Brain Processes", *Phys. Rev. E*, 61(4): 4194-4206.

Wigner, Eugene, 1961, "Remarks on the Mind–Body Question", in *The Scientist Speculates*, ed. I.J. Good, pp. 284-302, London: Heinemann.

4

Zeno Goes to Copenhagen

A Dilemma for Measurement-Collapse Interpretations of Quantum Mechanics

David J. Chalmers
Kelvin J. McQueen

Abstract: A familiar interpretation of quantum mechanics (one of a number of views sometimes labelled the "Copenhagen Interpretation"), takes its empirical apparatus at face value, holding that the quantum wave function evolves by the Schrödinger equation except on certain occasions of measurement, when it collapses into a new state according to the Born rule. This interpretation is widely rejected, primarily because it faces the measurement problem: "measurement" is too imprecise for use in a fundamental physical theory. We argue that this is a weak objection, as there may be many ways of making "measurement" precise. However, measurement-collapse interpretations face a more serious objection: a dilemma tied to the quantum Zeno effect. Is measurement

* Authors are listed in alphabetical order and contributed equally. Thanks to Scott Aaronson, Harald Atmanspacher, Adam Brown, Chris Fuchs, Jim Holt, Matt Leifer, Simon Saunders, David Wallace and to audiences at Interlaken (TSC), Lake Arrowhead (CQIN) and Tuscany (FQXi).

itself an observable that can enter superpositions? If yes, then the standard measurement-collapse dynamics is ill-defined. If no, then (at least if measurement is an observable), measurements can never start or finish. The best way out is to deny that measurement is an observable, but this leads to strong and revisionary consequences. This reinforces the view that there is no non-revisionary interpretation of quantum mechanics.

Keywords: Measurement problem, Copenhagen Interpretation, measurement-collapse interpretations, wave function collapse, quantum Zeno effect, Zeno dilemma.

1. Introduction

A familiar story about quantum mechanics runs as follows. Quantum-mechanical systems can be modelled by a wave function. Most of the time, the wave function evolves according to the deterministic Schrödinger equation. The wave function need not specify definite values for the position, momentum and other properties of the system. Instead, it may specify that the system is in a superposition of many different values for these properties. When one measures these properties, however, one always obtains a definite result. After measurement, the system's wave function is now in a new state that specifies this definite value. The result of the measurement and the resulting wave function are determined probabilistically by the pre-measurement wave function of the system according to the Born rule, which associates wave function amplitudes with probabilities.

The canonical version of this story was given by John von Neumann in *Mathematical Foundations of Quantum Mechanics* (1932/1955). Construed as an empirical apparatus for predicting the results of measurements, this story has been tremendously successful. The predictions made by the story have been borne out again and again, and it has been used to explain all sorts of phenomena. As a result, the empirical apparatus has long ago obtained the status of orthodoxy.

Because of this empirical success, it is natural to construe the story as a description of the reality underlying quantum mechanics. Taken at face value, the story suggests that quantum-mechanical reality is objectively described by a wave function with a bipartite dynamics. First, there is the Schrödinger evolution, which is linear, deterministic and constantly ongoing. Second, there is a process of collapse into a definite state, which is non-linear, non-deterministic and happens only on certain occasions of measurement.

This face-value interpretation of quantum mechanics (Schrödinger equation plus collapse on measurement) is often regarded as a sort of orthodoxy or at least as a starting point for interpreting quantum mechanics, if a starting point that is very frequently rejected. Among physicists, this view is often called the "Copenhagen Interpretation", associating it with the traditional heft of the Copenhagen school of quantum mechanics led by Niels Bohr and Werner Heisenberg.

Philosophers and historians of science more often use the "Copenhagen" label for Bohr's own quite different interpretation, which was based on his somewhat obscure principle of complementarity and did not invoke collapse.[1] To avoid this ambiguity, we will call the face-value interpretation the *measurement-collapse interpretation*, but we will occasionally

---

[1] The label "Copenhagen Interpretation" was introduced by Heisenberg (1955). See Howard (2004) for a history of how Heisenberg's approach differed from Bohr's and led to the contemporary use of the label as standing for the measurement-collapse interpretation. The label is also sometimes used for generic anti-realist views on which the wave function does not describe objective reality and for quietist views in the spirit of "shut up and calculate".

allude to the familiar Copenhagen label, for example, in our title.[2]

The measurement-collapse interpretation is widely rejected by theorists working in the foundations of quantum mechanics. Perhaps the most common reason for rejection arises from the original "measurement problem": the notion of "measurement" is ill-suited for use in a fundamental theory, as it is imprecise, ill-defined, or anthropocentric (Albert 1992; Bell 1990). As a result, theorists have focused on revisionary interpretations of quantum mechanics that give no special role to measurement. These include interpretations that give a role to collapse but not to measurement, such as the spontaneous-collapse interpretations developed by Ghirardi et al. (1986) and Pearle (1976, 1989). They also include interpretations that dispense with collapse altogether, such as Everett's (1957) many worlds interpretation and Bohm's (1952) hidden-variable interpretation.

We will argue in Section 2 that the standard reason for rejecting measurement-collapse interpretations is a weak one. It is true that the ordinary notion of "measurement" is imprecise. However, as with any imprecise term in physics, we can handle this issue by replacing it by something more precise that plays the same role in our theory. Replacing measurement with a range of different precise notions yields a range of different precise interpretations of quantum mechanics, each of which can be empirically tested in principle.

However, measurement-collapse interpretations face a more serious objection that (as far as we know) has not been noted previously. This objection arises from the quantum Zeno effect, which tells us that when we continuously measure an observable in a system, the value of that observable will never change. The

[2] Johnson (2010) suggests that as the two leading proponents of the measurement-collapse interpretation, von Neumann and Eugene Wigner, were both Hungarians, it should be called the "Budapest Interpretation". If that convention were adopted, this article might then be called "Zeno Goes to Budapest".

source of the quantum Zeno effect is the mathematical fact that for a system to evolve from one eigenstate (definite state) of an observable into another by Schrödinger evolution, it must always pass through superpositions of these eigenstates. Continuous measurement of an observable prevents these superpositions from arising, so prevents change between eigenstates.

The quantum Zeno effect was first described by Alan Turing (Gandy 1954) and was mathematically derived by Degasperis et al. (1974). Misra and Sudarshan (1977) called it "a Zeno's paradox for quantum theory". They regarded it as raising a genuine paradox for standard quantum mechanics on the grounds that we never observe the predicted freezing of quantum systems on continuous measurement. In a similar vein, Ballentine (1998: 343) says that measurement-collapse interpretations are "disproven by the simple empirical fact that continuous observation does not prevent motion".

In the ensuing years, most researchers have come to regard the Zeno phenomenon as non-paradoxical, for a number of reasons. First, weaker versions of the phenomenon involving slowing rather than freezing have been demonstrated experimentally (Itano et al. 1990). Second, it has been argued that the strong continuous measurements required for freezing are either practically or theoretically impossible (Nakazato et al. 1995). Third, it has been shown that a version of the Zeno effect follows from the Schrödinger equation alone, with or without the collapse postulate (Pascazio and Namiki 1994). As a result, the Zeno effect is widely held to be consistent both with empirical evidence and with all of the major interpretations of quantum mechanics.

We will argue that nevertheless, reasoning based on the Zeno effect raises a serious difficulty for measurement-collapse interpretations of quantum mechanics. This difficulty is quite distinct from the Misra–Sudarshan "paradox" and is not dissolved by the considerations mentioned above. Where the

Misra–Sudarshan "paradox" concerns the potential freezing of observables that are measured, the dilemma we are raising concerns the potential freezing of measurement itself.

To raise the problem, we can ask: can measurement itself enter superpositions? For example, can a particle be in a superposition of having its position measured and not having it measured? If it can, the standard dynamics is ill-defined, since the standard dynamics requires that collapse either happens or it does not, depending on whether measurement occurs. If it cannot, then the Zeno effect tells us that at least if measurement is itself a quantum observable, measurement states can never change, so that nothing can be measured after not being measured. Either way, the standard dynamics is not correct. In Section 3, we will set out this dilemma more carefully. In Sections 4-6 we look at the main options for escaping it, which require denying that measurement is a quantum observable.

Our conclusion is that endorsing a measurement-collapse interpretation requires some fairly radical revisions or additions to standard quantum mechanics. It requires either a strong form of dualism or treating measurement non-standardly as a special wave function property. This does not entail that no measurement-collapse interpretation is correct, but brings out the costs of such an interpretation more clearly. It also brings out that insofar as measurement-collapse provides the orthodox empirical apparatus for quantum mechanics, any tenable interpretation of quantum mechanics must be somewhat revisionary.

2. The Measurement Problem for Measurement-Collapse Interpretations

The standard objection to measurement-collapse interpretations is a version of the *measurement problem*: the notion of measurement is ill-suited for use in a fundamental theory, as it is imprecise, ill-defined or anthropocentric.

To illustrate the problem, we can ask questions such as: Does a rock make measurements? A camera? An ant? A cat? The ordinary notion of measurement leaves the issue unclear or ill-defined and thereby leaves the measurement-collapse dynamics of quantum mechanics unclear or ill-defined. Sometimes measurement is restricted to humans, which may yield a little more precision, but there is still some imprecision (for example, does unconscious perception count as measurement?). There is also now an issue of anthropocentrism: it is unclear why the fundamental physical dynamics of the world should give such a special role to humans. So at least with ordinary notions of measurement, the measurement-collapse dynamics seems to be imprecise and possibly anthropocentric as well.

We think the standard objection is a weak one. As with other imprecise notions used in physics, we can handle this issue by replacing it with something more precise: in particular, a precise mathematical criterion for when a given observable is measured. For example, Tononi (2008) has given a precise mathematical measure φ of information-integration in a system. We could define measurement so that only systems with φ above a certain precise threshold are measuring devices and an observable in another system is measured only when it becomes entangled with φ in the measuring system. This is just one example. There are an infinite number of other ways of making measurement precise.

In effect, the imprecise measurement-collapse interpretation can be seen as a template for a large number of more precise interpretations where "measurement" is replaced by some precise criterion for collapse. None of these interpretations are ill-defined or imprecise. Some of them may be anthropocentric, but many are not. If there is a problem in the vicinity, it is that many different precise interpretations are available and we do not know which of them is correct. But this is not really an objection to these interpretations. It is simply an invitation to further investigation.

Importantly, these precise measurement-collapse interpretations can all be empirically distinguished from each other. Different hypotheses about the locus of collapse make different predictions about where and when quantum superpositions and resulting quantum interference effects will be found and these predictions can be tested by experiments using interferometers and the like. Many of these experiments are not yet practically possible, but they are possible in principle. So, there is at least an in-principle empirical research programme of testing the many precise measurement-collapse interpretations to see which if any may be correct. The "imprecision" in the central notion of measurement simply amounts to a degree of freedom in our theories that is subject to empirical inquiry.

On one common understanding of measurement, it is equivalent to conscious observation. Given this understanding of measurement, the measurement-collapse interpretation leads to the *consciousness-collapse* interpretation (put forward by Wigner 1961), on which consciousness collapses the wave function. However, it is also possible to understand measurement quite independently of consciousness, in which case a measurement-collapse interpretation need give no special role to consciousness. In this paper, we are focusing on the broader class of measurement-collapse interpretations without assuming a connection to consciousness, but we will attend to consciousness-involving interpretations on occasion.

In formal terms, how can we understand measurement? Here is a fairly standard statement of the collapse postulate in quantum mechanics:

> Carrying out a "measurement" of an observable B on a system in a state $|A\rangle$ has the effect of collapsing the system into a B-eigenstate corresponding to the eigenvalue observed.

> Which particular B-eigenstate it collapses into is a matter of probability and the probabilities are given by a rule known as Born's Rule: $prob\ (b_i) = \langle A \mid B = b_i\rangle|^2$. – Ismael 2015: section 5

Here, the role played by measurement in the dynamics is that when an observable O of a system S is measured, S collapses into an eigenstate of O, with probabilities determined by the Born rule. We can think of measurement as a two-place property m of (system, observable) pairs. Here $m(S, O)$ obtains when the observable O is being measured in system S. For example, when the x-spin of a particle e is measured, $m(e, x\text{-spin})$ obtains.

The collapse postulate tells us that when $m(S, O)$ obtains, the wave function of S collapses onto an eigenstate of O according to the Born probabilities. As long as m is a precise property of (system, observable) pairs, the resulting dynamics will be precise and well-defined, at least setting aside worries arising from relativity (which requires an extensive treatment of its own) and from simultaneous measurement (where constraints will be needed in order to prevent simultaneous measurement of incompatible observables such as position and momentum).

On a traditional conception of measurement, one can think of the two-place relation $m(S, O)$ as deriving from a three-place relation $M(S^1, S, O)$ which holds when a (measuring) system S^1 is measuring observable O in a (measured) system S. On this conception, $m(S, O)$ obtains iff there exists a system S^1 such that $M(S^1, S, O)$ obtains. However, for our purposes there is no need to explicitly invoke the measuring system S^1 or the three-place relation M. We can obtain a simpler and more general treatment by staying with the two-place relation $m(S, O)$. That said, readers should feel free to think in terms of measuring systems by translating $m(S, O)$ into $\exists S^1 M\ (S^1, S, O)$.

In fact, the argument that follows does not require understanding m in terms of measurement or observation at all. In principle, any precise property m of (system, observable) pairs meeting the constraints mentioned above can serve as a trigger for collapse. There will be a different precise collapse dynamics for every choice of an underlying property *m*, so a wide range of precise interpretations is available. We might think of these interpretations as *triggered-collapse* interpretations, on which there is a trigger for collapse that may or may not involve measurement. (These contrast with spontaneous-collapse interpretations, on which collapse occurs without a trigger.) We will focus on measurement-collapse interpretations in what follows, but the analysis applies to triggered-collapse interpretations more generally.[3]

The original objections to measurement-collapse interpretations – that measurement is imprecise, ill-defined, or anthropocentric – do little to threaten an interpretation involving a precise property *m*. The residue of the first two charges is perhaps an objection from evidence: we do not have specific evidence that any of these specific interpretations is correct. But this is true of most interpretations of quantum mechanics and it provides little reason to reject the theories. The residue of the third charge is perhaps an objection from complexity: *m* is almost certainly a complex property of physical systems and other

---

[3] Taxonomy: As we understand them, spontaneous-collapse and triggered-collapse interpretations are both objective-collapse interpretations, on which collapse happens in objective reality. Triggered-collapse interpretations include measurement-collapse interpretations as a proper subset and also include views on which the trigger has nothing to do with measurement (such as Penrose's interpretation discussed later in the paper). Measurement-collapse interpretations include consciousness-collapse interpretations as a proper subset and also include views on which measurement has nothing to do with consciousness (such as the view von Neumann entertains on which measurement takes place in ordinary measuring devices). There can be some argument over cases: for example, does GRW count as a triggered-collapse interpretation because the size of a system serves as a trigger?

physical theories do not give a fundamental role to complex properties. It is true that this would make quantum mechanics unlike other physical theories to date, but it is unclear that there is any reason in principle that complex properties cannot play a role in fundamental physical dynamics.

There are also a few well-known problems for all collapse interpretations that apply to the measurement-collapse interpretations. These include the problem of consistency with relativity (Maudlin 2011) and the "tails" problem (McQueen 2015). These problems have not prevented spontaneous-collapse interpretations from being taken seriously, however, and the problems are not obviously any worse where measurement-collapse interpretations are concerned. For present purposes we will set those problems aside to focus on a problem that is distinctive to the measurement-collapse view.

3. The Zeno Dilemma

We can set things up for the Zeno dilemma by asking: can measurement be measured? Or more precisely: is there a quantum observable corresponding to $m(S, O)$? On the face of it, one would expect that there might be. On most understandings of measurement we can certainly observe one system measuring another, so if we understand m in terms of measurement one would expect it to be an observable. In quantum mechanics, the key quantum observables are quasi-classical properties of classical basis states, corresponding to Hermitian operators. On many natural ways of understanding measurement, it will be a quasi-classical property of this sort.

To convert the relation $m(S, O)$ into an observable, we need to define a numerical quantity $m_{S,O}$:

$m_{S,O} = 1$ if $m(S, O)$ obtains (i.e. if O is measured in S);

$m_{S,O} = -1$ if $m(S, O)$ does not obtain (i.e. if O is not measured in S).

If this quantity $m_{S,O}$ is an observable, there will be an associated Hermitian operator whose eigenstates are $|m_{S,O} = 1\rangle$ and $|m_{S,O} = -1\rangle$.

The measurement of observables in system *S* may depend on what is going on outside *S*, perhaps in a separate measuring system S^1. If so, $m_{S,O}$ will not itself be an observable of *S*, as observables of *S* depend only on *S* and not on matters external to *S*. Instead, $m_{S,O}$ will be an observable of a broader system, such as a combined system $S + S^1$ or the universe as a whole.

For now, we will assume that $m_{S,O}$ is an observable to see what follows. Later, we will consider the alternatives.

Assuming that $m_{S,O}$ is an observable, we can then pose the Zeno dilemma by asking: is $m_{S,O}$ open to quantum superposition? That is, can systems enter superpositions of eigenstates of $m_{S,O}$? For example, can an electron *e* and its position *p* fail to have a definite value of $m_{e,p}$, with the system instead being in a superposition of $|m_{e,p} = -1\rangle$ and $|m_{e,p} = 1\rangle$? Or put in terms of measurement, can a particle be in a superposition of the state of having its position measured and the state of not having its position measured?

If the answer is yes: then the standard measurement-collapse dynamics is ill-defined. The standard dynamics tell us that if $m(S, O)$ obtains, *S* collapses onto an eigenstate of *O* and if $m(S, O)$ does not obtain, *S* does not collapse. When *S* is in a superposition of $m_{S,O}$, there is no fact of the matter about whether or not $m(S, O)$ obtains and so the standard dynamics do not specify any fact of the matter about whether *S* collapses. The dynamics say nothing about what happens when the world is in a superposition of $m_{S,O}$, or when the system is in a superposition of being measured and not being measured. Perhaps one could suggest that the wave function undergoes a superposition of collapsing and not collapsing, but a moment's reflection reveals that this does not really make sense. Perhaps one could suggest that collapse requires an eigenstate of $m_{S,O}$, so that superpositions of $m_{S,O}$ never trigger collapse, but now there is the threat that the wave function will never collapse again. In any case, all of these options require going well beyond the standard dynamics, which assume that being measured or not is a binary and determinate matter.

If the answer is no, then $m_{S,O}$ can never change its value, so that a system can never come to collapse after not collapsing.[4] This reflects the quantum Zeno effect, which is often glossed as saying that when a quantum observable is continuously measured, its value can never change. If an observable is continuously measured, the measured system will always be in an eigenstate of that observable. The mathematics of Schrödinger evolution entails that a system cannot evolve from being in one eigenstate of an observable to another eigenstate without going through a non-eigenstate of that observable. So if systems can never enter superpositions of $m_{S,O}$ eigenstates, $m_{S,O}$ can never change under Schrödinger evolution. As a result, Schrödinger evolution can never lead from a state where the wave function does not collapse to a state where the wave function collapses and the measurement-collapse dynamics will fail.

In effect, if $m_{S,O}$ can never enter superpositions, it is as if $m_{S,O}$ itself were constantly being measured, so that $m_{S,O}$ always keeps a definite value whenever it would otherwise enter a superposition. The quantum Zeno effect tells us that in a case of "strong continuous measurement" like this, the continuously

---

4 If $m(S, O)$ is an observable that cannot enter superpositions, it is as if there is a superselection rule forbidding superpositions of $m(S, O)$. Thalos (1998) argues that superselection rules cannot explain the measurement processes, in large part on the grounds that superselected quantities cannot change over time. Her critique is not directed at measurement-collapse interpretations and does not discuss superpositions of measurement per se, but the current point can be seen as an application of Thalos's analysis to certain measurement-collapse views.

measured observable can never change precisely because it can never enter a superposition.

One can turn the Zeno problem into an inconsistent tetrad for measurement-collapse interpretations. Here $m_{S,O}$ as before is the condition under which collapse occurs: a system collapses into an eigenstate of O iff $m_{S,O} = 1$. We will say that an observable is *superposable* if it is possible for a system to enter a superposition of eigenstates of that observable. We will say that an observable is *changeable* if a system can have one value of that observable at one time and another value at a different time.

(1) $m_{S,O}$ is an observable.

(2) $m_{S,O}$ is not superposable.

(3) $m_{S,O}$ is changeable.

(4) If an observable is not superposable, it is not changeable.

These four claims are clearly inconsistent. Which should a proponent of the measurement-collapse interpretation reject? We will work through them in reverse order.

(4) is a mathematical property of quantum mechanics under Schrödinger evolution and collapse. One might suggest that a non-superposable observable could be changeable via collapse rather than via Schrödinger evolution, perhaps by measuring a different observable. However, this would require that a system in an eigenstate of $m_{S,O}$ collapses directly into a different eigenstate of the same observable, which is mathematically impossible. Measuring observable O_2 of a system in an eigenstate of an observable O_1 always leads either to the same eigenstate (if the two observables commute) or to a non-eigenstate of O_1 (if they do not).

Someone might suggest that violations of (4) for measurement are built into the special dynamics of measurement and collapse. For example, perhaps at the instant of measurement and collapse, measuring systems transit directly from a non-measurement eigenstate to a measurement eigenstate (e.g. from a "ready" eigenstate to an eigenstate in which a measurement result is recorded). This special dynamics will go beyond the standard wave function dynamics of Schrödinger evolution and collapse. On one version of the picture, measurement is autonomous from the underlying wave function so that it can vary independently. That version leads to the dualist picture discussed in Section 5. On another version of the picture, measurement depends on the underlying wave function so that the wave function of a measuring device will jump directly between eigenstates. This will require new wave function dynamics that will take some spelling out.[5]

It is very hard to deny (3), which says that $m_{S,O}$ is changeable. On any measurement-collapse interpretation there will be systems that undergo collapse when certain observables are measured and this collapse will happen at certain times and not at other times. Given that an observable O of system S collapses depending on the value of $m_{S,O}$, this requires that at least for some S and O, $m_{S,O}$ sometimes changes its value.

---

5 One common way to represent the measurement process (e.g. Albert 1992: chap. 4) involves a measurement device d measuring an electron e transitioning from a "ready" eigenstate to an eigenstate displaying a result as follows: $|ready>_d |\uparrow z>_e \rightarrow |up\,z>_d |\uparrow z>_e$. This presentation may make it seem that the device d evolves directly from the ready state to the collapse state without any problem. However, the problem arises with the transition. In accord with the collapse postulate electron e has already collapsed to $|\uparrow z>_e$. The collapsed electron then causes the device to enter the state $|up\,z>_d$, as in the transition above. Since the collapse postulate has done its job already, the transition must be achieved by the Schrödinger dynamics. Since $|ready>_d |\uparrow z>_e$ and $|up\,z>_d |\uparrow z>_e$ are orthogonal eigenstates, the Schrödinger dynamics must transition through intermediate superpositions of these eigenstates in order for this transition to occur.

Denying (2) may seem somewhat more attractive. The worry was that if $m_{S,O}$ is superposable, the dynamics will not be well-defined, but there are various options for fleshing out the dynamics here. Perhaps the most natural suggestion is that only eigenstates of $m_{S,O}$ trigger collapse. That is, system S collapses onto an eigenstate of O only when the overall system is in the eigenstate $|m_{s,o}=1\rangle$. Superpositions of $|m_{s,o}=-1\rangle$ and $|m_{s,o}=1\rangle$ are possible, but these superpositions never trigger collapse. This now provides a well-defined criterion for measurement.

For this view to work and to avoid the Zeno dilemma in ordinary measurement situations, superpositions of $m_{S,O}$ eigenstates must evolve by Schrödinger evolution into eigenstates which will then trigger collapse. The obvious worry is that there is little reason to think that superpositions will always evolve into eigenstates as required. In a typical case, we would expect superpositions of $m_{S,O}$ eigenstates to lead to more superpositions and eventually to decoherent components of the wave function in which the measurement activity in different components is quite different. On this picture, there is little reason to expect that ordinary measurement situations will lead to definite measurement outcomes.

On an alternative picture that denies (2), only certain sorts of superposition of $m_{S,O}$ eigenstates trigger collapse. For example, perhaps collapse takes place only on a sufficiently large superposition, or only with a sufficiently decoherent wave function. In effect, this is to say that collapse is triggered by an elaborated condition $m^1{}_{S,O}$ as a property that a system has when it is in a certain sort of superposition of $m_{S,O}$ eigenstates, where $m^1{}_{S,O}$ is a property of a wave function as a whole. However, we can now apply the quadrilemma above to m^1. In this version of the quadrilemma, we will deny (1) for the new property m^1, as it is a wave function property rather than a quantum observable (as discussed later). So this move does not really open up new space for resisting the quadrilemma. It is in effect equivalent to denying (1) for the triggering property, an important move that we will discuss shortly.

A third suggestion is that the measurement-collapse process may have an extended dynamics and that $m_{S,O}$ may be superposable during the post-measurement period. For a very simple example: perhaps a definite value of $m_{S,O}$ is required to trigger collapse, but then collapse takes place one second later. A non-standard post-measurement dynamics like this may help explain how measurement can be followed by non-measurement (the overall system is in $|m_{s,o} = 1\rangle$, this triggers collapse, the system enters a superposition of $|m_{s,o} = 1\rangle$ and $|m_{s,o} = -1\rangle$ and then collapses onto $|m_{s,o} = -1\rangle$. However, post-measurement dynamics does nothing to explain the crucial case in which non-measurement (ordinary Schrödinger evolution without measurement or collapse) is followed by measurement. Explaining the onset of measurement requires something quite different. Relatedly, one might consider departing from the standard Copenhagen dynamics by allowing collapse to be triggered stochastically. For example, $m_{S,O}$ may be a quantitative property yielding a rate or degree of collapse. This approach is subject to the same sort of dilemma – can $m_{S,O}$ and the associated rate or degree enter superpositions? Whether yes or no, the same issues arise. So this option does not really open new ground in dealing with the dilemma.

The remaining and best option is to deny (1), embracing interpretations on which measurement is not an observable and is therefore not subject to superposition and the Zeno effect. There are three fairly natural ways to do this.

First, we could say that measurement is a *classical* property. It is often held that classical properties are distinct from quantum observables and are not subject to the same principles. If so, measurement may not be subject to the quantum Zeno effect and the dilemma might be evaded.

Second, we could say that measurement is a *non-physical* property. The most natural way to do this is to endorse a mind–body dualism on which mental properties and physical properties are fundamentally distinct and hold that measurement involves a mental property which is not subject to quantum mechanical principles.

Third, we could say that measurement is a *wave function property*. This is a property of a quantum system that is determined by its whole wave function and which does not enter quantum superpositions. For example, the property of having a position superposed with a certain degree of spread is a wave function property of a particle. This property is not a quantum observable and does not itself enter superpositions. It nevertheless can straightforwardly change and is not subject to the Zeno effect. If measurement is a wave function property, the dilemma might be avoided.

There are various other ways that measurement could fail to be an observable, but they seem less promising for resisting the dilemma. Measurement could depend on a combination of non-commuting observables (such as position and momentum) so that it is not itself an observable, or it could depend on the state of a system across time. In these cases, the dilemma rearizes for the underlying observables (at a time or across time) on which measurement depends: if these components cannot be superposed, they cannot change and if they can, the dynamics is ill-defined. Measurement could also be a quantity such as entropy that is defined only relative to the knowledge of an observer, but then measurement will not give an objective criterion for collapse.

We will investigate each of the three main options (measurement as a classical property, a non-physical property, or a wave function property) in the following sections.

4. Measurement as a Classical Property

The first option is to say that measurement is a classical property that is not governed by quantum principles such as the quantum Zeno effect. A picture like this is suggested by some of Bohr's and Heisenberg's philosophical remarks about quantum mechanics, which stress that the classical realm is different in kind from the quantum realm and is subject to different principles. In particular, Bohr and Heisenberg stress that we need to treat an experimental apparatus as a classical system while treating the systems measured by the apparatus as a quantum system. On this picture, it is natural to treat measurement as a classical process that is not itself subject to quantum principles.

An extreme version of this option is *quantum–classical dualism*, which says that there are distinct and separate quantum and classical realms, neither of which is derivative from the other. On this view, fundamental reality involves both quantum entities and properties, governed by quantum dynamics and classical entities and properties, governed by classical dynamics. But this is not at all the picture given by quantum physics. Quantum physics tells us that fundamental physics is entirely driven by quantum principles and classical principles have no place at the fundamental level.

A more common picture of the quantum–classical divide is that the "classical" realm emerges derivatively and gradually from the quantum realm. It is widely held that this emergence of classical processes involves a process of decoherence, in which Schrödinger evolution leads quasi-classical branches of the wave function to become largely independent of each other. On a collapse interpretation, the emergence of classical processes will also centrally involve collapse, whereby one of these decoherent branches is selected as actual. This picture does not require a quantum–classical distinction at the fundamental level.

One might use this picture of emergent classicality to

respond to the Zeno dilemma. In particular, it may be suggested that measurement devices lie at the classical level and so are not subject to quantum dynamics such as the Zeno effect. An opponent might note that the Zeno effect does not seem to apply to macroscopic systems. One can continuously observe a moving car without the car freezing, for example. If so, one would expect that in macroscopic systems, measurements could also start and stop without freezing.

This response is tempting, but it is incorrect. The Zeno effect, understood as the claim that in order for a system to change between definite states of an observable, it must enter a superposition, is a mathematical property of quantum mechanics (under Schrödinger evolution with or without collapse) and applies equally to microscopic and macroscopic systems. Furthermore, the position of a macroscopic object can be regarded as a quantum observable. It is a property of a classical basis state that can in principle be measured and corresponds to a Hermitian operator. Of course, the position of a macroscopic object derives from positions and mass densities of simpler objects, so it is not a fundamental observable, but it is no less an observable for all this than the position of a molecule. Correspondingly, macroscopic objects can enter superpositions of position eigenstates. On an Everett-style interpretation of quantum mechanics, the position of a macroscopic object may enter large superpositions. And even on a collapse interpretation of quantum mechanics, the position of a macroscopic object must enter at least small superpositions in order to change. Of course, these superpositions will not typically be macroscopically detectable, but they will always be present.

Consequently, *if* we carried out a strong continuous measurement of the position of a macroscopic object so that the position could never enter a superposition, then the macroscopic object would never change its position. As discussed earlier, we never observe this effect, for the familiar reason that strong continuous measurements are difficult or impossible to perform. The same is true even at the microscopic level, where one never sees the extreme case of the Zeno effect when measuring the position of a particle, because we cannot perform strong continuous measurements. It remains a mathematical fact that for microscopic or macroscopic position to be changeable, it must be superposable. In the case of measurement, by contrast, we have stipulated (at least on the relevant horn of the dilemma) that measurement is non-superposable. As a result, measurement is unlike ordinary macroscopic properties which are superposable and which change only through superpositions. Instead, measurement is constrained to evolve exactly as if measurement was itself being strongly continuously measured, at least if measurement is an observable. It follows that measurement cannot start and stop. Furthermore, given that "classical" macroscopic properties such as position are still quantum observables, it is incorrect to say that measurement is not a quantum observable because it is classical. Perhaps, there is some other quite different reason to deny that measurement is a quantum observable, but this leads us to the options covered in the next two sections.

5. Measurement as a Non-physical Property

The second option holds that measurement is a non-physical property. On the most natural version of this view, measurement is a mental property which is distinct from any physical property and is not itself governed by quantum principles.

This sort of mind–body dualism is familiar in the quantum-mechanical context. Wigner (1961) appealed to mind–body dualism in his famous argument that consciousness collapses the wave function. Precisely what made consciousness suitable for this role, on his view, was that it is non-physical and therefore not governed by the usual quantum principles of superposition and Schrödinger evolution. In recent years, a dualist consciousness-collapse interpretation has been developed further by Henry Stapp (1993), who holds that measurement is an act of consciousness involving a free choice of what to measure.

Mind–body dualism is a familiar philosophical view which has some supporters. But to make a measurement-collapse view work, we need a very strong form of mind–body dualism on which the mind is strongly independent of the body. Descartes endorsed a strong form of substance dualism, on which the mind is a Cartesian ego that can exist independently of the body and whose state does not depend only on the state of the brain. By contrast, the forms of mind–body dualism that have been most widely discussed in recent years involve a sort of naturalistic property dualism, with mental properties that depend systematically on physical properties according to strict psychophysical laws. Naturalistic property dualism is better behaved than Cartesian substance dualism, but it makes it much harder to avoid the Zeno dilemma.

On a naturalistic property dualist view, there are systematic physical correlates of consciousness. On an especially well-behaved version of this view, for every state of consciousness *C*, there is a corresponding physical state *P* such that one is in *C* if and only if one is in *P*. For example, one may experience a pointer in one position if and only if one's brain is in state *P*1, while one may experience a pointer in another position if and only if one's brain is in state *P*2. There are also weaker versions where physical states correspond many–one to states of consciousness, but these end up raising the same issues.

Unfortunately, using standard property dualism with physical correlates of consciousness to ground a measurement-collapse view leads straight back to the Zeno problem. Presumably, we will say that wave function collapse will be triggered iff one is in a certain state *C* of consciousness (or perhaps a more complex state involving consciousness, but the issues will be the same). On the naturalistic property dualist view, one will be in state *C* iff one is in physical state *P*. We can now ask: can *P* enter a superposition? For example, can one's brain be in a superposition of states corresponding to *P* and not-*P*?

If *P* cannot enter a superposition, we are subject to the Zeno problem. *P* can never change and so *C* can never change either. So one can never move from lacking the relevant state of consciousness to having it and a measurement process can never begin.

If *P* can enter a superposition, then it is unclear that the measurement dynamics are well-defined. It is most natural to say that if one is in a superposition of *P* and not-*P*, then one's consciousness will be in a superposition of *C* and not-*C*. It is not obvious what it means to say that consciousness is in a superposition, but even if we can make sense of this, the dynamics are unclear in a familiar way. The original dynamics said that state *C* triggers collapse while not-*C* does not. On the face of it a superposition of the two will lead to a superposition of collapse and non-collapse, which does not make sense. To avoid the problem, something more is needed.

One could perhaps embrace a form of property dualism where the physical correlates of consciousness are wave function properties. For example, perhaps one is in a conscious measurement state if and only if one's brain is in a certain sort of superposition. This would avoid the Zeno dilemma in much the same way as taking measurement to be a wave function property avoids the dilemma. This strategy requires an unusual theory of consciousness, however, and it also requires an appeal to wave function properties as a trigger of collapse. As a result, it is not entirely distinct from the third option discussed below and it raises similar issues.

To avoid the Zeno problem without an appeal to the second option, one needs a strong form of dualism on which consciousness does not straightforwardly depend on states of the brain. It is worth noting that the same analysis applies to quantum–classical dualism. To avoid the Zeno problem entirely via quantum–classical dualism, one needs a strong dualism where classical states do not straightforwardly depend on quantum states.

If we adopt a strong form of mind–body dualism, there will be no perfect physical correlates of consciousness and consciousness will be somewhat autonomous from the brain. A view like this can allow that consciousness is always in a definite state even when the brain is in a superposition. Presumably entering certain states of consciousness will trigger a collapse in one's brain and in states of the world that are entangled with it.

This view avoids the Zeno problem, but it still raises many puzzles. For a start, it is quite unclear what the autonomous dynamics of consciousness will be once it does not depend entirely on physical dynamics. Stapp's version of the view requires consciousness to make free choices of which properties to measure, but he gives no account of this dynamics (which he calls "process 0") and instead takes it as primitive.

A relative of the Zeno problem may also still arise from causal connections between states of the visual cortex (say) and states of consciousness. Presumably the visual cortex is sometimes in a superposition of two states (representing an object in location *A* and location *B*, say), which gives rise to a definite conscious state (perceiving the object in location *A*, say) which leads to a collapse in visual cortex and the rest of the brain. But now there is a danger that the immediate physical antecedents of consciousness will themselves be subject to the Zeno effect, as was the case for physical correlates of consciousness earlier. Perhaps, there will be a small delay that allows these antecedents to enter brief superpositions and avoid the Zeno effect, but it will at least be a challenge to develop a dynamics that avoids the problem entirely.

Maybe, these problems can be solved, but it is clear that a very strong form of mind–body dualism is required. The standard quantum dynamics will be quite incomplete as an account of the dynamics of reality and we will need a separate mental dynamics. So, on this view the standard Copenhagen Interpretation will at best be incomplete.

6. Measurement as a Wave Function Property

The final option for avoiding the Zeno dilemma is to treat measurement as a wave function property. That is, the trigger of collapse is not an observable that can enter superpositions, but rather is a property of a quantum wave function as a whole.

For example, wave functions have many binary properties at times. They have certain patterns of amplitude, or they do not. They involve certain sorts of superpositions, or they do not. Wave functions also have many degreed properties at times. For example, a particle's wave function for position can involve greater or smaller degrees of superposition. The binary and degreed properties are not themselves subject to superposition. A system cannot be in a superposition of having a wave function with a certain amplitude distribution and not having such a wave function, or of having a large and a small degree of superposition.

As a result, treating measurement as a wave function property has the potential to avoid the Zeno problem. It can always be a definite matter whether a measurement is taking place and a wave function can evolve straightforwardly from a non-measurement state to a measurement state.

The hard questions for such a view are: just which wave function property triggers collapse and how exactly does the collapse process work? Certainly there is no suggestion in standard quantum mechanics that measurement is a special wave function property and intuitively we tend to think of measurement as a paradigm of a quasi-classical process. So, here we need to go beyond standard methods of thinking about quantum mechanics.

There are perhaps two especially natural approaches to understanding the trigger for collapse as a wave function property. On one approach, collapse is triggered by *decoherence*. When a wave function enters a sufficiently decoherent state relative to some basis, on which it is a superposition of largely non-interfering quasi-classical alternatives, the wave function collapses onto one of those alternatives. An observable of a system collapses when it becomes part of a decoherent quantum system. This *decoherence-collapse* interpretation has the promise of combining some of the virtues of interpretations involving decoherence and those involving collapse, but we set it aside here.

On the second approach, collapse is triggered by *superposition*. In particular, it is triggered by a sufficiently great degree of superposition of certain key observables.

The most well-known proposal along these lines has been made by Roger Penrose (2014). Penrose holds that collapse is triggered when space–time enters into certain superpositions involving sufficiently different structures. Here, the trigger for collapse is a wave function property: a certain degree of superposition of space–time structure. The collapse process itself is stochastic: greater degrees of superposition lead to higher probabilities of collapse. Penrose does not identify this wave function property with measurement and intuitively superpositions of space–time can take place without anything we ordinarily think of as measurement. But one could also apply his approach to other triggers for collapse that are more linked to standard measurement.

A generalization of this approach by Chalmers and McQueen (2022) holds that there is a special class of *superposition-resistant* observables associated with measurement (akin to pointer positions or perhaps states of a perceptual system) that are responsible for collapse. On a simple version of this approach, superposition-resistant observables can never be superposed, which leads to the Zeno problem. To avoid the problem, we can instead say that superpositions of these observables are unstable, so that large enough superpositions trigger a collapse toward an eigenstate of the observable with high probability. This will then also collapse any external systems that are entangled with the superposition-resistant observable.

This approach is somewhat revisionary insofar as it involves a fixed locus for collapse, whereas the standard measurement-collapse dynamics allow a variable locus of collapse (any observable can serve as the primary locus of collapse, if it is measured). In effect, on this framework $m_{S,O} = 1$ only when O is a special superposition-resistant property. We could perhaps define an extended notion of measurement that applies to any observable, so that O is measured iff it becomes entangled with a superposition-resistant observable, but the fundamental locus of collapse is still the superposition-resistant observable and not O.

Other non-standard pictures have been developed with wave function properties serving as triggers for collapse. In particular, Kremnizer and Ranchin (2015) define a scalar wave function property "quantum integrated information" and use this to determine the rate at which particles in a system collapse onto a position basis. This model departs even further from the standard Copenhagen dynamics, however, by invoking a scalar trigger for the rate of collapse and by always collapsing onto a position basis. The Kremnizer–Ranchin approach is closer in spirit to spontaneous collapse approaches of GRW and Pearle, with the difference that the rate of collapse is modulated by the scalar wave function property in question.

Still, an approach on which measurement is a wave function property is perhaps the best bet for a measurement-collapse interpretation that roughly fits the mould of the original Copenhagen Interpretation. If a wave function property $m_{S,O}$ serves as a deterministic trigger, the approach is compatible with the letter of the standard measurement-collapse interpretation: wave functions evolve according to the Schrödinger equation except when measurement occurs, when they undergo collapse according to the Born rule. This approach simply supplements the standard interpretation with a specific definition of measurement as a wave function property. This involves perhaps the smallest change to the standard measurement-collapse dynamics of any proposal we have seen, though the stipulations are still significant and the overall picture is non-standard.

7. Conclusion

We have seen that the Zeno problem poses a major challenge to Copenhagen-style measurement-collapse interpretations of quantum mechanics. Responding to it requires either adopting a strong form of mind–body dualism where conscious measurement does not precisely correlate with states of the brain, or adopting an unusual view on which measurement is understood as a special wave function property that triggers collapse. Both views deserve exploration, but they also require going well beyond the simple framework of the measurement-collapse dynamics.

It is a familiar point that interpretations of quantum mechanics such as those put forward by Bohm, Everett, Ghirardi et al. and Pearle are revisionary relative to the textbook account of quantum mechanics. One might have hoped that a precisified version of the measurement-collapse dynamics would be the best hope for a non-revisionary interpretation of quantum mechanics, but the Zeno dilemma suggests that any such interpretation must be somewhat revisionary. This reinforces the view that there is no adequate non-revisionary interpretation of quantum mechanics.

References

Albert, D.Z., 1992, *Quantum Mechanics and Experience*, Cambridge: Cambridge University Press.

Ballentine, L.E., 1998, *Quantum Mechanics: A Modern Development*, Singapore: World Scientific.

Bell, J.S., 1990, "Against 'Measurement'", *Physics World*, 3(8): 33.

Bohm, D., 1952, "A Suggested Interpretation of the Quantum Theory in Terms of 'Hidden' Variables I", *Phys. Rev.*, 85(2): 166-79.

Chalmers, D.J. and K.J. McQueen, 2022, "Consciousness and the Collapse of the Wave Function", in *Consciousness and Quantum Mechanics*, ed. S. Gao, Oxford: Oxford University Press.

Degasperis, A., L. Fonda and G.C. Ghirardi, 1974, "Does the Lifetime of an Unstable System Depend on the Measuring Apparatus?", *Nuov Cim A*, 21: 471-84.

Everett, H., 1957, "Relative State Formulation of Quantum Mechanics", *Rev. Mod. Phys.*, 29(3): 454-62.

Gandy, R., 1954, *Letter to M.H.A. Newman*. Turing Digital Archive. url: http://www.turingarchive.org/browse.php/A/8.

Ghirardi, G.C., A. Rimini and T. Weber, 1986, "Unified Dynamics for Microscopic and Macroscopic Systems", *Phys. Rev. D*, 34(2): 470-91.

Heisenberg, W., 1955, "The Development of the Interpretation of the Quantum Theory", *Niels Bohr and the Development of Physics*, ed. W. Pauli, L. Rosenfeld and V. Werokopf, London: Pergamon Press.

Howard, D., 2004, "Who Invented the 'Copenhagen Interpretation'?: A Study in Mythology", *Philosophy of Science*, 71: 669-82.

Ismael, J., 2015, "Quantum Mechanics", in *The Stanford Encyclopedia of Philosophy*, ed. E.N. Zalta, Spring, Metaphysics Research Lab, Stanford University (https://ploto.standard.edu/entries/qm/QuanMech).

Itano, W.M. et al., 1990, "Quantum Zeno effect", *Phys. Rev. A*, 41(5): 2295–2300.

Johnson, G., 2010, *Fire in the Mind: Science, Faith and the Search for Order*, New York: Knopf.

Kremnizer, K. and A. Ranchin, 2015, "Integrated Information-Induced Quantum Collapse", *Found Phys*, 45: 889-99.

Maudlin, T., 2011, *Quantum Non-Locality and Relativity*, 3rd edn, Oxford: Blackwell Publishing.

McQueen, K.J., 2015, "Four Tails Problems for Dynamical Collapse Theories", *Studies in History and Philosophy of Modern Physics*, 49: 10-18.

Misra, B. and E.C.G. Sudarshan, 1977, "The Zeno's Paradox in Quantum Theory", *Journal of Mathematical Physics*, 18(4): 756-63.

Nakazato, H. et al., 1995, "On the Quantum Zeno Effect", *Physics Letters A*, 199(1): 27-32.

von Neuman, John, 1932/1955, *Mathematical Foundations of Quantum Mechanics*, Princeton, NJ: Princeton University Press.

Pascazio, S. and M. Namiki, 1994, "Dynamical Quantum Zeno Effect", *Phys. Rev. A*, 50(6): 4582-92.

Pearle, P., 1976, "Reduction of the State Vector by a Non-linear Schrödinger Equation", *Phys. Rev. D*, 13(4): 857-68.

———, 1989, "Combining Stochastic Dynamical State-vector Reduction with Spontaneous Localization", *Phys. Rev. A*, 39(5): 2277-89.

Penrose, R., 2014, "On the Gravitization of Quantum Mechanics 1: Quantum State Reduction", *Foundations of Physics*, 44: 557-75.

Stapp, H., 1993, *Mind, Matter and Quantum Mechanics*, Berlin/Heidelberg: Springer.

Thalos, M., 1998, "The Trouble with Superselection Accounts of Measurement", *Philosophy of Science*, 65: 518-44.

Tononi, G., 2008, "Consciousness as Integrated Information: A Provisional Manifesto", *Biol Bull*, 215(3): 216-42.

Wigner, E.P., 1961, "Remarks on the Mind–Body Question", in *The Scientist Speculates*, ed. I.J. Good, pp. 284-302, London: Heineman.

5

Quantum-like Reality

Sudip Patra
Menas C. Kafatos

Abstract: In the last decade, there has been a serious surge of interest among physicists, mathematicians, cognitive scientists, philosophers and social scientists alike to explore the possibilities of extending mathematical and logical frameworks of quantum theory to human cognition. As a result, scholars are raising fundamental questions on the possible existence of genuine quantum features of the human mind and how it connects to the systems under observations. Applications of such models abound, in decision science, game theory, finance, engineering, biology and neuroscience. The present chapter provides a brief as well as deep summary of such frontier works. Here we propose a new conceptual framework based on contextuality and complementarity as appropriate for human cognition research.

Keywords: Quantum-like, Hilbert space, complementarity, contextuality, Copenhagen Interpretation, Bell inequalities, classical and quantum entanglements, quantum games, Quantum Bayesianism (QBism), quantum decision theory (QDT).

1. Introduction

IT IS a great opportunity for the authors of the present chapter to summarize some of the frontier studies in the quantum-like modelling paradigm applied to human cognition, particularly, as the current volume along with providing important aspects of contextuality and complementarity, related to the Copenhagen Interpretation and beyond, also brought up aspects of Henry P. Stapp's seminal contributions in understanding deep links between free will and quantum physics. Most important, the links between quantum mechanics (QM) and consciousness, particularly as to the role of the mind in bringing out aspects of physical reality. Moreover, the broader question of any possible role that QM plays in issues related to the overall field of consciousness and mind brings out foundational aspects in the epistemology and ontology of science and more specifically in QM. We note here that the term *quantum mechanics* used in the present work is more general than its usual historical meaning and encompasses the original QM of the early twentieth century as well as all consequent developments culminating in modern quantum field theory (QFT). It does not, however, include issues related to the unification of QM and QFT to general relativity (GR) and gravitation as these would go beyond the scope of the present chapter. We also provide some brief comments on this important issue facing modern physics in the latter parts of the chapter.

Quantum-like modelling[1] being (Busemeyer et al. 2006; Busemeyer et al. 2009; Dzhafarov et al. 2017; Haven and Khrennikov 2013; Haven et al. 2017; Khrennikov 2010; Patra and Ghose 2020, 2021; Yukalov and Sornette 2010) a relatively new strand of thinking, which overall can be assimilated

---

1 The phrase may mean both mathematical modelling using basic abstract quantum-theory framework and deeper philosophical concepts, particularly contextuality and complementarity, which are most relevant for cognition as a whole.

among various studies (Busemeyer et al. 2006; Busemeyer et al. 2009; Yukalov and Sornette 2010) was developed to describe the human mind, or the brain at a more physical level, using different constructs from quantum mechanics as well as more abstract mathematical frameworks (Ehtibar et al. 2017). The authors have pointed out in several publications that quantum-like is a generic term applicable to broad classes of human endeavours beyond cognition and biology, and in fact constitutes the most important characteristic of what one may term the nature of Reality. In our view, Reality is more fundamental and encompassing than Theories of Everything or whatever terms are used in physical science. Such theories generally are focused on unification of physical interactions or theories provided by physics. In the present work, capitalized nouns usually denote universal qualities or quantities beyond the usual grammatical conventions, such as (universal) Mind, etc.

Quantum-like modelling in the scientific and philosophical literature emerged from the intriguing earlier findings of neuroscientists and cognitive scientists for example (Kahneman 2011; Ellsberg 1961), that, in general the human mind defies classical Boolean logic and since classical Boolean logic can be embedded within the Kolmogorovian measure theory[2], more commonly known as classical probability theory (Haven et al. 2017), with extension to Bayesian decision framework, we can infer that studying the human mind needs a more comprehensive decision framework different from all such extant models. Recently, scientists have also proposed the rejection of Aristotelian logic of excluded middle when describing features of human behaviour or the behaviour of mind. The proposition we are making here is that since quantum

---

[2] It is surprising to note that historically quantum and set theory frameworks were built during the same decade, particularly von Neumann helped in building quantum framework as well as classical game theory based on Kolmogorov measure theory.

logic allows relaxation of the excluded middle proposition, it might be a better candidate for describing at least some core features of the human mind. The whole issue of what constitutes consciousness and mind is likely more natural to Platonic philosophical views and Socratic statements, particularly the admission of ultimately not knowing the nature of reality, which naturally fits with modern quantum views of non-classical reality, the role of measurement and, among others, the nature of relationship between objects and subjects [for a more philosophical study, refer (Ghose 2017)]. Quantum-like modelling then describes decision makers' mental or belief states as states in Hilbert space and also describes updating of such states based on either the projection postulate (Neumann updating rule or in appropriate context by the Luder updating rule (Aerts 2011), for example, while computing conditional probabilities), or in general using the positive operator value measures (POVM) (ibid.), for example, when there is "noise" in the overall decision-making situation.

It is significant that a large body of literature (as cited above) supports the proposal that human mind can really be considered to be quantum-like. This paradigm is, however, also agnostic about any "quantum brain" proposal as we find in the Orch oR model. Such proposals are in fact physicalist in their ontology as they presume an existing physical structure or framework (viz. the physical brain and the body) and stand apart from what is often termed as the idealist position, which takes as reality a basic mind-like ontic existence.

Even though it is often assumed that science is based on physical existence, this is by no means a given and in fact as the founders of QM assumed and demonstrated, goes counter to the most successful scientific theory, viz. QM and what followed it, QFT, as the mental aspects related to observation and measurement play a primary role. Even GR is fundamentally a non-physical ideation as repeatedly pointed out by Einstein (Rovelli 2018) and others since the "objects" of GR are non-physical, viz. space–time. It is our view here that the fundamental role of consciousness is justified by the best of modern science or to put it in another way, that quantum-like propositions form the ontology of modern science as well as modern philosophy.

The current chapter is thus divided into various subsections with the addition of an updated literature review: Section 2 briefly explores QM and quantum-like universal laws. Section 3 describes in more detail the main two foundations for our proposal of quantum-like reality, viz. complementarity and contextuality. Section 4 describes the Copenhagen Interpretation and some other competing views, along with the basic mathematical features of quantum-like reality related to human cognition. Section 5 delves into the Bohr–Kantian and Heisenberg perspectives on complementarity and contextuality. Section 6 describes "classical" entanglement or classical Hilbert space-based modelling of cognition and its applications. Section 7 provides a comparison between new models suggested in the broader spectrum of quantum-like reality. Section 8 provides further discussions for future studies. Finally, we provide mathematical formalisms in the Appendices.

2. Quantum Mechanics and Quantum-like Universal Laws

As modern physics is based on quantum mechanics (and the theory of relativity), it makes little sense to rely too much on the older physics, the so-called classical physics. At least, it is worth understanding the limitations of classical physics. As we emphasize here, quantum mechanics is not just a theory, it has a very practical nature and many applications (see specific applications described herein). The general, fundamental laws, on which quantum mechanics is based, are applicable to the entire physical universe; we can even claim that these laws apply everywhere, in the natural, mental, biological world, they apply to philosophies and sources of religions, in art, in the mental realm and attempts to understand emotions, everywhere. This is in agreement with the focus of the present book. As such, our conjecture is that quantum mechanics is based on the same general laws that apply to our daily activities. For considerations of life, QM explains how the sun, the source of radiant energy, shines, how photosynthesis works, it has much to do with the existence of life itself. Thanks to these laws, technology is flourishing with "smart" mobile phones. Quantum phenomena, such as entanglement, are expected to find fields of applications in future technologies. If we consider the terms *Nature* or *Universe* as the sum of the physical, biological, mental, social and spiritual realities, then should it not be important to observe and understand what are the general laws applicable to Nature? These laws are obvious in quantum phenomena, which is why QM is so useful beyond its mere applications. In other words, we emphasize that the laws of Nature, which are based on quantum mechanics, also apply primarily to life, they apply everywhere. To distinguish the microscopic realm from other levels, one notices that a more encompassing term is needed. Such a term is *quantum-like* which forms the main subject of the present chapter.

Specifically, all phenomena (especially quantum phenomena) are based on a small number of principles or *Laws*. Despite the fact that there are other specific laws of physics (such as the laws of electromagnetic and gravitational interactions), nevertheless, according to the quantum world view, the minimum number of such genera Laws is three. These general Physical Laws apply in everything we experience, in what we feel, in what we do, in what we encounter and in how we describe the physical universe and the Universe beyond the physical, which includes everything, including observation, measurements and subjectivity:

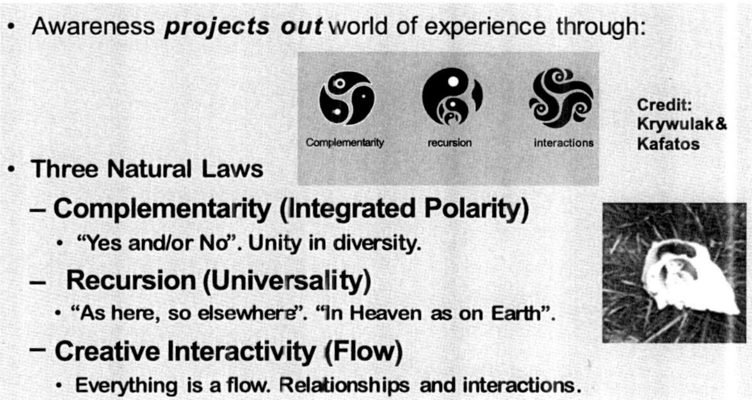

fig. 5.1: Three natural laws

The First Law is of **Complementarity** (a more common or everyday term would be *Integrated Polarity*, while *Complementarity* would be a more scientific term). According to this Law, opposites create pairs, providing unity through differentiation, the process of creating differences, such differences not being permanent. Its logical assumptions are "Yes and/or No" rather than the dialectical expression "Yes or No". This becomes more obvious when we look at *fig.* 5.1: A quantum behaves as a particle *or* a wave, which are opposites, therefore we can say that while a quantum behaves *either as a particle or as a wave*, according to quantum choices, its nature is a *particle and/or wave* (but never *both* under the same circumstances/conditions). To emphasize the point, in the quantum world, quanta are either localized (in which case we name them particles); or vibrations/oscillations (in which case we name them waves), but never both under the same conditions.

The Second Law is that of **Recursion** (a more common term would be *Universality*, while *Recursion* would be a more scientific term), a Law found in many traditions such as the tradition of the hermetic philosophers, who were followers of the legendary ancient philosopher Hermes Trismegistus, coming to us from worldwide ancient and more recent traditions during the Renaissance, mystical traditions, all stating the universal principle "As here, so elsewhere". "In Heaven, as on Earth". Without the Second Law, there would be no logic, there would be no mathematics, there would be no science. Because as scientists we believe that the universe can be studied, using logic and mathematics, it can be understood, in other words to put it in a way, from "here" we can learn about "there" (and of course vice versa).

The Third Law is that of **Interactivity** (which implies a *Flow of interactions*; the scientific term would be *Creative Interactivity*): "everything flows" as Heraclitus used to say. In QM, we are not talking about specific objects. Quantum field theory predicts that everything flows, everything vibrates or fluctuates. These interactions, these pulsations, affect everything, both those things that are "near us" and those that are "far away" from us. Every being, every person, every object in the universe interacts with something else. Through these interactions, we exist as human beings, as societies, as individual lives, we invent and develop economic, social and physical sciences, and as human beings we experience relationships, happiness and love.

We notice that the number three is very prevalent in the world, it exists everywhere in nature, such as, the three fundamental Laws. The most important triad is object–subject relationship linking them, which is the foundation of all theoretical, philosophical and artistic endeavours, to which we will devote a lot of attention as we proceed in our discussion.

Quantum mechanics makes some perhaps equally striking suggestions: First and foremost, reality, whatever that term means, is based on the wave nature of *quanta*. Quantum mechanics does not provide clear and unique answers, it only gives us *probability of events* to happen. In other words, quantum mechanical equations do not tell us when something will happen, only the probability of what *may* happen as a function of time. Quantum mechanics is *inherently* probabilistic (Bohr 1960; Don 2004; Josephson and Sorokin 2017) with *unpredictable results* rather *than just random effects* (or events): The laws of physics probabilistically predict potential outcomes of future results, not actual results. The complete description of a quantum system is generally described by the *wave function*, which allows for the future evolution of such a system. Because of the nature of the wave function itself describing any quantum system, "particles" are entangled with other particles, all objects in the universe are entangled. In addition, QM tells us that (physical) reality is neither given nor external and that it exists with specific attributes only when there is an observation. Quanta have no properties until observed, or as we shall see further down, information is associated with quanta, as such one can state that the universe is participatory, we do not just observe, we are involved in what is called "reality", as physicist John A. Wheeler used to say. Because the quantum world is essentially probabilistic, Nature also has the freedom to "answer" our questions in an unpredictable way for us. We can only calculate the probabilities of possible outcomes, i.e. what *can* be done, not what *will* happen.

The implication is that classical physics is essentially causal and leaves no room for free will and action on the part of the individual human. The classical world does not exist in an absolute sense, only in an approximate approach. It, however, appears to be true because of our senses and our mind.

A typical example in quantum mechanical experimental application is the well-known "double-slit experiment", see *fig.* 5.2. The wave particle complementary reality is mapped onto the right panel, the double-slit experiment. In fact, this experiment implies more than the wave particle complementarity: It entails, entanglement, non-locality and all non-trivial quantum properties (cf. Tegmark 2015). To determine whether the electrons are particles or waves, quantum scientists can set up

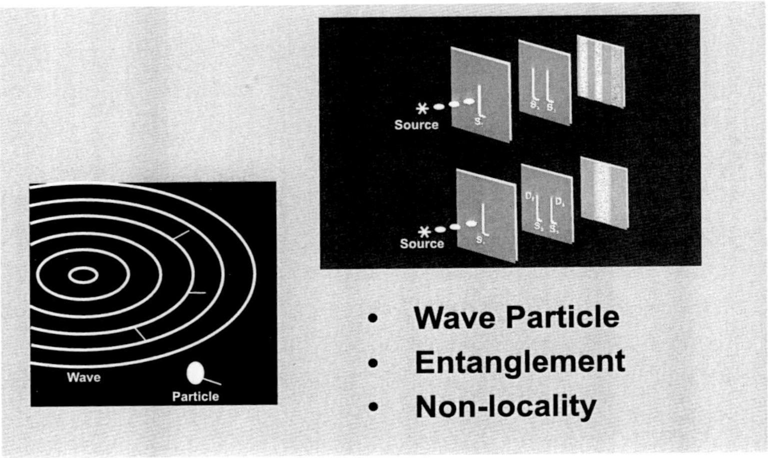

fig. 5.2: Quantum universe

and perform an experiment by sending a beam of electrons to a surface passing through two thin slits. The interesting thing about this experiment is that as the beam passes through the slits and falls onto the wall behind it, the electrons sometimes appear with a behaviour characteristic of particles, sometimes exhibit behaviour of waves. This has to do with the observer's individual choices during the experiment. In order to determine what really happened, scientists have the choice of placing a mechanism of observation next to each of the slits. This is in order to detect the electrons or the photons (the quanta) as they pass through, to understand what happened, whether an electron passed or did not pass through a particular slit? However, the electron acts as a particle only in this case. This occurs as if the electron "realizing" that it is being observed, decides to change its state! But how can this be explained? When in a separate case, quantum scientists do not place an observation mechanism in the two slits, then the wave pattern is observed. Starting with Niels Bohr, quantum physicists concluded that "observer mediation brings to light quantum reality". In other words, the electron can be either a particle or a wave, what will happen depends on the observational conditions, it depends on the observer's participation. *Quantum phenomena can be said to be contextual*. Therefore, one of the central and mysterious issues for quantum mechanics today is the so-called "observer effect". It is a great mystery because quantum mechanics considers a particle/quantum, e.g. say an electron, that it does not even exist, it does not exist as a particle with specific properties, until one observes it. Of course, even if no particular (human) observer is present, there are other observers. One can rightly ask, what happens if we remove *all* the observers? The possible conclusions that a possible reality applies in everything, as if the Observer exists everywhere. We are not talking about just humans or human-like observers. If this were the case, it would imply an anthropocentric world. We are talking about *any* observers, which of course includes human observers.

However, our present position, following the study of various quantum phenomena, is to extend the interpretation of Niels Bohr/Werner Heisenberg/Wolfgang Pauli/John von Neumann (Cassidy 2008; Heisenberg 1930), who collectively formulated the so-called Copenhagen Orthodox interpretation, a position one of us (cf. Kafatos and Nadeau 2000) developed the "Enhanced Orthodox interpretation" which, as its name indicates, enhances the currently popular standard or orthodox,

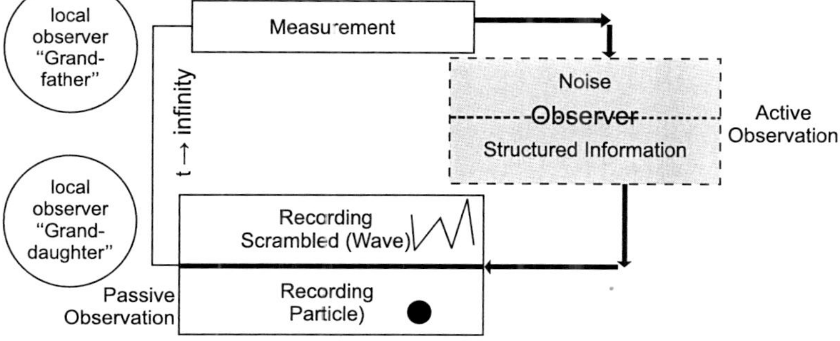

fig. 5.3: Qantum eraser experiments

Copenhagen Interpretation. The persistence of the Copenhagen Interpretation, specifically pushed by Bohr, which is that local observers are the only active participant-observers, may not be the whole picture to try to explain the results of some quantum experiments and this step is indeed a very big ontological step.

As we emphasize here, an important aspect of quantum mechanics with practical applications is the issue of measurement and observation, which imply the existence of an observer or observers. One possibility (Cassidy 2008) is that there may only one *Observer*, as the interpretation of the so-called "quantum eraser" experiments, seems to show (Kafatos and Kak 2015; Stapp 2007). A consequence of this experiment was schematically shown in *fig.* 5.3. Such an interpretation still requires that local observers exist to first set up and begin the experiment and also other observers, not necessarily the same ones, who return to see the results at the end of the experiment (the so-called "Grandfather" at the beginning and the so-called "Granddaughter" at the end, both referring to quantum observers). This possibility is not an inherent weakness, nevertheless it is a weakness that requires more explanation than provided by quantum mechanics alone. Note that the Grandfather sets up the relevant experiment, at any time *before* the experiment starts and therefore has no impact on the results. *Passive Observation* does not in any way influence the end results of the experiment. Only what happens in the *Active Observation* box influences the results of the experiment. Such a view opens up the overall metaphysical implications which the present book follows, which would be difficult for "Western" ontologies to adhere to, or to phrase it in another way, views based on an external, classical realism to accept. We see this phenomenon, denying that there is basically a vast world beyond the senses, occurring again and again.

In modern quantum mechanics, we claim that there is no real *self* (in other words the ego) in the sense of a material substance which does not change. We all are *processes* (following the Third Law). The ancient Greek philosopher Heraclitus taught that you cannot enter the same waters twice. This is what quantum mechanics says in a different way. Observations transform objects into reality and the Universe changes. Today one can look back at the development of quantum mechanics and in many ways ponder that it is really strange that QM which involves quanta/particles is essentially a *theory of the mind*. Today, we can express the statement that quantum mechanics is a theory of *how the mind generates* what we call reality.

In QM, emptiness and fullness are complementary truths. The quantum void is "empty", but it is also completely "full", complete, as far as it is possible, because it contains all possible outcomes. If, however, we believe that only the void exists, then we are wrong. Therefore, since the universe is participatory, observations always have some kind of a limit. This as we will see is where contextuality enters the picture. Boundaries are created through the process of observation, the limitations that ultimately manifest through our minds. But here is the question: How can the quantum world, which is non-local and entangled, appear classical, Newtonian, full of discrete objects? We need to identify the answer as to the role of the mind. Therefore, ultimately, human existence is very important. Could it be that the covering of quantum reality by the mind conceals the underlying Consciousness and blurs experience? Curiously, QM is basically about the nature of the field of the mind. Psychologists, cognitive scientists and brain scientists should perhaps study QM.

3. Review of Existing Literature on Quantum-like Modelling, Complementarity and Contextuality

3.1 ONTOLOGICAL FOUNDATIONS

We propose that quantum theory has many profound implications for understanding the nature of consciousness.

In Western literature, it is usually assumed that the term *consciousness* refers to "being conscious of (an object)". However, this is an ontological assumption and by no means self-evident, cf. the works of Kafatos and co-workers Kak, Kato, Nadeau, Narasimhan and Theise (Kafatos and Kak 2015; Kafatos and Kato 2017; Kafatos et al. 2015; Narasimhan and Kafatos 2016; Theise and Kafatos 2016). Consciousness and the role of the mind in what constitutes reality continue to challenge all of science. It is fair to say that, although much progress has been made in the understanding of the brain as a physical object of incredible complexity, not much progress has been achieved in understanding or even accounting for the most elementary subjective experiences that are usually assigned to the brain. The latter assumption, that mind is based on physical structures of the brain and the body, is actually an ontological statement of profound implications and not a priori given. Today, scientists in many polls (Kafatos and Narasimhan 2019) inquired about what are the two most important and unsolved topics facing modern science, respond that it is the nature of the universe and the nature of conscious experience, often termed *qualia*. It turns out that these two profound issues are closely related to each other. As such, what used to be in the domain of philosophy and metaphysics, specifically the origin of the mind and in more general terms the nature of consciousness, how consciousness itself arises, can now be approached by modern science. This is not just our view, it forms the basic underlying philosophy of the founders of QM, Planck, Bohr, Heisenberg, Pauli, Born, Dirac, Wigner, von Neumann, to name a few and even opponents of the Copenhagen Interpretation school of thought, including Einstein, Schrödinger, de Broglie, Bohm and others who prescribe to more realistic, but not necessarily physicalist, viewpoints (Cassidy 2008; Frauchiger and Renner 2018; Wheeler 1982).

We claim that rather than viewing these two great schools

of thought as irreconcilable, one should view them as the two main aspects of generalized complementarity, forming necessary aspects of Reality. Such ontological issues are at the foundation of modern QM and QFT, and are an integral part of modern science which not only *accommodates* the opposites but *requires* them. Here, we look at these issues and specifically the connection between quantum theory extending from the microcosm to cosmological scales and beyond, and assign them to *quantum-like Reality*. The "beyond" includes issues of consciousness, sociological, philosophical and even art fields, in other words the entire set of human experiences. We heavily rely on publications such as Kafatos 2015; Kafatos and Kak 2015; Kafatos and Kato 2017; Kafatos and Nadean 2000; Kafatos and Narasimhan 2019; Narasimhan and Kafatos 2016; Theise and Kafatos 2016.

The issue of consciousness presents a clear embarrassment to modern science. Despite the great successes of theoretical physics, cosmology and quantum field theory, despite the advances of molecular biology and brain science to just mention a few of the most successful scientific fields, we still do not have a comprehensive theory of consciousness. It is even more challenging than that, as we seem not to agree on a common framework of terms. Yet, any theoretical advance will have to involve an understanding and development of a suitable set of mathematical languages (Narasimhan and Kafatos 2016).

It is now an accepted construct from quantum measurement theory that observational choices in the laboratory determine the context of what is to be observed, we may even state (as Richard Feynman and John A. Wheeler would hold) that without observation, particles do not even have any properties. In the participatory quantum universe, as Wheeler (1982) would say, "no phenomenon is a phenomenon until it is an observed phenomenon" and as such, the observer's choices play a fundamental role. The observer is an integral part of the process of what is to be observed. Quantum theory opened the door to consciousness but did not provide a solution, except hints of what the next steps might be, or its applications in different fields (Lave 1962). Here quantum-like certainly means only mathematical or philosophical similarities with QM.

3.2 BOHR, HILBERT SPACE, QUANTUM-LIKE EXTANT MODELS AND CONCEPTS

One of the major areas in which decision science has been applied is economics and so-called "neoclassical economics"[3] is rather based on standard set theoretic formulation. Among the central axioms of neoclassical economics, which describes how rational utility optimizing behaviour should be, is the "sure thing principle", which means irrelevance of irrelevant alternatives while making a rational choice. For example, if Bob is asked whether he should buy a house if *X* wins the presidential election and he answers yes and again he answers yes when he is asked what if *X* loses, then the sure thing principle would hold that information regarding *X* winning or losing is irrelevant in the choice making. However, the same agent, i.e. Bob, might behave completely differently when the atmosphere is of uncertainty or ambiguity about the presidential election. Hence, under uncertainty, human choice making would not follow neoclassical predictions, which are based on full information conditions (certainly, there is a huge literature on information asymmetry and costly signalling, but uncertainty context is fundamentally different from information asymmetry context, since in such a context classical probability distribution or say Bayesian updating procedure might not work). Such violations can be found copiously in various areas of decision science, for example, in game theory. In the famous Prisoner

---

[3] We have used this example to demonstrate the contrast between such theoretical modelling and real cognition, overall our objective is to critique the standard framework of decision science.

Dilemma game[4] (Khrennikov 2016), in the full information context, it is simply irrelevant what the other player does or thinks in terms of cooperation or defection, since only the Nash equilibrium is to defect[5] (which is not Pareto optimal, hence the dilemma). However, numerous accounts (Khrennikov 2012) of real prisoners' dilemma game shows that in the context of uncertainty, such predictions of Nash equilibrium are non-trivial. Hence lies the question whether players are "irrational" under uncertainty context? (a standard response from behavioural game theory or decision models) or we are failing to describe genuine human behaviour under such contexts.

If quantum-like modelling holds, we can build a more comprehensive "non-Boolean" decision framework, which might describe choice making under uncertainty contexts as well as containing the standard predictions.

Before referring to the basic mathematical–logical framework of quantum-like modelling, let us also discuss some of the central concepts of the paradigm which draw upon some philosophical debates as found in the dense literature of quantum foundations.

Contextuality

It is well known in the foundations literature that one cannot escape the notion that quantum mechanics is contextual in

---

4 Prisoner's dilemma is a non-zero sum game where loss of one player does not mean symmetric gain of another player, such games are widely observed in evolutionary biological models too, economic theory is just a subset.

5 In the typical story of Prisoners' dilemma, both prisoners if "cooperate", i.e. do not confess individually to the police, then both get less punishment, which means greater welfare for them! It is only when both individually confess, which means "defect" or not cooperate, they both get jailed for more time, which is the bad equilibrium for them. This set-up has been used myriads of times in different economic/strategic circumstances.

nature (Dzhafarov et al. 2015). Certainly the original concept of contextuality can be stretched back to the Copenhagen school and particularly to Bohr.

There are attempts to describe non-local correlations and Bell inequality violations in terms of contextuality and, even in the recent quantum information theory literature, one observes that if one demands non-contextual measurement results along with the universality of quantum theory and that every measurement generates only a single outcome, then there would be paradoxical statements in Wigner's friend or related hybrid thought experiments.[6] Hence, current authors propose quantum theory to be "meta-contextual" in such cases.

We note that in human cognition literature, contextuality, is a debated topic with no final agreement. In fact, there are questions regarding the proper ways of formulating contextuality. One noted extant model, contextuality by default (CbD) builds up a robust framework based on a simple concept of defining contexts as measuring one random variable with another, hence pairs of random variables form a context. Hence, it is analysed in detail whether such contexts violate the principle of marginal selectivity, i.e. whether contexts influence the marginal probability distributions of random variables (Khrennikov and Basieva 2014). Recently authors (Dzhafarov et al. 2015) investigating the CbD framework have claimed evidence of contextuality in human cognitive experiments.

However, one might observe that Bohr's view of contextuality is deeper and one can think of "single variable" contextuality in such a case. In cognitive literature only recently (Aerts 2014) has the Bohr contextuality framework been suggested. We present a brief discussion of the same issue in the Appendix.

---

[6] The deeper problem is of "Heisenberg cut" the subjective or objective divide between observer–observed; it is suggested that observers are always to be kept outside the "black box" to avoid "self-referential" paradoxes.

3.3 HILBERT SPACE MODELLING AND NON-BOOLEAN LOGIC

Here some basic features of Hilbert space modelling and its application in human cognition are briefly described (Dzhafarov et al. 2015; Khrennikov and Basieva 2014; Khrennikov 2012, 2016).

We begin with a brief comparison between classical probability theory (CPT) and quantum probability theory (QPT). The main features of classical probability theory followed in classical mechanics and thermodynamics are as follows: Events are represented by sets, which are subsets of Ω sample space, sigma algebra of such subsets, a measure (probability) defined on the sample space, are the main features of the related Kolmogorov measure theory. Boolean logic is the type of compatible logic with CPT, which allows for deductive logic and basic operations like union and intersection of sets. Also, the De Morgan Laws of set theory are valid.

Conditional probability: $Prob\ (a \mid b) = \dfrac{prob\ (a \text{ and } b)}{prob\, b}$.

We note here that the conditional probability is a direct consequence of Boolean operations. CPT is very successful, but it has inherent assumptions which cannot be supported by modern QM.

The main features of QPT are: State space is a complex linear-normed vector space: Hilbert space; Finite/infinite D, symbolized as H, H is endowed with a scalar product (positive definite), norm and an orthonormal basis, non-degenerate. Any state can be visualized as a ray in this space.

Superposition Principle. It states that a general state can be written as a linear superposition of "basis states"; in information theory language, the basis states are |0> or |1>. Which is also termed as the computational basis, for example, as in case of spin measurements |0> and |1> which might mean up-down spin measurements, respectively, and then further QBIT states can be expressed as linear superposition of such basis states. For example, other basis states like diagonal basis states can be constructed out of such states. In the case of cognitive modelling 0 and 1 states might represent some responses to questions given a context, for example 0 represents "yes, I am happy" and 1 represents "no, I am not happy".

Measurement. Most of the times projection postulates; measurement implies projection onto a specific Eigen subspace. Probability, updating can be visualized as sequential projections on Eigen subspaces.

Non-Boolean logic is compatible with such state space structure, which means violation of commutation and associative properties. The details of Non-Boolean logic are shown in Appendix A.

3.4 QUANTUM-LIKE MODELLING OF BELIEF STATES

The cognitive modelling based on quantum probabilistic framework's main objective is assigning probabilities to events. The space of belief in a finite dimensional Hilbert space *H*, which is spanned by an appropriate set of basis vectors as follows:

Observables are represented by operators (positive operators/Hermitian operators) which need not commute; in other words, they do not necessarily follow the relationship

$$[A, B] = AB - BA.$$

Generally, any initial belief state is represented by the density matrix/operator, outer product of ψ with itself $\rho = |\psi\rangle\langle\psi|$, this is a more effective representation since it captures the ensemble of beliefs.

Pure States and Mixed States. Mixed states $\rho = \Sigma_i |\varphi i><\varphi i|$,[7]

[7] Here the sum is over all possible states, *ws* are the classical probabilities over the pure states, hence density matrix actually captures "ignorance" over the pure states, a combination of "epistemic" and "ontic" probabilities.

hence a mixed state is an ensemble of pure states with *ps* being the probability weights. Mixed states are considered the most common states in quantum systems.

Some properties of ρ are:

$\rho = \rho^D$, where *D* stands for complex conjugate transpose, for pure states ρ = ρ^2, (ψ, ρ ψ)>0: positivity, Trace ρ = 1.

Measuring the probability of choosing one of the given alternatives, which is represented by the action of an operator on the initial belief state.

While making a decision, the superposition state collapses to one single state (can be captured by relevant eigenvalues). One of the main principles of QM rests on obtaining observational outcomes and is based on the assumption that physical variables can be represented as Hermitian operators.

Observables in QPT represented by Hermitian operators can be described mathematically in the following way:

$$A = A^D.$$

$< A > =$ Trace (ρA), every time measurement is done, one of the Eigen values of the *A* is realized.

$A = \Sigma_i \, a_i P_i$ spectral decomposition rule: as are the Eigen values and *P*s are the respective projectors which project the initial state to the Eigen subspace with a specific value *a*.

Prob (a_i) = trace $(P_i \, \rho)$, where ρ is the density matrix representation.

As soon as the measurement is done the state is

$\rho' = P_i \rho P_i / trace(P_i \rho P_i)$ simultaneously updating the agents' belief state.

3.5 TOTAL PROBABILITY

One central implication of Hilbert space modelling of belief states in human cognition is the change in the well-known formula for total probability. To put it briefly, due to the amplitude representation of states and use of square of the amplitude or Born rule for computing probabilities, we end up having additive perturbative or "interference" terms in FTP, which is non-existent in classical probability theory. Here, we should mention that in the case of experimental cognitive studies such interference terms can be hyperbolic, in contrast to trigonometric terms in standard quantum physical set-ups. Here, we note that in cognitive experiments, when first responses from human decision makers are obtained, for example, in a real-life prisoner's dilemma set-up, where the players might either cooperate or defect, in the context of uncertainty (when the individual players cannot form any subjective beliefs for other players' action, given that players are not able to communicate). Then based on such data, conditional probabilities are calculated (as frequencies) and then such probabilities are checked against the predictions based on classical probability theory set-up. Any deviation is then described using FTP in the quantum probability framework, where the phase term for interference terms is reconstructed from data. Such phase terms are at times found to be in the form of Cosh and Sinh expressions.

3.6 FTP AND IMPLICATIONS IN COGNITIVE AND SOCIAL SCIENCES

We conclude this section with some observations on the implications of formula for total probability (FTP) in social sciences. Specifically, in financial decision making under contexts such as uncertainty or ambiguity, the FTP formulation can play an important, and yet not fully recognized, role in resolving some long-standing confusions regarding mechanisms through which market observables change. A market can be perceived as a network of agents, such that we can provide a finite dimensional Hilbert space description to the state of the market as a whole. Such a state can then undergo updating based on a similar description as we provided in the earlier sections.

For example, in neoclassical finance, there is a long-standing debate on the exact mechanism through which agents' beliefs about asset prices impact asset returns. As we have discussed earlier, there can be both pure state to pure state and mixed state updating of beliefs. Now in the latter case, we have a classical ensemble of beliefs (probability distribution over possible states) with no interference terms. Such a mixed state can be analogous to standard dispersion of belief description in finance, which in neoclassical finance has been studied statistically. However, if there is a resultant pure state of the market as a whole with interference terms (as described for the bivariate observables in the earlier sections), there is no analogous description in the standard finance literature since the standard decision-making models are again based on classical Boolean logic. In such a case the impact of phase factor in the FTP would be crucial on observables like asset prices. Recently, secondary market data has been used to reconstruct phase factors for game theoretic scenarios involving investors. Therefore, more generally we can contrast here between the standard Bayesian updating scheme as used profusely in cognitive studies and social sciences and the updating mechanism provided by the quantum-like scheme. Quantum-like cognitive modellings do have a probability updating scheme via Born's rule, which would also accompany updating of cognitive states. Here, a pertinent question would be why not use Bayesian updating only? There have been some problems with the pure Bayesian paradigm, which has been emphasized in the quantum-like modelling paradigm as follows:

a. Using standard Bayesian updating formula, which given prior credence of an event happening generates posterior beliefs or credence of such events based on new information being generated in the environment, suffers from the "zero prior" trap, which means if the prior knowledge for any event is very near 0, then no amount of belief updating would generate significant posterior probabilities. Using the Born rule would avoid the situation encountered.

b. Recently, in another work a breakthrough (Dzhafarov et al. 2015) has been shown, that use of the quantum-like framework, rather than pure Bayesian updating, generates a more expanded form of the so-called "common knowledge" theorem, with deep implications in economics and finance. Robert Aumann (1976) in his seminal paper proposed that given common priors and a common knowledge about posteriors of an event, Bayesian rational agents (which update according to Bayes rule) cannot agree to disagree any further on probabilities of any event occurring. Now this assumption is central to many asset pricing models/general equilibrium models in economics. However, it has been shown that if decision makers or observers have a quantum-like framework (it may be QBist or our framework/Vaxjo) for updating, then even if other conditions hold, agents can still agree to disagree. This also means under special conditions that one could recover Aumann's theorem. We believe this has deep implications for economics and social science as a whole.

4. Copenhagen School, Quantum-like Modelling, Human Cognition and Quantum Games

4.1 THE COPENHAGEN INTERPRETATION (CI) OF QM

It is the most popular interpretation of QM, named after the capital city of Denmark where Niels Bohr's institute is located. Bohr was the principal developer of the new quantum physics a century ago, and was joined initially by Werner Heisenberg and soon by other physicists in Europe, primarily Wolfgang Pauli, Max Born, Paul A.M. Dirac, Pascual Jordan, Eugene Wigner, etc. (Stapp 2007a). The actual name was given in the 1950s by Heisenberg. Today, CI is accepted as not a unique interpretation but a loose collection of diverse ideas and principles that form what is the quantum view of the universe. Principal among them is the principle of complementarity, the uncertainty principle, the correspondence principle for large quantum numbers and the Born rule of obtaining answers to specific calculations that can be tested in the laboratory. Even the two initial developers, Bohr and Heisenberg, did not espouse the same views. There are, of course, alternative interpretations, such as the many worlds interpretation, the de Broglie wave mechanics, the Bohmian theory and different modern developments. Many of these alternatives either insisted on realistic outcomes or challenged the basic probabilistic nature of quantum "events". In fact, it was Albert Einstein and his co-workers who raised the most serious challenges insisting on real events and Erwin Schröndiger who instead developed a highly successful wave mechanics that is the principal way that quantum mechanics is generally taught at universities.

In the CI, the act of observation plays a fundamental role in explaining the nature of reality. The so-called collapse of the wave function denotes the process through which quantum possibilities as calculated in the probability function become actualities in the "real" world of experience. The original Copenhagen school of physicists was later enriched by the work of John von Neumann and is now often referred to as the Orthodox Interpretation (heretofore and in agreement with Stapp (2007b, c) (Frauchiger and Renner 2018), we can also refer to it as standard QM).

In this standard Orthodox QM, there are two main types of processes as developed by von Neumann. Process 1 presents non-linear aspects of QM, wherein a "collapse" takes place upon observation, the actual outcome of which is unknown a priori. Process 2 is the predictable, linear time evolution of the wave function through the Schrödinger equation. The exact nature of collapse and what causes it remains a controversial topic to this day, but in the Orthodox Interpretation of QM, it is taken for granted that the act of observation is *essential* for the collapse of the wave function: out of a large set of possible outcomes, observation confers reality on the specific outcome of a measurement performed in the laboratory, such as determining the direction of the spin of a particle.

Even if the experimental process is automated, the participation of an observer remains essential, because we inhabit a participatory universe (cf. Wheeler 1982). The mind that plans, executes and undertakes an observation is termed here the (human) local observer, denoted by lower case *o*. This mind cannot be extracted from what is being observed. Observer *o* sets up the quantum observation or "probing action" to ask a question of Nature, which responds with its answer (Process 1) at some initial time. This answer is recorded by the measuring apparatus. S/he observes the outcome, which becomes an actuality, according to linear time evolution, or Process 2. The result can be recorded at a later time as a defined outcome. In the CI, observation causes the particular form of Nature's answer – e.g. particle or interference pattern in the double-slit experiment, as described in many references.

In the context of the CI, the crucial question arising from the double-slit experiment is whether the measurement requires a conscious observer. In the Orthodox QM world view, the answer is yes. A conscious observer is required because information itself is relevant in quantum experiments only through a human observer. Information, measurement and the setting up of experiments are intertwined human activities. The state of information without a mind to give it meaning is highly problematic. The relevant issues are explored below.

Though contextuality and complementarity were the central features of Bohr's own philosophy about quantum mechanics, Heisenberg's "interaction" picture appeared victorious and founded in some ways the basis for further developments in quantum physics. The Heisenberg "cut", the assumed distinction between classical observers or measuring devices and quantum systems to be observed or measured, has remained a central feature of Copenhagen paradigm, though stalwarts like Bell have clearly shown the arbitrariness of such divide (in Bell's own words "shifty divide"). There are two versions or attitudes towards the Heisenberg cut, one is objective (all the way to Planck level) and one is subjective. The present authors have shown recently how such different attitudes towards the quantum–classical divide might give rise to completely different answers to well-known Wigner's friend type paradoxes, or more hybrid paradoxes (often now called as FR paradoxes, Frauchiger and Renner 2018; Aerts 2014).

For us here, such a quantum-classical divide whether subjective or objective also, has implications for quantum-like modelling, particularly for the current state of affairs in quantum games. As mentioned above, in the quantum game literature we still hold that players are classical or their dynamics is still governed by a "Newtonian" framework, whereas resources they share might be truly quantum. However, it is unclear as of now what would become of quantum games (or game theory in general) if we hold quantum theory to be "universal".

4.2 ENTANGLEMENT OR "NON-LOCAL" CORRELATIONS IN HUMAN COGNITION

Hence, based on experimental findings of the Brussels group (Aerts 2014), a fuller understanding of human mind and cognition is called for. Popescu and his collaborators (1994, 1995) since long have demonstrated that it is theoretically possible to construct theories where stronger non-local correlations (violating the Tsirelson bound, for example) are possible without violating the no-signalling condition of Special Relativity, which also means that such a theory would be fundamentally non-deterministic. It is an open question whether human cognition or human mind might qualify. We recall here that non-locality might well be the foundational feature of reality (Tegmark 2015). Recently, Lee Smolin and other physicists have been working on formulating the quantum gravity theory where non-locality becomes a fundamental feature. In quantum physics, there is literature on two types of non-localities: The first, if we consider (as many dynamic collapse theories do, for example GRW) the wave function as an extended physical object in real space–time, then spontaneous collapse would violate the special relativity principle of "no universal Now". In the second, certainly non-local correlations between space-like separated events are occurring.

5. Bohr and Bohr–Kantian Ontologies

5.1 BOHR, KANT AND HEISENBERG

Bohr was strongly influenced by the eighteenth-century German philosopher, Immanuel Kant. Kant's philosophy has as a central feature of defending the objective basis of Newtonian world view against Hume's well-known scepticism. One may hold that Bohr used Kantian views in a modified form for describing quantum mechanics. One point we would like to make is that Bohr's original views might be placed in sharp contrast to text-book versions of Copenhagen (or various subschools of the Copenhagen camp), which is unfortunately less appreciated nowadays, since Bohr and Heisenberg have been wrongly clubbed together as the instrumentalist or operational viewpoint of quantum mechanics (many critics holding it as a fundamental anti-realist philosophy). This term was used by physicists opposed to Bohr's principles of complementarity and contextuality, to identify what they saw as the common features of the Bohr–Heisenberg interpretation as it emerged in the late 1920s.

Interestingly, after Heisenberg's uncertainty relations became established in 1927 and it was understood that at the heart of quantum physics there is the inevitable ontic randomness, due to the unalienable disturbance created by the experimental probe on the system measured, Bohr was not happy with the extant interpretations of quantum mechanics. More specifically, after the 1935 EPR paper, Bohr adopted the standard viewpoint that the state of the measuring device and the state of the object cannot be separated from each other during a measurement but they form a dynamical whole or an unanalysable whole.

Bohr viewed Heisenberg's relations as formal or mathematical expressions of the general notion that our understanding of atomic phenomena must be built on complementary descriptions emerging from incompatible experimental arrangements of a classical type, i.e. a type not subject to Heisenberg's indeterminacy or uncertainty relations.

Particularly, in the case of the double-slit experiment illustrated above, where the measuring apparatus or the experimental set-up in Bohr's language is still classical, it presents two mutually exclusive and complementary contexts, with one case having one slit open and the other having two slits open and hence the results are driven by that contextuality. In Bohr's own words:

> Consequently, evidence obtained under different experimental conditions cannot be comprehended within a single picture but must be regarded as complementary in the sense that only the totality of the phenomena exhausts the possible information about the objects. – Plotnitsky 2012

Hence, according to Bohr, contextuality and complementarity are deeply related to each other. Another aspect of Bohr's view is of central importance, which is that later he started considering contextuality–complementarity as the central feature of human cognition. In his own words:

> In introspection it is clearly impossible to distinguish sharply between the phenomena themselves and their conscious

> perception and although we may often speak of lending our attention to some particular aspect of a psychical experiment, it will appear on closer examination that we really have to deal, in such cases, with mutually exclusive situations. Such a comparison is, of course, in no way intended to suggest any closer relation between atomic physics and psychology, but merely to stress an epistemological argument common to both fields and thus to encourage us to see how far the solution of the relatively simple physical problems may be helpful in clarifying the more intricate psychological questions with which human life confronts us. – Plotnitsky 2012

We also mention here that Bohr's view of the Heisenberg Cut was of pure epistemic nature, with no ontological significance. Though it is true that Heisenberg Cut remains as a central feature of the Copenhagen camp, as we have mentioned elsewhere in this chapter also, even theorists who would like to build quantum-like modelling for cognition, etc. also assume such a Cut.

We also observe that in human cognition and social sciences in general, Bohr's views can be philosophically very appropriate, since the subjective states of individuals are in principle not accessible directly to other observers. Hence, the first-person experience (more deeply, "qualia") cannot be directly observed by another agent. Hence, what can be learned in an intersubjective environment is just responses to questions by agents under specific contexts.

Finally, when one talks about QM, one usually has non-relativistic particle mechanics in mind. What distinguishes the quantum mechanics of particles from the classical mechanics of particles is its ability to account for

i. interference phenomena,
ii. contextuality and complementarity, and
iii. entanglement.

This is achieved by describing a quantum state as a vector in a Hilbert space rather than by a point in phase space.

5.2 COMPLEMENTARITY AND CONTEXTUALITY

We also observe, based on the above discussion, that there were marked differences between the founders of the Copenhagen view, particularly between Heisenberg and Bohr. Specifically, this relates to the differences of views on complementarity, the concept which according to Pauli (Hendry 2012) defines modern quantum theory. Authors (Rovelli 1996) observed that many adherents to the Copenhagen view failed to grasp "complementarity" in the sense of Bohr, which means that there was never a single comprehensive view. The view of quantum theory being a theory of mutually exclusive experimental set-ups or contexts, which Bohr propounded throughout the 1930s, has become the standard view on complementarity. However, in the earlier lectures Bohr proposed the idea in relation to stationary states, not much mentioning the later complementarity–contextuality idea. While, the original idea of Bohr was in relation to conservation of energy and a space–time description of electron (position in a time instance), when Heisenberg "defended" Bohr's ideas he referred to the evolution of the wave function in time.

According to Heisenberg, complementarity consists of two exclusive modes of descriptions in QM, one, as outcomes of experiments in a classical language and two, in terms of Schrödinger's wave function evolution. This is interesting since, as Rovelli (1996, 2018) notes, Heisenberg's original paper in 1925 which officially started the QM literature, was certainly not based on a wave function ontology, rather on observables and relations between them (in terms of commutation algebra).

Lessons for cognitive modelling from the Copenhagen debates might be that there are apparently, mutually contradicting positions on the complementarity–contextuality framework, hence, it would be quite important to decide which of the formulations would be apt for describing human mind, or choice making under contexts.

5.3 OTHER APPROACHES IN QM

Generally speaking, there are two types of approaches for "interpreting" or "completing" the original QM and in fact its successor, QFT. The so-called "anti-realist" approach is one which has its roots in the Copenhagen tradition (e.g. Josephson and Sorokin (2017); Bohr (1960); Don (2004)) where the attempt is not to provide a more complete view of individual micro-world processes, but rather to interpret the standard quantum framework in different ways. QBism can be thought as one of such approaches, where any process of "measurement" is actually a subjective and personalist belief updating process, which converges with Born rule for probability updating, further here emergence of probability is epistemic rather than ontic, we present more details later.

The realist tradition, which comprises, the de Broglie–Bohm pilot wave theory, dynamical collapse theories and Multiverse theories, try to rather provide a complete ontological view of micro processes. Some authors have held that such theories are not QM, since they have either different ontologies and at times, or predicts more than standard quantum framework. We here just observe that some of these realist approaches, for example, the pilot wave theory where both wave and particles are real (wave acts as a guidance to particle which always has a definite location in space and evolves over time) hence, has a double ontology, have been used to model certain financial market processes.

6. Entanglement in Human Cognitive Processes

Very recently, however, various authors (including one of the present authors) have shown that a classical entanglement-based framework can be built for human cognition in general and quantum games in particular, which might also describe the "non-Boolean" features of behaviour. Such a framework has been named as classical optical modelling of human cognition (COM), which builds upon a widely noted phenomenon of "classical entanglement" in classical optics (where we do not introduce any quantum degree of freedom in describing light beams, e.g. photons). Classical entanglement can be differentiated from pure quantum entanglement as being coupling between different degrees of freedom of the same system, rather than spatially or temporally separated systems. Particularly, it has been known since long that Hilbert space modelling can be fruitfully exploited in describing classical polarized beams. One of the current authors has been involved in developing such a framework, where there are quite a few advantages as compared to pure quantum framework of human cognition, or its applications like quantum games. For example, in any cognitive model where we use the operator algebra or c^* algebra in full glory (defined on finite or infinite dimensional Hilbert space as the state space of the model), we have to encounter the presence of Planck's constant in the commutation relations between observables, which are represented as Hermitian operators. However, unlike pure quantum physics where Planck's constant plays a foundational role as the fundamental unit of action, in cognitive models or their applications it is certainly not clear what its role should be. Now we have shown (Patra and Ghose 2022) that usage of classical Hilbert space modelling where Lie brackets are used while expressing commutation relations, there is no need for usage of Planck's constant. Though basic results of quantum-like modelling in human cognition can still be preserved.

Another interesting feature in application of COM in quantum games is that since real players may use classically entangled systems (e.g. polarized beams) to achieve superior equilibrium outcomes, fragility of such systems go down, since classical entanglement, unlike the pure quantum case is stable against atmospheric decoherence.

Overall, the new approach or framework is based on the following steps:

1. The mathematical techniques of classical polarization optics.
2. The Bohr–Kant epistemology of "unanalysable wholeness" as explained above.
3. Luder's rule, which preserves pure states, for updation purposes.
4. The subjective interpretation of probability.
5. The formula for total probability (FTP) with the interference term.

7. Human Cognitive Modelling

Here, first we would like to point out the differences in different extant frameworks relevant for human cognitive modelling as below.

7.1 FTP GENERATED IN DIFFERENT VERSIONS OF QUANTUM-LIKE MODELS

The cognitive state as we have defined earlier, as an unanalysable whole, which has contextuality embedded in its description, can be provided a subjective epistemological interpretation as in QBism (Fuchs 2010). The QBist method has been to provide a subjectivist description to the state and use Born rule for further updating of states and evaluating probabilities. There have been multiple versions of QBism, one distinctive version being the Vaxjo version, which came up from the discussions since 2001.

Since we are contrasting between different quantum-like approaches, it is reasonable to question the validity of the QBist approach in cognitive modelling. QBism, as is widely known today, is fundamentally a subjectivist and personalist view on quantum mechanics overall. Many would like to place QBism in the anti-realist camp, where the aim is not to "complete" quantum mechanical description of reality by another realist theory of nature (in contrast to Pilot wave theory of de Broglie–Bohm, or various dynamical collapse theories or even many world Everettian quantum mechanics), but to interpret the standard framework of QM from a subjectivist perspective. QBism avoids any measurement problem in QM by proposing that any quantum state and updating of such state are just epistemic in nature, which means just knowledge update of the rational agents who use quantum theory for decision making, at times one can use the expressions "betting" or "gambling". Hence the use of probabilities, which coincide with the Born rule as in standard QM, is fundamentally subjective with credence for any event to occur in space–time, meaning even probabilities 0 and 1 can be treated as extremely high confidence for events not to occur or occur.

Recently, it has been shown that QBist propositions, for example, the use of Born rule or critically the use of a modified version of FTP, emerge from some basic decision theory-based arguments, particularly known as the "Dutch Book" argument. The associated argument is remarkably simple, suggesting that under no context, rational agents should take a sure loss. Here, however, we may question that since QBism is fundamentally based on rational utility maximizing agents (strikingly similar to the neoclassical framework in general) is it suitable for containing various "irrational" behaviours too?

We now proceed to provide a contrast between some quantum-like approaches to human cognition.

7.2 HUMAN COGNITION

Decision science or decision theory was initially based on classical set theory, with the main probability updating scheme as the Bayesian scheme. Bayesian formula for updating belief for rational agents is based on the assumption of rationality, which is also termed at times as the Dutch Book argument, the essence being that in no context a rational agent should take a sure loss. In social sciences, such a rational decision framework is provided a utility maximizing set-up, which in simple words mean that agents are updating their beliefs and making decisions (e.g. choosing between viable options) as if they are maximizing a utility function which is given for them based on their preference patterns.

However, with the advent of quantum-like modelling of cognition the standard Bayesian scheme is modified, at times agents are considered as quantum-Bayesian, which means that such agents use the non-Boolean logic set-up and Born's rule for updating belief states.

According to the QBist approach, quantum states can be represented by density operators, ρ, in Hilbert spaces as described above, which are finite dimensional and measurements are described by POVM. Symbolically, M_j, where j signifies individual agent's measurement experience. Hence, the individual probability, similar to degree of belief (which is widely used in social sciences like finance), of the outcome is given by $prob\ (M_j) = trace\ \rho M_j$. QBist perceive this rule to be a generalization of classical probability update. Hence, we briefly first explore the "Jeffrey Conditioning" framework for belief update in classical set-up.

According to the famous Bayesian framework of updating of subjective degree of beliefs, if H is a hypothesis to be tested conditioned on the E as the set of observed data, then:

$$p\ (H \mid E) = p\ (H\&E)/p(E),$$

where $1>p(E)>0$, the above expression can be further simplified as

$$p(H \mid E) = (p(H)/p(E)) \times p(E \mid H).$$

Here, the commutativity property of Boolean logic is assumed and also there is so-called "zero prior" trap of Bayesian logic, which means if the prior probability for H is already 0 or near 0, then any amount of updating will not generate any significantly large posterior. However, if keeping the subjective probability updating, agents update according to Born mechanism or rule, such a trap can be avoided. This point is important since in social sciences, mainly, financial market scenarios, exhibit rare events or so-called "black swans" which mean large updates from near 0 prior probabilities or degree of beliefs.

There can be two types of updating of subjective degree of beliefs, simple conditioning and a more pragmatic "Jeffrey Conditioning". In the former case, if the agent is absolutely certain of E happening, then the posterior belief $q(H) = p(H \mid E)$. However, this might seem to be an idealist case, hence in a more pragmatic scenario, if the posterior belief about E is updated as $q(E) > 0$, then we arrive at a formula for total probability, FTP, where the expression for FTP is

$$\text{FTP} = q(H) = q(E)\, p(H \mid E) + (1 - q(E))\, p(H \mid E')$$

and where E' signifies complement of E.

Based on this FTP, one can formulate the ratio of odds, which means, ratio of probabilities of H happening and H not happening and then use a rule that if that ratio > 1 then the collected data E can be treated as an evidence of H happening.

One of the main contributions of both the quantum-like framework and the QBist framework in decision-making theory is to generalize the above FTP, so as to incorporate "perturbative" terms which might explain deviations of real decision-making behaviours, than prescribed by classical probability framework or Game theory framework.

We refer to here two forms of FTP recently suggested – QBism FTP and Vaxjo FTP – and we then discuss how the present framework can contribute. Though Bayesianism is mentioned in the generalized formulations of FTP, the only commonality is the framework of subjective belief updating, the specific forms of FTP need not refer at all to the Bayesian updating formulas which are based on the Boolean logical set-up.

In the quantum-like framework, we can work with a complete set of hypotheses $\{H_j\}$ which is represented by POVMs. On the other hand, Vaxjo set-up, which is a statistical realist contextual set-up and where the observables are represented by Neumann–Leuder type operators with discrete spectral decompositions, the FTP formula (for simplicity for bivariate observables) can be derived based on a similar POVM approach which our framework also suggests. The interference terms we get in FTP for Vaxjo approach are quite intriguing, since it has been shown that for cognitive experiments, or real life game theory experiments, such interference terms can be "hyperbolic" in nature.

FTP Based on COM (Classical Optical Modelling) Set-up

Recently, one of the current authors has been working on a COM set-up for decision theory, where classical rather than fully quantum entanglement has been used as a feature to describe certain human mind behaviours. Such a framework can also be termed as quantum-like, where many of the features of quantum algebra are retained and simplified. For example, we do not need the full glory of Heisenberg algebras to describe human mind, at least on an epistemic level, not mentioning the quantum brain hypothesis.

FTP in COM set-up (Patra and Ghose 2022) is based on the geometrical description of sates on the unit Poincare sphere, the unit radius of the Poincare sphere would act as a substitute.

For the Born rule. There is a standard way to represent a general state corresponding to a point $(2\theta, 2\phi)$, in the standard basis c as in the following equation:

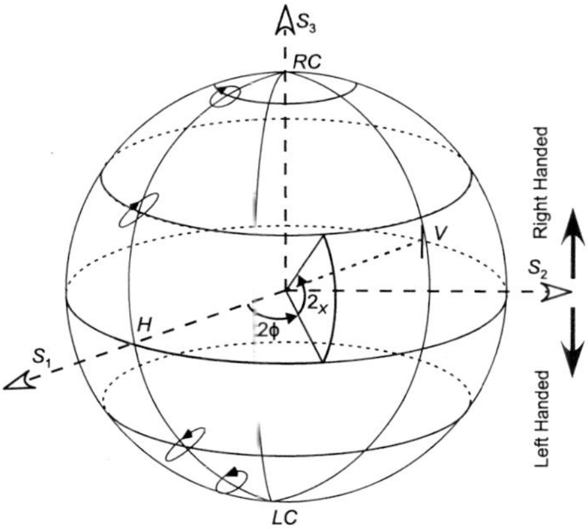

fig. 5.4: Poincare sphere

We consider the standard basis states spanning the finite dimensional separable Hilbert space used *as* $|0> = \binom{1}{0}$, and $|1> = \binom{0}{1}$, *then any general normalized state on the Poincare sphere is* $|\varphi> = cos\theta|0> + e^{i\varphi}sin\theta|1>$. This is a symbolic representation of any normalised state in this framework, for a given context *c*, where *c* refers to a chosen basis.

Hence, the coefficients of the basis states can be interpreted as probability amplitudes. Hence, considering another state on the sphere (2θ, 2ϕ') and taking their inner product, we define FTP, as: $FTP_{COM} = p_0 + p_1 + 2\sqrt{p_0 p_1}$ cosine δ, where $p_0 = \cos^2\theta$, $p_1 = \sin^2\theta$ and $\delta = \phi - \phi'$.

There are two interesting features of the FTP: one, since cosine δ can vary between –1 to +1, the FTP can be both greater or less than the classical range, again the FTP thus formulated is contextual in nature.

A question arises, how does COM differ from the QBist approach?

Since we have adapted the Bohr–Kantian view of the cognitive state (or quantum state or wave function in case of quantum mechanics), we agree with QBist that it does not represent any objective reality beyond the observer, that this state captures observer's state of knowledge which makes it fundamentally an epistemological or information theoretic problem. But then we do not fully agree with the QBists about completely subjective and personalized interpretation of probabilities obtained from the usage of the Born rule.

Also, as we have emphasized, it might not be necessary that state of the system being observed be updated always by "measurements", as in the case of classical optics, but certainly we can also describe via our framework of complex state updating like mixed state updating, which might be more relevant for cognition modelling or subjective decision making.

8. Conclusions

Quantum-like descriptions provide new powerful means to apply the successes of quantum mechanics beyond the original QM and even beyond the modern successor of quantum field theory (QFT) to essentially all levels of existence. This appears as a bold step but the work outlined here with specific examples and developments shows that this is necessary. It provides perhaps the foundation of developments across different fields in *interdisciplinary* and *transdisciplinary* scientific approaches. What used to be in the realm of speculation, albeit powerful philosophical developments can now successfully be applied in the *new science of human understanding*.

Based on the laws of the quantum universe, we hold the view that the quantum-like paradigm is a unified way to approach a vast number of phenomena and applications at the physical, mental, biological and sociological realms. This implies that the classical world of the five senses, although applicable in many phenomena, is obsolete or at least limited in an ontological sense. We presented the view that the quantum universe is much more natural to interconnection, non-locality, complementarity, a set of truths that form the whole, a reality in which the observer is central, the boundaries of observation providing the means to start exploration of next developments. In fact, we hold the view that there are no two worlds, the quantum world and the (seemingly classical) world of everyday life. There is only one world, the entire Universe that includes everything physical and non-physical, which cannot be described through the classical laws that we thought in earlier times were universal.

Complementarity and contextuality form the pillars of quantum-like Reality. It is, however, more challenging to expect that future developments of human understanding will be static and the same in the future as today. The expanded view we present here is that *the quantum-like paradigm* is adaptive and will allow future dynamical developments.

Moreover, as we have explored above, there seems to be departures from the orthodox quantum framework when it comes to describing fully the human mind. There are two levels of departures we can observe: one, the mathematical or descriptive level, where the state vector space may have to be more comprehensive, for example, the Fock space which can better describe "non-linear" features of the human mind. We also showed that the formalism in which simple orthogonal projection measures are utilized, may not capture decision making under all contexts, for example, when noise is present in the atmosphere. Therefore, as we have shown, to derive FTP, a more general class of measures, the so-called positive measures or POVM are often used.

The second level of departure from orthodox QM presents and even greater level of non-locality, as might be a characteristic feature of mind. The question arises: *Are non-linearities central features of cognitive models?*

We would like to conclude our exploration of quantum-like paradigm by observing some very recent trends, which might throw more light into "transdisciplinary" aspects. We note these recent trends first and then provide our own brief discussion for future research.

First, even mathematically (Kafatos 2015), while extending Hilbert space modelling with operator algebras, defined on it to human cognition, or even behavioural models like financial markets, we note a good use of non-Hermitian operators, which are more akin to non-linear versions of QM.

Transdisciplinary aspects of quantum-like modelling are apparent when we identify new findings on entanglement-like features in human cognition. Aerts (2014) has reported non-local correlations in the form of CHSH inequality violations in *human concept combinations* experiments. The authors have claimed such violations may occur in cognitive experiments where respondents have been asked to correlate between animals and sounds, they make (concept combinations), such that each random variable has binary values. What is remarkable is that CHSH inequality violations in some experiments have crossed Tsirelson's bound, which is the maximal entanglement case for quantum observables. We may either question such formulation or else need to think about human cognition as featuring non-local correlations placed beyond standard quantum framework.

More common place is the observation that while cognitive experiments violate the FTP or classical formula for total probability, standard trigonometric interference terms may not suffice since authors of such works do report hyperbolic interference terms with complex phase factors. These observations might open up the possibilities for a more comprehensive "non-linear" and non-Boolean human mind theory. As in quantum theory itself there are realist attempts of building dynamic collapse theories based on non-linear Schrödinger type equations, one can then ask whether there can be any clue for "completing" QM in a realist way by including human mind?

Finally, we would like to observe that there are alternative Bayesian or classical probability models with noise, which have also claimed to capture various "anomalies" in cognitive behaviour like "order effects" (where judgement of probability of a hypothesis depends on the order of information presented to the decision maker). Hence, one may raise the question why then quantum-like models are special? Here we would like to emphasize that our perspective in this work is not only focusing on technicalities which quantum-like models use, which might provide certain advantages with respect to classical counterparts, but more deeply, we like to propose that reality including cognition is overall quantum-like. There might be other non-Boolean logical perspectives, but questions of complementarity and contextualities would still remain, which we believe are described better in a general quantum-like framework as presented here.

Appendix A: Non-Boolean Logic:[8]

The main features of non-Boolean logic are the following: Boolean logic is based on the Kolmogorov measure theory, which can be described by a tuple: a sample space comprising events, sigma algebra of such events and a measure defined on the sample space. Sigma algebra comprise of all possible subsets of the events in the sample space including empty set. The central features of operations defined on the sample space are commutativity and associativity.

However, non-Boolean logic is such a logic (often described by Hilbert space modelling) where these two central axioms are relaxed. Hence, non-commutativity also means order of operation matter, in quantum physics such order effects are well known, for example, in classical physics observations or experimental results are non-contextual, but in quantum physics

---

[8] We also mention here that there are several other non-Boolean framework possible, for example, Clifford algebra, or Fuzzy logic, some of them have been used in quantum theory or decision theory alike.

order in which variables are measured impacts the final value of a variable measured.

As we have described in the chapter, order effects are central to cognition also, hence, a non-Boolean logic might describe it better.

The algebra of events is prescribed by quantum logic. Events form an event ring R, possessing two binary operations, addition and conjunction $P(A \cup B) = P(B \cup A)$ (this Boolean logic feature is invariant in Quantum logic). $P\{A \cup (B \cup C)\} = P\{(A \cup B) \cup (A \cup C)\}$ (associative, property also holds good) $A \cup \cdot A = A$ (idempotence) also holds good. $P(A \cap B) \neq P(B \cap A)$ (non-commutativity, incompatible variables), which also implies non distributive.

The fact that distributivity is absent in quantum logic was emphasized by Birkhoff and von Neumann in subsequent developments to the original developments. Suppose there are two events $B1$ and $B2$ that, when combined, form unity, $B1 \cup B2 = 1$. Moreover, $B1$ and $B2$ are such that each of them is orthogonal to a non-trivial event $A \# 0$, hence, $A \cap B1 = A \cap B2 = 0$. According to this definition, $A \cap (B1 \cup B2) = A \cap 1 = A$. But if the property of distributivity were true, then one would get $(A \cap B1) \cup (A \cap B2) = 0$. This would then imply that $A = 0$, which contradicts the assumption that $A \# 0$.

Appendix B

Here, we present a brief summary of FTP based on extant literature (particularly known as Vaxjo interpretation of FTP).

To get the modified FTP as in non-Kolmogorovian QDT set-up, we have to go through the concept of positive operator valued measure (POVM) operators as below:

A POVM is a family of positive operators $\{\{M_j\}$ such that $\Sigma_i M_i = I$ where I, is the unit operator.

It is convenient to use the following representation of POVMs:

Again,

$$M_j = V\text{x}V,$$

where $V_j : H \rightarrow H$ are linear operators.

A POVM can be considered as a random observable. Take any set of labels α1, ... , α*m*, e.g. for *m* = 2, α1 = yes, α2 = no. Then the corresponding observable takes these values (for systems in the state ρ) with the probabilities, $prob\ (\alpha_j) = trace\ (\rho M_j) = trace\ V_j \rho V_j^*$.

We are also interested in the post-measurement states. Let the state ρ was given, a generalized observable was measured and the value *αj* was obtained. Then the output state after this measurement will also be updated following quantum rules. Both order effects and interference terms in FTP can be demonstrated using POVM.

Consider two generalized observables *a* and *b* corresponding to POVMs $Ma = \{V\text{x}_j\ V_j\}$ and $Mb = \{W\text{x}_j\ W_j\}$, where $V_j \equiv V\ (\alpha_j)$ and $W_j = W(\beta_j)$ correspond to the values α_j and β_j.

For the consecutive *b*-measurement, the probability to obtain the value *b* = β is given $prob\ (\beta \mid \alpha) = trace\ \rho\ a\ (\alpha)\ Mb(\beta)$

$TrW(\beta)\ V(\alpha)\rho\ V\text{x}(\alpha)\ W\text{x}\ (\beta)/(TrV(\alpha)\ \rho V\text{x}(\alpha))$.

This is the conditional probability to obtain the result *b* = β under the condition of the result *a* = α. We set $p(\alpha, \beta) = pa(\alpha)\ p(\beta \mid \alpha)$.

Now since operators need not commute $p(\alpha, \beta) = p(\beta, \alpha)$, we recall that, for two classical random variables *a* and *b*, which can be represented in the Kolmogorov measure-theoretic approach, the formula for total probability (FTP) has the form $pb(\beta) = \Sigma\ pa(\alpha)\ p(\beta \mid \alpha)$.

Further, we restrict our consideration to the case of dichotomous variables, α = α1, α2 and β = β1, β2. Where in the

FTP formula, then we will have the general interference terms/ phase terms, which then make them non-classical.

References

Aerts, D., 2011, "Quantum Interference and Superposition in Cognition: Development of a Theory for the Disjunction of Concepts", in *Worldviews, Science and US: Bridging Knowledge and Its Implications for Our Perspectives of the World*, ed. D. Aerts, J. Broekaert, B. D'Hooghe and N. Note, Singapore: World Scientific.

———, 2014, "Quantum Theory and Human Perception of the Macro-world", *Frontiers of Psychology*, https://doi.org/10.3389/fpsyg.2014.00554.

Aerts, D., et al., 2019, *Quantum Entanglement in Physical and Cognitive Systems: A Conceptual Analysis and a General Representation*, arXiv:1903.09103 [q-bio.NC].

Aumann, R.J., 1976, "Agreeing to Disagree", *The Annals of Statistics*, 4(6): 1236-39.

Bohr, N., 1960, *The Unity of Human Knowledge: Philosophical Writings of Niels Bohr*, vol. 3, Woodbridge: Ox Bow Press.

Busemeyer, J.R., M.R. Matthew and Z. Wang, 2006, "A Quantum Information Processing Explanation of Disjunction Effects", in *Proceedings of the Annual Meeting of the Cognitive Science Society*, vol. 28, no. 28.

Busemeyer, J.R., Z. Wang and A. Lambert-Mogiliansky, 2009, "Comparison of Markov and Quantum Models of Decision Making", *Journal of Mathematical Psychology*, 53: 423-33.

Cassidy, D., 2008, *Quantum Mechanics 1925-1927: Triumph of the Copenhagen Interpretation*, ed. Werner Heisenberg, New York: American Institute of Physics.

Don, Howard, 2004, "Who Invented 'Copenhagen Interpretation'?: A Study in Mythology", *Philosophy of Science*, 71(5): 669-82.

Dzhafarov, E.N., R. Zhang and J. Kujala, 2016, "Is There Contextuality in Behavioural and Social Systems?", *Philosophical Transactions of the Royal Society, A: Mathematical, Physical and Engineering Sciences*, 374(2058): 20150009.

Ehtibar, N. Dzhafarov, Victor H. Cervantes and Janne V. Kujala, 2017, "Contextuality in Canonical Systems of Random Variables", *Philosophical Transactions of the Royal Society A: Mathematical, Physical and Engineering Sciences*, 375, 20160389, arXiv:1703.01252.

Ellsberg, D., 1961, "Risk, Ambiguity and the Savage Axioms", *Quarterly Journal of Economics*, 75(4): 643-69.

Frauchiger, D. and R. Renner, 2018, "Quantum Theory Cannot Consistently Describe the Use of Itself", *Nature Communications*, 9: art. no. 3711.

Fuchs, C.A., 2010, *QBism: The Perimeter of Quantum Bayesianism*, arXiv arXiv:1003.5209.

Ghose, P. (ed.), 2017, *Einstein, Tagore, and the Nature of Reality*, London: Routledge.

Haven, Emmanuel and Andrei Khrennikov, 2013, *Quantum Social Science*, Cambridge: Cambridge University Press.

Haven, E., T. Robinson and A. Khrennikov, 2017, *Quantum Methods in Social Science*, Singapore: World Scientific.

Heisenberg, W., 1930, *The Physical Principles of the Quantum Theory*, tr. K. Eckhart and F.C. Hoyt, New York: Dover (repr. 1949).

Hendry, J., 2012, *Creation of Quantum Mechanics and the Bohr–Pauli Dialogue*, Dordrecht: D. Reidel.

Josephson, P. and A. Sorokin, 2017, "Physics Moves to the Provinces: The Siberian Physics Community and Soviet Power, 1917-40", *British Journal for the History of Science*, 50(2): 297-327.

Kafatos, M. and G.C. Kato, 2017, "Sheaf Theoretic Formulation for Consciousness and Qualia and Relationship to the Idealism of Non-dual Philosophies", in *The Necessary Conjunction of the Western and Eastern Thought Traditions for Exploring the Nature of Mind and Life*, ed. P.L. Simerov et al. **(Special Theme Issue Integral Biomathics. *Prog. Biophy. Mol. Biol.* 131 C. Elsevier, ISSN: 00796107, 242-50).**

Kafatos, M. and Narasimhan, 2019, "The Observer and Access to Information in the Quantum Universe", invited chapter, in *Quanta and Mind: Essays on the Connection between Quantum*

Mechanics and Consciousness, ed. Jose Acacio De Barros and Carlos Montemayor, Synthese Library (https://urldefense.proofpoint.com/v2/url?u=http-3A__www.springer.com_series_6607&d=DwIFaQ&c=TwQYWVcq0sGbkW5mKeqBpQ&r=3Z0LsbAnx59haR5D1UNC0QhJ756PCgyjJGMGCD6BI-4&m=pE6XIPP2shqL9lAISBhE5OF-plHhee62v87EdAWwoWs&s=zcxQpMV41vsk0jGZ-gB22eq2_88kknRNd8ICWlN3dBtM&e=

Kafatos, M. and R. Nadeau, 2000, *The Conscious Universe: Parts and Wholes in Physical Reality*, New York: Springer.

Kafatos, M.C. and S. Kak, 2015, "Veiled Nonlocality and Cosmic Censorship", *Physics Essays*, 28: 182-87; http://physicsessays.org/browse-journal-2/product/1242-9-menas-c-kafatos-and-subhash-kak-veiled-nonlocality-cosmic-censorship-and-local-observations.html and http://arxiv.org/abs/1401.2180

Kafatos, M.C. et al., 2015, "Biofield Science: Current Physics Perspectives", *GAHMJ*, 4: 25.

Kafatos, M.C., 2015, "Fundamental Mathematics of Consciousness", *Cosmos and History: The Journal of Natural and Social Philosophy*, 11(2): 175-88.

Kahneman, Daniel, 2011, *Thinking Fast and Slow*, New York: Farrar, Strauss and Giroux.

Khrennikov, A., 2010, *Ubiquitous Quantum Structure*, Berlin/New York/Heidelberg: Springer-Verlag.

Khrennikov, A., 2012, "Quantum Probabilities and Violation of CHSH-inequality from Classical Random Signals and Threshold Type Detection Scheme", *Progress of Theoretical Physics*, 128(1): 31.

Khrennikov, A., 2016, "Why Quantum?", in *The Palgrave Handbook of Quantum Models in Social Science: Applications and Grand Challenges*, ed. E. Haven and A. Khrennikov, pp. 321-34, London: Palgrave Macmillan.

Khrennikov, A. and I. Basieva, 2014, "Possibility to Agree or Disagree from Quantum Information and Decision Making", *J. Math. Psych*, 6263: 115.

Lave, Lester B., 1962, "An Empirical Approach to the Prisoner's Dilemma", *Quarterly Journal of Economics*, 76: 424-36.

Narasimhan, A. and M.C. Kafatos, 2016, "Wave Particle Duality: The Observer and Retrocausality", *Quantum Retrocausation III*, ed. Daniel P. Sheehan, AIP Conference Proceedings, 1841: 040004-1, 9 pages.

Patra, S. and Partha Ghose, 2020, "Quantum-like Modelling in Game Theory, Quo Vadis?: A Brief Review, *Asian Journal of Economics and Banking*, December 4.

———, 2021, "Classical Optical Modelling of Prisoner's Dilemma", accepted manuscript, preprint.

———, 2022, "Classical Optical Modelling of Social Sciences in a Bohr–Kantian Framework", in *Credible Asset Allocation, Optimal Transport Methods, and Related Topics*, ed. S. Sriboonchitta, V. Kreinovich, W. Yamaka, TES 2022, Studies in Systems, Decision and Control, vol. 429. Springer, Cham. https://doi.org/10.1007/978-3-030-97273-8 16.

Plotnitsky, A., 2012, *Niels Bohr and Complementarity: An Introduction*, Springer Science and Business Media.

Popescu, S., 1994, "Bell's Inequalities versus Teleportation: What is nonlocality?" *Phys. Rev. Lett*, 72: 797.

———, 1995, "Bell's Inequalities and Density Matrices", *Phys. Rev. Lett*, 74: 2619.

Rovelli, C., 1996, "Relational Quantum Mechanics", *Int. J. Theor. Phys*, 35: 1637-78.

———, 2018, "Physics Needs Philosophy, Philosophy Needs Physics", *Found. Phys.*, 48: 481-91.

Stapp, H.P., 2007, "The Quantum-classical and Mind-brain Linkages: The Quantum Zeno Effect in Binocular Rivalry", arXiv preprint arXiv:0710.5569.

———, 2007a, "Quantum Mechanical Theories of Consciousness", in *The Blackwell Companion to Consciousness*, ed. M. Velmans and S. Schneider, pp. 300-12, Malden, MA: Blackwell.

———, 2007b, "Quantum Approaches to Consciousness", in *The Cambridge Handbook of Consciousness*, ed. P.D. Zelago, M. Moscovitch and E. Thompson, pp. 881-908, Cambridge: Cambridge University Press.

———, 2007c, *Mindful Universe: Quantum Mechanics and the Participating Observer*, New York: Springer.

Tegmark, Max, 2015, *Our Mathematical Universe*, New York: Knopf.

Theise, N.D. and M.C. Kafatos, 2016, "Fundamental Awareness: A Framework for Integrating Science, Philosophy and Metaphysics," *Communicative & Integrative Biology*, 9(3): 00-00 e1155010-19

Wheeler, J., 1982, "The Computer and the Universe", *International Journal of Theoretical Physics*, 21: 557-72.

Yukalov, V. and D. Sornette, 2010, "Decision Theory with Prospect Interference and Entanglement", *Theory and Decision*, 7: 283-328.

6

Bohr, QBism and Beyond

Ulrich Mohrhoff

Abstract: QBism advocates not only a subjective Bayesian interpretation of probability but also a subjective interpretation of the events to which, and on the basis of which, probabilities are assigned by quantum mechanics. It made me look more closely at the original writings of Niels Bohr and discover that Bohr came tantalizingly close to adopting a QBist stance and that the different versions of the so-called Copenhagen Interpretation misrepresent Bohr's views in various degrees. Not only QBism and Bohr but also Schrödinger attribute the objectivity of science to intersubjective agreement, but only Schrödinger addressed the need to explain the "far-reaching structural similarity" between the contents of our respective "spheres of consciousness" that makes intersubjective agreement possible. To explain this, Schrödinger invoked the philosophy of the Upaniṣads, according to which reality is relative to consciousness. Instead of a single mind-independent reality, there are different poises or structures of consciousness, in which different relations between subject and object obtain. This potentially answers several deep-seated problems in the philosophy of mind, such as Husserl's paradox of human subjectivity and the conundrum of intentionality. I show how this explanation is supported by quantum mechanics.

Keywords: Bohr, consciousness, evolution, involution, Kant, the One, QBism, Schrödinger, Upaniṣads.

Introduction

THE beginning of the twenty-first century saw the launch of a radically epistemic interpretation of quantum mechanics (QM), by Carlton Caves et al. (2002). Initially conceived as a generalized personalist Bayesian theory of probability called "Quantum Bayesianism", it has since been re-branded as "QBism", the term David Mermin (2017) prefers, considering it

> as big a break with twentieth-century ways of thinking about science as Cubism was with nineteenth century ways of thinking about art.

The big break lies not in the emphasis that the mathematical apparatus of QM is a probability calculus [which, after all, is the common denominator of all existing formulations of the theory (Styer et al. 2002)] but in this *plus* a radically subjective Bayesian interpretation of probability *plus* a radically subjective interpretation of the events to which and on the basis of which, probabilities are assigned by "users" (of QM) or "agents" (in a quantum world).[1]

I am indebted to QBism for two reasons: It made me

i. come round to seeing that there is no difference between observations qua experiences and observations qua measurement outcomes, which explains why measurements are necessarily irreversible and outcomes definite; and

---

[1] While Fuchs and Schack prefer the term "agent", Mermin prefers the term "user", to emphasize that QBists regard QM as a "user's manual" (Mermin 2017).

ii. look more closely at the original writings of Niels Bohr and discover

   a. that Bohr came tantalizingly close to adopting a QBist stance, and

   b. that the different versions of the "Copenhagen Interpretation"[2] misrepresent Bohr's views in various degrees.

Mermin lists four stages of acceptance a radical new idea goes through:

1. it is nonsense;
2. it is well known;
3. it is trivial; and
4. I thought of it first.

He thinks that by now stage (2) is well underway: a growing minority of philosophically-minded physicists are beginning to maintain that there is nothing very new in QBism, that it is, in fact, just another version of the Copenhagen Interpretation. Unsurprisingly, therefore, QBists distance themselves not only from the Copenhagen Interpretation but also from Bohr's views. Section 1 addresses common misconceptions (shared by QBists) about Bohr's unique views, which "are almost universally either overlooked completely or distorted beyond recognition – this by philosophers of science and scientists alike" (Hooker 1972) – and Section 2 shows that where the irreversibility of measurements and the definiteness of outcomes are concerned, Bohr and QBism are on the same page.

In Section 3 it is argued that the shapes of things resolve

[2] The "Copenhagen Interpretation" only emerged in the mid-1950s, in response to David Bohm's (1952) hidden-variables theory and the Marxist critique of Bohr's alleged idealism, which had inspired Bohm (Chevalley 1999). The term "Copenhagen Interpretation" first appeared in print in Heisenberg (1955).

themselves into more or less indefinite spatial relations and that these relations are reflexive: they are the self-relations of a single relatum. In support of this, it is argued that this single relatum is also

i. the *sole* substrate of all properties measured or experienced, and

ii. the *sole* causal agent responsible for all clicks and more generally for all successful measurements.

Section 4 introduces the concept of "the One", which is central to the philosophy of the Upaniṣads. It has been invoked by Schrödinger to explain the "far-reaching structural similarity" between the contents of our respective "spheres of consciousness" by positing that "we are all really only various aspects of the One". Section 5 shows how Husserl's paradox of human subjectivity and another major conundrum in the philosophy of mind – to wit: the problem of intentionality – can be resolved along Upaniṣadic lines, and Section 6 outlines the Upaniṣadic theory of evolution and its response to the knotty problem of evil.

1. QBism and Bohr

While QBism, as propounded by Fuchs et al. (2014), agrees with Bohr "that the primitive concept of *experience* is fundamental to an understanding of science", and while Mermin admits that Bohr "delivered some remarkably QBist-sounding pronouncements", QBists believe that what Bohr meant by "experience" was (as Mermin puts it) "the objective readings of large classical instruments and not the personal experience of a particular user of quantum mechanics". To this, Fuchs et al. add that

> [b]eing objective and independent of the agent using them, instruments miss the central point of QBism, giving rise to the notorious measurement problem, which has vexed physicists to this day. – 753

These assertions raise several issues:

1. What exactly did Bohr mean by "experience"?
2. What is the intended meaning of "objective"?
3. Which measurement problem do Fuchs et al. have in mind?
4. What role did instruments play in Bohr's thought?

As to 1: Carl Friedrich von Weizsäcker, who referred to himself as "a student of Bohr and Heisenberg" (2014a), defined "experience" via the following statements (2014b): "we can learn from the past for the future"; "this learning can be formulated in terms of concepts"; "there are therefore things such as ... recurring events which we can recognize with recognizable words". This, I believe, is a good as any clarification of what Bohr meant by "experience", for example, when he wrote:

> In our description of nature the purpose is not to disclose the real essence of the phenomena but only to track down, so far as it is possible, relations between the manifold aspects of our experience. – *BCW* 6: 296[3]

Or

> [w]hen speaking of a conceptual framework, we merely refer to an unambiguous logical representation of relations between experiences. – *BCW* 10: 84

Von Weizsäcker's definition highlights the inextricability of the subjective and objective aspects of experience. The recurring events occur in my personal experience. The ability to recognize them with recognizable words, on the other hand, involves a common language, a common repertoire of concepts and publicly available objects to which this language and its concepts refer.

---

[3] These references are to volume and page number(s) of the *Collected Works of Niels Bohr* (1972–2008).

As to 2: To Bohr, "the emphasis on the subjective character of the idea of observation [was] essential" (*BCW* 10: 496). Because of this, grounding the objectivity of the new theory became a major concern for him:

> From a logical standpoint, we can by an objective description only understand a communication of experience to others by means of a language which does not admit ambiguity as regards the perception of such communications.
>
> – *BCW* 10: 276

> Faced with the question of how … we can achieve an objective description, it is decisive to realize that however far the phenomena transcend the range of ordinary experience, the description of the experimental arrangement and the recording of observations must be based on common language.
>
> – Ibid. 10: 158

If, as Bohr affirmed, "[t]he description of atomic phenomena has … a perfectly objective character" in spite of "the subjective character of all experience" (*BCW* 6: 279; 7: 259), it was

> in the sense that no explicit reference is made to any individual observer and that therefore … no ambiguity is involved in the communication of information. – *BCW* 10: 128

When Mermin refers to "the objective readings of large classical instruments" and when Fuchs et al. describe instruments as "objective and independent of the agent using them", they attribute to instruments and their readings a mind-independent reality. Bohr, on the contrary, in denying that the objective character of atomic phenomena was predicated on the experience of any *individual* observer, just as clearly affirmed that it was predicated on the collective (shared and agreed upon) experience of communicating observers. His meaning of "objective", therefore, is of the weaker, intersubjective kind. It does not apply to a mind-independent external reality. Bohr would not have denied the origination of objective experience in our respective personal experiences.[4]

As to 3: QM has two measurement problems, one "BIG" and one "small" (Pitowsky 2006). The crucial difference lies in the interpretation of the wave function ψ. Considered as a tool for assigning probabilities to the possible outcomes of possible measurements, on the basis of information derived from the actual outcomes of actual measurements, ψ has two obvious dependencies. It depends continuously on the time t of the measurement: if this changes, the assigned probabilities generally change as well. And it depends discontinuously on the outcomes that constitute the assignment basis: if the information on the basis of which probabilities are assigned changes, so do the probabilities assigned. Transmogrified into a physical entity that exists at every moment of time and evolves from earlier to later times, ψ thus has two modes of evolution: between measurements it changes continuously and predictably, whereas at the time of a measurement it generally changes discontinuously and unpredictably.

In dynamics (the general study of the changes of physical states), there are changes that are considered normal and thus not in need of explanation, and there are changes that need to be explained. For Aristotle, being at rest was normal, hence motion needed to be explained. For Newton, uniform motion was normal, hence acceleration needed to be explained. For Einstein, motion along the geodesics of curved spacetime was normal, hence geodesic deviation needed to be explained. If ψ is taken for

---

4 For Mermin (2017), the objective world is "the common external world we have all negotiated with each other", which originates "in the private experiences we try to share with each other through language". QBists and Bohr thus agree not only about the origin of the objective world in our private experiences but also about the role that our common, object-centred language plays in its construction.

an evolving physical state, then by the same logic its continuous evolution is normal, while its discontinuous change at the time of a measurement (its "collapse" or "reduction") needs to be explained. This is the BIG measurement problem, a.k.a. "the disaster of objectification" (van Fraassen 1990).[5]

For Bohr, there was no BIG measurement problem. This may be gleaned from his insisting that

> the physical content of QM is exhausted by its power to formulate statistical laws governing observations obtained under conditions specified in plain language. – *BCW* 10: 159

The very idea of conceptually dividing a measurement into a unitary physical process (nowadays referred to as "pre-measurement") and a non-unitary one (nowadays called "objectification") was anathema to him. Did he then give rise to the small measurement problem? On the contrary, he *solved* it. The small measurement problem is the question why measurements provide factual rather than merely conditional information. As I shall argue in Section 2, Bohr's answer to this question was the same as that which is now vigorously promoted by QBists: measurement outcomes, being experiences, possess the incontrovertible definiteness and irreversibility of experiences.

As to 4: Bohr accepted Kant's (1998: 115) premise that (i)

---

5 If the wave function is reified and the measurement apparatus treated as a quantum system, the measurement process ends with a state that only provides conditional information. It does not lead to the "objectification" of one of the possible outcomes. It only tells us that *if* the apparatus indicates that the measured observable has the value *a* (or *b*, or *c*), *then* the measured observable has the value *a* (or *b*, or *c*). One would need a second apparatus to find out what the first apparatus actually indicates and so on ad infinitum. This state of affairs is known as "von Neumann's catastrophe of infinite regression" (DeWitt 1970).

> space and time are only forms of sensible intuition and therefore only conditions of the existence of things as appearances.[6]

And (like Kant) he insisted that all physical concepts owe their meanings to the logical (or grammatical) structure of our thought (or language) and to "our ordinary forms of perception". By "our ordinary forms of perception" Bohr meant

> the conceptual structure upon which our customary ordering of our sense-impressions depends and our customary use of language is based. The basis of this ordering is, certainly, the possibility for recognition and comparison and accordingly the usual description of nature is characterized by the attempt to express all experience by stating the locations of material bodies and changes of location with time relative to a coordinate system defined in the traditional manner by means of measuring rods and clocks. – *BCW* 10: xxxv-vi

In other words, he meant a system of concepts that allows us to unambiguously identify (recognize and compare) objects in space and time. This is the very system of concepts the applicability of which was to Kant a precondition of the possibility of objective knowledge, which to Kant meant knowledge of an effectively subject-independent system of objects.

But Bohr also insisted that

> the facts which are revealed to us by the quantum theory … lie outside the domain of our ordinary forms of perception.
> – *BCW* 6: 217

So, how can we talk about these facts? Kant (1998: 115) went on to argue that (ii)

---

[6] "Intuition" is the standard translation of the German word *Anschauung*, which covers both visual perception and visual imagination. Perception is sensible, i.e. filled with actual sensations, imagination is not.

> we have no concepts of the understanding and hence no elements for the cognition of things except insofar as an intuition can be given corresponding to these concepts.

And that therefore (iii)

> we can have cognition of no object as a thing in itself, but only insofar as it is an object of sensible intuition, i.e. as an appearance.

Bohr could not have agreed more, insisting as he did that meaningful physical concepts have not only mathematical but also visualizable content. Such concepts are associated with pictures, like the picture of a particle following a trajectory or the picture of a wave propagating in space.

In the classical theory, a single picture could accommodate all of the properties a system can have. When quantum theory came along, that all-encompassing picture fell apart. Unless certain experimental conditions obtained, it was impossible to picture the electron as following a trajectory (which was nevertheless a routine presupposition in setting up Stern–Gerlach experiments and in interpreting cloud-chamber photographs) and there was no way in which to apply the concept of position. And unless certain other incompatible experimental conditions obtained, it was impossible to picture the electron as a travelling wave (which was nevertheless a routine presupposition in interpreting the scattering of electrons by crystals) and there was no way in which to apply the concept of momentum.

If the visualizable content of physical concepts cannot be described in terms of compatible pictures, it has to be described in terms of something that *can* be so described, and what can be so described are the experimental conditions under which the incompatible physical concepts are employed. Bohr settled on the nexus between pictures, physical concepts and experimental arrangements as key to "the task of bringing order into an entirely new field of experience" (Bohr 1949). What essentially distinguishes the experimental conditions from the quantum systems under investigation is their accessibility to direct sensory experience. What Bohr added to Kant's theory of science was his insight that empirical knowledge was not necessarily limited to what is *directly* accessible to our senses and that, therefore, it does not have to be *solely* a knowledge of objects of sensible intuition. It can also be a knowledge of something that is not an object of sensible intuition but instead is constituted by experimental conditions, which themselves are constituted by objects of sensible intuition. To Bohr, instruments thus interface two aspects of reality (or "realities"):[7]

---

[7] In previous publications (e.g. Mohrhoff 2014, 2017) I interpreted the difference between a non-contextual classical domain and a contextual quantum domain as the difference between the *manifested* world and its *manifestation*. Instead of being constituent parts of the manifested world, subatomic particles, non-visualizable atoms and partly visualizable molecules play an instrumental role in the world's manifestation. They mark the stages of a transition from the undifferentiated unity of a single substance to a world that allows itself to be described in the object-oriented language of classical discourse. Two questions arose in this framework. First, how are we to describe the intermediate stages of this transition, at which the definiteness of properties and the distinguishability of objects are not yet fully realized? My answer to this question was (and still is) that whatever is not *intrinsically* definite and distinguishable can only be described in terms of probability distributions over what *is* intrinsically definite and distinguishable, to wit: the possible outcomes of measurements. This went a long way towards explaining why the general theoretical framework of contemporary physics is a probability calculus, and why the events to which it serves to assign probabilities are measurement outcomes. And second, what accounts for the intrinsic definiteness of measurement outcomes? It is not enough to argue, as I did at the time, that the measurement apparatus is needed to define the values that quantum observables can possess, or to make properties →

- A reality that is directly accessible to sensory experience, which can be described in ordinary (object-centred) language using concepts whose meanings are rooted in the logical or grammatical structure of our thought or language and in the spatio-temporal structure of human sensory experience.
- A reality that is not directly experienced by us, to which neither the physical concepts at our disposal nor the language of objects can be applied, except by an intrinsically ambiguous extrapolation via measurement procedures.

When quantum theory came along, it at first seemed to require a radical departure from the classical universe of discourse staked out by Kant. According to Brigitte Falkenburg (2007: 28-29),

> quantum mechanics is neither compatible with the traditional concept of substance (that is, the principle of attributing properties to property carriers) nor with the principle of causality in its usual application to individual systems and processes. These traditional principles belong to the classical universe of discourse, but they are at odds with the structure of quantum phenomena.

What actually happened when QM came along, however, was not that the classical universe of discourse had to be replaced but only that it had to be *expanded*. It so to speak acquired windows into another domain of reality, the domain of quantum

---

← available for attribution to quantum objects. As QBism has convinced me, the measurement apparatus is also needed to *indicate* the actually possessed value of a quantum observable or the actually possessed property of a quantum object, and no property or value can be indicated in the absence of a sentient observer to whom it is indicated. The reason why the properties of the manifested world are intrinsically definite is that the manifested world is an *experienced* world. It is manifested *to us*.

phenomena,[8] which Bohr did not venture to explore, insisting instead that "the quantum-mechanical formalism ... represents a purely symbolic scheme permitting only predictions ... as to results obtainable under conditions specified by means of classical concepts" (*BCW* 7: 350-51).[9]

And he stressed that quantum theory necessitates "the greatest caution as regards all questions of terminology" (*BCW* 7: 316). He especially warned of the ambiguity of such phrases as

i. "disturbing a phenomenon by observation", and
ii. "creating physical attributes to objects by measuring processes".

As to (i): If the terminology of quantum phenomena is used consistently, then nothing – at any rate, nothing we know how to think about – happens between the preparation of a system and the subsequent observation. Any story purporting to detail a course of events in the intervening interval – including any

---

8 Here is what Bohr meant by a "(quantum) phenomenon":

"All unambiguous interpretation of the quantum mechanical formalism involves the fixation of the external conditions, defining the initial state of the atomic system concerned and the character of the possible predictions as regards subsequent observable properties of that system. Any measurement in quantum theory can in fact only refer either to a fixation of the initial state or to the test of such predictions and it is first the combination of measurements of both kinds which constitutes a well-defined phenomenon." – *BCW* 7: 312

9 What Bohr meant by "classical concepts" (or "the terminology of classical physics" [*BCW* 7: 349]) was not something proprietary to classical physics. He meant the "elementary physical concepts" (*BCW* 7: 394) that owe their meanings to the spatio-temporal structure of human sensory experience like position, orientation and those which are defined in terms of invariances under space–time transformations.

intervening "disturbance" – is inconsistent with "the essential wholeness of a quantum phenomenon", which

> finds its logical expression in the circumstance that any attempt at its subdivision would demand a change in the experimental arrangement incompatible with its appearance.
> – *BCW* 10: 278

As to (ii): If the dichotomy of objects and attributes created for them by measurements is ambiguous, then, arguably, this is because not only the attributes obtained by measurement but also the objects themselves are constituted by the experimental conditions under which they are observed. More recently, this point was forcefully made by Falkenburg (2007: 205-06):

> [O]nly the experimental context (and our ways of conceiving of it in classical terms) makes it possible to talk in a sloppy way of *quantum objects*. ... Bare quantum "objects" are just bundles of properties which underlie superselection rules and which exhibit non-local, acausal correlations. ... They seem to be Lockean empirical substances, that is, collections of empirical properties which constantly go together. However, they are only individuated by the experimental apparatus in which they are measured or the concrete quantum phenomenon to which they belong. ... Without a given experimental context, the reference of quantum concepts goes astray. In this point, Bohr is absolutely right up to the present day.

2. Bohr and the Irreversibility of Measurements

Certain passages in Bohr's writings, such as the following, make it seem as if he attributed the irreversibility of measurements to irreversible amplification effects or processes.

> The circumstance that such marks [as are produced by the impacts of electrons on a photographic plate] are due to irreversible amplification effects endows the phenomena with a peculiarly closed character pointing directly to the

> irreversibility in principle of the very notion of observation.
> – *BCW* 10: 120

> Far from involving any special intricacy, the irreversible amplification effects on which the recording of the presence of atomic objects rests rather remind us of the essential irreversibility inherent in the very concept of observation.
> – *BCW* 7: 390

> The fact that the amplification devices used in the production of such marks involves essentially irreversible processes presents no new observational problem, but merely stresses the element of irreversibility inherent in the definition of the very concept of observation. – *BCW* 10: 212

The non-negotiable foundation of Bohr's deliberations was "the irreversibility in principle of the very notion of observation" or "the essential irreversibility inherent in the very concept of observation". And given the stress Bohr laid on "the subjective character of the idea of observation" (*BCW* 10: 496), it should be clear that by "observations" he did not mean the subject-independent readings of measuring devices but the private experiences from which we have built "the common external world we have all negotiated with each other" (Mermin 2017). If "the quantum-mechanical formalism ... represents a purely symbolic scheme permitting only predictions ... as to results obtainable under conditions specified by means of classical concepts" (*BCW* 7: 350-51), then the only way to make sense of Bohr's apparent invocations of irreversible amplification effects or processes is as a concession to the quantum-state realist who interposes a unitary physical process or "pre-measurement" between the "fixation of the initial state" and "the test of such predictions [as can be extracted from the initial state]" (*BCW*: 312, see Note 8.

Bohr also appears to demand on occasion that the experimental conditions be specified "by means of bodies like diaphragms and photographic plates so large and heavy that the statistical element in their description can be neglected" (*BCW* 10: 212), or that the following be used as measuring instruments:

> Rigid bodies like diaphragms, lenses and photographic plates sufficiently large and heavy to allow an account of their shape and relative positions and displacements without regard to any quantum features inherently involved in their atomic constitution. – *BCW* 10: 165

So we have to ask ourselves: what were Bohr's intentions in invoking, in lieu of the essential irreversibility of human sensory experience, the size and weight of the measurement apparatus?

Recall that grounding the objectivity of science was a major concern for Bohr as well as for Kant. Having asserted that "we can have cognition of no object as a thing in itself, but only insofar as it is an object of sensible intuition, i.e. as an appearance", Kant (1998: 115) went on to affirm:

> Even if we cannot *cognize* these same objects as things in themselves, we at least must be able to *think* them as things in themselves. For otherwise there would follow the absurd proposition that there is an appearance without anything that appears.

If the only relevant context is human experience, or if the reach of human sensory experience is unlimited (as classical physics takes it to be), it is easy to forget about the human context of the scientific enterprise. It is possible to transmogrify calculational tools into objective physical processes with some measure of consistency (Mermin 2009). But if the experimental context is relevant as well, or if the reach of human sensory experience is limited, then the elision of the subject is much harder. In the situation contemplated by Kant, *all* properties are accessible to direct sensory experience. This allows them to be organized into an effectively free-standing causally evolving system of interacting objects. In the situation contemplated by Bohr, there are two kinds of properties to reckon with:

(i) the outcome-indicating properties of measuring devices, and (ii) the properties indicated by them, and neither is capable of being organized into an effectively freestanding system of objects.

The properties indicated cannot be organized into such a system because they only exist if and when they are indicated, and the outcome-indicating properties presuppose beings to whom something can be indicated. The elision of the subject thus appears to be a lost cause, and so does the transmogrification of calculational tools into physical mechanisms or natural processes. If one nevertheless wants to establish the irreversibility of measurements without invoking the essential irreversibility of human sensory experience, one has no choice but to invoke such "macroscopic" features as the size and/or weight of the measurement apparatus.

So why did Bohr invoke such features? Was it to appease the naive realistic inclinations of lesser minds? Or did he do it in order to indicate the price one had to pay (but which he personally was not willing to pay) for exorcising every possible reference to human sensory experience? My suggested answer is "yes" to both questions.[10]

3. The One According to Quantum Mechanics

The first to give a dynamic explanation of extension and impenetrability was the Serbo-Croatian polymath Roger Boscovich (Bošković). On the basis of his study of collisions, Boscovich (1922) arrived at an atomic theory in which matter was reduced to a dynamic system of relations between identical dimensionless "points of force" lacking mass and substantiality. His *A Theory of Natural Philosophy*, first published in 1758, was well known and remained influential for 150 years. His work inspired Faraday's lines of force, it advocated a relational

---

[10] For a more detailed and slightly different argument leading to the same conclusion, see Mohrhoff (2019).

view of space and it accounted for the stability of objects in terms of equilibria between attractions and repulsions. While Boscovich arguably achieved the complete elimination of pre-existent forms, classical point mechanics, for which he laid the foundation, retained them in the shape of point masses. The first theory to provide a complete dynamical reduction of form is QM. If a quantum object has a form, this consists of indefinite spatial relations between component parts.[11] If it lacks components, it also lacks a form.[12]

If the shapes of quantum objects – including molecules and eventually everything we tend to think of as "made from" atoms and molecules – can be accounted for in terms of spatial relations between (ultimately) *formless* relata, then we can invoke the principle of the identity of indiscernibles and regard these spatial relations not as relations between a multitude of relata but as the *self-relations* of a *single relatum*.

It is not a new idea that particles *of the same type* are numerically identical, in the sense of being (multiple aspects of) one and the same thing. In his Nobel lecture, Feynman recalled:

> I received a telephone call one day at the graduate college at Princeton from Professor Wheeler, in which he said, "Feynman, I know why all electrons have the same charge and the same mass." "Why?" "Because, they are all the same electron!"

---

11 Saying that a physical quantity is indefinite is the same as saying that it can only be described by assigning nontrivial probabilities to the possible outcomes of an unperformed measurement of it.

12 According to the current standard model of particles and forces, some quantum objects, including electrons and quarks, are fundamental in the sense of not being composed of other quantum objects. While such objects are often described as pointlike, this can only mean that they lack internal structure, which is another way of saying that they lack component parts.

My claim, on the other hand, is that "the miraculous identity of particles of the same type", which according to Misner et al. (1973: 1215) is to be regarded "not as a triviality, but as a central mystery of physics", need not be confined to particles of the same type.

To see this, consider (to begin with) an elastic scattering event featuring a pair of incoming particles "in" the states $|1\rangle$ and $|2\rangle$ and a pair of outgoing particles "in" the states $|A\rangle$ and $|B\rangle$.[13] If the two particles are of the same type, we can say that initially there are two things with the respective properties 1 and 2, and that subsequently there are two things with the respective properties A and B, but we cannot say that there are two separate *enduring* things. Quantum statistics forbids it.

While admitting that the locations at which particles are detected sometimes "form chains that give the illusion of permanent beings", Schrödinger (2014: 131-32) was adamant that

> [a]toms – our modern atoms, the ultimate particles – must no longer be regarded as identifiable individuals. – Ibid.: 162

> When you observe a particle of a certain type, say an electron, now and here, this is to be regarded in principle as an *isolated event*. Even if you do observe a similar particle a very short time later at a spot very near to the first and even if you have every reason to assume a *causal connection* between the first and the second observation, there is no true, unambiguous meaning in the assertion that it is *the same* particle you have observed in the two cases. ... It is beyond doubt that the question of "sameness", of identity, really and truly has no meaning. – Ibid.: 121-22, original emphases

A typical particle detector consists of zillions of individual detectors each monitoring a relatively small region of space or spacetime. Compared to the number of actual clicks elicited

---

13 For brevity's sake the customary phraseology of "being *in*" such and such a state is used in lieu of the more correct mouthful.

during each experimental run, the total number of possible clicks (or droplets, or whatever else makes up a track) is therefore enormous. This, along with the conservation of energy and momentum, makes it possible to observe tracks and to identify the type of particle associated with each track.[14] But Schrödinger was right: there are no *true* individuals; at best there are FAPP individuals, to use Bell's (1990) familiar acronym for "for all practical purposes".

The qualification "FAPP" becomes necessary whenever classical features are obtained by ignoring quantum features. Here the quantum feature ignored is the uncertainty relation for position and momentum. Because the locations of the clicks are "fuzzy" enough, the correlations between the clicks make it possible FAPP to imagine a continuous path, to imagine a particle following it and to imagine that this causes the clicks that make up the observed track. If continuous paths could actually be observed, the connection between particle types and individual particles would be unequivocal. Because particles do not follow continuous paths,[15] the connection can be made only FAPP.

---

14 A track makes it possible to measure such quantities as its radius of curvature (in a magnetic field), the particle's time of flight, its kinetic energy and/or its energy loss through ionization and excitation. Measuring three of these quantities is sufficient in principle to positively identify the particle type (Grupen and Shwartz 2008).

15 "[W]e assume – following a habit of thought that applies to palpable objects – that we could have kept our particle under *continuous observation*, thereby ascertaining its identity. This habit of thought we must dismiss. *We must not admit the possibility of continuous observation*. Observations are to be regarded as discrete, disconnected events. Between them there are gaps which we cannot fill in." – Schrödinger 2014: 131, original emphases

In the context of our elastic scattering event, the question "Which outgoing particle is identical with which incoming one?" has no answer. It is meaningless. Meaningless questions typically arise from wrong assumptions. In this case the wrong assumption is that initially there are two particles with the respective properties 1 and 2 and that subsequently there are two particles with the respective properties *A* and *B*. To avoid asking the meaningless question, we may follow Schrödinger and deny the existing of particles altogether (Bitbol 2007). Alternatively, we can avoid asking "Which is which?" by assuming instead that initially there is one thing, which is observed to have the properties 1 *and* 2 and that subsequently the *same* thing is observed to have the properties *A* and *B*.

Let us rerun our scattering experiment with particles of different types α and β. The initial states are now $|\alpha, 1\rangle$ and $|\beta, 2\rangle$, the final states are $|\alpha, A\rangle$ and $|\beta, B\rangle$, say. While it is customary in this case to say that we are dealing with two *enduring* things, this cannot be advanced as the reason *why* we observe a particle of type α and a particle of type β both initially and in the end. On the contrary, it is the latter fact that allows us to entertain the belief that we are dealing with two enduring things. This belief has the same FAPP status as the belief that the clicks that make up a track indicate the presence of a single enduring individual. What remains strictly assertible is that there is *one* thing, which is initially observed in possession of the property pairs (α, 1) and (β, 2), and which is subsequently observed in possession of the property pairs (α, *A*) and (β, *B*). Nothing therefore stands in the way of conceiving of the spatial relations which make up the formal aspects of quantum objects – and eventually the formal aspects of all objects – as reflexive relations entertained by a *single* relatum and to posit this as the *sole* substrate of *all* properties measured or experienced. Let us call it "the One".

What is more, while associating a unique causal agent with the clicks that make up a particular track is warranted only

FAPP, associating a *single* causal agent with *every* click (not only those that make up a particular track) is warranted without qualification. If in spite of the fortuitousness of clicks – i.e. undeterred by their lack of a cause in the experienced world (Ulfbeck and Bohr 2001) – we adhere to the principle of causality, we, in fact, will have to acknowledge the existence beyond this world of a causal agent responsible for every click in this world. And if we do, we will be able to identify the One – the sole substrate of all properties observed – as being also the *sole* causal agent responsible for *all* clicks and more generally for *all* successful measurements.[16]

4. The One According to Schrödinger and the Upaniṣads

In an essay written during the last year of his life, Erwin Schrödinger (1964) expressed astonishment at the fact that despite "the absolute hermetic separation of my sphere of consciousness" from everyone else's, there is "a far-reaching structural similarity between certain parts of our experiences, the parts which we call external; it can be expressed in the brief statement that we all live in the same world". This similarity, Schrödinger avowed, "is not rationally comprehensible. In order to grasp it we are reduced to two irrational, mystical hypotheses," one of which is "the so-called hypothesis of the real external world". Schrödinger left no room for uncertainty about what he thought of this hypothesis: To invoke

> the existence of a real world of bodies which are the causes of sense-impressions and produce roughly the same impression

---

16 Every measurement is genuinely fortuitous not merely with regard to its specific outcome (which may in fact be predictable) but more fundamentally with regard to its *occurrence*. There are no causally sufficient conditions for the success of an attempted measurement. The redundancy typically built into a measurement apparatus can maximize the likelihood of success, but it can never guarantee success.

> on everybody ... is not to give an explanation at all; it is simply to state the matter in different words. In fact, it means laying a completely useless burden on the understanding.

While we can compare the relevant contents of our respective spheres of consciousness through communication, we have no access to this real world of bodies and no way of knowing how it relates to our experiences.

The second of the two hypotheses, the one Schrödinger endorsed, was that "we are all really only various aspects of the One". The multiplicity of minds, he wrote in a different work (Schrödinger 1992a), "is only apparent, in truth there is only one mind. This is the doctrine of the Upanishads. And not only of the Upanishads".

The Upaniṣads are ancient Sanskrit texts, which contain many central concepts and ideas of classical Indian philosophy. Here "the One" refers to the Ultimate Subject, from which we are separated by a veil of self-oblivion. The same veil, according to the Upaniṣads, also prevents us from perceiving the Ultimate Object, as well as its identity with the Ultimate Subject. It prevents us from perceiving that the world is something that the One (qua Ultimate Object) manifests to itself (qua Ultimate Subject) – and therefore to us who are but "various aspects of the One".[17]

---

[17] Schrödinger (1992b) adds that if "to Western thought this doctrine has little appeal", it is because our science "is based on objectivation, whereby it has cut itself off from an adequate understanding of the Subject of Cognizance, of the mind", and that "this is precisely the point where our present way of thinking does need to be amended, perhaps by a bit of blood-transfusion from Eastern thought. That will not be easy, we must beware of blunders – blood-transfusion always needs great precaution to prevent clotting. We do not wish to lose the logical precision that our scientific thought has reached and that is unparalleled anywhere at any epoch."

If at bottom we are all the same subject – without being aware of it, except by a genuinely mystical experience that is hard to come by – then we have to conceive of two poises of consciousness or modes of awareness, one in which the One manifests the world to itself aperspectivally, as if experienced from no particular location or from everywhere at once, and one in which the One manifests the world to itself perspectivally, as if experienced by a multitude of subjects from a multitude of locations within the world.[18]

5. The Paradox of Human Subjectivity

Schrödinger (1964: 69) would have agreed with both QBism and Bohr about the role that language plays in establishing the rationally inexplicable correspondence between, as he put its "the content of any one sphere of consciousness and any other, so far as the external world is concerned". But if the spatial relations that make up the shapes of things are reflexive and thus entertained by a single relatum, or if there is a single substance underlying every property measured or experienced, or if there is a single causal agent responsible for every outcome-indicating event, then there has to be more to that correspondence than is warranted by language. If my sense impressions did not agree with yours, it would be impossible for my description of

18 An aperspectival consciousness features prominently in the work of Jean Gebser (1986) and in the philosophy of Sri Aurobindo (2005). Such a consciousness lacks the distantiating viewpoint of our perspectival outlook. The subject is where its objects are, for it knows them by identity, by being them. This means that space as we know it does not yet exist. The familiar dimensions of phenomenal space (viewer-centred depth and lateral extent) come into being in this secondary poise, in which the One views the world in perspective. Objects are then seen from "outside", as presenting their surfaces. Concurrently, the dichotomy between subject and object becomes a reality, for a subject identified with an individual form cannot be overtly identical with the substance that constitutes all forms.

my impressions to agree with your description of yours. What remains unexplained by language is *why* my impressions agree with yours to such an extent that we are able to compare our respective descriptions.

How the world we construct on the basis of our experiences is related to whatever it is that induces experiences in us has been a central issue throughout the history of philosophy. The issue can be stated in the form of a dilemma, whose two horns are:

i. the existence *of* consciousness *in* what appears to be a material world, and
ii. the existence *in* consciousness *of* what appears to be a material world.

Edmund Husserl (1970: 178) referred to it as "the paradox of human subjectivity: being a subject for the world and at the same time being an object in the world".

Starting from the first horn (and focusing on perception), we can gain an understanding of the causal chains that lead from objects in the physical world to firing patterns in brains, but then we find ourselves stymied by the notorious "explanatory gap" (Levine 2001: 78) between neural processes and conscious experience.[19] Starting from the second horn, we can gain an

[19] Here is how the problem was formulated by Hilary Putnam (1987: 7-8): "How does the familiar explanation of what happens when I 'see something red' go? The light strikes the object (say, a sweater) and is reflected to my eye. There is an image on the retina. ... There are resultant nerve impulses. ... There are events in the brain, some of which we understand thanks to the work of Hubel and Wiesel, David Marr and others. And then – this is the mysterious part – there is somehow a 'sense datum' or a 'raw feel'. *This* is an *explanation*? An 'explanation' that involves connections of a kind we do not understand at all ... and concerning which we have not even the sketch of a theory is an explanation through something more obscure than the phenomenon to be explained."

understanding of the general structure of empirical knowledge, its dependence on the logical structure of rational thought and the spatio-temporal structure of human sensory experience, but then we find ourselves stymied by the same explanatory gap met from the other side: the goings-on in our brains – as far as they are empirically accessible to us – are themselves objects of sensory experience, and objects of sensory experience cannot be uncritically identified with whatever it is that induces sensory experiences in us.

Here is how Husserl's paradox is resolved by the philosophy of the Upaniṣads: reality is relative to consciousness and consciousness comes in different poises, in which different relations between subject and object obtain. In the aperspectival poise, the One contains the world; in the perspectival poise, the One is multiply contained in it. This potentially answers a slew of further questions, such as for instance the conundrum of intentionality: how can anything in the world, such as a neural firing pattern, represent – or even refer to or be about – anything else in the world?

In the view of the Upaniṣads, all knowledge, all experience is founded on identity. What ultimately exists, independently of anything else, is indistinguishably (i) a consciousness that contains, (ii) a substance that constitutes, and (iii) an infinite quality and delight (*ānanda*) that experiences and expresses itself in form and movement.

If the One is essentially this infinite, self-existent quality and delight, it is easy to understand why the One would adopt a multitude of standpoints within the world that it manifests to itself: a mutual creative self-experience offers a greater variety of delight than a solitary one. If the One adopts a multitude of localized standpoints, knowledge by identity takes the form of direct knowledge: each individual knows the others directly, without mediating representations. But if the One identifies itself with each particular form *to the exclusion of* every other form, then the knowledge of other forms gets reduced to an indirect knowledge, i.e. a direct knowledge by the individual of some of its own attributes (think electrochemical pulses in brains), which serve as representations of external forms.

An idea that has been dominant throughout history (and still is so today) is that representations are encodings. Much has been learned about the processes by which the brain extracts information from the images falling on the retinas (Enns 2004; Hubel 1995). This information is said to be encoded in patterns of electrochemical pulses, and if these patterns are to be experienced as (or to give rise to experiences of) a world extended in space and time, they have to be *decoded* or *interpreted*. The decoding or interpretation presupposes, inter alia, acquaintance with the expanse of space and the passing of time and such acquaintance is not something that neural processes can provide.[20]

Some, like Bickhard and Richie (1983), are intent on repudiating the interpreter. What is actually required, however, is an understanding of the nature of the interpreter and the basis of its interpretive capacity, such as the Upaniṣadic theory of existence can provide. On this theory, the incomplete

---

20 Like the colour of a Burmese ruby, spatial extension is a quality that can only be defined by ostentation – by drawing attention to something of which we are directly aware. If you are not convinced, try to explain to my friend Andy, who lives in a spaceless world, what space is like. Andy is good at math, so he understands you perfectly if you tell him that space is like the set of all triplets of real numbers. But if you believe that this gives him a sense of the expanse we call space, you are deluding yourself. *We* can imagine triplets of real numbers as points embedded in space; he cannot. *We* can interpret the difference between two numbers as the distance between two points; he cannot. At any rate, he cannot associate with the word "distance" the phenomenal remoteness it conveys to us. And much the same goes for time. Time passes and the only way to know this is to be aware of it.

quantitative information afforded by neural firing patterns is supplemented by a qualitative direct knowledge that springs from a subliminal source, as *fig.* 6.1 suggests. Our indirect knowledge would not be possible if it were not supported by a subliminal direct knowledge, even as direct knowledge would not be possible if it were not founded on identity. In the words of Sri Aurobindo (2005: 560-61) – arguably the most qualified modern interpreter of Upaniṣadic thought:

> In the surface consciousness knowledge represents itself as a truth seen from outside, thrown on us from the object, or as a response to its touch on the sense, a perceptive reproduction of its objective actuality. ... Since it is unable to ... observe the process of the knowledge coming from within, it has no choice but to accept what it does see, the external object, as the cause of its knowledge. ... In fact, it is a hidden deeper response to the contact, a response coming from within that throws up from there an inner knowledge of the object, the object being itself part of our larger self.

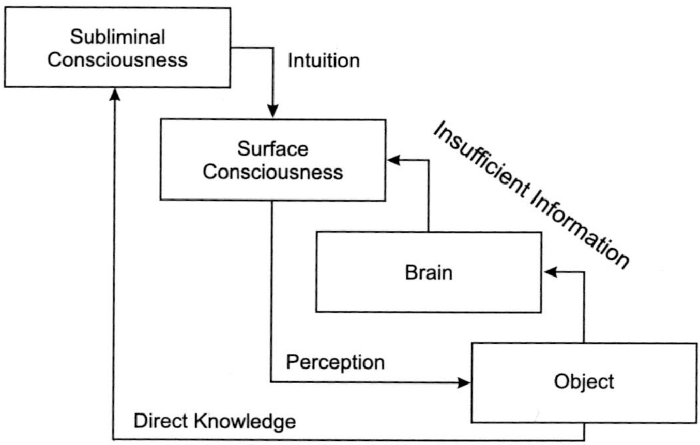

fig. 6.1: Our indirect (hence representative) knowledge is the meeting point of information flowing inward from the external object and information flowing outward from a subliminal source within

6. Evolution

I suppose we can all appreciate the advantage of an ontology that has at its core an infinite Quality/Delight, over a framework of thought according to which what is ultimately real is a multitude of entities (fundamental particles or space–time points) lacking intrinsic quality or value. In many traditions such a multiplicity is fittingly referred to as "dust". But why would the One not only adopt a multitude of standpoints but also identify itself with each to the apparent exclusion of the others?

From the point of view of the Upaniṣads, evolution presupposes *involution* and involution consists in a stepwise departure from the original status of the One as at once an all-containing consciousness, an all-constituting substance and an infinite quality/value/delight. The first step towards involution is individuation. By a multiple concentration of its creative consciousness, the One adopts a multitude of knowing and determining standpoint. The multiple concentration of consciousness may be inclusive, or it may be exclusive. Involution begins when the knowing and determining individuals lose sight of their mutual identity and, as a result, lose access to the aperspectival view of things. Carried further, involution renders consciousness implicit in its aspect of formative force. Carried still further, it renders formative force implicit in inanimate forms. And carried to its furthest extreme, it renders the principle of form implicit in a multitude of formless entities. And since these formless entities are indistinguishable and therefore (by the principle of the identity of indiscernibles) numerically identical, involution ends with the One effectively deprived of its innate consciousness and self-determining force – the Ultimate Subject, infinitely creative, rendered implicit in the Ultimate Object. This (or something much like it) is how the stage for the adventure of evolution was set.

This, then, is the question: What can justify such an adventure, considering all the pain and suffering that (in hindsight) it entails? Certainly not an extra-cosmic Creator imposing these evils on his creatures. But the One of the Upaniṣads is no such monster; it imposes these things on itself. But still – why? Imagine for a moment that you are all-powerful and all-knowing. Could you experience the joy of winning a victory, of overcoming difficulties and oppositions, of making discoveries, of being surprised? You could not. To make all of this possible, you impose limitations on your inherent power and knowledge. In the words of Sri Aurobindo:

> a play of self-concealing and self-finding is one of the most strenuous joys that conscious being can give to itself, a play of extreme attractiveness. There is no greater pleasure for man himself than a victory which is in its very principle a conquest over difficulties, a victory in knowledge, a victory in power, a victory in creation over the impossibilities of creation. ... There is an attraction in ignorance itself because it provides us with the joy of discovery, the surprise of new and unforeseen creation. ... If delight of existence be the secret of creation, this too is one delight of existence; it can be regarded as the reason or at least one reason of this apparently paradoxical and contrary Lila. – 2005: 426-27

Līlā is a term of Indian philosophy which describes the manifested world as the field for a joyful sporting game made possible by self-imposed limitations.

If the force at work in the world is an *infinite* force working under self-imposed constraints, we can stop being spooked by the quantum-mechanical correlation laws. There is no need for a mechanistic or naturalistic explanation of the working of an infinite force. What we need to ask is why the force at work in the world works under the particular constraints that it does and to this question there are definite answers.[21]

---

[21] A world about which anything coherent can be said requires sufficiently stable, re-identifiable forms. If these are to be manifested by means of spatial relations between relata that lack →

References

Bell, J.S., 1990, "Against 'Measurement'" in *62 Years of Uncertainty*, ed. A.I. Miller, pp. 17-31, New York: Plenum.

Bickhard, M.H. and D.M. Richie, 1983, *On the Nature of Representation*, New York: Praeger.

Bitbol, M., 2007, "Schrödinger against Particles and Quantum Jumps," in *Quantum Mechanics at the Crossroads*, ed. J. Evans and A.S. Thorndike, pp. 81-106, Berlin: Springer.

Bohm, D., 1952, "A Suggested Interpretation of the Quantum Theory in Terms of 'Hidden' Variables", *Physical Review*, 85: 166-93.

Bohr, N., 1949, "Discussion with Einstein on the Epistemological Problems in Atomic Physics", in *Albert Einstein: Philosopher-Scientist*, ed. P.A. Schilpp, New York: MFJ Books.

———, 1972–2008, in *Niels Bohr: Collected Works*, gen. ed. L. Rosenfeld, E. Rüdinger, F. Aaserud, Amsterdam: Elsevier.

Boscovich, R., 1922, *A Theory of Natural Philosophy*, Cambridge, MA: MIT Press.

Caves, C.M., C.A. Fuchs and R. Schack, 2002, "Quantum Probabilities as Bayesian Probabilities", *Physical Review A*, *65*: 022305.

Chevalley, C., 1999, "Why Do We Find Bohr Obscure?", in *Epistemological and Experimental Perspectives on Quantum Physics*, ed. D. Greenberger, W.L. Reiter and A. Zeilinger, pp. 59-73, Dordrecht: Kluwer.

DeWitt, B.S., 1970, "Quantum Mechanics and Reality", *Physics Today*, 23(9): 30-35.

← spatial extent, the spatial relations, as well as the corresponding relative momenta, must be indefinite, uncertainty relations must hold, the relata must be fermions – in short, something very much like quantum mechanics must hold (Mohrhoff 2009). And if the manifested world is, in addition, to contain individuals capable of telling stories about sufficiently stable, re-identifiable objects, the standard model and general relativity will hold at least as effective theories (Mohrhoff 2018: chap. 25).

Enns, J.T. , 2004, *The Thinking Eye, the Seeing Brain: Explorations in Visual Cognition*, New York: Norton.

Falkenburg, B., 2007, *Particle Metaphysics: A Critical Account of Subatomic Reality*, Berlin: Springer.

Fraassen, B.C. van 1991, "The Problem of Measurement in Quantum Mechanics", in *Symposium on the Foundations of Modern Physics*, ed. P. Lahti and P. Mittelstaedt, pp. 497-503, Singapore: World Scientific.

Fuchs, C.A., N.D. Mermin and R. Schack, 2014, "An Introduction to QBism with an Application to the Locality of Quantum Mechanics", *American Journal of Physics*, 82(8): 749-54.

Gebser, J., 1986, *The Ever-Present Origin*, Athens, OH: Ohio University Press.

Grupen, C. and B. Shwartz, 2008, *Particle Detectors*, chap. 9, Cambridge: Cambridge University Press.

Heisenberg, W., 1955, "The Development of the Interpretation of the Quantum Theory", in *Niels Bohr and the Development of Physics*, ed. W. Pauli, pp. 12-29, Oxford: Pergamon Press.

Hooker, C.A., 1972, "The Nature of Quantum Mechanical Reality: Einstein versus Bohr", in *Paradigms & Paradoxes: The Philosophical Challenge of the Quantum Domain*, ed. R.G. Colodny, pp. 67-302, Pittsburgh, PA: University of Pittsburgh Press.

Hubel, D.H., 1995, *Eye, Brain, and Vision*, San Francisco, CA: W.H. Freeman.

Husserl, E., 1970, *The Crisis of European Sciences and Transcendental Phenomenology*, Evanston, IL: Northwestern University Press.

Kant, I., 1998, *Critique of Pure Reason*, ed. and tr. P. Guyer and A.W. Wood, Cambridge: Cambridge University Press.

Levine, J., 2001, *Purple Haze: The Puzzle of Consciousness*, Oxford: Oxford University Press.

Mermin, N.D., 2009, "What's Bad about This Habit", *Physics Today*, 62(5): 8-9.

———, 2017, "Why QBism Is not the Copenhagen Interpretation and

What John Bell Might Have Thought of It", in *Quantum [Un] Speakables II: 50 Years of Bell's Theorem*, ed. R. Bertlmann and A. Zeilinger, pp. 83-93, Berlin: Springer.

Misner, C.W., K.S. Thorne and J.A. Wheeler, 1973, *Gravitation*, San Francisco: W.H. Freeman.

Mohrhoff, U., 2009, "Quantum Mechanics Explained", *International Journal of Quantum Information*, 7: 435-58.

———, 2014, "Manifesting the Quantum World", *Foundations of Physics*, 44(6): 641-77.

———, 2017, "Quantum Mechanics in a New Light", *Foundations of Science*, 22: 517-37.

———, 2018, *The World According to Quantum Mechanics: Why the Laws of Physics Make Perfect Sense After All*, 2nd edn, Singapore: World Scientific.

———, 2019, "Niels Bohr: Objectivity and the Irreversibility of Measurements", *Quantum Studies: Mathematics and Foundations*. https://doi.org/10.1007/s40509-019-00213-6.

Pitowsky, I., 2006, "Quantum Mechanics as a Theory of Probability", in *Physical Theory and Its Interpretation: Essays in Honor of Jeffrey Bub*, ed. W. Demopoulos and I. Pitowsky, pp. 213-39, Dordrecht: Springer.

Putnam, H., 1987, *The Many Faces of Realism*, LaSalle, IL: Open Court.

Schrödinger, E., 1964, "What Is Real?", in E. Schrödinger, *My View of the World*, Part 2, Cambridge: Cambridge University Press.

———, 1992, *What Is Life?: With Mind and Matter & Autobiographical Sketches*, Cambridge: Cambridge University Press.

———, 1992a, "The Arithmetic Paradox: The Oneness of Mind", in Schrödinger, 1992, pp. 128-39.

———, 1992b, "The Principle of Objectivation", in Schrödinger, 1992, pp. 117-27.

———, 2014, *Nature and the Greeks and Science and Humanism*, Cambridge: Canto Classics.

Sri Aurobindo, 2005, *The Life Divine*, Pondicherry: Sri Aurobindo Ashram.

Styer, D.F., M.S. Balkin, K.M. Becker, M.R. Burns, C.E. Dudley, S.T. Forth, J.S. Gaumer, M.A. Kramer, D.C. Oertel, L.H. Park, M.T. Rinkoski, C.T. Smith and T.D. Wotherspoon, 2002, "Nine Formulations of Quantum Mechanics", *American Journal of Physics*, 70: 288-97.

Ulfbeck, O. and A. Bohr, 2001, "Genuine Fortuitousness: Where Did That Click Come From?", *Foundations of Physics*, 31(5): 757-74.

Weizsäcker, C.F. von, 2014a, "Possibility and Movement: A Note on Aristotelian Physics", in *Carl Friedrich von Weizsäcker: Major Texts in Philosophy*, ed. M. Drieschner, pp. 127-37, Heidelberg: Springer.

———, 2014b, "The Unity of Physics as a Philosophical Problem", in *Carl Friedrich von Weizsäcker: Major Texts in Physics*, ed. M. Drieschner, pp. 67-71, Heidelberg: Springer.

7

Quantum Paradoxes:

To Resolve or to Acquiesce?

Ruth E. Kastner

Abstract: At the dawn of the Quantum Age, Erwin Schrödinger presented his Cat Paradox as a *reductio ad absurdum* of the problem of measurement in quantum theory in its standard formulation. Later, Eugene Wigner accentuated the paradox by considering himself and a Friend as among the correlated systems allegedly described by quantum theory but lacking any principled account of the conclusion of a "measurement". This basic problem facing the standard formulation has recently been brought to a head by the latest, most grotesque version of the same paradox by Frauchiger and Renner. This situation entails two basic options for researchers:

1. To regard the problem of measurement as inevitable, as something to which we should acquiesce as a feature of some "appropriate lesson" of quantum theory; or

2. to regard it as a symptom of a fundamental, but curable, problem afflicting the standard formulation of quantum theory.

I briefly critique option (1) and explore option (2), proposing that the simplest and most elegant solution has been overlooked due to deeply-seated metaphysical and cultural ground rules that are overdue for critical examination.

Keywords: Quantum measurement, Wigner's Friend, non-unitarity, quantum possibility, Direct Action Theory, quantum electrodynamics.

1. Introduction

AT THE dawn of the Quantum Age, Erwin Schrödinger presented his Cat Paradox as a *reductio ad absurdum* of the problem of measurement in quantum theory in its standard formulation. Nicolas Gisin correctly notes:

> The quantum measurement problem [is] a serious physics problem. Serious because without a resolution, quantum theory is not complete, as it does not tell how one should – in principle – perform measurements. – 2017: 207

This basic problem facing the standard formulation has never gone away. Instead, it has recently been brought to a head by the latest, most grotesque version of the same paradox by Frauchiger and Renner (2018). Based on an elaboration of the Wigner's Friend variant of the paradox, Frauchiger and Renner construct a contradiction in which a set of internal observers (at the level of the "Friend") must disagree with an external set of observers (on the level of "Wigner") regarding the Born probability for an outcome of a specific observable that could, in principle, be subject to empirical test.

The ambiguity inherent in the standard formulation of quantum theory concerning whether – and if so, when and how – measurement really yields a specific outcome is what leads to this inconsistency. This author has analysed the source of the inconsistency elsewhere and argued that the FR Paradox shows us that the measurement problem continues to plague standard, unitary-only approaches to quantum theory (Kastner 2020a). By unitary-only, in this context, I mean formulations that do not provide any quantitative, real non-unitarity that physically applies to the process of measurement, but which instead assume that the unitary evolution, referred to as "Process 2" by von Neumann, is the only process for which there is a quantifiable physical account (as opposed to a mere "Projection Postulate").

There have been a variety of responses to the Frauchiger–Renner construction, most of which discuss ways to evade the inconsistency within the unitary-only quantum paradigm (e.g. Nurgalieva and del Rio 2018; Sudbery 2016; Tausk 2018). To date, all responses (of which this author is aware) appear to assume that "real quantum theory" has only unitary dynamics and that any non-unitarity associated with "real quantum theory" is either epistemic or simply an ad hoc postulate with no physics behind it. So, while some authors take into account "non-unitary theories" as possible solutions to FR, they all consider such theories as different from "real quantum theory", exemplifying them by the Ghirardi–Rimini–Weber (1986) model that incorporates ad hoc changes to the unitary evolution (whether in the Schrödinger or Heisenberg pictures) to force collapse. But, as noted in Kastner (2020a), this is not in fact the case; there is (at least) one non-unitary theory that is both formally and empirically equivalent (at the level of Born probabilities) to quantum theory: the Transactional Interpretation (TI). Thus, unitary-only propagation is not in fact forced upon us by "real quantum theory". While details of the natural non-unitarity arising in TI are explicated elsewhere (e.g. Kastner 2018, 2020b; Kastner and Cramer 2018), Section 3 provides a brief overview of how the non-unitarity arises.

In this paper, it is proposed that the FR paradox should be regarded as a symptom of a fundamental, but resolvable, problem afflicting the standard unitary-only formulation of quantum theory and that Gisin is right in insisting on the need for an unambiguous definition of "measurement" within real, genuine quantum theory (not some other theory that is not empirically equivalent or that adds *ad hoc* changes). Entrepreneur Paul Arden (2003) once remarked:

> If you can't solve a problem, it's because you're playing by the rules.

Specifically, I argue herein that in fact quantum theory *really does* contain physical non-unitarity that does not need to be added as an ad hoc "tweak" to the theory that changes it to a different theory from quantum theory. This non-unitarity has been hidden from view because of an inappropriate metaphysical picture of field behaviour (and an attendant failure to distinguish between real and virtual quanta). This persistent, but probably wrong, conception of field behaviour is anchored in deeply seated metaphysical and even cultural ground rules that are overdue for critical examination. Thus, the real lesson of FR is that real quantum mechanics is *not* unitary-only. It only appears that way because of inappropriate ground rules that need to be acknowledged and discarded.

2. Traditional Quantum Theory Hampered by Non-Obligatory Rules

What do I mean by "the standard formulation of quantum theory" and "playing by the rules"? First, as noted above, the standard formulation assumes unitary-only dynamics, i.e. it assumes that quantum theory has no real, physical, non-unitarity subject to a quantitative theoretical description. To the extent that a standard approach includes any non-unitarity, it is confined to an *ad hoc* "projection postulate" (PP) for which there is no quantitative theoretical model. Since the advent of decoherence theory in the unitary-only (UO) approach and attendant claims that UO decoherence suffices as an account for measurement outcomes, it has become less fashionable to employ the projection postulate and many researchers tacitly assume an Everettian picture, in which the projection postulate is omitted. However, it is important to remember that decoherence alone, in a unitary-only account, does not solve the measurement problem. This point is emphasized by G. Bacciagaluppi in a discussion of decoherence in the *Stanford Encyclopedia of Philosophy* (2016):

> Unfortunately, naive claims of the kind that decoherence gives a complete answer to the measurement problem are still somewhat part of the "folklore" of decoherence and deservedly attract the wrath of physicists (e.g. Pearle 1997) and philosophers (e.g. Bub 1997, chap. 8) alike.[1]

But, in fact, real quantum theory can be understood as having intrinsic non-unitarity that is subject to quantitative analysis and that serves to define "measurement". One hint of this fact, obtainable only at the relativistic level, is that the vacuum-to-vacuum scattering matrix for a single current, based on the Feynman propagator, is non-unitary. This point has been discussed by Breuer and Petruccioni (2000: 40-41) and is further considered in Section 3.

The reason that the intrinsic non-unitarity of quantum theory has been hidden is because of the second set of acknowledged ground rules, which involve a particular metaphysical picture of field behaviour. Specifically, according to these rules, quantum state propagation is taken as unilateral; i.e. as dependent only on an emitter. We can think of this as the "baseball pitcher" view of field propagation: it assumes that nothing happens unless a single player initiates the action. After that, *everything* happens; i.e. nobody needs to figuratively "catch the ball" for it to complete its trajectory. In terms of quantum state propagation in the form of some field Ψ, it is assumed that there is no need

---

1 Bacciagaluppi, Guido, 2016, "The Role of Decoherence in Quantum Mechanics", in *The Stanford Encyclopedia of Philosophy* (Fall 2016 edn), ed. Edward N. Zalta, URL = <https://plato.stanford.edu/archives/fall2016/entries/qm-decoherence/>.

for a response or absorption of the field in order for it to be generated and to proceed on a well-defined trajectory. In this picture, *emission is active, while absorption is passive* (or not even required).

The above is the standard way of looking at field propagation in physics. The problem, however, is that it does not actually account for radiative processes, e.g. the loss of energy by a radiating charge or the gain of energy by an absorbing charge. The usual remedy for this shortcoming of the unilateral propagation picture is to assume an ad hoc "free field" in order to force these processes to conform to empirically observed radiation damping effects. This issue was discussed in detail by Wheeler and Feynman (1945, 1949), who proposed an entirely different theory of field behaviour – the "absorber" theory or "direct action" theory of fields – in order to render a more natural description of radiative processes. We turn to that picture in the next section.

Before doing so, it should be noted that the usual unilateral picture of field propagation is a classical, local picture, based on the kinds of processes we observe at the macroscopic level. As such, it arguably amounts to imposing classical preconceptions on the quantum level. Specifically, it assumes a particular kind of locality: the idea that physical influences always travel at no more than light speed. However, quantum theory has nonlocal features (e.g. EPR correlations). In critically examining the locality constraint, it is important to distinguish between information transfer (as in nonlocal quantum correlations) and *energy* transfer (amounting to controllable signalling). The former, termed "passion at a distance" by Shimony, is allowed in quantum theory, while the latter is not and that is what allows "peaceful coexistence" between quantum theory and relativity.

Standard quantum field theory makes no fundamental distinction between information transfer and energy transfer and imposes wholesale locality through a "bucket brigade" picture of field propagation, involving the assignment of an independent mechanical set of "field oscillators" to every spacetime point. These oscillators, described by creation and annihilation operators, act as a localized "bucket brigade" assumed to carry influences locally and continuously from one place to another. Standard approaches to non-relativistic quantum theory retain this metaphysical assumption of unilateral and local overall state propagation, even though, of course, quantum theory exhibits non-local correlations between entangled subsystems.

3. Uncovering Real Non-Unitarity in Quantum Theory

As noted above, a different (non-unilateral) theory of field propagation naturally accounts for radiative damping: the "Absorber Theory" or "Direct Action Theory (DAT), first proposed by Wheeler and Feynman (1945, 1949); but it is less known and less popular. One reason for its lack of acceptance is its denial of the usual picture of local, unilateral propagation of energy, which makes it counterintuitive. It rejects the "bucket brigade" picture of propagation, i.e. the idea that propagating influences are always localized and mediated through an independent mechanical system. It has been termed an "action-at-a-distance" theory, although that characterization has connotations that do not really apply to the specifics of the DAT, which does involve field generation by sources. So the "action" is indeed propagated between charges, but not in the usual local way. Specifically, in the DAT there is field propagation which is nonlocal, in that the field does not require a "medium" in the usual sense. In the quantum relativistic version of the DAT, for example, there is no independent system of field oscillators.

The DAT is the foundation of an alternative formulation of quantum theory first proposed by Cramer (1986): the

Transactional Interpretation (TI), as mentioned in Section 1. This formulation has been extended to the relativistic domain, termed RTI, by the present author (e.g. Kastner 2018, 2022). The essence of the DAT is that the elementary fields are time-symmetric, i.e. half-retarded and half-advanced. At the non-relativistic level, absorbers respond to emitted fields such that advanced effects from the emitter and retarded effects from the absorber are cancelled. In terms of quantum states, in a measurement interaction an emitter generates an "offer wave" (OW), which corresponds to the solution to the Schrödinger equation, $|\psi\rangle$. Absorbers respond to the OW with a corresponding adjoint field, called a confirmation wave (CW). The latter is not acknowledged in standard quantum theory and has counterintuitive features, in that it is a solution to the advanced (conjugate) Schrödinger equation. However, this overlooked interaction is what leads to non-unitarity, as we will see below (*figs* 7.1-7.3).

If there is more than one absorber involved in this process, each receives a component of the OW. So, for example, if there are 3 absorbers involved, *A*, *B*, *C*, each receives the component $\langle A|\psi\rangle|A\rangle$, etc.:[2]

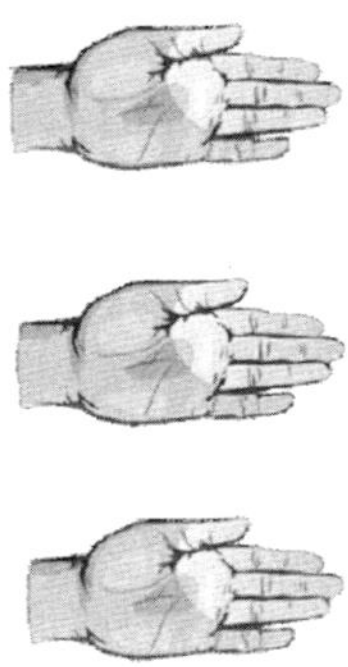

$$\langle A | \psi \rangle \, | A \rangle$$

$$\langle B | \psi \rangle \, | B \rangle$$

$$\langle C | \psi \rangle \, | C \rangle$$

fig. 7.1: Offer waves

[2] There is also the applicable Hamiltonian, which serves to direct separate components to each of the absorbers via unitary interactions (such as elastic scattering).

Absorbers respond by generating the adjoint (advanced) form of each of these components, i.e.:

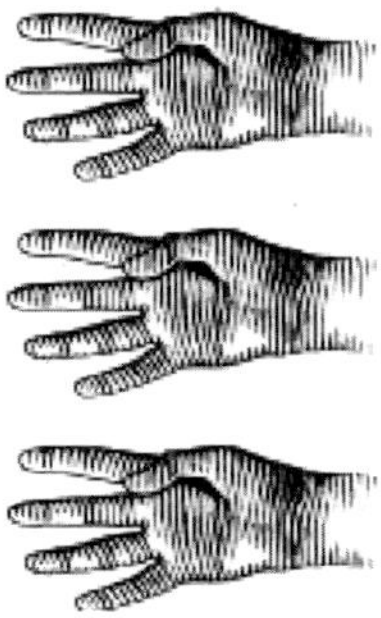

$\langle \psi | A \rangle \langle A |$

$\langle \psi | B \rangle \langle B |$

$\langle \psi | C \rangle \langle C |$

fig. 7.2: Confirmation waves

The interaction of each OW and CW components can be visualized as a "handshake", hence the name "Transactional Interpretation". This interaction, which has no classical counterpart, is the physical referent of the quantum probabilistic description. It is described by the outer product of the OW and CW, i.e. a weighted projection operator:

$| \langle A | \psi \rangle |^2 | A \rangle \langle A |$

$| \langle B | \psi \rangle |^2 | B \rangle \langle B |$

$| \langle C | \psi \rangle |^2 | C \rangle \langle C |$

fig. 7.3: Incipient transactions. Note that these are weighted projection operators, where the weights are the Born Rule

Each "handshake" is an incipient transaction. This is a possible transfer of energy (all the energy contained in the state $|\psi\rangle$) – but only one of these can be actualized. This actualization of a single outcome out of many possible ones is "quantum collapse" or objective reduction of the quantum state. Since the weights of the incipient transactions correspond to the Born Rule, TI is a collapse theory that is completely equivalent to standard quantum theory at the level of probabilistic predictions. This fact refutes the usual assumption that an explicit collapse theory must be different from quantum theory. It should also be noted that the creation of the set of incipient transactions, described by weighted projection operators as in *fig*. 7.3, provide the physical referent for von Neumann's "Process 1" or transformation of a pure state to a proper mixed state. The "reduction" to a particular actualized outcome can be understood as a form of weighted spontaneous symmetry breaking. There are no ad hoc hidden-variables here; the theory is truly indeterministic.[3]

It can now be seen that TI provides a cure for the FR inconsistency: F sees a definite outcome because there is one and W describes the situation accordingly – which means that uses a proper mixed state for F and his lab and never constructs the "absurd" macroscopic superposition corresponding to the Schrödinger's Cat or Wigner's Friend paradoxes. For more details on the circumstances triggering absorber response, which lead naturally to the micro/macro transition corresponding to our experience, see Kastner (2018) and Kastner and Cramer (2018).

At the relativistic level, the Feynman propagator D_F (constructed in an ad hoc way in standard quantum field theory) actually expresses non-unitarity. This is because it is a complex quantity with real and imaginary parts:

---

3 Implications for free will of the indeterministic actualization of an outcome are explored in Kastner 2016b.

$$D_F = \bar{D} - \frac{i}{2} D_1 \cdot \tag{1}$$

Therefore, the interaction Lagrangian based on it has real and imaginary parts. Explicitly, the Lagrangian is:

$$\frac{1}{2} \sum_{i,j} j_i^{\mu}(x)[\bar{D}(x-y) - \frac{i}{2} D_1(x-y)] j_{\mu,j}(y) \,. \tag{2}$$

Keeping in mind that the scattering matrix S is given by:

$$S = Pe^{-ij} \,, \tag{3}$$

where j is the action based on the Lagrangian, the complexity in (2) implies that S is non-unitary. The non-unitarity inherent in this interaction remains hidden in standard quantum field theory, but is revealed in the direct action theory, which provides a specific physical account for the non-unitary aspect of D_F. In fact, the intrinsic (but hidden) non-unitarity of standard quantum theory has already been noted by Breuer and Petruccioni (2000: 40-41). These authors discuss non-unitary of the S-matrix in a vacuum-to-vacuum transition for a subset of all interacting currents and argue that this is the basis for decoherence in quantum measurement. These authors take note of the fact that the Feynman propagator D_F contains an imaginary part due to the effective "free field" D_1 (whose existence as a component of D_F has no natural explanation in standard field theory, but does in the DAT; see Kastner and Cramer 2018). For a single current, the vacuum-to-vacuum scattering amplitude $S(D_1)$ corresponding to this component is:

$$S(D_1) = \exp\left(-\mathrm{Im}(D_F)\right) = \exp\left(-\frac{1}{4} \int j^{\mu}(x) D_1(x-y) j_{\mu}(y)\, d^4x\, d^4y\right). \tag{4}$$

We can use this expression to find the probability that no photon is emitted by the current, since the vacuum-to-vacuum probability associated with that component is

$$\left|S(D_1)\right|^2 = \epsilon^{-\bar{n}} < 1 \,, \tag{5}$$

where $\bar{n}$ is the average number of real photons emitted (corresponding to twice the integrand in (4)). Thus, the above probability will be less than one (and $S(D_1)$ therefore non-unitary) whenever $\bar{n}$ is different from zero. This explicit violation of unitarity obtains at the level of the S-matrix for a single current – i.e. when final absorption of the emitted photon(s) by other current(s) is not taken into account.[4] Since Breuer and Petruccioni are working with standard quantum field theory, they are not assuming specifically a direct action theory in order to obtain these results, although they do note that the real part of D_F corresponds to the basic time-symmetric interaction of the Wheeler–Feynman theory. This demonstrates that standard quantum field theory has hidden implicit non-unitarity. All that is required to make it explicit is to work in the Wheeler–Feynman DAT model and note that one gets the "free field" imaginary part of D_F from absorber response to the emitted time-symmetric field (a process overlooked in the standard approach).

4. Why Is the Transactional Solution Overlooked?

The above is just a quick review of TI and the more recent developments of RTI. It has been established in the literature that TI and RTI provide a physical, quantitative account of measurement, satisfying Gisin's concern as quoted above. That is, TI provides a specific non-unitary physical interaction corresponding to "measurement", which distinguishes measurement-type interactions from unitary interactions (such as elastic scattering not involving transfer of real energy). The relativistic form of TI, RTI, naturally finds the non-unitarity in the generation of the D_1 term in Feynman propagator and gives a quantitative indeterministic law governing the occurrence of the required interaction – essentially, decay rates.[5] Moreover,

---

4 The present author discusses the dependence of genuine (as opposed to for all practical purposes) decoherence on non-unitarity in Kastner 2019.

5 See Kastner 2020b and Kastner and Cramer 2018 for further quantitative details.

this account also explains why we do not see macroscopic superpositions (Kastner 2018). So, we seem to have a clear solution to the measurement problem here. Why is this solution still being generally overlooked?

First, there has long been a stigma attached to the "absorber theory" or DAT for historical reasons, which could be summarized as follows:

> Wheeler and Feynman were two smart guys who abandoned their direct action theory.

The first response to this sort of concern is to note that in fact Wheeler had returned to it with enthusiasm in 2003, when (with Wesley) he promoted the direct action theory as a possible approach to quantum gravity:

> [The Wheeler–Feynman theory] swept the electromagnetic field from between the charged particles and replaced it with "half-retarded, half advanced direct interaction" between particle and particle. It was the high point of this work to show that the standard and well-tested force of reaction of radiation on an accelerated charge is accounted for as the sum of the direct actions on that charge by all the charges of any distant complete absorber. Such a formulation enforces global physical laws and results in a quantitatively correct description of radiative phenomena, without assigning stress-energy to the electromagnetic field. – Wesley and Wheeler 2003: 427

It is also important to recall in this regard that the reason that Wheeler and Feynman originally lost interest in the DAT was because their main concern in developing it was to solve the problem of self-energy. When they realized that some form of self-action was necessary at the quantum level, this purpose no longer seemed to be served. However, as this author has noted elsewhere (Kastner 2016a), the self-action applying to the quantum form of the DAT is not self-energy; it is only self-force and this feature of the DAT becomes very useful for solving consistency problems of standard quantum field theory (Kastner 2015).

Having established that the reluctance of Wheeler and Feynman to further develop their direct action theory is no reason to consider it inadequate, we turn now to another reason for the general disregard of the transactional picture: its purported refutation by Maudlin (2002). In fact, the Maudlin challenge has now been multiply refuted (Kastner 2014; Marchildon 2006); and it completely evaporates when the fully relativistic level (RTI) is considered (Kastner 2019). In particular, at the relativistic level, the "slow-moving offer wave" required for the objection does not exist.

Besides the lingering, but unjustifed, worries about Wheeler and Feynman's attitudes and the Maudlin scenario, more deeply-seated cultural views need to be identified and their pervasive influence recognized. First, recall a foundational concept of Asian thought and culture: the duality of Yin and Yang (*fig*. 7.4).

fig. 7.4: Yin and Yang

These elements are complementary aspects of reality that are seen as balancing and even interpenetrating one another. In Asian metaphysics, there is no process in nature that is without both elements. Yang (symbolized by the white area) is the element corresponding to initiating, giving and creating, while Yin (symbolized by the black area) is the element corresponding to responding, receiving and dissolving.

With the help of this concept of Yin and Yang, it can be seen that the unilateral propagation picture is an approach consisting of "all Yang and no Yin". This preponderance of the initiating, creating, Yang element and neglect of the responding, receiving Yin element characterizes much of Western thought and metaphysics. It is taken for granted that objects or substances can be created autonomously (the Yang element) and have an independent existence and career without any element of Yin. Yet this contradicts much of what we actually see in the world. For example, if we want to have tulips in our garden, we cannot just toss the bulbs out. They must be received in the earth and interact with the soil in specific and crucial ways in order for anything to grow. Similarly, there are always two elements in a financial transaction: the seller and the buyer. Nobody sells a house (Yang) without someone buying and receiving it (Yin). However, the standard approach to field propagation takes all physical processes as Yang-only. Exemplifying this attitude is the idea that a photon can be emitted unilaterally and continue on autonomously, without ever being absorbed. In contrast, in the direct action theory, *both* Yin (response; reception) and Yang (initiation; emission) are required for the photon to exist. A photon, which is a transfer of energy from one system to another, can no more exist based on a unilateral impulse than someone can sell a house without a buyer.[6]

This Western cultural exaggeration of Yang at the expense of Yin impedes scientific progress in other areas. Pioneering research by anthropologist Emily Martin (1991) revealed that reproductive biologists had long been pursuing and promoting a highly inaccurate model of ovum fertilization in mammals. This model assumed that sperm were highly adept swimmers who unilaterally sought out the egg and competed against one another for the victory of (single-handedly) penetrating the egg. The egg was assumed to be completely passive, contributing nothing to the process. It was not until the mid-1980s that some researchers looked more closely into the process of fertilization and found out, quite by accident, that:

---

[6] Quantitative details on how one can indeed have a real photon both emitted and absorbed are provided in Kastner and Cramer (2018) and further discussed in Kastner (2021), which refutes the idea that a real photon must have an infinite lifetime.

> the egg is not merely a large, yolk-filled sphere into which the sperm burrows to endow new life. Rather, recent research suggests the almost heretical view that sperm and egg are mutually active partners. – Schatten and Schatten 1984: 51

Martin's paper, entitled "The Egg and the Sperm: How Science Has Constructed a Romance Based on Stereotypical Male/Female Roles", laid out in great detail how laden the standard reproductive narrative was with metaphors of sperm as strong, brave, autonomous conquerers and the egg as a weak, dependent, passive object to be conquered. However, the work by Schatten and Schatten revealed that in fact, fertilization was a team effort. Sperm were actually not very adept swimmers at all and the egg actively signalled with various chemical signals to guide the sperm to it; without that help, sperm got lost in dead ends. Fertilization itself involved the collaborative creation of structures connecting the sperm and the egg, rather than a unilateral "harpooning" of the egg by a sperm. Fertilization is now finally understood to be a mutual, transactional process.

Perhaps it is time to consider whether the same sorts of metaphysical and cultural habits of thought that long blinded researchers to what was really going on in reproductive biology may be making us blind to what is really going on in quantum theory. If we say "no" to these tacit but stubborn Yang-heavy ground rules and allow due consideration of the more balanced, Yin/Yang direct action model of fields, we get a solution to the measurement problem, including a full theoretical account of von Neumann's "Process 1" non-unitary measurement transition and a natural physical basis for the Born Rule. And we escape for good from all of the Schrödinger's Cat *reductio* absurdities that arguably stem from considering only the Yang aspects of Nature.

Finally, what connection does the Relativistic Transactional Interpretation have to issues of mind and consciousness? A key feature of RTI that distinguishes it from extant models is its interpretation of quantum states as pre-spacetime *possibilities* subject to actualization, where the latter corresponds to the occurrence of a measurement outcome. The domain of quantum possibility is represented by Hilbert space, while actuality corresponds to the spacetime manifold of concrete events. Unlike deterministic hidden-variable models or block world ontologies, the transactional picture has genuine becoming in the form of the transformation of possibility into actuality. This process of "collapse" or reduction involves the wholly indeterministic "choice" of a particular outcome, where there is no causal mechanism for the choice. One can view this either as a form of spontaneous symmetry breaking; or, more intriguingly, as evidence that at some level, Nature is "choosing", which attributes to it a form of intention. While formal RTI takes no position on issues of mind, it is reasonable to conjecture that mental processes could be identified with the quantum level of possibility. Thus, besides the opening for genuine free will afforded by inherent indeterminism (nothing is "fated" to occur), one could trace the ultimate origins of intentional and perceptual functions of the mental level to the domain of quantum possibilities. Might quantum entities be elementary forms of consciousness?

References

Arden, Paul, 2003, *It's Not How Good You Are, It's How Good You Want to Be*, London: Phaidon Press.

Breuer, H.P. and F. Petruccioni, 2000, *Relativistic Quantum Measurement and Decoherence: Lectures of a Workshop Held at the Institute Italiano per gli Studi Filosofici*, Berlin: Springer.

Bub, J., 1997, *Interpreting the Quantum World*, Cambridge: Cambridge University Press; corrected edition, 1999.

Cramer, J.G., 1986, "The Transactional Interpretation of Quantum Mechanics", *Reviews of Modern Physics*, 58: 647-88.

Frauchiger, D. and R. Renner, 2018, "Quantum Theory Cannot Consistently Describe the Use of Itself", *Nature Communications*, 9, art. no. 3711.

Ghirardi, G.-C., A. Rimini and T. Weber, 1986, "Unified Dynamics for Microscopic and Macroscopic Systems," *Phys. Rev.* D, 34: 470-91.

Gisin, N., 2017, "Collapse: What Else?", arXiv:1701.08300.

Kastner, R.E. and J.G. Cramer, 2018, "Quantifying Absorption in the Transactional Interpretation", *International Journal of Quantum Physics*, 4: 210-22. https://arxiv.org/abs/1711.04501.

Kastner, R.E., 2014, "Maudlin's Challenge Refuted: A Reply to Lewis", *Studies in History and Philosophy of Modern Physics*, 47: 15-20. Preprint version: http://arxiv.org/abs/1403.2791

———, 2015, "Haag's Theorem as a Reason to Reconsider Direct-Action Theories", *International Journal of Quantum Foundations*, 1(2): 56-64. arXiv:1502.03814.

———, 2016a, "Antimatter in the Direct action Theory of Fields", *Quanta*, 5(1): 12-18. arXiv:1509.06040.

———, 2016b, "The Born Rule and Free Will", in *Probing the Meaning of Quantum Mechanics: Superposition, Dynamics, Semantics and Identity,* ed. C. DeRonde et al., pp. 231-43, Singapore: World Scientific (2016), Preprint version: http://philsci-archive.pitt.edu/11893.

———, 2018, "On the Status of the Measurement Problem: Recalling the Relativistic Transactional Interpretation", *Int'l Jour. Quan. Foundations*, 4(1): 128-41.

———, 2019, "The Relativistic Transactional Interpretation: Immune to the Maulin Challenge", in *Probing the Meaning of Quantum Mechanics: Information, Contextuality, Relationalism and Entanglement*, ed. C. de Ronde et al., Singapore: World Scientific. arXiv:1610.04609.

———, 2020a, "Unitary-Only Quantum Theory Cannot Consistently Describe the Use of Itself: On the Frauchiger–Renner Paradox", *Foundations of Physics*, 50: 441-56.

———, 2020b, "Why the Quantum Absorber Condition Is Not a Light-Tight Box". Preprint, https://rekastner.files.wordpress.com/2020/02/light-tight-box-preprint.pdf

———, 2021, "The Relativistic Transactional Interpretation and the Quantum Direct Action Theory", https://arxiv.org/abs/2101.00712; excerpt from Kastner 2022.

———, 2022, *The Transactional Interpretation of Quantum Mechanics: A Relativistic Treatment*, Cambridge: Cambridge University Press.

Marchildon, L., 2006, "Causal Loops and Collapse in the Transactional Interpretation of Quantum Mechanics", *Physics Essays*, 19: 422.

Martin. E., 1991, "The Egg and the Sperm: How Science Has Constructed a Romance Based on Stereotypical Male/Female Roles", *Signs*, 16: 485-501. https://web.stanford.edu/~eckert/PDF/Martin1991.pdf.

Maudlin, T., 2002, *Quantum Nonlocality and Relativity: Metaphysical Intimations of Modern Physics*, 2nd edn (1996, 1st edn), London: Wiley-Blackwell.

Nurgalieva, N. and L. del Rio, 2019, "Inadequacy of Modal Logic in Quantum Settings", in *15th International Conference on Quantum Physics and Logic*, ed. Giulio Chiribella and Peter Selinger, (QPL 2018), vol. 287 of EPTCS, pp. 267-97, 2019. arXiv:1804.01106.

Pearle, P., 1997, "True Collapse and False Collapse", in *Quantum Classical Correspondence: Proceedings of the 4th Drexel Symposium on Quantum Nonintegrability, Philadelphia, PA, USA, 8-11 September 1994*, ed. Da Hsuan Feng and Bei Lok Hu, pp. 51-68, Cambridge, MA: International Press. [Preprint available online].

Schatten, G. and H. Schatten, 1984, "The Energetic Egg", *Medical World News*, 23: 5.

Sudbery, A., 2016, "Single-World Theory of the Extended Wigner's Friend Experiment", *Foundations of Physics*, 47(5): 658-69.

———, 2019, "The Hidden Assumptions of Frauchiger and Renner", *Int. J. Quant. Foundations*, 5: 98. arXiv:1905.13248.

Tausk, D.V., 2018, "A Brief Introduction to the Foundations of Quantum Theory and an Analysis of the Frauchiger-Renner paradox", preprint, https://arxiv.org/abs/1812.11140

Wesley, D. and J.A. Wheeler, 2003, "Towards an Action-at-a-Distance Concept of Spacetime", in *Revisiting the Foundations of Relativistic Physics: Festschrift in Honor of John Stachel*, ed. A. Ashtekar et al., Boston Studies in the Philosophy and History of Science (Book 234), pp. 421-36, Dordrecht: Kluwer Academic Publishers.

Wheeler, J.A. and R.P. Feynman, 1945, "Interaction with the Absorber as the Mechanism of Radiation", *Reviews of Modern Physics*, 17: 157–61.

———, 1949, "Classical Electrodynamics in Terms of Direct Interparticle Action", *Reviews of Modern Physics*, 21: 425–33.

8

The Epistemic View of Quantum Reality

Subhash Kak

Abstract: Classical reality is described in terms of objects and things and their mutual relationships. On the other hand, in the case of quantum reality, the collapse of the state in an interaction assigns a unique position to the observer. These two disparate views are based on different logics of representation, the history of which can be traced back to Greek and Indian thought. In this chapter, we first summarize the early evolution of these ideas and then go beyond the implicit dependence of the quantum theory framework on the mathematical apparatus of calculus and vector spaces, by delving one layer deeper to an information-theoretic understanding of symbol representation. We examine some epistemic implications of the fact that, mathematically, *e*-symbol representation is optimal and three symbols are more efficient than two symbols and this optimality leads to the idea that space itself is *e*-dimensional and not three-dimensional. We also discuss the principle of veiled non-locality as a way to understand the split between the observer and the physical process. By considering how information is obtained from a quantum system, we argue that consciousness is not computable, which means that it cannot be generated by machines.

Keywords: Epistemology; observer-centred reality; first digit phenomenon; consciousness.

Introduction

PHYSICS is the search for a mathematical basis for the observed phenomena. But the mathematical structure often comes with implicit entities and unstated assumptions about reality. For example, in classical mechanics, the observer's sentience lies outside the explanatory power of the theory, and space and time are considered absolute. In general, abstract entities of a theory may be mapped to intuitive notions in different ways, leading to divergent interpretations. Broadly speaking, these interpretations fall into the epistemic and the ontic categories. In the epistemic view, one is speaking of the knowledge obtained from the experiment without going into the ultimate nature of reality, whereas in the ontic view one is describing reality as a particular assemblage of objects, together with their mutual relationships and evolution in time. These two represent fundamentally different intuitions in physics and they have a prehistory that goes back to ancient thought.

The Copenhagen Interpretation (Bohr 1958; von Neumann 1955) of quantum mechanics is an epistemic understanding in which the observer remains outside the experiment, thus dividing the world into the domains of physical objects and that of observers. Although, it has long been the dominant view amongst quantum theorists, many have felt disquiet that it brings in consciousness as an element of the interpretation and, consequently, several alternative interpretations have been advanced. Of these, the ontic many worlds interpretation (MWI) (Zurek 2003) seeks to explain the observer as a separate physical system also governed by the laws of quantum mechanics (QM).

The ontic understanding of reality becomes problematic when one speaks of information, fundamental to many theories in physics, since it involves properties of ensembles or wholes that cannot be reduced to a field, which is essential for a theory based on local variables. Although neuroscience accepts the doctrine of the identity of brain and mind, and sees the mind emerge from the complexity of the interconnections, others assert that there is no logical reason why complexity should lead to such a new phenomenon. The situation is complicated by the fact that there is no specific neural correlate of consciousness (Zeki 2003). Furthermore, seeing the universe as a machine leaves out participants who have agency.

In the epistemic Copenhagen Interpretation, the physical universe is separated into two parts: the first part is the system being observed and the second part is the human observing agent, together with the instruments. The agent is, therefore, an extended entity described in mental terms that includes not only his apparatus but also instructions to colleagues on how to set up the instruments and report on their observations. The orthodox version of Copenhagen Interpretation excludes causal interaction between mind and body; in this view, mental and physical phenomena are two aspects of the same reality like two sides of a coin (Kafatos and Nadeau 2000; Kak 2018; von Neumann 1955).

The Heisenberg cut (also called the von Neumann cut) is the hypothetical interface between quantum events and the observer's information, knowledge or awareness. Below the cut everything is governed by the state or wave function, whereas above the cut one must use classical description. Operationally, it is a dualist position, where there is a fundamental divide between observers and objects. The placement of the cut between the subject and the object depends on the nature of the interaction between the two.

The arbitrariness of the cut has come in for criticism and spurred the development of other interpretations, but it is a device for aggregating the effects of the mind or minds associated with the observational regime and it appears to be a reasonable way to separate the inanimate from the animate especially since the brain itself may be viewed as a machine.

In the ontic view of the wave function there is no collapse of the wave function and the interaction is described in terms of decoherence, which occurs when states interact with the environment producing entanglement (Penrose 1994; Zurek 2003). By the process of decoherence, the system makes transition from a pure state to a mixture of states that the observer ends up measuring. The problem of collapse of the wave function is sidestepped by speaking of interaction between different subsystems. But since the entire universe is also a quantum system, the question of how this whole system splits into independent subsystems arises. Operationally, the split into subsystems is to an extent the choice of the observer and it serves about the same function as the Heisenberg cut of Copenhagen Interpretation. Note that the ontic view has no place for minds, which can at best be taken as traces of mathematical operations, thus ruling out agency.

Other less popular interpretations include various hidden variable theories (e.g. Bohm 1980), consistent histories, modified dynamics and the transactional interpretation (Jaeger 2009; Kastner 2013; Penrose 2004). Another idea is to assume that quantum mechanics is incomplete and there is a yet-to-be-discovered deeper theory that agrees with it in the microscopic world and with the classical theory in the macroscopic world.

The principle of least action (PLA), according to which Nature is optimal and thrifty, has played a key role in the axiomatization of physical theories (Feynman and Hibbs 1965; Stöltzner 2003). Using this principle, a true dynamical trajectory of a system is found by computing all trajectories that the system could possibly take, computing the action for each of these trajectories and selecting the one with the least action as the true trajectory (Feynman 1985). PLA is about dynamics and its complementary aspect is that of representation, which comes in even before dynamics is considered. The representation can be concerning structure or data or both and it comes into physical reasoning both in logic and also counting.

When it comes to dynamics, some see the logic of choosing between two alternatives, made famous in Wheeler's (1990) memorable phrase *it from bit* as the bedrock upon which physical reasoning rests. There are many proposals that information in terms of bits (one-in-two) is the fundamental basis of physical reality and that the universe is a digital machine (e.g. Zurek 2009), but others argue that this claim is not consistent with quantum mechanics (Penrose 1989). Complicating this picture is the reality that counting is at the basis of observations, but binary choices are not optimal (Kak 2018) and space itself may be viewed as being *e*-dimensional (Kak 2020, 2021c).

In this chapter, we first present the historical antecedents to the rival ideas of epistemic and ontic nature of reality. Then we review the argument that shows that three-way logic is superior to the two-way one and then examine its implications for the understanding of experimental results related to the three-slit experiment. The principle of veiled non-locality is discussed as a way to understand the split between the observer and the physical process and it is shown how an ontic scheme cannot be the basis of effective evolution. By considering how information is obtained from a quantum system, we argue that consciousness is not computable, which means that it cannot be generated by machines.

A Brief Historical Excursus

The first person to use the term "physics" in the sense it is understood now is Aristotle (384–322 BCE). Motivated perhaps by biology, he conflated change in biological and physical domains. He defined motion as the actuality of a potentiality, which is strictly true only for the "motion" of a living organism. Motion defined this way requires the assumption of an absolute frame and other imaginary schema. He gave example of four types of change, viz. change in substance, quality, quantity and place.

Aristotle's ontic system was extremely influential for nearly 2,000 years in the intellectual life of the Western world for he was embraced by the orthodoxy in both Christianity and Islam. As physics is fundamental to cosmology, his thoughts had a profound impact on the history of Western science (Ackrill 1981).

According to Aristotle, the sun, moon, planets and stars are embedded in perfectly concentric *crystal spheres* that rotate at fixed rates. The celestial spheres are made up of the element ether which supports uniform circular motion. He took the terrestrial objects to be composed of four other elements that rise or fall. The earth, the heaviest element and water, fall toward the centre of the universe; hence the earth and the oceans constitute our planet. At the opposite end the lightest elements, air and fire, rise up and away from the centre and this led to the geocentric model of the solar system. As we know, this set the stage for a challenge to this model by Copernicus and Galileo and the subsequent rise of classical physics. But the system that replaced Aristotle's was also an ontic one.

A few centuries before Aristotle, around 600 BCE, Kaṇāda in India anticipated two of the three laws of motion and he attempted to create a formal system that includes space, time, matter, as well as observers (Dasgupta 1992). Kaṇāda's most impressive assertion is that "all that is knowable is based on motion", which gives centrality to physics in the understanding of the universe.

In the text called the *Vaiśeṣikasūtra* (Kak 2016b), Kaṇāda defines categories for space–time–matter and for attributes related to perception by sentient agents. He asserts that these six categories are sufficient to describe everything in the universe from concrete matter to the abstract atom.

The six categories are: substance, quality, motion, universal, particular and inherence (which relates to observation). The first three of these have objective existence and the last three are a product of the observer's interaction. Universals are recurrent generic properties in substances, qualities and motions. The mind is not an empty slate; the very constitution of the mind provides some knowledge of the nature of the world.

Of the six categories, the basic one is that of substance and the other five categories are the ones that the mind associates with the substance. Thus, observers belong to the system in an integral fashion. If there were no sentient beings in the universe then there would be no need for these categories.

There are nine classes of substances, some of which are non-atomic, some atomic and others all-pervasive. The non-atomic ground is provided by the three substances of ether, space and time, which are unitary and indestructible; a further four, earth (P), water (Ap), fire (T) and air (V) are atomic composed of indivisible and indestructible atoms; the eighth is the self or consciousness, which is omnipresent and eternal; and, lastly, the ninth, is the mind, which has atomic dimensions. The atoms are abstractions that should not be confused with the elements of the same name.

Why are there only four kinds of basic atoms? Consider gold in its solid form; its mass derives principally from the P atoms. When it is heated, it becomes a liquid and therefore there should be another kind of atom already in gold which makes it possible for it to take the liquid form and this is Ap. When heated further, it burns and this is when the T atoms get manifested. When heated further, it loses its mass ever so slightly and this is due to the loss of the V atoms.

It is significant that consciousness is listed before mind, suggesting that it is the medium through which mind's apprehensions are received. By including consciousness and mind in his scheme where all the properties of matter are to be obtained by the study of motion and qualities of matter, Kaṇāda put unique emphasis on the observation process and thus the scheme is fundamentally epistemic. A related tradition called Vedānta, in which the observer plays a fundamental role, influenced Schrödinger in his development of wave mechanics (Moore 1989).

Three-way Choice and Counting

Since coding of coordinates is fundamental to physical theory and a part of what the experimenter chooses to do, let us consider numerical data or coordinate locations, to an arbitrary base r. Given that the probability of the use of the r symbols may rightly be taken to be the same and equal to $1/r$, the information associated with each symbol is log r. The efficiency of the coding scheme per symbol, $E(r)$, is (Kak 2021a):

$$E(r) = \frac{\ln r}{r}. \tag{1}$$

To find the value of r for which the above expression is maximal we take its derivative with respect to r and equate that to zero. This yields the condition that $\ln r = 1$, from which we conclude that the optimal base is e, with $E(e) = 0.368$ nats or 0.531 bits. Table 8.1 provides $E(r)$ for some of the values of r that range from 2 to 10.

The efficiency is quite close to the maximum for $r = 3$ (a value of 0.528 bits as compared to the optimal value for e which is 0.531 bits), with the next best value coming at the bases 2 and 4 (where it is 0.500 bits). The efficiency at $r = 3$ is superior to that at $r = 2$ by 5.6 per cent. After this the values decline monotonically as shown in *fig*. 8.1.

Table 8.1. Efficiency of Coding for Certain Bases

b	2	e	3	4	5	8	10
$E(r)$ nats	0.347	0.368	0.366	0.347	0.322	0.260	0.230
$E(r)$ bits	0.500	0.531	0.528	0.500	0.465	0.375	0.331

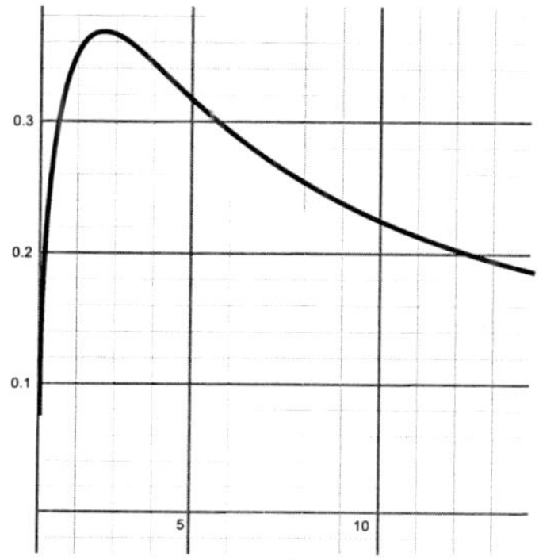

fig. 8.1: Efficiency of number bases, 2 through 10

The optimal value *e* is not convenient for representation of integers and since conceptual schemes use integers, this may be a reason why these schemes appear to fall short.

The basis used in physics may be related to the choices made in terms of alternatives, in which, assuming linearity, the influence of one is added to that of another. Examples of this are the two-body problem of classical physics and the two-slit experiment of quantum theory. In classical physics, the general version of the two-body problem can be reduced to a pair of one-body problems, allowing it to be solved completely. By contrast, the three-body problem (and, more generally, the *n*-body problem) cannot be solved in terms of first integrals, except in special cases. Paralleling this, one could ask if the three-slit variant to the double-slit experiment provides new understanding since the three paths may be taken to correspond to 3 digits of the ternary system.

It is noteworthy that the fundamental constants of physics and a host of other natural data follow the Newcomb–Benford law on first digits (Hill 1998) according to which the leading digit d ($d \in \{1, \ldots, r-1\}$) for number to the base r, $r \geq 2$, occurs with probability as a logarithmic function:

$$P(d) = log_r\left(1 + \frac{1}{d}\right). \quad (2)$$

Table 8.2: First Digit Data from a Variety of Natural Phenomena

	First Digit Frequencies								
	1	*2*	*3*	*4*	*5*	*6*	*7*	*8*	*9*
NB's Law	30.1	17.6	12.5	9.69	7.92	6.69	5.80	5.12	4.58
Fundamental physics constants	34.0	18.4	9.2	8.28	8.58	7.36	3.37	5.21	5.52
Geomagnetic field	28.9	17.7	13.3	9.40	8.10	6.90	6.10	5.10	4.50
Geomagnetic reversals	32.3	19.4	13.9	11.80	5.30	4.30	3.20	5.40	4.30
Fermi space teles. fluxes	30.3	17.9	13.0	9.90	7.60	6.96	5.23	5.23	2.72
Pulsars rotation freq.	33.9	20.7	12.7	7.60	5.30	5.00	4.94	4.67	4.88

This may be derived by summing together many uniform random variables with varying support (Hill 1995). The first row of Table 8.2 lists these frequencies for base 10, the rest of the data on the first digits related to different phenomena is adapted from Sambridge (2010).

The mathematical explanation is that of counting that stops at different counts and the probability distribution is obtained by summing over all such counts. This notion may also be seen as the basis of self-similarity in natural phenomena.

Since the first digit phenomenon is true for a variety of natural phenomena including fundamental physical constants, one may conclude that counting is a foundational attribute of reality. But unlike the large difference of information that was found between the use of bases 2 and 3, the corresponding difference in optimality for counting for these two bases is not particularly large (Hayes 2001).

The Three-slit Experiment

Let us consider particles with the wave function $\varphi\ (r, t)$. According to the Born rule (e.g. Penrose 1994; Sinha et al. 2015), which is a fundamental axiom of quantum mechanics, the probability density to find a particle at position r and at time t is given by

$$p\,(r,t) = \varphi^{*}\,(r,t)\,\varphi(r,t) = |\,\varphi(r,t)\,|^{2} \tag{3}$$

In the two-slit experiment, if $\varphi_A\,(r)$ and $\varphi_B\,(r)$ represent the wave function associated with slits A and B at the location r, then the wave function for both slits open is a superposition of the different paths given by $\varphi_{AB}\,(r) = \varphi_A\,(r) + \varphi_B\,(r)$. Let $p_A = |\,\varphi_A\,|^2$ and $p_B = |\,\varphi_B\,|^2$ be the probabilities with the slits A and B open.

The probability of detection, p_{AB}, is:

$$\begin{aligned} p_{AB}\,(r) &= |\varphi_{AB}\,(r)\,|^2 = |\,\varphi_A\,|^2 + |\,\varphi_B\,|^2 + \varphi_A{}^{*}\,\varphi_B + \varphi_B{}^{*}\,\varphi_A \\ &= p_A + p_B + I_{AB}, \end{aligned} \tag{4}$$

where I_{AB} is the interference term which may be written as

$$I_{AB} = p_{AB} - (p_A + p_B).$$

For three slits, A, B and C, if we only consider pair-wise interference, the probability p_{ABC} is given by:

$$p_{ABC} = p_A + p_B + p_C + I_{AB} + I_{AC} + I_{BC} \tag{5}$$

The interference term is:

$$\begin{aligned} I_{ABC} &= p_{ABC} - (p_A + p_B + p_C + I_{AB} + I_{AC} + I_{BC}) \\ &= p_{ABC} - p_{AB} - p_{BC} - p_{AC} + p_A + p_B + p_C. \end{aligned} \tag{6}$$

This expression is entirely described by probabilities involving only one and two slits. Any contribution from higher-order interference terms (i.e. a path involving the three slits) is quantified by the Sorkin parameter (1994):

$$\varepsilon = p_{ABC} - p_{AB} - p_{EC} - p_{AC} + p_A + p_B + p_C, \tag{7}$$

which should be identically zero if only the direct paths through the three individual slits are considered. Sinha et al. (2010) evaluated ε experimentally in a three-slit experiment with photons and found the magnitude of three-path interference to less than 10^{-2} of the expected two-path interference, thus ruling out third- and higher-order interference. But recent experiments have found (Sawant et al. 2014) that the Sorkin parameter is a non-zero quantity which indicates that the three-way behaviour cannot be directly obtained by adding different two-way results.

This non-zeroness has been seen as a consequence of the non-classical paths such as loops through the slits but it can also be ascribed to the use of the three-way representation that cannot be obtained by simply adding together various two-way representations (Quach 2017). Considering the significance of this problem, further investigation is needed to determine whether its origin is in the limitations of the underlying logic.

Dimensionality of Space

The dimension of a mathematical space is the minimum number of coordinates, or bins, needed to specify any point within it. Mathematicians have defined dimension of a space to be the least integer n for which every point has arbitrarily small neighbourhoods whose boundaries have dimensions less than n. Space is taken to be three-dimensional in physics for that seems the most obvious thing to do and the idea of the four dimensions of space–time is that events are not absolutely defined spatially and temporally, but rather are relative to the motion of the observer.

The three-dimensionality of the common intuition in terms of length, breadth and height is a consequence of our experience. Under certain conditions, it becomes necessary to consider non-integer dimensions as in the emergence of scale invariant and fractal phenomena like turbulence, human physiology, medicine, neuroscience and engineered networks (Kak 2021d). The most commonly used measures are the box-counting, information, packing and the Hausdorff dimensions. In general, these dimensions measure the apparent density of the given set and in conformity with common sense a non-integer space is less dense than the one with the immediately higher integer (Kak 2021b).

Since the notion of dimension applies to physical reality at all conceivable scales, one must consider both the objective view in terms of the physical location of things within the space and the subjective view in terms of the motions of the objects as defined by an underlying dynamic that leads to the locations. As an application of this idea the discrepancy between the early and late universe estimates of the Hubble constant may be explained away if one recognizes that the early universe model provides the true *e*-dimensional estimate, whereas the late universe model imposes a three-dimensional gloss on the measurement (Kak 2020).

Another corollary of this theory is that one may view the evolution of the universe to be driven by the changing dimensionality *d* with corresponding changes in the value of *G*, the gravitational constant. In this view, the gravitational attraction will begin to rise from dimensionality, *d*, equal to 2 and peak at some value of *d* between 2 and 3 (Kak 2021c). Assuming symmetry, we can take the value of peak gravitation attraction to be given by $d = 2.5$. If we take a quadratic relationship between *d* and *G*, we can write:

$$G(d) = 4G_m(5d - d^2 - 6)\,. \tag{8}$$

We know from astronomical records that the expansion of the universe began to accelerate 9.8 billion years after the Big Bang (time 0 for our equation) and we propose that this happened as the drag of the gravitational attraction opposing the expansion due to the potential singularity of time = 0 began to weaken. This implies that the peak $G = G_m$ occurred at $d = 9.8$ billion years.

By change of units, $t = ad + b$, we get an equation for change in *G* with respect to time in billions of years. To solve for *a* and *b*, we use the conditions $d = 2.5$ corresponds to $t = 9.8$ and, $d = 2$ corresponds to $t = 0$. Solving, we get that $a = 19.6$ and $b = -39.2$. Therefore,

$$G(t) = \frac{G_m}{96.04}(19.6t - t^2)\,. \tag{9}$$

The optimal value of $d = e$ is obtained for $t = ae + b = 14.078$ billion years. Considering that the estimated age of the universe is 13.77 billion years, the above expressions imply that the gravitational constant will plateau in about another 300 million years.

The Observation Process

Einstein, Podolsky and Rosen (EPR) (1935) argued from the philosophical position of realism that quantum mechanics could not be considered a complete theory since for an entangled pair of particles that are far apart from each other, the measurement on one causes the second to change its wave function. This influence projected non-locally across what could be a vast distance is against our common sense expectation of a physical process. Although EPR did not use the phrase "non-locality" in their paper, it is clear that this feature of quantum mechanics was behind their assertion that it could not be a complete theory. As a realist, one cannot accept that a measurement at one location, which in principle is arbitrarily far from the second location, can influence an object at this second location.

Bell considered the question if the property being measured was fixed at the time the pair of entangled particles was produced or whether the random collapse took place at the time of measurement after the particles had separated. He showed that if measurements were made independently in three different directions, the constraints on probability for the quantum case were different than for the classical case (Bell 1988). Bell's theorem is taken to mean that quantum theory cannot be mimicked by introducing a set of objective local "hidden" variables. It follows that any classical theory advanced in place of quantum mechanics will be non-local.

Those who approach the subject from the position of realism offer the possibility that the collapse of the state function of two remotely situated entangled objects will leave some trace in terms of local process explanations that will call for a theory that goes beyond current quantum theory, for if a signal travels faster than the speed of light, then there is a frame in which it travels backwards in time.

The complementarity of aspects, such as wave and particle, may be seen as a consequence of the ability of the observer to make different kinds of choices. The particle view is the one imposed on reality by the mind governed by a classical mode (Kafatos and Nadeau 2000). Non-locality is a significant issue when one takes the particle picture, together with local interaction, to be the underlying reality.

Language underpins our constructions of reality both in the apprehension of our intuitions and the interpretation of mathematical theories. The issue of knowability is complex: even though terms are defined precisely in a mathematical theory, one still needs to interpret the variables in an experiment to connect them to theory.

Evolution in quantum theory proceeds in two different ways: first, by the unitary evolution of the Schrödinger equation; and second, by the non-unitary reduction of the wave function by the process of measurement. The results of the measurement depend on the questions posed by the measurement apparatus. The outcomes of the measurement are classical variables for they are well-defined values quite unlike the superpositions of the quantum variables (Zeh 1970).

Another fundamental issue related to knowability is the limitation on what can be inferred about the system. According to Copenhagen Interpretation, quantum mechanics only provides probabilities of observing values of measurement variables (Bell 1988). From a philosophical view, its framework represents a computational procedure that allows us to obtain information from beneath a veil that covers reality (d'Espagnat 2003).

Veiled Non-locality

The multiplicity of the interpretations of quantum mechanics is a consequence of the difficulty of conceiving of the same "object" in terms of the mutually contradictory intuitions of particle and wave in different situations. Since single objects also produce interference patterns in the double-slit experiment (Tonomura et al. 1989), either some kind of a wave phenomenon is taken to be at the basis of particles that is masked by the mathematical formalism that requires complex probability amplitudes to be associated with individual objects or it is assumed that there is a pilot wave accompanying the particles, but both these, as well as other approaches, lead to a variety of difficulties (Zeh 2010). Last, in consideration of measurement, the observer is by himself – or in terms of the measurement equipment that may be considered his extension – both a part of the experimental system and outside of it (Wigner 1967).

The idea that reality is veiled (d'Espagnat 2003) is equivalent to the conception of a deeper implicate order (Bohm 1980). I have modified this to a principle of veiled nonlocality (PVN) (Kak 2014) that explains why we do not have loophole-free experimental evidence in support of nonlocality in spite of much research effort. Although quantum mechanics is a nonlocal theory as expressed, for example, in the property of entanglement between remote particles, it is also consistent with the no-signalling theorem according to which no useful information can be sent to remote places. According to PVN, which is a stronger assertion than the non-signalling theorem, the loopholes will never be closed and experimental verification of nonlocality that excludes local realistic explanations will not be found.

Veiled nonlocality does not imply a local realistic basis to quantum theory. Our mind operates by the classical picture and it uses whatever artefacts are necessary that make the classical picture of reality remain consistent. But it does not exclude the possibility that non-locality can leave traces that can be measured.

Consider a known wave function that has been prepared in the laboratory. It has extension, i.e. it is described across space and time. Since this extension collapses into a local attribute, what is the process by which this collapse takes place and might this be apprehended by our instruments? For entangled pair of particles that are far apart, we will have to postulate processes that travel faster than the speed of light, contradicting relativity. If instantaneous information transfer cannot take place, we can yet see correlations that can only be explained by means of non-local processes. PVN ensures that we will be able to advance local explanations for the process or ascribe the results to coincidence.

PVN cannot be negated when the wave function of the objects is known for even for that case there are imponderables. Although one can prepare a quantum state precisely, in reality, there exist problems related to initialization and lack of knowledge of the environment and decoherence that affects the state of the system in uncertain and uncontrollable ways. This means that uncertainty relations will continue to be central in the analysis of the evolution of the system.

In principle, macroscopic systems may also be quantum and we cannot rule out that our conception of the universe and its laws and our analysis is a result of the limitations of the capacities of our cognitive systems (Gautam and Kak 2013). Even if the classical agents of our mind are based on quantum collectives (Kak 2016a), we cannot negate the fact that the elementary perceptions at the basis of our knowledge of this world have classical form. Some see the observer's consciousness playing a role in the transition from the quantum to the classical world (Stapp 2007; Wigner 1967), others find that problematic since consciousness cannot be defined in an objective sense.

Copenhagen Interpretation vs Many Worlds Interpretation (MWI)

Veiled non-locality facilitates choice between the two main interpretations of the wave function:

i. it represents objective reality in a mathematical form, and

ii. although sometimes the wave function may describe the system fully, in the general case it only encodes information about the potential outcomes of the experiment together with their probabilities.

If the wave function has ontological reality, then it is conceivable that an experiment will show the nonlocality, but if the wave function only encodes information about outcomes then it is unlikely that nonlocality will be revealed.

Within the mathematical framework, observable quantities are represented by Hermitian operators and their possible values are the eigenvalues of these operators. The act of observation reduces the wave function to one of its component states and it is the outcome associated with the application of the measurement operator on the state. From the philosophical perspective the reduction of the wave function in a random fashion is a feature very different from that of its evolution although this jump may be viewed as not taking place in the physical world but rather in our knowledge of the system.

If Copenhagen Interpretation is the view of the universe with the observer in the privileged position, then MWI is the outside realistic view. In Copenhagen Interpretation, the wave function represents the knowledge of the experimenter, whereas in MWI the wave function is the complete reality. If Copenhagen Interpretation is the subjective view, MWI is the objective view.

The inside-out and the outside-in are like the complementary wave and particle viewpoints already considered in Copenhagen Interpretation. The outside-in view of MWI might present a consistent picture but it means that observers are zombies and in this, it is similar to a conception of reality as nothing more than a collection of *things*. In such a picture, there is no room for minds with agency and the whole universe operates as a giant computer with the choices solely determined by the environment.

The inside-out view of Copenhagen Interpretation admits the possibility that somehow "free will" plays a role in the choice that emerges during a measurement (of course, this narrative is relevant only in a limited set of possibilities). Since the cut between the classical and the quantum may be made at different points, it does not exclude the explanation that the outcomes of the experiment are a result of the decoherence caused by the environment.

The problem of measurement is linked with the idea of "free will". If the brain is viewed as a neural machine, its response to a stimulus is determined by its current internal state and, therefore, it cannot act acausally and exercise free will. Consciousness, if taken to be an emergent phenomenon, provides a false sense of agency by assigning its intervention an earlier time than is correct, as indicated by experiments (Libet et al. 1983).

Many physicists, perhaps a majority, have an intuitive realistic world view and consider a quantum state as a physical entity. Its value may not be known, but in principle they assume that the quantum state of a physical system is well defined. This view, as mentioned earlier in the chapter, leads to various paradoxes. When correctly used, quantum theory does not yield contradictory answers to a well posed question; it is only the misuse of quantum concepts, guided by a pseudorealistic philosophy, that leads to paradoxical results.

If MWI is the machine view of the universe, in Copenhagen Interpretation the observer's subjective experience is evidence that agency exists and other sentient beings also possess it. The various differences in Copenhagen Interpretation and MWI are summarized in Table 8.3.

Table 8.3: Differences between the Copenhagen Interpretation and the Many Worlds Interpretation

	CI	*MWI*
Wave function	State of knowledge of the system	Mathematical representation of reality
Measurement	Change in the knowledge of the system based on observations made	Decoherence of the system induced by the environment
Observers	Create representations of the universe	Observers merely record results; observers are like zombies
Reality	Constructed out of measurements	Reality exists outside of agents

Many points of difference between Copenhagen Interpretation and MWI are of a philosophical nature without implications as far as physical experiments are concerned. In a universe only of "things" which excludes "being", the problem of "free will" is unsolvable and in a theoretical framework based on causality, "free will" is paradoxical.

From the perspective of sentient beings, objects are not primary; what is primary are mental feelings and perceptions. Newer theories of physics consider information as primary, but there can be no information unless there is consciousness that can recognize this information. This consciousness (or being) may exist in a plane different from regular spacetime.

Accepting mental states as primary building blocks of reality leads to questions such as: Are the worlds of mind (consciousness) and matter separate? In the Vedāntic model, consciousness is viewed as interpenetrating the material world and guiding its evolution indirectly (Moore 1989) in a manner similar to the Quantum Zeno Effect (Misra and Sudarshan 1977).

In the ontic view of the wave function, decoherence causes the system to make transition from a pure state to a mixture of states that the observer is able to measure (Zurek 2003). The process of decoherence in no way negates the Copenhagen Interpretation picture, for it merely shifts the cut away in such a way that the system under observation and the measurement apparatus are on the same side. The experimenter is not describing reality ontologically; rather, he is obtaining knowledge about it and this depends on the nature of his interaction with the system. The knowledge informs his mind and consideration of this information creates a sense of overarching knowledge.

The idea of a computation determined by the environment is not, in itself, surprising. Consider ants in random motion on a mountainside so that some are able to reach the mountaintop. The fact of having reached the top is a consequence of the nature of the environment and it cannot be ascribed to the intention of the ant. It is in that sense that the environment reduces the dynamics of the system. But if the environment itself is random, no such discernible "computation" can occur.

Mind and Computability

To the extent that machines used in experiments are physical systems, they are extensions of human agents. The agent is further associated with internal states and a cultural context. Although some physicists believe that all phenomena must be reducible to physics, others have suggested that one needs different kinds of descriptions. Popper and Eccles (1984) believed one needs three different worlds, each with its own language, to understand reality. In their classification, World 1 is the world of physical objects and states, World 2 is the world of subjective states such as thoughts, memories and emotional states and World 3 is knowledge in an objective sense. These worlds deal with outer sense, inner sense and culture and spirit (or self), respectively. Eccles even argued that the self controls the brain.

Information requires an observer for whom the prior expectations are changed once a message has been received. The central idea here is that of computation of global states and an underlying structure of data within which the message must be examined. An observer cannot analyse data without models and expectations on measurements. The observer, therefore, must not only belong to Eccles Worlds 1 and 2, but also World 3. The observer must have complex stable structures that are entangled not only within its subsystems but also with the environment. This implies that the assumption that the environmental systems are randomly phased as assumed by Zurek is not valid. What is true of the external environment is also valid of the internal environment (structure) of the observer. One may assert that whatever is observed is predicated on the capacity of the cognitive systems to make such observation. One may also take particular characteristics of reality to be a consequence of the nature of the cognitive system of the human agent.

Although there are many ways to look at information, it is common to view scientific information or knowledge within the context of specific areas that allows us to understand relationships between variables, find laws and make predictions, where some of the phenomena are deterministic and others are random. Another perspective is to consider the nature of the language in which knowledge is expressed. Different areas of science have their own specialized languages and across fields the languages are not always consistent. This inconsistency points to the gaps that exist in the understanding of reality.

The classical system can be observed since it can be isolated from other systems – and from the observer – due to the local nature of interactions. In contrast, since interactions in quantum mechanics are nonlocal, subsystems cannot be isolated within a system. Such isolation is essential for the observer to recognize his or her own identity that requires some knowledge of the environment in advance.

If systems cannot be completely separated before the observation begins, observation should be impossible. From another perspective, the need for global states (related to World

3 aspects of observation) in the observation process implies that the measurement of one system by another by unitarity alone cannot be reduced to the Turing machine formalism.

Let us consider the implications of viewing the brain as a machine consistent with the physicalist position that consciousness is either an emergent property or an epiphenomenon (Baars 1997). One may further assume that computers can capture the abstract causal organization of other systems and thus of the brain (Gamez 2008). Panpsychism, the view that mind is to be found everywhere, is another position that has recently become popular in academic circles (Koch 2014), but it is too extravagant in associating mind even with a straw or a rock. Broadly speaking, both physicalism and panpsychism associate mind with matter, although they do it in different ways.

From a computational perspective, it is counter-intuitive that a small subset of activity in the brain in terms of abstract thought is able to capture the workings of the physical world. This happens even though brain function is accompanied by the reorganization of its very structures during learning and function (Kak 2016a), which goes beyond the Turing machine model on which the von Neumann architecture of digital computers is broadly based (Penrose 1989).

Organisms do not create representations of visual or other stimuli (Chemero 2009) and store them in short-term and long-term memories. If experiences cannot be accessed, they cannot be described as data (whether digital or chemical), which is a requirement in processing by a computer. The processing by the brain must thus be non-computable by a machine and the emulation of cognition by computer must therefore be different from how the brain does it.

The American psychologist James J. Gibson showed years ago (Gibson 1979) that brain processing is not passive like that of a computer, but an active process between the subject and the environment. When perceiving an object, we attend to its properties to see what we can do with it. The mind actively explores the environment to find elements that guide the performance of one action or the other. This information, called ecological information, is unique to the subject and it does not lend itself to the information processing model.

Another perspective on this is that the most mundane memory tasks involve multiple and very large areas of the brain (Gilboa et al. 2004). Skill learning and expertise involve reorganization and plastic changes (Chang 2014), which cannot be mapped into a computer with fixed architecture.

Although learning cognitive tasks may require attention and concentration, once the learning is complete they can be performed literally automatically. The learning apparently leads to training of neural networks that convert the computational problem into one of classification and recognition. It should thus be possible to replicate the processing in a machine of tasks that involve computations in the neural circuitry of the brain. But raw awareness appears to be a phenomenon that is different from cognitive processing (Kak, A. et al. 2016).

Attempts at mimicking the workings of the brain in the design of conscious machines face formidable scientific and engineering obstacles. Architectures that copy models of brain function have been investigated (Haikonen 2012). These architectures include distributive agents and the global workspace theory (GWT) (Baar 1988; Shanahan 2006). In the GWT separate parallel processes compete to place their information in the global workspace whose contents are broadcast to a multitude of receiving processes. Since globally broadcast messages can evoke actions in receiving processes throughout the network, the global workspace may be used to exercise executive control to perform voluntary actions. This roughly mimics some brain functions without addressing the nature of consciousness.

Postulating a physical substrate of consciousness to be at the basis of complex patterns of activity has been called the integrated information theory (IIT) (Tononi et al. 2016). But it amounts to correlations in physical processes that cannot by themselves be the origin of awareness. Complex causally connected behavioural patterns can also be seen in social networks, but they are properly analysed within the framework of an ecological system without recourse to the concept of consciousness.

In the standard neuroscience view, mind emerges from the interoperation of the various modules in the brain and its behaviour must be completely described by the corresponding brain function, even though there is no evidence for any specific neural correlate of consciousness. Counterintuitive characteristics of the mind may be ascribable to underlying quantum processes, but although quantum mechanics might indeed play a role in brain processes, there is no compelling reason to assume that quantumness is associated with the phenomenon of consciousness.

Reality is comprehended in consciousness and not directly in terms of space, time and matter. Consciousness is the doorway that shows us the world and makes self-knowledge possible and it is the source of creativity although it is constrained by the habits and limitations of the mind (Freeman 1999). Although we are unable to define consciousness as a mathematical property of a system, the quality of its manifestation in a natural system depends on structure and different modes of processing. Consciousness and the material world complement each other and consciousness may influence material evolution as in the Quantum Zeno effect.

The statement that consciousness is the ground on which experience is evoked variously may appear to be a principle that is no different from that of gravity that works on objects differently depending upon their location. But this does not rule out the possibility that the structure of the mind makes it impossible to know reality completely.

We think of ourselves as being outside of the physical world. Even our conceptions of the universe are as if we are not a part of it and in the words of Schrödinger (1951: 95-96):

> We do not belong to this material world that science constructs for us. We are not in it; we are outside. We are only spectators. The reason why we believe that we are in it, that we belong to the picture, is that our bodies are in the picture. Our bodies belong to it.

If this sense of being outside of the physical world is true, it would be impossible to emulate it by hardware and processing that is within the world. It also follows that it will not be a computational property of the physical elements that comprise the system. Since consciousness is global, it must be non-algorithmic.

Can consciousness be defined as the capacity to know with certainty that one is conscious? This appears to be a circular definition and it hinges on hard-to-define concepts such as "knowledge" and "belief". Consider HM, the guy who lost all new memory with the bilateral resection of medial temporal lobe and his ability to hold beliefs and knowledge was greatly impaired (Squire 2009), yet, without doubt, he had all hallmarks of consciousness.

We can look for the non-computability of consciousness from its parallel to the unsolvability of the halting problem. Let us define "consciousness" as some privileged state of the mind that makes its processes halt (we do not bother to specify it beyond this description) and its contents registered (which is what we imply by awareness). Humans can get into the state of "awareness" at any time, which means that the earlier computation has halted and this is irrespective of the initial state of the immediately preceding process. The exceptions to this are if a person is sleeping or unconscious as in coma. But such halting to arbitrary input is impossible from a computability point of view. Therefore, it follows that consciousness is not computable (Kak 2019).

The consideration of information (or entropy) in physical theory, which is commonly done in many branches of physics, implies an unstated postulation of consciousness. Information cannot be reduced to local operations by any reductionist programme. It requires the use of signs derived from global properties and the capacity to make choices which, in turn, implies agency. Such agency will be consistent with physical law only if it does not involve the expenditure of energy. There are different ways by which interaction between matter and consciousness may be considered and these include the questions of information and that of dynamics.

As quantum mechanics, unlike classical physics, involves non-local correlations, the premise may be advanced that workings of consciousness that are associated with a brain must also have a nonlocal component (Kafatos and Kak 2015). To seek the physical trace, induced by consciousness associated with humans and other sentient subjects, one would need to look for probabilities that do not conform to local expectations.

Concluding Remarks

In classical physics, the future of a system is completely known in principle, given the initial conditions and the assumption that the computations are made by an observer who is located outside of the system. For classical mechanics to be universally true, this requires that the behaviour of the observer must also be viewed as being completely predictable which negates the idea of free will. Since the very act of observation requires making a choice, observers and the observation process lie outside of classical physics.

The situation is essentially the same in quantum mechanics for the unobserved system, which evolves deterministically by the Schrödinger equation. The consideration of observation as unfolding of the entanglement between the system and the apparatus (or the observer) into a statistical mixture of classical pointer states has circularity built into it since we expect the state to evolve preferentially into the classical states. Neither does it address the question why the system and the apparatus were separate at the beginning of the measurement given the universe itself has an evolving state function that overarches the evolution of the subsystems.

We argued that while collapse of the state function in QM is best described as a nonlocal process, this nonlocality is veiled. This has important implications for quantum information processing and the development of quantum computers. In practical terms, it compels us to view that the wave function represents our lack of knowledge rather than the reality.

If the case is made that entanglement or nonlocality is at the basis of the superiority of quantum computing algorithms, then the effective veiling of this nonlocality will preclude its exploitation in any practical implementation scheme. This veiling will manifest itself in terms of noise and errors that will be impossible to control thus making effective computation unattainable.

Nonlocality lies outside the framework of classical science and, therefore, its actual occurrence is problematic in making sense of the world. But veiled nonlocality, which appears to be consistent with the Copenhagen Interpretation, saves us from this difficulty. It creates the space in which human agency sees its actions as consistent with class ical explanations.

Considering the question of logical categories, we showed that absolute optimality is unachievable as it corresponds to a non-integer, irrational value. Since ternary categories are more efficient than binary ones, one may need to posit certain physical questions not in terms of "yes" or "no", but rather with an additional category. This third "indeterminate" category may be seen as the origin of non-classical aspects of reality.

Consciousness cannot intervene in physical law but it can change the probabilities in the evolution of quantum processes, without changing the dynamics and this provides an explanation of how consciousness can be reconciled with the physical law. It appears to be a privileged state of the mind that makes brain processes halt and its contents registered at arbitrary time instants. Since such halting to arbitrary input is impossible from a computability point of view, we conclude that consciousness is not computable.

References

Ackrill, J.L., 1981, *Aristotle the Philosopher*, Oxford: Oxford University Press.

Baars, B., 1997, *In the Theater of Consciousness*, New York: Oxford University Press.

Bell, J.S., 1988, *Speakable and Unspeakable in Quantum Mechanics*, Cambridge: Cambridge University Press.

Bohm, D., 1980, *Wholeness and the Implicate Order*, London: Routledge.

Bohr, N., 1958, *Atomic Physics and Human Knowledge*, New York: Wiley and Sons.

Chang, Y., 2014, "Reorganization and Plastic Changes of the Human Brain Associated with Skill Learning and Expertise", *Frontiers in Neuroscience*, 8: 35.

Chemero, A., 2009, *Radical Embodied Cognitive Science*, Cambridge, MA: MIT Press.

Dasgupta, S., 1992, *A History of Indian Philosophy*, Delhi: Motilal Banarsidass.

Einstein, A., B. Podolsky and N. Rosen, 1935, "Can Quantum Mechanical Description of Physical Reality Be Considered Complete?", *Physical Review*, 47: 777-80.

d'Espagnat, B., 2003, *Veiled Reality*, Boulder, CO: Westview Press.

Feynman, R.P. and A.R. Hibbs, 1965, *Quantum Mechanics and Path Integrals*, New York: McGraw Hill.

———, 1985, *QED: The Strange Theory of Light and Matter*, Princeton, NJ: Princeton University Press.

Freeman, W., 1999, *How Brains Make Up Their Minds*, London: Phoenix.

Gamez, D., 2008, "Progress in Machine Consciousness", *Consciousness and Cognition*, 17: 887-910.

Gautam, A. and S. Kak, 2013, "Symbols, Meaning and Origins of Mind", *Biosemiotics*, 6: 301-09.

Gibson, J.J., 1979, *The Ecological Approach to Visual Perception*, Boston: Houghton Mifflin Harcourt.

Gilboa, A., G. Winocur, C. Grady, S. Hevenor and M. Moscovitch, 2004, "Remembering Our Past: Functional Neuroanatomy of Recollection of Recent and Very Remote Personal Events", *Cerebral Cortex*, 14: 1214-25.

Haikonen, P., 2012, *Consciousness and Robot Sentience*, Singapore: World Scientific.

Hayes, B., 2001, "Third Base", *American Scientist*, 89: 490-94.

Hill, T.P., 1995, "A Statistical Derivation of the Significant-digit Law", *Statistical Science*, 10: 354-63.

———, 1998, "The First-digit Phenomenon", *American Scientist*, 86: 358-63.

Jaeger, G., 2009, *Entanglement, Information and the Interpretation of Quantum Mechanics*, New York: Springer.

Kafatos, M. and S. Kak, 2015, "Veiled Non-locality and Cosmic Censorship", *Physics Essays*, 28: 182-87.

Kafatos, M. and R. Nadeau, 2000, *The Conscious Universe*, New York: Springer-Verlag.

Kak, A., A. Gautam and S. Kak, 2016, "A Three-layered Model for Consciousness States", *Neuro Quantology*, 14: 166-74.

Kak, S., 2014, "From the No-signaling Theorem to Veiled Non-locality", *Neuro Quantology*, 12: 12-20.

———, 2016a, "Communication Languages and Agents in Biological Systems", in *Biocommunication: Sign-Mediated Interactions between Cells and Organisms*, ed. R. Gordon and J. Seckbach, pp. 203-26, London: World Scientific Publishing.

———, 2016b, *Matter and Mind: The Vaisheshika Sutra of Kaṇāda*, Mississauga, ON: Mount Meru Publishing.

———, 2018, "On Ternary Coding and Three-valued Logic", *arXiv*:1807.06419.

———, 2019, "Is Consciousness Computable?", *Neuro Quantology*, 17: 71-75.

———, 2020, "Information Theory and Dimensionality of Space", *Scientific Reports*, 10: 20733.

———, 2021a, "The Base-e Representation of Numbers and the Power Law", *Circuits Syst. Signal Process*, 40: 490-500.

———, 2021b, "The Intrinsic Dimensionality of Data", *Circuits Syst. Signal Process*, 40: 2599–2607.

———, 2021c, "Asymptotic Freedom and Noninteger Dimensionality", *Scientific Reports*, 11: 1-5.

———, 2021d, "Fractals with Optimal Information Dimension", *Circuits Syst. Signal Process*, 40.

Kastner, R., 2013, *The Transactional Interpretation of Quantum Mechanics*, Cambridge: Cambridge University Press.

Koch, C., 2014, *The Quest for Consciousness: A Neurobiological Approach*. Pasadena, CA: Roberts & Company Publishers.

Libet, B., C.A. Gleason, E.W. Wright and D.K. Pearl, 1983, "Time of Conscious Intention to Act in Relation to Onset of Cerebral Activity (Readiness-potential): The Unconscious Initiation of a Freely Voluntary Act", *Brain*, 106: 623-42.

Misra, B. and E.C.G. Sudarshan, 1977, "The Zeno's Paradox in Quantum Theory", *Journal of Mathematical Physics*, 18: 756-63.

Moore, W., 1989, *Schrödinger: Life and Thought*, Cambridge: Cambridge University Press.

von Neumann, J., 1955, *The Mathematical Foundations of Quantum Mechanics*, Princeton, NJ: Princeton University Press.

Penrose, R., 1989, *The Emperor's New Mind*, New York: Oxford University Press.

———, 1994, *Shadows of the Mind*, New York: Oxford University Press.

———, 2004, *The Road to Reality*, New York: Alfred A. Knopf.

Popper, K. and J.C. Eccles, 1984, *The Self and Its Brain: An Argument for Interactionism*, London: Routledge.

Quach, J.A., 2017, "Which Way Double-slit Experiments and Born Rule Violation", *Phys. Rev.*, A 95: 042129.

Sambridge, M., H. Tkalčić and A. Jackson, 2010, "Benford's Law in the Natural Sciences", *Geophys. Res. Lett.*, 37: L22301.

Sawant, R., J. Samuel, A. Sinha, S. Sinha and U. Sinha, 2014, "Nonclassical Paths in Quantum Interference Experiments", *Phys. Rev. Lett*, 113: 120406.

Schrödinger, E., 1951, *Native and the Greeks*, Cambridge: Cambridge University Press.

Shanahan, M., 2006, "A Cognitive Architecture that Combines Internal Simulation with a Global Workspace", *Consciousness and Cognition*, 15: 443-49.

Sinha, A., A.H. Vijay and U. Sinha, 2015, "On the Superposition Principle in Interference Experiments", *Scientific Reports*, 5: 10304.

Sinha, U., C. Couteau, T. Jennewein, R. Laflamme and G. Weihs, 2010, "Ruling Out Multi-Order Interference in Quantum Mechanics", *Science*, 329: 418.

Sorkin, R.D., 1994, "Quantum Mechanics as Quantum MeasureTheory", *Modern Physics Letters*, A9: 3119-27.

Squire, L.R., 2009, "The Legacy of Patient H.M. for Neuroscience", *Neuron*, 61: 6-9.

Stapp, H.P., 2007, *Mindful Universe*, Berlin: Springer-Verlag.

Stöltzner, M., 2003, "The Principle of Least Action as the Logical Empiricist's Shibboleth", *Studies in History and Philosophy of Modern Physics*, 34: 285-313.

Tonomura, A., J. Endo, T. Matsuda, T. Kawasaki and H. Ezawa, 1989, "Demonstration of Single-electron Buildup of an Interference Pattern", *Am. J. Phys*. 57: 117-20.

Tononi, G., M. Boly, M. Massimini and C. Koch, 2016, "Integrated Information Theory: From Consciousness to Its Physical Substrate", *Nature Reviews Neuroscience*, 1: 450-61.

Wheeler, John A., 1990, "Information, Physics, Quantum: The Search for Links", in *Complexity, Entropy and the Physics of Information*, ed. W. Hubert Zurek, New York: Addison-Wesley.

Wigner, E.P., 1967, *Symmetries and Reflections*, Bloomington, IN: Indiana University Press.

Zeh, H.D., 1970, "On the Interpretation of Measurement in Quantum Theory", *Found Phys*, 1: 69-76.

———, 2010, Quantum Discreteness Is an Illusion", *Found. Phys*, 40: 1476.

Zeki, S., 2003, "The Disunity of Consciousness", *Trends Cogn. Sci*, 7: 214-18.

Zurek, W.H., 2003, Decoherence, Einselection and the Quantum Origins of the Classical", *Rev. Mod. Phys*, 75: 715-75.

———, 2009, "Quantum Darwinism", *Nature Physics*, 5: 181-88.

9

Gödel's Incompleteness Theorems, Complementarity and Fundamental Awareness

Neil D. Theise
Goro C. Kato
Menas C. Kafatos

Abstract: Gödel's Incompleteness Theorems have had a wide applicability beyond the usual scope of formal logic, inclusive of broadening the theoretical, philosophical and cultural approaches to understanding the relationship of consciousness to the universe. In particular, idealist perspectives, such as the fundamental awareness model (FAM) of reality discussed herein, are fostered. FAM posits a ground of non-dual fundamental (pure) awareness that, in differentiating into subject and object dualities, gives rise to the manifest physical universe. A consequence of FAM is the support for Bohr's concepts of a universal "complementarity". Implication of Gödel's Incompleteness Theorems are reviewed as foreground to demonstrating how mathematical formalizations of FAM meaningfully relate to Gödel's theorems. First, it is shown that using a simple mathematical formalism that eventually ties to Hilbert space geometry expresses an underlying arithmetic foundation and, therefore, is explicitly subject to the Incompleteness Theorems. Second, using temporal topos methods to model the relationship of FAM to consciousness in the physical universe provides an alternate strategy for proving Gödel's theorems. With both approaches we are thus able to conclude that Gödel's theorems are the direct expression and implication of the universal complementarity implicit in FAM.

Keywords: Gödel, incompleteness, temporal topos, fundamental awareness, idealism, consciousness, complementarity, subject–object relationship, duality, non-duality, complexity, emergence, Hilbert space, Buddhism, Śaivism, Advaita Vedānta, mysticism, Kabbalah, category theory, Platonism.

Gödel, Fundamental Awareness and Mathematical Models

GÖDEL'S Incompleteness Theorems have had a wide applicability beyond the usual scope of formal logic in which they were first proposed (Theise 2023). The field of consciousness studies is among these. That consciousness is now presented as a reasonable subject for scientific discourse has been heavily influenced by the ideas put forth by philosopher John Lucas (1961) and by physicist and Nobelist Roger Penrose (1989), both of whom invoked Gödel's theorems to question whether consciousness could be reduced to a merely computational outcome of the complex functioning of the brain as an assumed physical machine.

Both scholars suggested that since the proofs themselves could only have been formulated through the intuitions of Gödel's human mind and not through strictly computational processes, they are not only about arithmetic principles, but simultaneously about the processes that enclose it – proofs regarding the possibility of proofs. Of course, the issue of the role of intuition for the obtaining of human knowledge goes much further back to ancient philosophical systems and representations of reality, such as those found in Buddhism, non-dual Vedānta, Triadic Śaivism known as Kashmir Śaivism, Taoism, Shamanic and monotheistic mystical cultures (Theise and Kafatos 2016; Theise 2023) and also include Gödel's own Platonic idealist perspective (Gödel 1995; Goldstein 2005; Tait 2001, 2005).

Gödel's Incompleteness Theorems proved that some formal systems "within which a certain amount of elementary arithmetic can be carried out" (Raatikainen 2013) necessarily could not be both complete and consistent. Any system that was complete would always contain contradictory statements, while any system that contained only non-contradictory time statements would not contain all true statements. Such statements are either *true but unprovable from within the system* (the system thereby being incomplete); or *false and provable* (the system thus being inconsistent).

Both Lucas and Penrose noted that since Gödel-unprovable statements can be proved by human mathematicians, but not from within the formal system itself, human minds do not function as formal algorithmic systems. Thus, the human mind cannot be a product of a computer-like functioning of the brain, even if that were feasible. Indeed, there is really no a priori reason why the notion that the brain is merely a computer would be valid, other than cultural prejudice or philosophical preference, which we will critically discuss further, below. The appropriateness of applying Gödel's theorems has been critiqued, to be sure, though others have supported their applicability (Hadley 2010; Shear and Sims 2018).

It is within the context of bridging contemporary science with philosophy as well as with metaphysics/mysticism (i.e. speculations born of first person experiences) that we have recently proposed a *Fundamental Awareness* framework for understanding consciousness (Theise and Kafatos 2016). We consider the ground of being to be a field of non-dual

Pure Awareness, i.e. *Awareness of Awareness*, which is in a complementary relationship with duality/differentiation. This concept is:

1. in keeping with core strands of Western philosophy (inclusive of ideas from Plato, Spinoza, Kant, Schopenhauer, Hegel, Whitehead; most recently, Kastrup) that have provided arguments in a modern philosophical context for the validity of what we state herein (Kastrup 2018, 2019);
2. consistent with, if not directly implied by orthodox quantum mechanics, relativity and complexity theory; and
3. reflective of deep first person experiences (and the philosophies born of these).

Subsequently, the mathematization of Theise and Kafatos' Fundamental Awareness framework by Kafatos and Narasimhan (2016) resulted in a formal Fundamental Awareness Model (FAM). These authors, using approaches from Hilbert space, category theory and calculus of indications, showed that if Awareness is fundamental in the universe, then mathematical frameworks are likely to be best suited to reveal its fundamental aspects. They explored and summarized in general terms mathematical formalisms that may take us as close as possible to conscious Awareness, beginning with the primary relationships between the observer and the observed. Such mathematical frameworks, built on fundamental mathematical languages of our interactions with the universe, need to be further developed with consciousness being the fundamental dynamic. This is further developed in this work.

It is important to emphasize that our approach is not an actual expression in terms of mathematics of the activity *within* non-dual Fundamental Awareness, as understood in lineages of mystical practice such as Vedāntic (Prabhavananda and Isherwood 1978), Buddhist (Klein and Wangyal 2006; Berzin 2008), Śaivist (Dyczkowski 1992, 1994) and Kabbalist (Scholem 1941; Idel 1988) traditions. In these, there ultimately can be no such mathematical formalisms, or for that matter any linguistic description, as the non-dual is beyond such attempts to describe it. However, the actual emanation of duality from Fundamental Awareness can be described verbally and captured mathematically as we will see below. This, again, gets us as close as is possible to a formal framework, realizing that, ultimately, even such approaches are bound to leave out the most important aspect of fundamental Awareness: its total, boundless freedom to create, sustain and re-absorb all existence, beyond space and time (Theise and Kafatos 2016).

We also note that there are other mathematical approaches to Fundamental Awareness such as explored by Kafatos and Kato (2017). They advocate seeking mathematical formalisms for the workings of an underlying universal consciousness or Fundamental Awareness that do not rely on specific interpretations of quantum mechanics (QM) and originate in a branch of category theory, viz. temporal (*t*-)topos. They propose that *t*-topos provides such a framework in which the difference between a subject and an object involves the direction of a morphism in a category. Clearly, this approach of Kafatos and Kato involves complementarity as it addresses relationships between the subject and the object, and qualities of experience. The resulting formalism of Kafatos and Kato (2017) provides powerful ways to address Fundamental Awareness and associated experiences or qualia. In other words, there may very well be multiple ways to mathematize Fundamental Awareness. However, the connection to Gödel advocated here brings in additional elements of not bounding Awareness in a formal mathematical system. In other words, mathematical systems can only go so far and cannot provide the implied freely expressible qualities of experience.

Gödel's Incompleteness Theorems: Historical Context and Brief Review

We now turn to Gödel in general and specific ways to further develop the rigour and implications of these FAM mathematical models. First, in general ways, there is a set of cultural conditions that frame our investigations, including a complete contextual overview of Gödel's own Platonism, the Incompleteness Theorems' expression of that stance, and their precise and definitive explosion of the cultural imperatives of the Logical Positivists of the Vienna Circle, around the first part of the twentieth century (Goldstein 2005). Indeed, while speculations such as those of this FAM (and other idealistic or panpsychist perspectives) are often deemed a priori "unscientific", the Incompleteness Theorems provide the cultural and intellectual milien in which this critique dissolves.

Furthermore, as Gödel intended, mathematical formalisms – such as the Gödel type statements – are examples of mathematical Platonic ideals, existing *prior to and beyond* our formal systems' capacity to capture them (Gödel 1995; Goldstein 2005; Parsons 1995). We interpret these concepts as inherent in the complementary relationship between the non-dual Fundamental Awareness and the duality of the knowable universe that emanates from it; not merely embedded *within* the fabric of the universe (i.e. within space, time, matter and energy), per se, non-duality is what *underlies* that fabric (Theise and Kafatos 2016). Space and time, matter and energy are the manifestations of the dualities arising from the non-dual. Non-dual Fundamental Awareness gives experience to conscious observers through countless levels of qualia, the inherent objective sets of what constitutes the universe. Of course, since Awareness is non-dual, even the so called "observers" are part of universal Awareness. The issue of observers, whether they themselves are quantum systems or exist "outside" the quantum system being observed, is debated in different schools of thought under the general rubric of the Copenhagen Interpretation as discussed in the Introduction to this volume.

GÖDEL, THE VIENNA CIRCLE AND THE LIMITATIONS OF EMPIRICISM

The Vienna Circle of philosophers, under the leadership of Moritz Schlick, comprised a group of philosophers, social scientists, mathematicians and physicists, in particular Hans Hahn, Philipp Frank, Otto Neurath, Olga Hahn-Neurath, Viktor Kraft, Theodor Radacovic, Gustav Bergmann and Rudolf Carnap (Stadler and Uebel 2012). A primary aim of the group was to define the limits of what may or may not be reasonable topics for philosophical and scientific discourse; the philosophical ideas were often referred to as *Logical Positivism*. This enterprise essentially intended to eliminate any hint of "metaphysics" or intuitive knowledge, however derived, from contemporary thought. They did so by establishing two essential tests for knowledge of the external world: was it derived from empirical observations made in reproducible scientific experiments or could it be expressed mathematically as a provable, formal system of logic? Certainly from Newton onward, generations of experimentalists were the foundational figures for scientific empiricism, though many (particularly Newton the alchemist, himself) would not have agreed with Vienna Circle's absolutist reification of the sola primacy of scientific method for notions of "truth".

On the formal logic side of the Vienna Circle mission, a precursor work was the *Principia Mathematica* of Russell and Whitehead: a system of formal logic from which, it was hoped, all mathematical truths could be derived (Whitehead and Russell 1910). Its three volumes were perhaps the ultimate attempt to formulate the kind of system for which the Vienna Circle hoped. However, flaws leading either to incompleteness or inconsistency of the system were recognized early on by the authors themselves (particularly with attempts by Russell to redress some of these) and by others (Wittgenstein of particular note) (Whitehead and Russell 1925, 1927; Wittgenstein 1922).

The cultural impact of the core views of the Vienna Circle philosophers (though there were many differences between them) would not have been extended so universally had they been able to stay safely in Vienna, unchallenged by the rising tides of history that destroyed their community. With the murder of Schlick in 1936 and the subsequent Nazification of academic life in Austria, prior to and following the *Anschluss*, the annexation of Austria, those philosophers who could flee did so. They found refuge in major academic centres in the United States and in England. It was in part through this diaspora that by the mid-century the ideas of the Logical Positivists spread as a dominant philosophy of science despite the ultimate negation of their aims, from within (by Gödel) and from without (Uebel 2006).

By "from without" we refer to QM, the still reigning model of reality derived from empirical observation, one of the fundamental knowledge tests for Logical Positivism. It is no small paradox that one certain blow to the Vienna Circle mission was provided by the scientific community itself. At the core of the Logical Positivist position is the assumption that scientific method is defined by the separation of the subjective observer from the object of examination, i.e. empiricism. QM reveals the complete lack of such separation at the most fundamental levels of existence and thus, in a sense, effectively dooms the entire Vienna Circle mission.

But the Vienna Circle did not engage QM. Lord Alfred North Whitehead did and, despite his prior efforts with *Principia Mathematica* (and perhaps because of those efforts' failure), offered this famous rebuke to the Logical Positivists:

> There persists ... [a] fixed scientific cosmology which presupposes the ultimate fact of an irreducible brute matter,

> or material, spread through space in a flux of configurations. In itself such a material is senseless, valueless, purposeless. It just does what it does do, following a fixed routine imposed by external relations which do not spring from the nature of its being. It is this assumption that I call "scientific materialism". Also it is an assumption which I shall challenge as being entirely unsuited to the scientific situation at which we have now arrived. – Whitehead 1925: 17

More fundamental was the challenge presented by Gödel. As described above, Gödel's theorems rendered the Logical Positivist mission obsolete. Statements within formal systems that are true, yet unprovable from within the system, affirm the role of intuition in mathematics, without which formal theorems do not stand by themselves. In other words, the world cannot be described, captured and "proven" as a machine-like exercise in producing theorems from postulates. While Gödel might have bridled at some extended implications of his own work, he reasserts the importance of intuition in scientific understanding structures and functions of the universe and reopens science to at least consider the embracing of insights from philosophy and metaphysics.

It is likely that Gödel's understanding of his intuitions, which were both the source and method of proof of the Incompleteness Theorems, pointed to intellectual process as his primary mode. But intellectual intuitions are not the only kind from which important insights into the nature of existence can derive (Theise 2006; Theise and Kafatos 2016). Insights or, more precisely, experiences – from within deep contemplation or obtained through extreme physical states or with the use of certain psychoactive chemicals and entheogens – are also profoundly rich sources of data for construction of a theory of consciousness.

Gödel himself noted the potential implications of his work in this regard, as he wrote to his mother:

> It was something to be expected that sooner or later my proof will be made useful for religion, since that is doubtless also justified in a certain sense. – Letter of 20 October 1963

His work makes it possible to scientifically propose an idealist model of consciousness, but his Incompleteness Theorems do more than that as we will now discuss.

GÖDEL, COMPLEMENTARITY AND FUNDAMENTAL AWARENESS

In FAM, we have postulated that the universe is, using Koestler's (1967) word, a "holarchy" of self-organizing systems. They emanate from Fundamental Awareness as the ground of being, Spinoza's "one substance" of which all existence is comprised (Theise and Kafatos 2016). The properties of this postulated non-dual Awareness reflect classical insights from contemplative traditions such as, for example, Vedānta and Śaivism (in which Fundamental Awareness is described as *Brahman* or *Parama Śiva*), Lurianic Kabbalah (*Ein Sof*) and Buddhism generally (the *Absolute* or *One Mind*) and Tibetan practice particularly (*Mind of Clear Light*). While cultural perspectives shape the metaphors used to describe this indescribable realm in these traditions, they all agree that when the mind perceives its own deep nature, what it perceives is a luminous, boundless, profoundly creative, non-dual and Fundamental Awareness.

In brief, the gradual evolution of the division into subject and object, in its most primitive stages as differentiation *within* Fundamental Awareness, eventually requires literal separation into subject and object, which necessarily implies dimensional distance, at least dimensions of space and time. And, thus, space–time itself implicitly arises as duality emanates from non-duality, in keeping with principal ideas expressed by Kant and by Schopenhauer. This space–time at the physical level is none other than that described by Einstein. As application of QM to the structure of space–time makes evident, it is not an empty vacuum, but is energy rich. This energy produces mass in a "quantum foam", out of which arise the smallest subatomic entities (though there is no consensus as yet about the nature of these smallest entities, strings or otherwise, or a theory that unites all interactions including gravity) (Greene 2000). These smallest entities, interacting with each other, give rise to higher scales of organization and size, i.e. the particles of the Standard Model (and perhaps others). In turn, these interact and self-organize into, amongst other structures and phenomena, atoms, which in turn self-organize into molecules and, on upward, to the larger scale structures of living things (Theise and Kafatos 2013b) and of planets and planetary systems, stellar systems, galaxies, the universe as a whole.

Of course, we should note here that in the modern quantum field theory as well as in string theory, the quanta are not particles as first envisaged. The "boundaries", of a localized particle in space–time, are more ranges of vibration. Thus, constitutive panpsychism is excluded from consideration since there are no such things as particles and no combining of such micro-level conscious entities into higher-level subjects of experience. As such, there is bound to be interpenetration of scales of existence, or the structures in the quantum universe would be fuzzier than taken in a classical world.

It is in these successive levels of self-organization that we have previously identified a universal aspect of "complementarity" (Theise and Kafatos 2013b) that was first fully expressed by Bohr in the Como Lectures of 1927 (Bohr 1937). Each level of scale may be viewed either as comprising a "thing" or arising from interactions of smaller things: so a physical body at the everyday scale is a solid *thing* (with all the sense of a skin-bounded self that comes along with that), but is also, simultaneously, a very large community of single cells that are self-organizing into tissues, organs, etc. (and most of which are not even "our own" human cells, but bacteria and other microbials of the microbiome. One might say that "everything only looks like a thing" (Theise 2017). As we have previously analysed, there is no reified "thing" to be found at any level of scale (Jantsch 1980; Theise 2005, 2006, 2009, 2019; Theise and Kafatos 2013b, 2016). We believe that this is at least a significant aspect of Bohr's complementarity as it applies across all levels of scale (Theise and Kafatos 2013b). In FAM, we take one more step and say that the entire manifest universe is in complementarity with the non-dual Fundamental Awareness (Theise and Kafatos 2016).

Not only is "thingness" scale-dependent, but "boundaries" are scale-dependent as well (Theise and Kafatos 2013b, 2016). At the everyday scale, our bodies appear bounded by our skin, but at the cellular scale the outer reaches of our microbiomes would constitute our boundary (which may therefore include multiple living entities living in community within an extended microbiome, such as families, pets, infestations) (Theise and Kafatos 2013b). At the atomic scale, since every atom in our bodies is derived from ingesting, breathing or drinking atoms from the planet, the bodily boundary becomes all compassing of the planet as a whole: we are not simply beings living on a planet (though we are that, too), but the atoms of the planet self-organizing into living things that think of themselves as separate – a version of Lovelock's Gaea hypothesis. The further down in scale, the wider the boundaries get, ultimately, in the

fig. 9.1: Two faces or a vase?

quantum realm, leading to the non-locality and entanglement that Einstein predicted, but which rankled him so and to boundaries that encompass all existence.

A useful image is that of the classic "two faces/vase" drawing (*fig.* 9.1). The image shows two faces gazing at each other across a space. Or is that a vase surrounded by the ground field on either side? Which is it? Of course, it is both. The holarchical description, to be complete, requires both "two faces" and "a vase"; however, no "model" or "theory" of the image can contain both – one most always choose a perspective, either one sees two faces or one sees a vase. Thus, the images are complementary or represent a "complementarity".

Likewise, a complete description of existence requires the QM wave/particle complementarity, though any attempt at examination reveals only one or the other. Indeed, any scientific description of something must begin with selection of an object of study and the boundary conditions of that object. But the object-nature and its boundaries are scale and perspective dependent; every selection of scale and perspective, while capturing some aspects of the object of study will necessarily exclude others.

Gödel's Incompleteness enters here. There is always some aspect of study of a system examined or, more specifically, described mathematically that while "true" is necessarily excluded from any specific empirical or logical description of that object. This applies to logical statements, but in our view it would extend to the empirical side as well. For example, in quantum mechanics logical or mathematically expressed theoretical descriptions and empirical descriptions are intertwined. As such, scientific theories and mathematical formalisms will always be perspective dependent (for example in QM they are observer-made choices carrying out specific measurements of a quantum system). Therefore, no formal system or empirically derived theory can capture the holarchy of all the nested, self-organizing systems emanating from Fundamental Awareness that comprise existence. Gödel's Incompleteness is, *at least metaphorically*, an expression of all the complementarities that FAM postulates as inherent and universal through all levels of scale of the cosmos and of the most fundamental complementarity of all, the of the non-dual and its emanated dualities.

We believe, however, that the formal mathematization provided by application of the formalism presented here, to the evolution of subject–object separation within Fundamental Awareness, takes the application of the Incompleteness theorems beyond mere metaphor. Likewise, using *t*-topos to model the relationships of Fundamental Awareness to existence mediates another way to prove the Incompleteness Theorems.

MATHEMATICAL FORMALISM, I-NESS AND THAT-NESS, RĀMĀNUJAN AND ŚAIVISM

Of all contemplative systems which we have reviewed in detail, Rāmānujan's version of Vedānta and Kashmir Śaivism specify the most details regarding how the non-duality differentiates into subject–object duality through successive stages. Specifically, we take into account Rāmānujan and Śaivite intuitions regarding the differentiation within and from non-dual Fundamental Awareness and follow the views previously proposed (Kafatos 2015; Kafatos and Narasimhan 2016). We then build upon these concepts to show that working with physical theories alone will not lead to a framework of consciousness and such efforts are doomed to fail.

The starting point is an *ontological assumption, an axiomatic* approach similar to all mathematical formalisms: Here, *universal Awareness operates at every level of reality through three "laws", complementarity (as described above), process or creative intra-/ interactivity (the arising of emergent properties and structures from self-organizing behaviours), and recursion (emergence at ever higher levels of scale and, accordingly, self-similarity across all scales)* (Theise and Kafatos 2013a, b, 2016). Through these laws, Fundamental Awareness, which otherwise would be unmanifest and unknowable, emanates the universe giving rise to all the qualia of subjective experiences and constituting the Awareness within which qualia are perceived. In this model, qualia are not a problem to be solved by a theory of consciousness, but the nature of all existence itself, including the brains that materialists privilege as the source of mind.

In the mathematical formalism,

$\perp\top$ is the symbol for absolute undifferentiated Consciousness,

$\perp$ is the symbol for Subject, i.e. $\perp$ = "I", and

$\top$ is the symbol for Object, i.e. $\top$ = "That".

Moreover, the A symbol is "Am". We then use the convention $A \perp = \perp$"I Am". While $\top A^{+} = \top$ means "That Am". "I Am" is existence of Subject, what we term *I-ness*; while "That Am" is existence of Object, what we term *That-ness*. Subject and Object are *not* yet differentiated, they form the primordial qualia relationship between what eventually will become a separated object from subject, the *fundamental complementarity* or primal complementarity of qualia. The adjoint A^{+} is introduced here to indicate that A and A^{+} commute, or $A\ A^{+}$ is *identical* to $A^{+} A$, in other words the direction of the relationship between $\perp$ and $\top$ does not matter. We note that the convention used here can eventually carry over to standard Hilbert space convention, which will have the advantage that it can bring forward a familiarity with quantum formalism and the relationships between the observer carrying out measurements and the (quantum) observed system. As QM is the only physics we have that fundamentally relates to observation, the connection of I-ness to That-ness is akin to the relationship between observed and observed in quantum measurement theory (the reader can refer to Kafatos 2015 for further details).

There are *five universal and logical (mathematical) statements*:

I

That

I (Am) That

That (Am) I

I (Am) **That.**

Where the bold indicates primary or dominant aspect of the subjective–objective relationship, realizing that at these five levels, unity still prevails.

In *fig.* 9.2, the subject–object relationships are shown, in unity, where the tendencies to separate are still latent. As shown

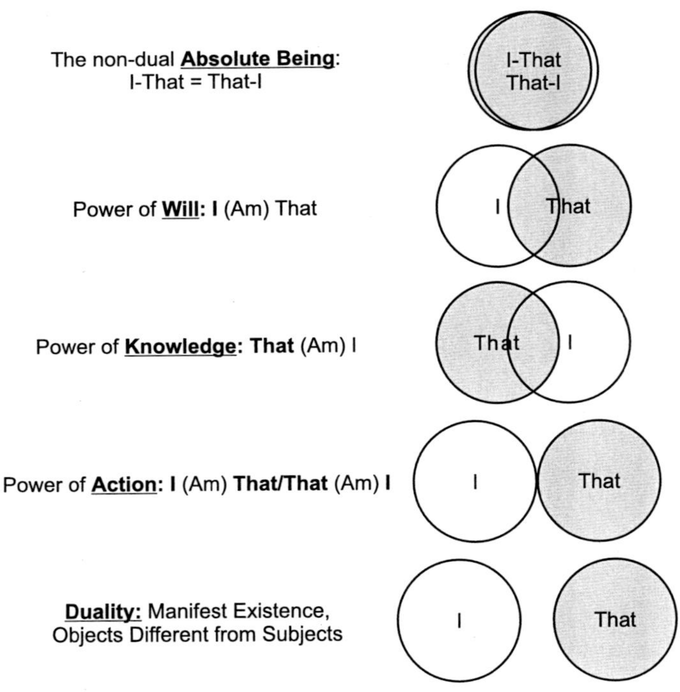

fig. 9.2: Open circles indicate subjectivity ("I-ness"), filled circles indicate objectivity ("That-ness")

in previous works (Kafatos 2015; Kafatos and Narasimhan 2016; and following Śaivism and Rāmānujan), at the first two levels, the subjective (what we term *I-ness*) and the objective (what we term *That-ness*) are totally integrated in pure *Unity*. At level 3, the primary force to manifest brings forth the *intent*: I-ness is beginning to be more prominent ("I intend to...") though the two entities are still in unity. At level 4 the primary force to manifest brings forth the *knowledge*: That-ness is beginning to be more prominent ("That to know..."); unity still prevails. At level 5, I-ness and That-ness are in perfect balance, neither one being more prominent and beginning to manifest *action*. These five levels of pure subjectivity and pure objectivity will, subsequently, fully manifest as subjective selves and separate objects, fully separated (level 6).

All three fundamental laws – Complementarity, Recursion, Creative Interactivity – are operating at these five levels (see *fig.* 9.2 through Will, Knowledge and Action):

> For example, complementarity is operating as the fundamental relationship between the Subject and Object, etc. However, as we move next to the level of symmetry breaking of the above universal relationships in which the Subject and Object become separated a certain *veiling* of Awareness occurs which we posit is manifest in quantum non-locality.
>
> – Kafatos and Kak 2015

The simple logical statements presented above break down as this differentiation becomes more instantiated, the universal $\perp$ and $\top$ (again we emphasize that these expressions for *I-ness* and *That-ness* can then carry over to quantum formalism as specific case for interaction of observer with observed system in quantum measurements) now becoming limited or bounded subjects and limited objects; simultaneously, the mathematics becomes much more complex, instead of **0** and **I**, we now have an infinite set of mathematical entities equivalent to vectors, representing infinitely many sentient beings, interacting with each other and sensing objects. What occurs is the logical statement **I** (Am) **Not** that, or **Not That** (Am) I. Here the symmetry breaking that applied to the first four levels is complete, which we posit allows space, time, energy and mass to arise. We then speak of limited will (of subjects), limited knowledge (of objects) and limited action (between subjects and objects), providing an account of qualia in individual experiences.

The world appears as classical, composed of separate subjects and objects. However, the general principles of complementarity, recursion and sentience still hold but now in an infinitely complex set of entities. The universe is then born. In summary, non-dual Fundamental Awareness produces the dualities of object–subject relationships, descriptions of which may develop from the practice of contemporary science, inclusive of mathematical physics – such activities involve dynamics as utilized by our minds and intellect to provide the qualia of understanding of our environment. Finally, when the Subject–Object identity breaks down, we also have the universal Observer (O; Subject) that *appears* to be separate from the individual observer (o), in space–time. It is remarkable that quantum eraser experiments actually reveal this separation (Kim et al. 2000; Narasimhan et al. 2019).

The next steps of development would be to connect the above formalism to *experiences* of the world by conscious entity as outlined in Kafatos and Kato (2017). This will be explored in future work.

TEMPORAL TOPOS AND FUNDAMENTAL AWARENESS

Next, we shall focus on the *t-topos* methods. In physics, as a parameter we use time *t*, which appears, for example, in the Schrödinger equation (stated in language as expressing the rate of change of the wave function with respect to time *t* equals the Hamiltonian operated on the wave function). However, such a parameter t is an arbitrary time. Not only for the wave particle duality of a quantum, but also in the study of consciousness, specifically the role of mind interacting with a quantum system through specific measuring processes, the concept of "Nowness" plays an important role, i.e. "Now" should be distinguished from any other time. In describing the states characterized by energy ε, one cannot develop a theory by letting t_1, t_2 and t_3 be corresponding to the past, the present and the future, since the uncertainty principle is involved in the process from t_2 to t_3, and linear time as such breaks down; we handle this enigma by introducing the concept of a temporal site, i.e. a parameter t of a parameter object of a temporal site. Namely, we consider a temporal site as a parameter category over which the sheaf τ associated with time is defined. Specifically, sheaf τ associated with time has a temporal site as its domain category. A temporal site S is defined as a category with a Grothendieck topology with the temporal topos theoretic restrictions. See Kato (2004, 2005, 2010, 2013, 2017) for those restrictions. In the theory of temporal topos $S^\wedge$, even a parameter time t is the image (or the value) of time-associated sheaf τ defined on the temporal site S, which is also called a generalized time category, which is abbreviated as t-site. See Kato (2013, 2017) for general references for t-topos and t-site. That is, a category is not enough to capture the Nowness; one needs the notion of a t-site S as a parameter category indicating "when". What we need for applications to fundamental aspects of quantum physics, we need a t-topos (i.e. sheaves) parameterized over a t-site. For those applications, see the above references.

A humorous popular saying is that our world is on the back of a turtle T_1 which is standing on another turtle T_2 and under that turtle T_2 there is another turtle T_3, maybe even ad infinitum. A theory with a finite number of axions with no internal contradictions, i.e. a consistent logical axiomatic system, has a weak spot; using those axioms, the theory is not capable to prove with finite number of steps that there do not exist contradictions. It would take an infinite set of steps to try to accomplish that.

In terms of temporal topos (which is abbreviated as *t*-topos) methods, for any entity *Q* as an object of *t*-topos *S*^, which can be representing either an animate or inanimate entity, we first have the fundamental commutative diagram coming from our *t*-topos theoretic ontological view as follows:

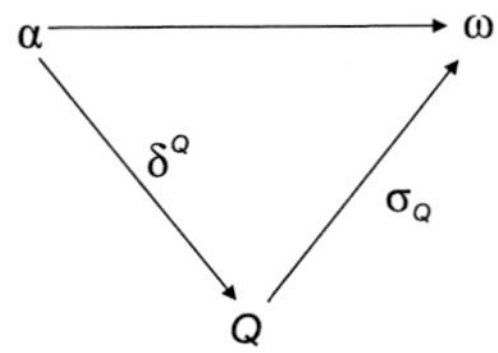

(*)

where sheaf α is an initial object and spacetime sheaf ω = (κ, τ) is a terminal object of *t*-topos S^ and where δ^Q and σ_Q are uniquely determined morphisms from α and ω, respectively. Note also that the horizontal morphism in diagram (*) is $\delta^\omega = \sigma_\alpha$, which follows directly from the definitions of an initial object and a terminal object. The *t*-topos theoretic interpretation of the ontological universe is the *t*-topos *S*^, where each object *Q* of *S*^ should be associated with the *t*-topos theoretic ontological reality diagram (*), abbreviated as a *t-tred*. That is, the ontological universe consists of *t*-treds. The physical universe is the right half of diagram (*), i.e. half of *t*-tred. On the other hand, the left half of diagram (*) is for the cognitive universe. In the various aspects and views from the traditionally established philosophies, sheaf α seems to be capable of playing the roles for "One Substance", *Brahman*, "One Mind" depending how one pays attention to sheaf α itself, or unique morphism δ from sheaf α, or even to the commutativity of diagram (*). Our view is, as noted earlier, that fundamental reality cannot be captured as a machine-like exercise from a set of axioms, i.e. the right half of (*). That is, we need to consider the entire diagram (*), not only the space–time aspect ω but also the cognitive aspect α. One cannot have one without the other. Notice also that since sheaves α and ω are constant functors, they exist (generalized time, i.e. *t*-site object) time independent.

We refer to Kato and Nishimura (2020, 2021) for applications of sheaf α for self-organization and emergence aspect in bio-cognitive science. For the role and applications of *t*-topos to quantum theory, see Kato (2004, 2005, 2010, 2017). In diagram (*), the uniquely determined morphism δ^Q from sheaf α is regarded as the consciousness (morphism) of entity *Q*. Also note that in diagram (*), three objects and morphisms are in *t*-topos *S*^, viz. objects are presheaves and morphisms are morphisms of functors (i.e. natural transformations) defined over the *t*-site *S*. Over an object *V* in *S*, diagram (*) becomes

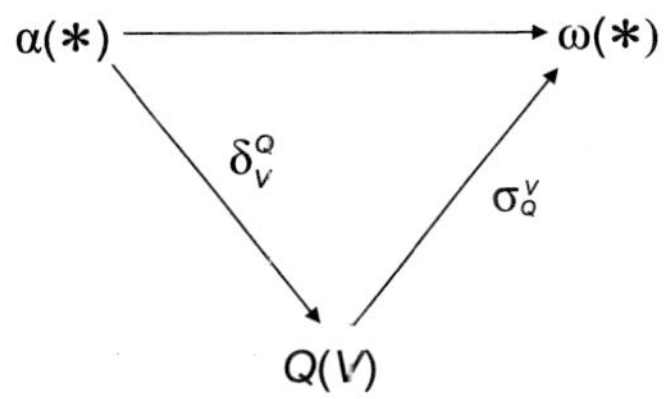

(*V)

Recall initial and terminal objects in the functor category *S*^ are constant functors. Namely, as we noted earlier, α(*V*) = α(*W*) for any objects *V* and *W* in the *t*-site *S*, which indicates the constant existence of sheaf α, which may be said to be a representation of Fundamental Awareness here or, as referred to in prior works (Kafatos 2015; Kafatos and Kato 2017; Kafatos and Nadeau 2000; Kafatos and Narasimhan 2016; Kato and Nishimura 2020, 2021; Nadeau and Kafatos 1999; Struppa et al. 2002), Universal Consciousness, independent of not only regular time *t*, corresponding to $\tau(U)$, $U \in Obj(S)$, but also independent of generalized time as an object of *t*-site *S*. Then δ_V^Q is the consciousness of *Q* over generalized time period $V \in Obj(S)$. The term awareness includes of course being conscious of the "other" as well as the "self". The *fundamental* aspect refers to the underlying ground of reality, while *universal* refers to unrestricted global aspects that apply everywhere or being conscious of all possible objects that exist.

We note (1) that generally speaking, an initial object A in any category C is characterized (i.e. defined) by the following universal morphism property; for an arbitrary object $X \in Obj(C)$, there exists a uniquely determined morphism $f^X: A \to X$. Using this definition alone, one can prove that for another initial object A', there is an isomorphism between A and A' as follows. First regard A as an initial object of category C, then by the definition of A being an initial object of C, uniquely determined morphism $f^{A'}: A \to A'$ exists. Next regard A' as an initial object of category C. Then we have a uniquely determined morphism $f^A: A' \to A$. Consider the composition of those morphisms $f^{A'} \circ f^A: A' \to A'$. By the definition of a category, there is a morphism, the identity morphism $1^{A'}: A' \to A'$. However, regarding A as an initial object again, such a morphism is unique. Consequently, we have $f^{A'} \circ f^A = A' = 1^{A'}$. Similarly, one gets $f^A \circ f^{A'}: A' = 1^A$, proving A is isomorphic to A'.

Note also any terminal objects are isomorphic as well. As references for categories and sheaves, see Schubert (1972), Gelfand and Manin (1996), Kato (2006). We also note (2) that in diagram (*), for the uniquely determined horizontal morphism $\alpha \to \omega$ is $\delta^\omega = \sigma_\alpha$, that if there exists a morphism from ω to α, i.e. the reverse direction $\alpha \leftarrow \omega$, then it is an isomorphism, whose proof will not be given since such a proof is similar to the one done in (1).

Next, we will define an important notion of a mnemonic morphism. See Kato and Nishimura (2021) for an application of a mnemonic morphism to cognitive science. For a (non-t-linear) morphism $U \to V$ in t-site, we have the canonically (i.e. functorially) induced morphism $Q(V) \to Q(U)$ for $Q \in Obj(S^\wedge)$. A mnemonic morphism is defined as a non-canonical morphism $q_V^U : Q(U) \to Q(V)$ satisfying the commutativity $\delta_U^Q \circ q_V^U = \delta_V^Q$ of the following triangular diagram:

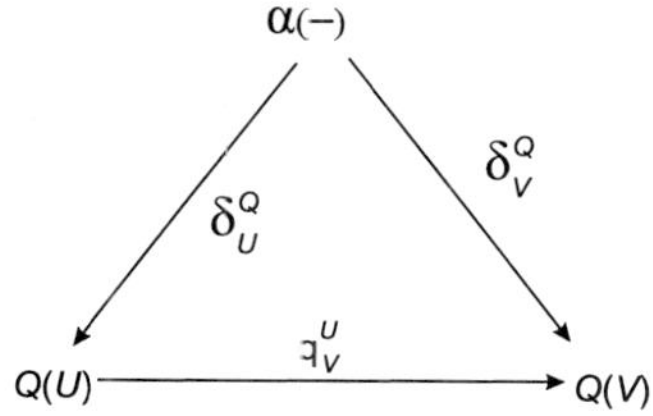

First, since Q is a conscious entity, like a human being, who does the logical processes as in the intuitions of Gödel's human mind (see Introduction), we associate a pre-sheaf Q corresponding to a conscious entity together with δ as in diagram (^*), where various δ* corresponding to axioms themselves and derived propositions, properties, or consequences from axioms. Second, since logical consistency is not only a time-independent concept, but also *t*-site object independent, in diagram (^*) we do not evaluate Q at any object of *t*-site; see diagram (*E) below.

RELATIONSHIPS OF MODELS OF FUNDAMENTAL AWARENESS TO GÖDEL

Gödel's Incompleteness Theorems prove incompleteness in any formal system if that formal system contains within it a proof of arithmetic. Thus, if our mathematical formalism to Fundamental Awareness developed in previous works (cf. Kafatos 2015) and summarized above, can prove arithmetic, Gödel's Incompleteness Theorems, by definition, apply. Furthermore, the Incompleteness Theorems would therefore not only assert the necessity of applying complementarity, but indeed *be* the assertion of complementarity as a fundamental and inescapable aspect of all existence from any and every perspective and scale, including logical and spatial scales, just as Bohr intuited.

Indeed, the *I That* description of Fundamental Awareness and its emanation of non-duality prove arithmetic, as follows: The formalism is based on the existence of two fundamental quantities, which reduce to 0 and 1 (referring to object and subject, or *I* and *That*). We note that what is assigned to 1 and 0 is in a sense arbitrary as, in Fundamental Awareness, the subject and the object are interchangeable. In either case, as such, a numerical basis is established.

We note here that 0 and 1 are not the usual prime numbers but can be considered as *complementary* entities, we may say they are "proto-numbers". One can be taken as existence (in the subjective sense) and the other as non-subjective or objective existence. Being in one of the two, displaces the other, although in the spirit of complementarity, *implies* the other. The proto-numbers 1 and 0 can also be taken as existence and emptiness.

In the primordial mathematics suggested here, two entities (*proto-numbers*) exist, complementing each other, with no separation. The relationships can repeat forever ("*I–That*", "*That–I*", "*I–That/That–I*"), "*I*-ness" senses itself as itself, the "*That*-ness" just being part of the Subjective Self with a tendency that will eventually break down the Unity. In the first four levels, there is no preferred logical direction of symmetry breaking, the *I*-ness and That-ness are interchangeable. Yet, in a latent way, the two proto-numbers will give rise to separation and the objectification of the universe. Thus, we assert that Gödel's Incompleteness theorems apply to this mathematization of the emanation of duality, of existence, from the ground of non-dual, Fundamental Awareness. Gödel's theorems are thus not just reflective of the Law of Complementarity, but are the direct expression and implication of it.

As for *t*-topos, we may precisely restate Gödel's theorems in this mathematical language. Consider a system A with axioms $A_1, A_2, \ldots, A_n$ and let P be the totality of all the propositions $\{P_k\}$, $k = 1, 2, \ldots, m$, where $m \geq n$, decidable from the system of axioms $A_1, A_2, \ldots, A_n$. Let $\delta^1, \delta^2, \ldots, \delta^m$ be uniquely determined morphisms from α to Q, which correspond to propositions P_k, $k = 1, 2, \ldots, m$. The Incompleteness Theorem of Gödel can be stated in terms of *t*-topos as follows:

A comprehensive treatment for the following E in terms of the descent theory for the system A will appear in Kato (2024), one can construct a relevant proposition E so that there *does not* exist a mnemonic morphism p from Q to Q to make the following diagram commutative:

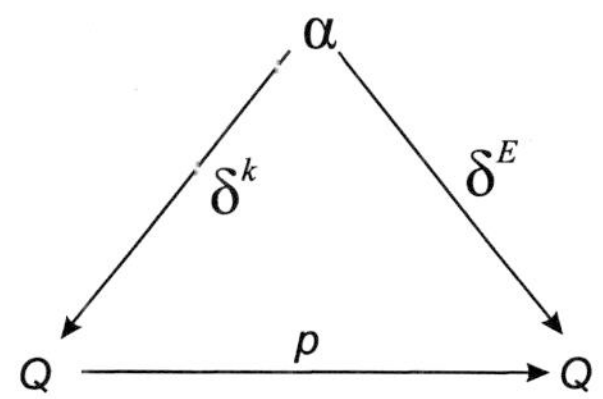

(*E)

for any $k = 1, 2, \ldots, m$, where δ^E is the uniquely determined morphism from α to Q corresponding to the undecidable proposition E. If there were such a mnemonic morphism for any proposition E, then such a mnemonic morphism would imply the commutativity in (*E). Consequently, we get $p \circ \delta^k = \delta^E$, indicating δ^E, corresponding to proposition E, follows from proposition corresponding morphism δ^k and the mnemonic morphism p corresponding to logical processes.

These considerations that Gödel's Incompleteness Theorems represent a profound mathematical–logical expression of fundamental aspects of existence are not separate from other recent works, such as that of Dourdent demonstrating that QM paradoxes arise from "a lack of metaphysical distancing" and "might just be instances of a fundamental undecidability, contributing to a quantum Gödelian hunch" (Dourdent 2020). As Dourdent quotes Wheeler (as presented in Fuchs 2017: 127):

> Physics is not machinery. Logic is not oil occasionally applied to that machinery. Instead, everything, physics included, derives from two parents and is nothing but cathode-tube image of the interplay between them. One is the "participant". The other is the complex of undecidable propositions of mathematical logic.

In other recent work, Nurgalieva and Renner (2021) examine how contemporary thought experiments regarding QM shed light on the paradoxes of QM, such as Maxwell's demon. They consider formulations of QM as an expression of *agents* who participate in a self-organizing (complex?) system performing the analyses, such as how "Wigner's friend" Alice is both an agent of observation outside her experimental apparatus and a participatory agent with Wigner who is considering her, from outside, as part of the experimental set-up. The fluidity of boundaries as described above, depending on point of view, is thus reaffirmed here. The authors suggest that multiagent experiments are consistency tests for physical theories:

> If a proposed physical theory is supposed to be universal, then it must be possible to model agents, i.e. users of the theory, as physical systems within that theory. In other words, the theory must be able to describe its own users! This immediately raises questions of consistency. For example, an agent Bob may not only reason directly about a particle, but he may as well use the theory to describe how another agent Alice reasons about the same. Within a consistent theory, such indirect reasoning should be allowed and not lead to contradictions.
>
> Nurgalieva and Renner 2021: 194

In their analysis, one of their proposed methods for assessing thought experiments "appears to have similarities to Gödel's incompleteness result" in that "both of them use a self-referential statement [...] to arrive at their respective conclusions". They acknowledge that:

> while Incompleteness Theorems show that it is *impossible to prove* that a given theory is consistent within the theory itself [their argument] proves that the rule system [...] *is not* consistent. In this sense, [their] argument yields a converse statement to Gödel's theorem (authors' emphases).
>
> – Ibid.: 195

Summary

Gödel's Incompleteness Theorems have been used by Penrose (1989) and Lucas (1961) to question whether consciousness could be reduced to merely algorithmic computational models, opening up a philosophically, mathematically and scientifically valid consideration of idealist/panpsychist hypotheses regarding the nature of consciousness. We have proposed a framework for understanding consciousness that integrates contemporary science, dominant strands of Western philosophy and experiential data/insights from diverse spiritual, often contemplative practices. This "Fundamental Awareness Framework" posited a non-dual field of pure Fundamental Awareness that emanates the duality of the existent universe. Mathematization of that framework, two approaches to which are summarized here, one with an approach using logical relationships between the subject and the object, and reflective of the emanation of duality from the non-dual as expressed by Rāmānujan and Śaivite philosophies, the other using *t*-topos to describe relationships between Fundamental Awareness and an emanated physical universe. These mathematical approaches to Fundamental Awareness relate to the ideas of Penrose and Lucas, further elaborating on relationships of Gödel's Incompleteness Theorems to consciousness.

In the general framework, non-dual Fundamental Awareness undergoes repetitive symmetry breaks which lead to subject–object separation in which space and time, matter and energy arise. We have previously described how the self-organization of these emanated structures reflect three "laws" (see also Patra and Kafatos, Chap. 5 of this book): *complementarity*, reflective of the complementary nature of I-ness and That-ness in the non-dual field as it differentiates; *process*; the intra- and interactive processes that result in emergent self-organization; and *recursion*, the repetitive cycling through such self-organization and emergence through increasing levels of scale and complexity

(Theise and Kafatos 2016). These are all reflected in mathematical formalisms of FAM (Kafatos 2015; Kafatos and Narasimhan 2016) and by *t*-topos (Kafatos and Kato 2017).

In particular, we have demonstrated that the formal system of FAM can now be assessed in terms of Gödel's Incompleteness Theorems: it is sufficient to prove arithmetic and therefore the theorems apply. Likewise, the description through *t*-topos of Fundamental Awareness directly provides an alternate approach to expressing the theorems themselves. Thus, we conclude that Gödel's Incompleteness Theorems are the direct expression and implication of the inherent universal complementarity of the non-dual emanating existence implicit in FAM.

Our demonstrations of *two* models of Fundamental Awareness also show that there is likely to be a whole class of Fundamental Awareness models that a framework would entail. To put it in another way, it seems that a generalization of Gödel necessitates a number (finite or infinite?) of different, but equivalent mathematical models. This would be akin to the situation encountered in early QM between the Heisenberg and the Schrödinger pictures which formed a strong impetus for Bohr's complementarity. These are intriguing questions to be further investigated.

Our thesis here, that the generalization of Gödel entails the fundamental aspect of mind in determining the structure, properties and nature of objective reality, is in concordance with the original quantum views of the founders of QM. More fundamentally perhaps, it brings together mathematics and the role of the conscious, self-aware mind, in a unified way shaping the experiences or qualia and underscores that mathematical languages are a most powerful means for humans to interact with the universe and efforts to understand it.

References

Berzin, A., 2008, *Berzin Archives Glossary*. [Online] http://www.berzinarchives.com/web/en/about/glossary/glossary.html_80737397.html (accessed on 6 March 2008).

Bohr, N., 1937, "Causality and Complementarity", *Philosophy Science*, 4: 289-98.

Dourdent, H., 2020, "A Gödelian Hunch from Quantum Theory", arXiv:2005.04274v1 [quant-ph] accessed on 7 May 2020).

Dyczkowski, M.S.G., 1992, *The Aphorisms of Siva*, Albany, NY: SUNY Press.

———, 1994, *Spandakarika ("The Stanzas of Vibration")*, Varanasi: Dilip Kumar Publishers.

Fuchs, C.A., 2017, "On Participatory Realism", in *Information and Interaction: Eddington, Wheeler and the Limits of Knowledge*, ed. I.T. Durham and D. Rickles, pp. 113-34, Switzerland: Springer.

Gelfand, S.I. and Yu. O. Manin, 1996, *Methods of Homological Algebra*, Berlin: Science + Business Media.

Gödel, K., 1995, *Collected Works III: Unpublished Essays and Lectures*, ed. S. Feferman, J. Dawson, S. Kleene, G. Moore, R. Solovay and J. van Heijenoort, pp. 321-22, Oxford: Oxford University Press.

Goldstein, R., 2005, *Incompleteness: The Proof and Paradox of Kurt Gödel*, New York: W.W. Norton & Company.

Greene, B., 2000, *The Elegant Universe: Superstrings, Hidden Dimensions, and the Quest for the Ultimate Theory*, New York: Vintage.

Hadley, R., 2010, "The Essential Role of Consciousness in Mathematical Cognition", *Journal of Consciousness Studies*, 17(1-2): 27-46.

Idel, M., 1988, *Kabbalah: New Perspectives*, New Haven and London: Yale University Press.

Jantsch, E., 1980, *The Self-Organizing Universe*, Oxford: Pergamon.

Kafatos, M. and R. Nadeau, 2000, *The Conscious Universe: Parts and Wholes in Physical Reality*, New York: Springer-Verlag.

Kafatos, M.C. and S. Kak, 2015, "Veiled Nonlocality and Cosmic Censorship", *Physics Essays*, 28: 182-87.

Kafatos, M.C. and G.C. Kato, 2017, "Sheaf Theoretic Formulation for Consciousness and Qualia and Relationship to the Idealism of Non-dual Philosophies", in *The Necessary Conjunction of the Western and Eastern Thought Traditions for Exploring the Nature of Mind and Life*, ed. P.L. Simeonov, A. Gare, K. Matsuno, A. Igamberdiev and A. Hawkey, Special Theme Issue Integral *Biomathics. Prog. Biophy. Mol. Biol.*, 131C: 242-50.

Kafatos, M.C. and A. Narasimhan, 2016, "Mathematical Frameworks for Consciousness", *Cosmos and History: The Journal of Natural and Social Philosophy*, 12(2): 150-59.

Kafatos, M.C., 2015, "Fundamental Mathematics of Consciousness", *Cosmos and History: The Journal of Natural and Social Philosophy*, 11(2): 175-88.

Kastrup, B., 2018, "The Universe in Consciousness", *Journal of Consciousness Studies*, 25(5-6): 125-55.

———, 2019, "Analytic Idealism: A Consciousness-only Ontology", Doctoral Dissertation, Radboud University, Nijmegen.

Kato, G. and K. Nishimura, 2020, "Toward a Descent Theoretic Formulation for Organization and Emergence: An Initial Object Sheaf α Hypothesis and Its Consequence", *Journal of Integrated Creative Studies*, no. 2020-004-a (June issue).

———, 2021, "Time and Mnemonic Morphism", in *Creative Complex Systems: From Constructive Destruction to Destructive Construction*, ed. Kazuo Nishimura, Masatoshi Murase, Kazuyoshi, Yoshimura, forthcoming, Springer.

Kato, G., 2004, "Elemental Principles of *t*-Topos", *Europhysics Letters*, 64(4): 467-72.

———, 2005, "Elemental t.g. Principles of Relativistic *t*-Topos (Presheafification of Matter, Space and Time)", *Europhysics Letters*, 71(2): 172-78.

———, 2006, *The Heart of Cohomology*, Dordrecht: Springer.

———, 2010, "*u*-Singularity and *t*-Topos Theoretic Entropy", *International Journal of Theoretical Physics*, 49(8): 1952-60.

———, 2013, *Elements of Temporal Topos*, Theschoolbook.com.

———, 2017, "Topos Theoretic Approach to Space and Time", in *Space, Time and the Limits of Human Understanding*, ed. S. Wuppuluri and G. Ghirardi, pp. 313-26, Cham, Switzerland: Springer.

———, 2024, *Categorical and Shcut Theoretic Methods in Epistemology and Philosophy of Sciences*, Berlin: Springer.

Kim, Y-H., R. Yu, S.P. Kulik, Y.H. Shih and M. Scully, 2000, "A Delayed "Choice" Quantum Eraser", *Physical Review Letters*, 84(1): 1-5.

Klein, A.C. and T. Wangyal, 2006, *Unbounded Wholeness*, Oxford: Oxford University Press.

Koestler, A., 1967, *The Ghost in the Machine*, London: Huchinson.

Lucas, J., 1961, "Mind, Machines and Gödel", *Philosophy*, 36.

Nadeau, R. and M.C. Kafatos, 1999, *The Non-local Universe: The New Physics and Matters of the Mind*, Oxford: Oxford University Press.

Narasimhan, A., D. Chopra, M.C. Kafatos, 2019, "The Nature of the Heisenberg von Neumann Cut: Enhanced Orthodox Interpretation of Quantum Mechanics", *Activitas Nervosa Superior*, 61: 12-17.

Nurgalieva, N. and R. Renner, 2021, "Testing Quantum Theory with Thought Experiments", https://doi.org/10.3929/ethz-b-000475588.

Parsons, C., 1995, "Platonism and Mathematical Intuition in Kurt Gödel's Thought", *Bulletin of Symbolic Logic*, 1(1): 44-74.

Patra, S. and M.C. Kafatos, 2021, "Quantum-like Modelling", *Present Volume.*

Penrose, Roger, 1989, *The Emperor's New Mind: Concerning Computers, Minds and the Laws of Physics*, Oxford: Oxford University Press.

Prabhavananda, S. and C. Isherwood, 1978, *Shankara's Crest-jewel of Discrimination (Vivekachudamani) by Sankaracarya*, Hollywood: Vedanta Press.

Raatikainen, P., 2013, "Gödel's Incompleteness Theorems", [Online] *Stanford Encyclopedia of Philosophy* (accessed on 2020).

Scholem, G., 1941, *Major Trends in Jewish Mysticism*, New York: Schocken Books.

Schubert, Horst, 1972, *Categories*, Berlin/Heidelberg: Springer.

Shear, J. and N. Sims, 2018, "Going Outside the System: Gödel and the 'I-it' Structure of Experience", *Journal of Consciousness Studies*, 25(5-6): 179-201.

Singh, J., 2018, *Pratyabhijñāhṛdayam* (*The Secret of Self-recognition*), Delhi: Motilal Banarsidass.

Stadler, F. and T. Uebel (eds), 2012, *Wissenschaftliche Weltauffassung. Der Wiener Kreis. Reprint of original edition with translations*, Vienna: Springer.

Struppa, D.C., M.C. Kafatos, S. Roy, G. Kato and R.L. Amoroso, 2002, "Category Theory as the Language of Consciousness", *Noetic Journal*, 3(3): 271-81.

Tait, W., 2001, "Gödel's Unpublished Papers on Foundations of Mathematics", *Philosophia Mathematica*, 9(1): 87-126. Reprinted in Tait 2005, pp. 276-313.

———, 2005, *The Provenance of Pure Reason: Essays in the Philosophy of Mathematics and Its History* (*Logic and Computation in Philosophy*), New York: Oxford University Press.

Theise, N.D. and M. Kafatos, 2013a, "Sentience Everywhere: Complexity Theory, Panpsychism and the Role of Sentience in Self-organization of the Universe", *J. Consciousness Exploration Res*, 4: 378-90.

———, 2013b, "Complementarity in Biological Systems: A Complexity View", *Complexity*, 18(6): 11-20.

———, 2016, "Fundamental Awareness: A Framework for Integrating Science, Philosophy and Metaphysics", *Communicative & Integrative Biology*, 9(3): e1155010-19.

Theise, N.D., 2005, "Now You See It, Now You Don't", *Nature*, 435: 1165.

———, 2006, "From the Bottom Up: Complexity, Emergence and Buddhist Metaphysics", *Tricycle*, 15: 24-26.

———, 2009, "Beyond Cell Doctrine: Complexity Theory Informs Alternate Models of the Body for Cross-cultural Dialogue", *Ann N Y Acad Sci.*, 1172: 263-69.

———, 2017, "Everything Only Looks Like a Thing" [Online] https://youtu.be/jaGuSZz-Fzw Science and Non-Duality Conference (1 September 2017).

———, 2019, "Microscopes and Mystics: A Response to Stuart Kauffman's Call to "Re-enchantment", in *Awakening: Exploring Spirituality, Emergent Creativity and Reconciliation*, ed. V. Neufeld Redekop and G. Redekop Neufeld, London: Lexington Books.

Theise, N., 2023, *Notes on Complexity: A Scientific Theory of Connection, Consciouness, and Being*, New York: Spiegel & Grau.

Uebel, T., 2006, "Vienna Circle", [Online] *Stanford Encyclopedia of Philosophy* (accessed on 2 April 2020).

Whitehead, A.N. and B. Russell, 1925 and 1927, *Principia Mathematica*, (1925: vol. 1; 1927: vols 2-3), Cambridge: Cambridge University Press.

———, 1910, *Principia Mathematica*, Cambridge: Cambridge University Press.

Whitehead, A.N., 1925, *Science and the Modern World*, New York: Macmillan.

Wittgenstein, L., 1922, *Tractatus Logico-Philosophicus*, tr. C.K. Ogden, London: Routledge & Kegan Paul.

Wong, H., 1995, *Reflections on Kurt Gödel*, Cambridge, MA: The MIT Press.

10

Complexity Theory and Quantum-like Qualities in Biology

Neil D. Theise

Abstract: Founders of quantum mechanics (QM), in particular Bohr, Pauli and Schrödinger, suggested that just as classical physics was required to encompass the stranger elements of QM, such as complementarity and uncertainty, similar re-evaluations would be necessary for biology. Complexity theory as a way to analyse biological systems provides possible responses to these intuitions, suggesting biological correlates to these concepts from QM reflecting possible "measurement problems" and that separation of subject and object might only be a useful fiction for reductive science even at classical biological scales. Systems biology requires precisely the same accommodations to the nature of "the real" as QM required. In this regard, the QM founders, in particular Bohr, Heisenberg, Pauli and Schrödinger, were several generations ahead of the biologists of the rest of the twentieth century. We argue that direct correlates to QM forms of observational/measurement issues, such as complementarity and uncertainty, can be recognized in such an understanding of complex biologies. Moreover, this analysis suggests that the phase space of "adjacent possibles" for a biological complex system from which one "actual" is selected in each passing moment of the systems evolution is an equivalent to the "collapse of the wave function" of possible quantum realities into an "actual" particle upon observation. Similarly, complexity reveals the contingent nature of boundaries and thus raises interpretive questions regarding the location of a boundary between QM and classical realms sometimes described as the Heisenberg or von Neumann "cut". Whether these properties of biological systems are of a different origin or order of meaning from those seen in QM, or, instead, arise directly from QM level principles as they scale upward into self-organizing biological systems, remains unsettled.

Keywords: Heisenberg, Bohr, Schrödinger, Pauli, uncertainty, complementarity, quantum, entanglement, complexity theory, self-organization, emergence, measurement problem, wave function, holarchy.

Introduction

DESPITE earlier belief that biological systems were "too wet and warm" (Koch and Hepp 2006; Tegmark 2000) for quantum mechanics (QM) to play a significant role, "quantum biology", exploring how quantum effects are essential for the normative functioning of complex biological systems has become a pioneering field of inquiry (Arndt et al. 2009; McFadden and Al-Khalili 2018). Quantum tunnelling is essential for enzyme catalysis (Kohen et al. 1999; Masgrau et al. 2006; Page et al. 1999), may underlie the diversity and sensitivity of olfactory sensations (Turin 1996) and has been invoked for understanding genetic mutations (Löwdin 1963). Avian navigation seems to depend, in part at least, on quantum entanglement (Cai et al. 2010; Gauger et al. 2011; Ritz et al. 2004). Long-lived quantum coherence may play an essential role in photosynthesis (Collini et al. 2010; Engel et al. 2007; Lee et al. 2007).

The founding fathers of quantum physics, were drawn to consider biology, particularly Bohr and Schrödinger, but not, at least at first, to seek out how their newly discovered, strange quantum processes were mechanistically important to biology. Rather, they more generally sought out the possibility that a new kind of biology might be in the offing, as their physics was clearly a new kind of physics, departing, along with Einstein's relativity, from classical Newtonian mechanics. They wrote philosophical speculations regarding how general scientific principles revealed by their efforts might be at play beyond the quantum realm. Niels Bohr's evolving concepts about complementarity at the heart of the Copenhagen Interpretation led him to speculate about a universal complementarity principle of which QM complementarity was merely one specific form (Bohr 1937; McKaughan 2005; Roll-Hansen 2000):

> Thus the existence of life itself would have to be regarded in biology, both as regards the possibilities of observation and of definition, as no more subject to analysis than the existence of the quantum of action in atomic physics. – Bohr 1937

Indeed, inspired by his attendance of Bohr's 1932 lecture on "Light and Life" (Bohr 1933), Max Delbruck turned his attention from QM to biology, specifically virology, coaxed by an intuition that biological complementarity might reveal itself at structures that exist at the seeming boundary between non-living and living things (McKaughan 2005; Roll-Hansen 2000).

Erwin Schrödinger reflected upon the question of "What is Life?", asserting that

> living matter, while not eluding the "laws of physics" as established up to date, is likely to involve "other laws of physics" hitherto unknown, which however, once they have been revealed, will form just as integral a part of science as the former. – Schrödinger 1944

Thus, in his contemplation of the special cases of living systems, Schrödinger was not predicting quantum effects within biological systems to explain their functioning; he was anticipating revolutionarily new concepts that would be added to the current, now foundational QM.

Wolfgang Pauli was also interested in the implications of QM for biology, to some extent focusing on the inseparability of the subject and the object as distilled in the Copenhagen Interpretation. Contrasting with Albert Einstein's perennial disapproval of the imperfections of QM due to the "measurement problem" and the accompanying irreducible "uncertainty", Pauli wrote:

> […] Einstein was regarding as an imperfection of wave mechanics within physics what was an imperfection of physics within life.
>
> – Meier 2001

Science, in views like these, was therefore not a definitive guide to reality, but simply aggregated perceptions that approximate reality, but cannot completely specify it in any single moment:

> The precondition for a description of phenomena independently of the mode of their observation is no longer fulfilled and physical objects acquire a two-valued, or many-valued and therefore symbolic character.
>
> – Pauli 1950 in Enz and von Meyenn 1994

For Pauli, this would include objects that were alive (van Speybroeck 2009).

What was perhaps missing for these QM founders to fully explore biology was a mathematical framework that could codify biological systems. The various mathematical tools that helped the twentieth-century physicists to codify the rules of QM (e.g. wave and matrix mechanics) and relativity (e.g. non-Euclidean geometries, tensor calculus) were insufficient for living systems. It was not until the developments of chaos theory, fractal mathematics and, eventually, complexity theory, that mathematics could attempt to capture the dynamical nature of life. It is through the lens of such mathematical approaches that we can begin to explore the founders' intuited affinities between the seemingly strange implications of QM and those to be discovered, eventually, in biology, across all scales in which biology displays itself, from biomolecules to cells, to tissues, organs and bodies, to systems of living beings in communities, cultures and ecosystems.

A Complexity Primer

Complexity theory concerns the nature of systems of interacting individuals or "agents" which, fulfilling some basic criteria, tend to self-organize into self-perpetuating, adaptive structures (for more extensive reviews (see Theise 2006; Theise and D'Inverno 2004; Theise and Harris 2006; Theise and Kafatos 2013). These structures are referred to as "emergent properties" or, simply, "emergence". The basic criteria include:

- *Numerical sufficiency*: There must be sufficient members interacting to generate emergent properties, though how many is sufficient depends on the nature of the agents involved. A correlate is that the more agents there are, the more complex the emergent properties may become. For example, 25 ants will generate a colony, 250 a more complex one, 2,500 will be yet more complex. Or, a few cells in the right culture conditions can become an organoid, more cells, for example in decellularized tissue or organ matrices, can become tissues or organs. A village is not a city is not a megalopolis. Also, the greater the number, the greater the diversity of interactions leading to potentially greater complexity.
- *Predominance of homeostatic feedback mechanisms*: Negative feedback loops will keep interactions within homeostatic zones that promote sustainability and facilitate healthy adaptation. Positive feedback loops may be present and serve useful purposes in the near term (e.g. a fever in response to infection), but they cannot predominate. If

they do, while there may still be emergent properties, these are likely to be energy expending and self-limited, rather than adaptive (e.g. cancer, economic bubbles, war fevers).

- *All interactions are local*: There is no global sensing. Interactions are local between individual interacting agents. While emergence may appear "designed" from the top-down, it is not; the appearance of design arises from the bottom-up. Even when global sensing is thought to exist (e.g. totalitarian regimes), they are never completely global (e.g. the rise of revolutions that the regimes fail to anticipate or recognize until it is too late). While top-down influences may also occur, the agents at the "top" are as influenced by those at the "bottom" as are the reverse. In fact, there is no actual "top" or "bottom" – complex systems are multinodal webs that are interconnected locally through multidirectional interactions.
- *Limited randomness*: If there is too much randomness in a system, then there is no capacity for sustained self-organization and emergence. If there is too little, then the system behaves more like a machine and loses the capacity to change its organizational structures in response to a changing environment. When the environmental changes exceed the ability of system to adapt, there will be a mass extinction event. This low-level randomness underlies the abilities of a system to explore what the pioneer of complexity theory, Stuart Kauffman, has termed "the adjacent possibles" (Kauffman 1995, 2019), alternate, novel modes of self-organization some of which may, eventually, be important for community adaptation and survival.

The mathematical details of complexity theory are beyond the scope of this review. However, the principles are, as seen above, simple. One corollary worth noting, additionally, derives from the underlying mathematics and it is not directly obvious without these mathematical underpinnings. Mathematically, complex systems are said to lie at the boundary between perfect order and fractal chaos or, as Norman Packard first referred to it: "the edge of chaos" (Packard 1988). Sometimes referred to as a "poised realm" between stability and chaos, it is delicate in its balance, but rich in its creativity and information storage, a mathematical region in which, as author Roger Lewin (1999) described it, "chaos and stability pull in opposite directions".

The boundary itself is, indeed, fractal, the implications of which are important. Because of the randomness in the system, inevitably, given enough time, as the system evolves, there will be a movement out of that zone of criticality and there will be a population collapse, a mass extinction event. In other words, precisely those conditions that make a system adaptive and "alive" are those that will eventually lead it to fall into a too rigid form of order or into chaos, resulting in an inability to adapt, i.e. death.

With these concepts and the underlying mathematics that they summarize, one can begin to explore how there are, as some of the foundational thinkers of QM intuited, parallels of a non-mechanistic biology with "strange" characteristics that are clear, yet still not widely appreciated let alone accepted in contemporary biology practice. However, there is clearly a generational shift taking place regarding how biological systems develop and behave, indeed how they interrelate across scales of organization. This transition holds out great promise. We will now consider biological equivalents of "the measurement problem", uncertainty, complementarity and superposition.

Measurement Problems and Cellular Uncertainty

Measurement problems in biology are found at all levels of scale, but the cell is a robust entry point for their discussion. Cell doctrine, the foundational theory of what we know as "Western" biology and medicine, holds that cells are the fundamental building blocks of living things, irreducible "atoms" of Greek philosophy, made visible by the invention of the microscope. Prior to the capacity to examine tissues at the microscopic level, it was an open philosophical debate as to whether bodies were comprised of endlessly divisible fluids or of some ultimately indivisible "atom" (Harris 2000). With microscopes and the visualization of cell walls (plants) and cell membranes (non-plants), the debate was settled: the walls/membranes defined what appeared to be empty boxes, which cannot, of course, be subdivided into smaller boxes. Since these structures appeared empty, like the cells of monks or prisoners, that name was applied and "cell doctrine" was born. As years would pass and chemical stains were developed to reveal these empty interiors, the "furniture" was filled in – nuclei and other organelles – but the name and concept remained.

Through the end of the millennium, there was some bias among cell biologists that cell behaviours and differentiative fate paths were largely deterministic (Morrison and Weissman 1994), based on concepts that epigenetic changes and gene activation/repression patterns were largely, if not always, irreversible. However, the development of cloning and studies in stem-cell plasticity, some demonstrations of which won the 2012 Nobel Prize, overturned those notions (Daley 2012). One culminating demonstration of adult cell plasticity came in 2001 with multiorgan plasticity deriving from a single, clonally explanted bone marrow cell (Krause et al. 2001). Commentary on these and other results recognized a biological variation of Heisenberg's uncertainty principle: that any attempt to observe a cell seemed likely to alter the nature of the cell at the time of observation (Potten and Loeffler 1990; Theise 2003, 2006; Theise and Harris 2006; Theise and Krause 2001, 2002).

The foundations of this argument lay in the exquisite sensitivity of a cell to any form of manipulation or identification.

Just as Heisenberg's thought experiments regarding the impossibility of measuring both position and momentum in a particular dimension of a particle, actual experimental data was accumulating that cells could not be isolated and probed for "what type of cell it is"; initially this was thought to be merely analogy to Heisenberg: "cellular uncertainty" (Potten and Loeffler 1990; Theise 2003, 2006; Theise and Harris 2006; Theise and Krause 2001, 2002).

Indeed, Richard Lewontin (2000) had stated at the time, "the inside and the outside co-determine the cell". The cell was becoming recognized as having no inherent identity or behaviour independent of the environment in which it finds itself. Any experimental procedure which isolated a cell for study, within the bounds of possibility at that time, at least, would necessarily disturb that environment and therefore, potentially, lead to changes in the nature of the cell's functions or even its differentiative fates (Theise 2006; Theise and Harris 2006). Whether the simplest act of venipuncture to isolate cells from the blood or enzymatic digestion and mechanical dissociation to derive them from tissues, there would be no way to avoid forms of interaction that would lead to alterations in gene expression and, thus, changes in the nature of the cell.

As with Heisenberg's initial discussions of uncertainty, the question for cellular uncertainty was, at first, whether this was merely a limit of current experimental methodologies or a fundamental principle. For Heisenberg: were the limits of uncertainty in QM merely technical?

The answer, ultimately, was "no". Quantum uncertainty reflected not an insufficiently sensitive technology, but a fundamental quality of existence. At first, cellular uncertainty also seemed merely analogous to Heisenberg's, but was, indeed, merely a difficult technological problem to solve. Could there be, for example, at least theoretically, a "perfect MRI machine" that could analyse the precise location and activity of every molecule in a cell without disturbing it, so that the cell could be described in full without interference (Potten and Loeffler 1990)? As was true for Heisenberg, however, the limitation turns out to not be merely technical, but inherent in the nature of biological reality.

Complexity theory would reveal a rationale for this position, but to determine that complexity principles apply, one more aspect of cell behaviour must be explored: whether cells are deterministic or stochastic in their behaviours (Kurakin 2005a, b; Theise 2006; Theise and Harris 2006). Indeed, while cell plasticity research progressed at the turn of the millennium, parallel attention was paid to the nature of gene regulation: accumulating evidence showed that the determinative gene restrictions that underlay the assumption of deterministic cell fates could all be flexibly changed through epigenetic modifications (Bruniquel and Schwartz 2003; Collas 1998, 2003; Cuthbert et al. 2004; Davis et al. 1987; Shi et al. 2004; Wang et al. 2004; Xie et al. 2004; summarized in Theise and Harris 2006). No gene activation or restriction was rigid and permanent. Cells had ample ways to remodel gene expression and the nature of all that the cell was and could do seemed completely malleable. Indeed, the 2012 Nobel prizes to John Gurdon for cloning and Shinya Yamanaka for induced pleuripotent stem cell technology were recognitions precisely of this flexibility (Daley 2012).

Combining this undermining of irreversible gene expression with the experiment-induced uncertainty described above, one arrives at the necessity that, indeed, determinism is not the rule. Determinism might have been a useful reductionist tool for examining cell behaviours in the laboratory, but for intact tissues and organisms, cell behaviours depend on whether the tissue or organism is physiologically normal or stressed by injury or disease. Likewise, if the cell is removed from a tissue or body for study, its nature is dependent on the mode of isolation and the experimental conditions under which it is examined. These concepts were the death of cellular determinism.

Finally, then, one may say that cells do, indeed, fulfil all the criteria for being a complex system: numbers and diversity of cells and their interactions governed generally by homeostatic feedbacks, without a globally sensing single cell or cell clusters and containing the limited randomness indicated by epigenetic/ genetic plasticity. Thus, like any complex system, while one could predict the existence of emergent properties that would define cells' natures, those precise natures could never be predicted with confidence. Cellular uncertainty is inherent, not contingent on any possible future technological progress.

A Generalized Biological Uncertainty

Approaching biological entities through the lens of complexity theory is sufficient to move from the association from cellular uncertainty as a metaphor to a direct analogy. At a large scale, seemingly self-inherent structures, like a colony of ants, a murmuration of starlings, a baitball of fish, are easily seen to not be *things* in and of themselves, but *phenomena* arising from smaller things, the ant/fish/bird bodies that comprise them. It depends on the scale of observation. Likewise, at a still coarse level of examination, the bodies themselves appear to be things, though examination at the microscopic level reveals them to be phenomena arising from smaller things, the cells that comprise them.

Do cells have a self-inherent nature, as Cell Doctrine suggests? Obviously, from these points of view, they do not (Theise 2005). Cells at the nanoscopic level dissolve, losing their "thingness", to be seen clearly as molecules (macromolecules, small molecules) and atoms/ions afloat in aqueous solution. These atoms and molecules also fulfil all those complexity criteria, the numbers, the homeostatic feedbacks and the local interactivity; at this level of scale, some of the quenched disorder arises from how Brownian motion plays an unavoidable role in molecular movements and energies (Theise and Harris 2006).[1]

---

[1] In this way, somewhat surprisingly, perhaps, the least honoured →

The importance of Brownian motion in biological systems was introduced by Toshio Yanagida (Yanagida et al. 2000) examining the role of ATP in single pairs of actin and myosin filaments. The dogma had been that the binding of ATP to the myosin filament and the bending of that elbow with its release of energy was sufficient to explain the stepwise motion of the myosin along the actin. The aggregate effect of that in the vast numbers of such pairs within a muscle cell (myocyte) would be contraction of the cell and, in turn, muscular contraction. Yanagida's studies demonstrated however that the energy of movement was provided by the inescapable Brownian motion induced by the kinetic energy of the water molecules at normal body temperature. The ATP did not propel the movement, it "quenched the disorder" into directional movement. This kind of phenomenon is now recognized in the functions of many different so-called "molecular motors", sufficiently so to say that cells are emergent properties arising from self-organizing biomolecules in water[2] (Ishii et al. 2004; Yanagida et al. 2007; Yanagida and Ishii 2017).

In turn, biomolecules (like all molecules) are comprised of self-organizing atoms, with the inherent constrained stochasticity of chemical interactions. In turn, atoms are composed of self-organizing subatomic particles that are subject to the constrained

← paper of Einstein's "Annus Mirabilus", on Brownian motion, now takes on fundamental import for the understanding of biology in a way not much appreciated for most of the first century of its existence.

[2] Moreover, surprisingly, it suggests that the energy derived from food is not to always provide the energy of our physiology. At least in part, it is the Brownian motion of our molecules in their aqueous environment that provides the energy for physiologic processes. Thus, also, a reason for the careful regulation of body temperature in complex organisms is revealed: too much heat and the Brownian motion cannot be quenched, too little and it is insufficient.

stochasticity of QM itself. Likewise, casting our gazes upward, we see that communities of bodies self-organize into larger scale structures – the colonies and flocks and baitballs already mentioned, or into local ecosystems, or into the composite global ecosystem of James Lovelock's and Lynn Margulis' Gaia hypothesis (Lovelock 2003; Margulis 1993).

Thus, in any biological system, from the everyday scale down through microscopic, nanoscopic and quantum scales of existence, there is no single category of *thing* which has inherent existence in any biological system; all biological structures and properties that have an appearance of inherent existence at one level of scale are clearly merely phenomena which arise from interactions of lower scale agents (Theise and Kafatos 2013). Their natures always manifest only at a specific, selected observational perspective. In turn, these appearances inescapably depend on the measurement issues familiar at the quantum level.

For our purposes, there are no biological systems, or parts thereof, that have inherent, consistently determined, properties. Emergent self-organization – adaptive, self-sustaining, but prone to inevitable collapses – governs all such systems across all scales. Therefore, biological uncertainty, like Heisenberg's uncertainty, is inherent, not merely a technological limitation.

Biological Complementarity and Beyond

This dependence on scale for the appearance of a biological entity as a thing vs a phenomenon arising from smaller things, explicitly invokes a "complementarity" that is not dissimilar to that which pertains at the quantum level (Theise 2005; Theise and Kafatos 2013). On the other side of scales, for large objects, Kafatos and Nadeau (2000) showed complementarity also applies to astronomical scales, all the way to the universe itself. No single description of an entity/process captures the entirety of the reality: particles vs waves, thing vs phenomena. There is no element of a biological system that does not partake of the incompleteness[3] of any specific point of view or method of interrogation of the system, very much in keeping with the views of Bohr and Pauli and, perhaps, Schrödinger's, as quoted above. Biological complementarity arises from the nature of biological beings as self-organizing systems and reflects necessary limitations of descriptions of their features/behaviours that are dependent on the time, technique and scale of observation.

Biological complementarity indicates

> that no single technique or perspective allows comprehensive viewing of all of a biological entity's complete qualities and behaviours; instead, complementary perspectives, necessarily and irrevocably excluding all others at the moment an experimental approach is selected, would be necessary to understand the whole. Systems biology and complexity theory reveal that, as in the quantum realm, experimental observations themselves limit our capacity to understand a biological system completely because of scale-dependent "horizons of knowledge" [...]. Specifically, observational selection is inherently, irreducibly coupled to observed biological systems as in the quantum realm. These nested systems, beginning with biomolecules in aqueous solution all the way up to the global ecosystem itself, are understood as a seamless whole operating simultaneously and complementarily at various levels.
>
> – Theise and Kafatos 2013: 11

This correlates with Pauli's prediction that some objects would have a "many valued" set of complementary observable properties, reflecting every possible scale of observation from the Gaian level through to the quantum realm, a more elaborate situation than seen in the frequently dual complementarities at the QM level such as particle/wave duality. The "horizons of knowledge" delineate the contingent boundaries between

---

[3] Perhaps reflective of Gödelian incompleteness; see this volume, Theise, Kato and Kafatos.

different scalar perspectives (Kafatos 2009; Kafatos and Nadeau 2000; Kafatos and Nassikas 2011; Nadeau and Kafatos 1999). Continuing:

> This selection of an observational stance is inseparable from descriptions of biology in accordance with views of thinkers such as von Neumann, Wigner and Stapp that even at levels of scale governed by classical physics, at biological scales, observational choice remains inextricably woven into the establishment, in the observational moment, of the present conditions of existence. – Theise and Kafatos 2013

These conceptual shifts are not merely theoretical or metaphorical. They should inform the interpretations of otherwise reductive research data. The study of cells isolated from a body in vitro are not the same cells as they were inside the body: an altered environment means an altered cell. The cell membrane is not an unchanging structure that keeps the inside separate from the outside. Far from it. And as we have already noted, the "cell" is also, complementarily, self-organized atoms and molecules which are necessarily in dynamic interplay with the atoms and molecules of whichever environment they find themselves in, dissolving the notion of a boundary between them. (Theise 2005).

Similarly, many diseases are now understood to reflect dynamic changes between a host organism and its microbiome. In one sense, the microbiome is decidedly "outside" the body of the host organism. But in other ways, they are just a single colony of cells interacting with each other coequally, even though they are vastly distant in terms of where they sit on the evolutionary tree. Concepts of symbiosis from Lynn Margulis are central to this aspect of biological behaviours (Margulis 1981; Sagan 2021). Contemporary understandings of physiology and pathobiology are being forced, implicitly, to encounter these complementarities, though explicit recognition of them is only just starting to emerge.

Similar views have been explored from a variety of theoretical perspectives. In developmental systems theory, Susan Oyama (2000), relates the intimacy of environment and biological form reflecting these same principles. Howard Pattee stated that "biological systems need both (rate dependent) structural and (rate independent) informational concepts for their description, suggesting that biological structures and information were an aspect of biological complementarity" (Pattee 1979a, b; Umerez 2001). Kafatos and Nadeau (2000) demonstrate that most, perhaps all, fields of study depend on complementarity frameworks and must therefore be foundational to the universe, not just biology. Similar concepts arise easily by relating biological networks of interacting agents to Markov blankets (Kirchhoff et al. 2018). Material engagement theory likewise explores such concepts (Malafouris 2004). Thus, this complex systems theory formulation of biological complementarity may, indeed, itself, be in complementarity with these adjacent views.

Scale/Perspective Dependence of Boundaries: Heisenberg's Cut

Once one views all biological structures as contingent phenomena arising from interactions at smaller scales, definitions of boundaries likewise then become contingent. At the everyday scale, we are bounded by our skin. At the cellular scale, our bodies are understood as communities of cells, the majority of which (~ 50 per cent) do not carry "our own" DNA, but are comprised of microorganisms, mostly bacteria, that make up our microbiomes, without which we cannot exist as living, human beings (Berg et al. 2020). At this level of scale, our boundary extends significantly beyond our skin, through shedding of our skin cells from the surface (much of the "dust" of any room one inhabits) and depositing bacteria on any surface (door knob, keyboard, eating utensil, etc.) or other living thing (spouse, child, pet, etc.) that we touch. Indeed, it is now understood that cohabitating humans and their pets comprise one single, unified microbiome that encompasses several large islands of otherwise distinct human and associated pet cells forming *holobionts* (Simon et al. 2019). At the cellular level, our boundaries are as wide as our physical environment and the other living beings with whom we share those spaces.

At the molecular level our boundaries are wider still. The most ready example is how we breathe out CO_2 which the planetary plant mass absorbs, in turn producing the oxygen for us to breathe. At the molecular level, our boundaries encompass the entire biomass of the planet. At the atomic level, there is no atom in our bodies that we have not breathed, drunk, or eaten from the planet; thus, while may think of ourselves as separate entities on the planetary rock that we call Earth, it is equally valid that we are the planet's atoms which have taken 3½ billion years to self-organize into beings that think they are separate. So, at the atomic level, our boundaries are as wide as the entire mass, organic *and* inorganic of the planet itself (as per Lovelock and Margulis). Finally, at the quantum level, where quantum non-locality reveals itself, we find our boundaries extending to the quantum limits of the entire universe.

If boundaries are scale/perspective dependent, then an answer to the puzzle of the Heisenberg–von Neumann cut" (Atmanspacher 1997; Stapp 2017) becomes apparent. This "cut" is the hypothetical boundary between infinitesimal levels of scale at which quantum events occur and the larger scales where classical physics and the separation of subject (experimenter) and object (e.g. Schrödinger's cat) occur. Von Neumann went from this hypothetical situation to ask where in the human body this cut *actually* exists, where the interface between physical phenomena involved in perception interface with how the mind manifests that perception (Narasimhan et al. 2019). Either way, the cut is understood as a boundary. But if there is no reified, inherent boundary between human subject and object (Schrödinger and his cat), if all boundaries, as we have demonstrated, are contingent, there can be no fixed "cut", from Heisenberg's view or von Neumann's.

Wave Functions and Kauffman's "Adjacent Possibles"

Much discussion and debate surrounds the concept of the "collapse of the wave function" upon observation of a quantum system. Depending on the interpretation of QM, this collapse may be an actual event or merely a mathematical expression of a result, but unreflective of an actual underlying process. Either way, there seems to be an analogous aspect of biological systems.

Stuart Kauffman coined the term "adjacent possibles" for the range of *possible* changes that *might* arise within a complex system's emergent properties as a result of the quenched disorder of the system (Kauffman 1995, 2019). The low level random events in the system may give rise to changes in emergent properties that are neutral in regard to the environment, adaptive or destructive. Kauffman considered these changes to represent Darwin's "preadaptations" or Gould's "exaptations", alterations that precede the environmental changes that set the stage for the natural selection between them and other, non-adaptive changes which fail to contribute to evolutionary development (Gould and Vrba 1982; Ridley 2004).

The adjacent possibles thus generate a kind of phase space around any current complex system. Every biological system in every single instant, explores a wide (though not infinite) array of "adjacent possible" changes to its emergent properties. It is only in the arrival of the next moment and the next and the next, that the range of adjacent possibles becomes limited to the *actual* possible. We propose that, in some fashion, this actual possible derives from the adjacent possibles in the way that, in "collapse of the wave function", the actual particle with its actual properties is recognized. In the quantum realm, it is the instance of observation that leads to collapse. In the complex realm, it is with each arrival of the present moment that collapse of the adjacent possibles into the actual occurs.

Summary and Conclusions

Using complexity theory as a way to analyse biological systems provides possible responses to questions and intuitions of many of the founding generations of QM that biology required revisions that would include variations of the measurement problem and, ultimately, recognition that subject–object separation was only a useful fiction for reductive science. Their intuitions pointed to what we now see arriving from the opposite approach to reductivism; systems biology requires precisely the same accommodations to the nature of "the real" as QM required. In this regard, the QM founders, in particular Bohr, Pauli and Schrödinger, were several generations ahead of the biologists of the rest of the twentieth century. It is in this new century that the contingent and complex natures of biological systems are only starting to be appreciated.

We argue that direct correlates to QM types of observational/ measurement issues, such as complementarity and uncertainty, can be recognized in such an understanding of complex biologies. Moreover, this analysis can provide biological correlates to such recognizable puzzles as the "collapse of the wave function" and the nature of the Heisenberg–von Neumann "cut".

Whether these properties of biological systems are of a different origin or order of meaning from those seen in QM, or, instead, arise directly from QM level effects as they scale upward into self-organizing biological systems, remains unclear. The work of the coming generations is to assimilate these concepts into "orthodox" biology, much in the way that the work of assimilating QM into classical physics continues to the present day. The assimilation is made ever more urgent by the exponentially growing current, very real threats of pandemics, ecosystem level toxicities, and mass extinctions of large portions of the global ecosystem.

The way out of these troubles depends on this more creative and robust understanding of biology as hierarchies – or "holarchies", as Arthur Koestler (1967) more precisely labelled them – of systems that are not merely predictable machines, but "wholes" that are magnificently creative and truly and unpredictably greater than the sum of their parts. While mass extinctions, as noted, are inherent in every complex system(s), the optimistic note is to be found in that exquisite sensitivity to conditions in the poised realm of complexity. It is within our power to find the interventions that will allow us to transcend the already demonstrable smaller extinctions, into a more sustainable, creative, adaptive future, for every human and for the entire living world.

References

Arndt, M., T. Juffmann and V. Bedral, 2009, "Quantum Physics Meets Biology", *HFSP Journal*, 3(6): 386-400.

Atmanspacher, H., 1997, "Cartesian Cut, Heisenberg Cut and the Concept of Complexity", *World Futures*, 49(3-4): 333-55.

Berg, G., D. Rybakova, D. Fischer, T. Cernava, M-C., Champomier Vergès, T. Charles, X. Chen, L. Cocolin, K. Eversole, G.H. Corral, M. Kazou, L. Kinkel, L. Lange, N. Lima, A. Loy, J.A. MacKlin, E. Maguin, T. Mauchline and M. Schloter, 2020, "Microbiome Definition Re-visited: Old Concepts and New Challenges", *Microbiome*, 8(1): 103.

Bohr N., 1933, "Light and Life", *Nature*, 133: 421-23 (pt 1), 457-59 (pt 2).

———, 1937, "Causality and Complementarity", *Philos Sci*, 4: 289-98.

Bruniquel, D. and R.H. Schwartz, 2003, "Selective, Stable Demethylation of the Interleukin-2 Gene Enhances Transcription by an Active Process", *Nat Immunol*, 4: 235-40.

Cai, J., G.G. Guerreschi and H.J. Briegel, 2010, "Quantum Control and Entanglement in a Chemical Compass", *Phys Rev Lett*, 104: 220502.

Collas, P., 1998, "Cytoplasmic Control of Nuclear Assembly", *Reprod Fertil Dev*, 10: 581-92.

———, 2003, "Nuclear Reprogramming in Cell-free Extracts", *Philos Trans R Soc Lond B Biol Sci*, 358: 1389-95.

Collini, E., C.Y. Wong, K.E. Wilk, P.M. Curmi, P. Brumer and G.D. Scholes, 2010, "Coherently Wired Light-harvesting in Photosynthetic Marine Algae at Ambient Temperature", *Nature*, 463: 644-47.

Cuthbert, G.L., S. Daujat, A.W. Snowden, E. Erdjument-Bromage, T. Hagiwara, T. Yamada, R. Schneider, P.D. Gregory, P. Tempst, A.J. Bannister and T. Kouzarides, 2004, "Histone Deimination Antagonizes Arginine Methylation", *Cell*, 118: 545-53.

Daley, G.Q., 2012, "Cellular Alchemy and the Golden Age of Reprogramming", *Cell*, 151: 1151-54.

Davis, R.L., H. Weintraub and A.B. Lassar, 1987, "Expression of a Single Transfected cDNA Converts Fibroblasts to Myoblasts", *Cell*, 51: 987-1000.

Engel, G.S., T.R. Calhoun, E.L. Read, T.K. Ahn, T. Mancal, Y.C. Cheng, R.E. Blankenship and G.R. Fleming, 2007, "Evidence for Wavelike Energy Transfer through Quantum Coherence in Photosynthetic Systems", *Nature*, 446: 782-86.

Enz, C.P. and K. von Meyenn (eds), 1994, *Wolfgang Pauli: Writings on Physics and Philosophy*, Berlin: Springer.

Gauger, E.M., E. Rieper, J.J.L. Morton, S.C. Benjamin and V. Vedral, 2011, "Sustained Quantum Coherence and Entanglement in the Avian Compass", *Phys Rev Lett*, 106: 040503.

Gould S.J. and E.S. Vrba, 1982, "Exaptation: A Missing Term in the Science of Form", *Paleobiology*, 8: 4-15.

Harris, H., 2000, *The Birth of the Cell*, New Haven, CT: Yale University Press.

Ishii, Y., M. Nishiyama and T. Yanagida, 2004, "Mechano-chemical

Coupling of Molecular Motors Revealed by Single Molecule Measurements", *Curr Protein Peptide Sci*, 5: 81-87.

Kafatos, M. and R. Nadeau, 2000, *The Conscious Universe: Parts and Wholes in Physical Reality*, New York: Springer.

Kafatos, M. and A.A. Nassikas, 2011, "Retrocausation, Minimum Contradictions and Non-locality", in *Quantum Retrocausation: Theory and Experiment*, vol. 1408; ed. D.P. Sheehan, AIP Conference Proceedings; pp. 291-96, Maryland: American Institute of Physics,

Kafatos, M., 2009, "Cosmos and Quantum: Frontiers for the Future". *J Cosmol*, 3: 511-28.

Kauffman, S.A., 1995, *At Home in the Universe: The Search for Laws of Self-Organization and Complexity*, New York: Oxford University Press.

———, 2019, *A World Beyond Physics*, New York: Oxford University Press.

Kirchhoff, M., T. Parr, E. Palacios, K. Friston and J. Kiverstein, 2018, "The Markov Blankets of Life: Autonomy, Active Inference and the Free Energy Principle", *J.R. Soc. Interface*, 15: 20170792.

Koch, C. and K. Hepp, 2006, "Quantum Mechanics in the Brain", *Nature*, 440: 611.

Koestler, A., 1967, *The Ghost in the Machine*, New York: Macmillan.

Kohen, A., R. Cannio, S. Bartolucci and J.P. Klinman, 1999, "Enzyme Dynamics and Hydrogen Tunneling in a Thermophilic Alcohol Dehydrogenase", *Nature*, 399: 496-99.

Krause, D.S., N.D. Theise, M.I. Collector, O. Henegariu, S. Hwang, R. Gardner, S. Neutzel and S.J. Sharkis, 2001, "Multi-organ, Multi-lineage Engraftment by a Single Bone Marrow-derived Stem Cell", *Cell*, 105: 369-77.

Kurakin, A., 2005a, "Self-organization vs Watchmaker: Stochastic Gene Expression and Cell Differentiation, *Dev Genes Evol*, 215: 46-52.

———, 2005b, "Self-organization versus Watchmaker: Stochastic Dynamics of Cellular Organization", *Biol Chem*, 386: 247-54.

Lee, H., Y.C. Cheng and G.R. Fleming, 2007, "Coherence Dynamics in Photosynthesis: Protein Protection of Excitonic Coherence", *Science*, 316: 1462-65.

Lewin, R., 1999, *Complexity: Life at the Edge of Chaos*, Chicago: University of Chicago Press.

Lewontin, R., 2000, "It Ain't Necessarily So: The Dream of the Human Genome and Other Illusions", *New York Review of Books*, New York.

Lovelock, J., 2003, "Gaia: The Living Earth", *Nature*, 426: 769-70.

Löwdin, P.O., 1963, "Proton Tunneling in DNA and Its Biological Implications", *Rev Mod Phys*, 35: 724-32.

Malafouris, L., 2004, "The Cognitive Basis of Material Engagement: Where Brain, Body and Culture Conflate", in *Rethinking Materiality: The Engagement of Mind with the Material World*, ed. E. DeMarrais, C. Gosden and C. Renfrew, pp. 53-62, Cambridge: McDonald Institute Monographs.

Margulis, L., 1981, *Symbiosis in Cell Evolution*, San Francisco, CA: Freeman, W.H.

———, 1993, "Gaia in Science", *Science* 259: 745.

Masgrau, L., A. Roujeinikova, L.O. Johannissen, P. Hothi, J. Basran, K.E. Ranaghan, A.J. Mulholland, M.J. Sutcliffe, N.S. Scrutton and D. Leys, 2006, "Atomic Description of an Enzyme Reaction Dominated by Proton Tunneling", *Science*, 312: 237-41.

McFadden, J. and J. Al-Khalili, 2018, "The Origins of Quantum Biology", *Proc Royal Soc A*, 474: 1-13.

McKaughan, D.J., 2005, "The Influence of Niels Bohr on Max Delbruck: Revisiting the Hopes Inspired by "Light and Life", *Isis*, 96: 507-29.

Meier, C.A. (ed.), 2001, *Atom and Archetype: The Pauli/Jung Letters, 1932-58*, Princeton, NJ: Princeton University Press.

Morrison, S.J. and I.L. Weissman, 1994, "The Long-term Repopulating Subset of Hematopoietic Stem Cells Is Deterministic and Isolatable by Phenotype", *Immunity*, 1: 661-73.

Nadeau, R. and M. Kafatos, 1999, *The Non-Local Universe: The New Physics and Matters of the Mind*, Oxford: Oxford University Press.

Narasimhan, A., D. Chopra and M.C. Kafatos, 2019, "The Nature of the Heisenberg–von Neumann Cut: Enhanced Orthodox Interpretation of Quantum Mechanics", *Activitas Nervosa Superior*, 61: 12-17.

Oyama, S., 2000, *The Ontogeny of Information: Developmental Systems and Evolution*, 2nd edn, Durham, NC: Duke University Press.

Packard, N.H., 1988, "Adapatation Toward the Edge of Chaos", in *Dynamic Patterns in Complex Systems*, ed. J.A.S. Kelso, AI J. Mandell, and M.F. Shlesinger, pp. 293-301, Singapore: World Scientific.

Page, C.C., C.C. Moser, X. Chen and P.L. Dutton, 1999, "Natural Engineering Principles of Electron Tunnelling in Biological Oxidation-reduction", *Nature*, 402: 47-52.

Pattee, H.H., 1979a, "The Complementarity Principle and the Origin of Macromolecular Information", *Biosystems*, 11: 217-26.

———, 1979b, "Complementarity vs Reduction as Explanation of Biological Complexity", *Am J Physiol*, 236: R241-R246.

Pauli, W., 1994, *Writings on Physics and Philosophy*, ed. C.P. Enz and K. von Meyenn, Berlin: Springer.

Potten, C.S. and M. Loeffler, 1990, "Stem Cells: Attributes, Cycles, Spirals, Pitfalls and Uncertainties – Lessons for and from the Crypt", *Development*, 110: 1001-20.

Ridley, M., 2004, *Evolution*, Hoboken, NJ: Wiley-Blackwell.

Ritz, T., P. Thalau, J.B. Phillips, R. Wiltschko and W. Wiltschko, 2004, "Resonance Effects Indicate a Radical-pair Mechanism for Avian Magnetic Compass", *Nature*, 429: 177-80.

Roll-Hansen, N., 2000, "The Application of Complementarity to Biology: From Niels Bohr to Max Delbruck", *Hist Stud Phys Biol Sci*, 30: 417-42.

Sagan, D., 2021, "From Empedocles to Symbiogenetics: Lynn Margulis's Revolutionary Influence on Evolutionary Biology", *Biosystems*, 204: 104386.

Schrödinger, E., 1944, *What Is Life?: The Physical Aspects of the Living Cell*, Cambridge: Cambridge University Press.

Shi, Y., F. Lan, C. Matson, P. Mulligan, J.R. Whetstine, P.A. Cole, P.A. Casero and Y. Shi, 2004, "Histone Demethylation Mediated by the Nuclear Amine Oxidase Homolog LSD1", *Cell*, 119: 941-53.

Simon, J.C., J.R. Marchesi, C. Mougel and M.A. Selosse, 2019, "Host-microbiota Interactions: From Holobiont Theory to Analysis", *Microbiome*, 7: 5.

van Speybroeck, L., 2009, "Exploring Pauli's (Quantum) View on Science and Biology", in *Recasting Reality: Wolfgang Pauli's Philosophical Ideas and Contemporary Science*, ed. H. Atmanspacher H. Primas, Berlin/Heidelberg: Springer.

Stapp, H. , 2017, *Quantum Theory and Free Will*, Heidelberg: Springer.

Tegmark, M., 2000, "Importance of Quantum Decoherence in Brain Processes", *Phys Rev E*, 61: 4194-4206.

Theise, N.D., 2003, "Stem Cell Research: Elephants in the Room", *Mayo Clinic Proc*, 78: 1004.

———, 2005, "Now You See It, Now You Don't", *Nature*, 435: 1165.

———, 2006, "Implications of 'Post-modern Biology' for Pathology: The Cell Doctrine", *Lab Invest*, 86: 335-e44.

Theise, N.D. and M. D'Inverno, 2004, "Understanding Cell Lineages as Complex Adaptive Systems", *Blood Cells Mol Dis*, 32: 17-20.

Theise, N.D. and R. Harris, 2006, "Postmodern Biology: (Adult) (Stem) Cells Are Plastic, Stochastic, Complex and Uncertain", *Handb Exp Pharmacol*, 174: 389-408.

Theise, N.D. and M. Kafatos, 2013, "Complementarity in Biological Systems", *Complexity*, 18: 11-20.

Theise, N.D. and D.S. Krause, 2001, "Suggestions for a New Paradigm of Cell Differentiative Potential", *Blood Cells Mol Dis*, 27: 625-31.

———, 2002, "Toward a New Paradigm of Cell Plasticity", *Leukemia*, 16: 542-48.

Turin, L., 1996, "A Spectroscopic Mechanism for Primary Olfactory Reception", *Chem Senses*, 21: 773-91.

Umerez, J., 2001, "Howard Pattee's Theoretical Biology: A Radical Epistemological Stance to Approach Life, Evolution and Complexity", *Biosystems*, 60: 159-77.

Wang, Y., J. Wysocka, J. Sayegh, Y.H. Lee, J.R. Perlin, L. Leonelli, L.S. Sonbuchner, C.H. McDonald, R.G. Cook, Y. Dou, R.G. Roeder, S. Clarke, M.R. Stallcup, C.D. Allis and S.A. Coonrod, 2004, "Human PAD4 Regulates Histone Arginine Methylation Levels via Demethylimination", *Science*, 306: 279-83.

Xie, H., M. Ye, R. Feng and T. Graf, 2004, "Stepwise Reprogramming of B Cells into Macrophages", *Cell*, 117: 663-76.

Yanagida, T. and Y. Ishii, 2017, "Single Molecule Detection, Thermal Fluctuation and Life", *Proc Jpn Acad Ser B Phys Biol Sci*, 93: 51-63.

Yanagida, T., K. Kitamura, H. Tanaka, A. Hikikoshi Iwane and S. Esaki, 2000, "Single Molecule Analysis of the Actomyosin Motor", *Curr Opin Cell Biol*, 12: 20-25.

Yanagida, T., M. Ueda, T. Murata, S. Esaki and Y. Ishii, 2007, "Brownian Motion, Fluctuation and Life", *Biosystems*, 88: 228-42.

11

Biologists Ponder: Omnipresent Consciousness?

Implications for Animal Mind, Human–Animal Relationships and Animal Well-Being

Carolyn A. Ristau
Eric G. Strauss

Abstract: As biologists, we cannot claim to fully understand the proposed quantum basis of consciousness. We can, however, ponder the implications of assuming a universal consciousness. How might animal research be changed? We suggest that by assuming the likelihood of conscious entities, we would expand the breadth and depth of questions asked about animal mind. Experimental design would be more sensitive; objective criteria for results would still be required. Humans, assuming that animals are conscious, have feelings, suffer, experience delight and are capable of complex relationships with humans and other animals, would be moved to treat the animals with greater compassion and respect. Similarly, legislative policies would change to take account of these possibilities.

But daunting questions remain: What is/is not conscious?

What are characteristics of the "receptacles" of consciousness, of the variety of consciousnesses?

Keywords: Conversation, consciousness, animal mind, human–animal relationship, Carolyn Ristau, Cognitive Ethology, Griffin.

Introduction

AS BIOLOGISTS, we cannot claim to fully understand the proposed quantum basis of consciousness. We can, however, ponder the implications of assuming a universal consciousness. How might research concerning animals be changed? How might our relationships with animals be altered and what different policies and legislation might we enact? What assumptions would underlie and guide those matters?

We should note that our assumptions about universal consciousness are not the same as those proposed by the Copenhagen Interpretation of quantum mechanics (QM) as discussed in this volume. Copenhagen Interpretation is an approach more sympathetic to Eastern philosophical views of a "oneness", of consciousness underlying all that exists. Our stance derives from a view that is rooted in non-spiritual, indeed atheistic, approaches to the study of the biological world. We could term it more "Western", notwithstanding the fact that there are many Eastern scientists who would follow our approach. Our stance does not preclude religious or spiritual beliefs held by a scientist; we simply do not utilize such in our biological explanations. There may well come a time when biologists will be more accepting of the Copenhagen Interpretation and utilize those principles in their scientific endeavours.

BRIEF HISTORY OF THE STUDY OF ANIMAL CONSCIOUSNESS UNIQUE, LANGUAGE-USING HUMANS

First, however, we think it useful to ask how scientists and philosophers have been considering the issue of consciousness over the centuries, as it pertains to other beings, in particular non-human animals. Although we cannot truly know what another human is thinking or feeling, which is a solipsistic philosophical attitude, we do assume that other humans, being like us, are conscious. They sense, they reason, they experience emotions. However, we have long considered ourselves to be unique and superior beings, distinct from the non-human, the animals. Our use of language has been considered a distinguishing feature of humankind, by which we create words or symbolic representations of the internal and external world, are assisted in our thinking, communicate to each other and can, by means of grammatical rules, create an infinite number of communications or sentences. As a means to communicate thoughts and feelings, language could also help provide supportive evidence of the consciousness of a being other than oneself.

What of the non-human animals? Concerns about *animal* mental abilities have existed over the centuries, considered by numerous philosophers, including Aristotle, Descartes and many contemporary philosophers of mind. To the seventeenth-century Descartes, animals were unthinking, unfeeling; indeed robots, though he did not use that more contemporary term. Animals, he said, reflexively responded to stimuli. Since presumably, they did not feel pain, animal cruelty was not an issue. Descartes dictum, *cogito, ergo sum* ("I think, therefore I am") placed great emphasis on the significance of thinking as a criterion for human's uniqueness. And thinking was assumed to be conscious. Humans had a soul; animals did not (Descartes 1989).

But how unique are humans? In the nineteenth century, Darwin's *The Origin of Species* and the work of his contemporary, Alfred Russel Wallace, placed humans along an evolutionary continuum, joined by a shared evolutionary history and ontogeny (Darwin 1872; Wallace 1858). Their theories were based on careful observations of the similarities in structure and physiology of many species, even of their behaviours. The continuum was nevertheless a "ladder", perhaps, even a tree, but with humankind at the apex. In a lesser known work, *The Expression of the Emotions in Man and Animals*, Darwin (1872) described astonishingly similar demeanours, bodily postures and particularly facial expressions which he took to be conveying emotions. Humans were not only along a continuum of abilities with animals, but that continuum included mental states. Discussions of "soul" had drifted out of the analysis.

As a staunch supporter of the impressive cognitive and emotional capacities of animals, Romanes gathered many examples of animal behaviour supporting these views. His enthusiasm led him to offer both careful observations and overinterpreted anecdotes. There was backlash; the pendulum swung. Work in the laboratories of Wilhelm Wundt in Germany (Wundt 1873-74) and then of Edward Titchener in the US led to creation of the field of Experimental Psychology (Titchener 1901-05). The human "mind" was to be examined in carefully controlled laboratory situations, not in the everyday world, not in the "field". Stimuli, such as brightness or loudness, would be calibrated and humans would report the "contents of consciousness" by introspection. Thus, the "structure" of mind would be revealed from a limited, but highly controlled *laboratory* perspective.

THE BEHAVIOURISTS, THEN COGNITION

But these sometimes quite varying personal reports led to a quest for "observables", external behaviours and other measurements that could be verified by independent third-party observers. B.F. Skinner led the "Behaviourist" movement, beginning in the US with the publication of *The Behaviour of Organisms* (1938) and holding sway over human and animal studies for over half a century. No mental states were to be part of any robust scientific explanation. Sometimes "intervening variables" were introduced between a stimulus and a response; non-behaviourists might instead term them mental states, perhaps fear, hunger, etc. Any behaviour, decreed Skinner, could be "instrumentally conditioned" with the appropriate reward or punishment. "Classical conditioning", as discovered by Ivan Pavlov (1960), was also involved, insofar as a stimulus that preceded another could come to provoke the same response as the second. Pavlov's dogs who learned to salivate to the sound of a bell that preceded food is the well-known example. According to these dicta, all behaviour, animal and human, were purported to be explained by these two classes of conditioning.

But mentation intervened. Simply put, Pavlov's dogs did not really give the same response to the bell as to the food; they did not eat it. The simple association of a stimulus and a reward was *not* adequate for that stimulus to elicit the same response as the reward. There was *not* a simple, direct neural connection between the preceding stimulus and the reward stimulus. With an ingenious set of experiments, Robert Rescorla reinterpreted classical conditioning as a cognitive event, whereby the first stimulus, under certain conditions, *predicts* the occurrence of the second. Significantly, it was *not* the mere association of two stimuli that mattered, but the *contingency*, i.e. the predictive value of the first stimulus (Rescorla 1967, 1988).

Cognitive studies, however, skirted the issue of consciousness when possible, certainly when discussing animals. Physical models were introduced to explain the brain's communication processes. Whereas the responses of Pavlov's dogs might be described in terms of a brain constructed somewhat like a telephone system, cognitive connections were said to be conducted in a brain that had complex computer structural networks (the "hardware") with neural impulses travelling according to complex computer-like programmes (the "software"). Although completely embedded in the tissues of neural metabolism, the idea of a possible "software" suggested to some a truly emergent suite of characteristics and the possibility of a shared "understanding" or "processing" of conscious ideas.

GRIFFIN'S QUESTION OF ANIMAL AWARENESS

And then, in this brief and admittedly selective history, we note that a book appeared in 1976, *The Question of Animal Awareness* by Donald R. Griffin. Griffin had excellent credentials: Harvard Biology Department Chair; head of The Rockefeller University Institute for Animal Behaviour; discovered echo-location by bats, the process by which they use ultrasound to detect objects, navigate around obstacles and hunt insects and he was the recognized world leader in those studies. He had endured decades of disbelief and ridicule with the bat research, his studies of bird migration and his promoting von Frisch's "discovery of honey bees" communicative dances. And, in each case, Griffin had been proven correct (Ristau 2005; in prep.).

Now he was daring to propose that, just as there was evolutionary continuity between humans and animals in so many domains, might there also be continuity in mental abilities? Might animals be aware, conscious beings, who thought and had feelings? Shouldn't scientists be examining this possibility? Instead of rejecting animal awareness out of hand, shouldn't we as scientists consider the hypothesis that we do not know whether animals are conscious and attempt to gather evidence on either side of that possibility?

Griffin proposed exploring several lines of evidence for this new field of cognitive ethology:

1. possible neural correlates of consciousness;
2. versatility of organisms in adapting to new challenges for which they had not been either genetically prepared or had pertinent learning experiences; and
3. communication by animals that can be interpreted as reporting subjective experiences (Griffin 1976, 1984, 2001).

Among his colleagues, there were actually whispers of "early senility". (A forerunner, Darwin's book, *Expressions of the Emotions in Man and Animals*, had, conveniently, largely been forgotten over the decades.) Many leapt into the ferment. Philosophers of science were among them. Ernst Nagel (1974) considered the question, "What is it like to be a Bat?" and said we cannot know the answer. He postulated that there are subjective facts about conscious experience that can be known only from that subjective perspective, not by an outsider, not from a third person perspective. Other philosophers who had been considering the subject of consciousness further expanded their efforts into animal minds, for example, Jonathan Bennett (1983), Daniel Dennett (1983), John Searle (1980), Ned Block (1995) and Ruth Millikan (1998); these particular articles referenced being published with commentaries from many fields.

Other theorists, many forgotten, had long been considering possible details of an animal's consciousness. The existence of different world views, indeed different life spaces, occupied by various species had already been emphasized by the Baltic German biologist, Jakob von Uexküll in a publication (1909/1985). His theory of "Umwelt" described how species sense, prioritize and interact with the environment differently. Thus, the "same environment" is being perceived and lived in differently by different beings. Not only do non-human species' sensing capacities differ from humans and from each other, but so do the senses emphasized and means of gathering, integrating and utilizing the sensory information. Somehow, though he established the field of biosemiotics and influenced philosophers, in particular, Martin Heidegger, he did not persuade the scientists of animal behaviour or philosophers to focus on studies of Umwelt. Although, in the modern fields of the life sciences, ranging from behavioural ecology to epigenetics, individual variation is considered a critical component of most research studies.

Consciousness: Criteria and Origins

A persistent question in all these examinations was what might be the criteria for consciousness in a non-human? Among the possible lines of supportive evidence, Griffin (1976, 1984, 2001; Griffin and Speck 2004), suggested:

1. The versatility of animal communication, including symbolic communication, long considered to be unique to human linguistic communication. Allowing for the possibility of such communication begins to undermine the barrier between human and animal mentation and also offers us a glimpse into a non-human psyche.
2. Examples of the abilities of animals to adapt their behaviour to novel and complex circumstances and to solve problems, shreds the notion of merely reflexive behaviour by non-humans as proposed by Descartes and others.
3. Might animals have goals, purposes? Might they be able to understand the purposes of another, i.e. the philosophical problem of "Other Minds" (Harnad 2016) and even use such information to their own advantage, for example, by deception? Given the evolutionary continuity of human and animal, what kinds of mental capacities might we expect to find in non-humans?
4. And as Griffin suggested, let us search for neurophysiological correlates of consciousness, possible indices of consciousness in humans; can they be found in non-humans?

From the neuroanatomical concerns arose the evolutionary concerns; how did consciousness originate? This question has been termed by the philosopher David Chalmers (1996), the "hard problem of consciousness", how subjectivity can emerge from matter. Some contemporary views consider that consciousness arose several times and followed distinct paths. Those who propose the existence of consciousness in the "lowly" creatures, emphasize a more phenomenological concept of consciousness, the *experience* of pain, emotions. These aspects might be controlled by more ancient rostral parts of the brain, more likely to be available to more "lowly" creatures. Adding senses to that concept of consciousness, such as odours, vision and sound, would have to utilize some other brain parts as well. Those who espouse a more cognitive concept of consciousness include not only problem solving and reasoning, but perhaps abilities to think of the past and plan for the future and even self-awareness. Such theorists emphasize the importance of more frontal and cortical structures and neural activity.

Still the question haunts; how did consciousness begin? Today's two dominant views argue in terms of structural organization and complexity of neural networks vs the dynamics of neural activity, such as synchronization. At some point (what point?) in the development of more and more complicated connections between cells or neurons, suddenly consciousness; alternatively, at some kind of dynamics, suddenly consciousness. A miracle of sorts, questioned by the physicists in this volume as having begun well before life evolved.

Tononi, who originated integrated information theory (IIT) counters such views by attempting to *specify* the characteristics of a conscious experience, seeing, as Descartes did in *cogito, ergo sum*, "thinking" as the central defining tenet. In fact, Tononi views are broader, for, in his proposals, consciousness is not defined by "thinking", but includes the intrinsic *phenomenon* of experience. From the characteristics of a conscious experience, Tononi and Koch (2015) claim to have deduced the necessary properties of any physical system that has some degree of consciousness. They stress that consciousness will vary in "quantity" in different entities and can be measured in units they have termed phi. A digital computer, for example, will not be conscious; it has the wrong structure; it has no causal powers. "Consciousness is a system's ability to be acted upon by its own state in the past and to influence its own future" says Koch, i.e. it has causal powers (Ball 2019). A computer can create only simulations. However, these assumptions treat all computational processing as a "black box" and do not take into account the most recent advances in machine learning. Certainly, computational advances allow experience (incoming signals or outcomes) to alter future interpretations and response (e.g. speech recognition). The challenges to answering this question of a conscious computer lie both in deficiencies in understanding the neural mechanisms of human consciousness and of how those characteristics are mimicked by a computational platform (Signorelli 2018).

Koch's views are closest to those of the Copenhagen Interpretation and its more recent reconsideration. He believes "that consciousness is a fundamental, elementary property of living matter. It cannot be derived from anything else." Indeed, in Koch's view, "we are surrounded and immersed" in consciousness (Ball 2019). Neurophysiologically, the IIT model of Tononi and Koch predicts that correlates of consciousness are likely to be found in the sensory areas, further to the back of the brain.

A major opposing viewpoint is the global workspace theory (GWT) which proposes that sensory information is gathered into a brain space in the cortical regions. The areas considered most likely are the parietal and frontal lobes of the cortex, where, presumably, the nervous activity or "neural correlates of consciousness" would also be found. Specifically, distinctive neural activity, occurring 300-400 msec. after a stimulus, is thought to be the neural marker indicating that the global workspace is broadcasting the information that makes us consciously aware of that stimulus.

Still other theories can be broadly classified as either first order or higher order theories (HOTs). The first order theories propose that mind is simply the brain's cognitive processing of information. Something, as yet unknown about the *dynamics* of the elements of that process leads to consciousness. HOTs stipulate that after the information is integrated, something is *added* by the mind to produce consciousness (Ball 2019).

Yet another approach emphasizes a cellular basis of consciousness (CBC). Arthur Reber (1996, 2016, 2018) makes a case for cellular-based sentience arising from the very first living single-celled organism, the prokaryotes, while Lynn Margulis (2001) has proposed a similar theory of a "microbial mind". The CBC model argues that sentience emerged with life itself. The most primitive unicellular species of bacteria are conscious, though it is a sentience of a basic kind.

Initially, Reber considered that only animals have minds, though they are tiny and limited in scope. He considered very potent examples, such as the behaviour of a single-celled amoeba. It can detect toxins in its environment, food and move away or towards such stimuli by protoplasmic flow. It has a "front", a part of the moving cell that is more sensitive to light. In the plant/animal distinction, it is classified as "animal". I Carolyn Ristau, always delighted in confounding my students on the first day of my animal behaviour courses, by describing the amoeba's behaviour in detail and asking the class to identify the species. They would be quite astonished to hear that I was describing a single-celled amoeba.

Reber proposes that once sentience arises from the first living, mobile organism, it develops through evolution into the more complex states we term consciousness. In his theory, mobility is essential, as a means to gather enough information, acquire food and leave dangerous situations. But, as has been argued (Ristau 2016a), when life originated, most likely in the sea, the water was flowing and brought with it information and food. Why should mobility allow for sentience while immobility does not? Apparently, the work of Baluška and other molecular botanists is beginning to persuade Reber that perhaps those early one-celled "plants" might also be sentient (Baluška and Reber 2019).

In our roles extrapolating the possibilities of the Copenhagen Interpretation, we would consider the possibility of the amoeba as a sentient being, a tiny-minded creature, as it would provide a novel subject for future biophysical experimentation. In our more usual roles as biologists and a cognitive ethologist, we would be considerably more hesitant.

Universal Consciousness?

With our current toolbox, biologists have no scientifically satisfying answer. The nexus of physics and biology will require a common language of interpretation in order to proceed. However, this is novel, but not unique. Biologists surrendered the Bohr model of the atom as quantum interpretations superseded. Our understanding of the cell membrane was modernized by the application of electro-physics to the Davson–Danielli Model ... What then? As noted, at this point in the long history of science that has passed and is yet to be, we both do not feel we can either adequately understand the proposed, modified Copenhagen Interpretation of a quantum basis for consciousness nor can we adopt what appears to us to be the more spiritual stance of accepting an underlying consciousness that *is* all things. Yet, we are in a conundrum. We fully accept that consciousness exists, however it is that we specifically choose to describe and define it. At least some non-human entities appear to be conscious, more and more of them as further scientific inquiries are conducted. Thus, not having an answer to the possible origins of consciousness, we will, at least, entertain the possibility of a universal consciousness and examine the implications that ensue for the study of animal behaviour and animal mind.

We shall consider the possibility that there might be a fifth force in the universe. Four elemental forces are described in the widely accepted "Standard Model" of atomic physics. The theory describes three of the four fundamental forces and classifies the elementary particles. These forces, along with gravity, drove the evolution of our universe and keep it together: the "strong" nuclear force binds the atom's nucleus together; the weak force is the mechanism of interaction between the subatomic particles and responsible for radioactive decay; the familiar electromagnetic force is light and electricity and magnetism; and, finally, there is the mysterious force of gravity, still baffling. It does not fit neatly into the Standard Model. Physicists' quest for the grand unifying theory of everything is simply stymied by gravity, as well as by other phenomena.

We do admit that simply stipulating this fifth force of consciousness is not all that much different from requiring a large or small miracle in all the other explanations of consciousness proffered so far. But it, perhaps, is the more plausible.

Implications of Universal Consciousness on Evolutionary Studies

If universal consciousness or a fifth force exists, much as the philosopher David Chalmers (1995, 1996) has suggested, what, for example, might be the implications for evolutionary studies? No longer do we have to search for the miracle to be discovered in the complexity of structure of a cellular/neuronal network, nor for neural processes similar to those occurring in a conscious human, nor whether the entity is to be classified as an animal and thus potentially conscious or a plant and thus never possibly conscious. As a fifth force, consciousness exists. Different entities can be receptacles for different aspects of consciousness depending on their characteristics. The analogy is simplistically similar to that of a radio that can receive certain restricted ranges of wavelengths on each station. Likewise, it is analogous to different organisms which are sensitive to distinct bands of electromagnetic wavelengths. Examples are the honeybees' sensitivity to ultraviolet light which reflects off certain flowers, revealing paths that lead to the location of pollen or nectar on the flower; many other species are also UV sensitive. And many species, not humans, can detect and produce ultrasonic acoustic frequencies, some just clicks, others a wide range of frequencies. The species include some insects, such as grasshoppers and some moths, certain frogs, some birds such as swiftlets and oil birds, some mammals such as dolphins (*Delphinus*), porpoises (*Phocoenidae*) and other toothed whales (*Odontoceti*), and even rats (*Rattus*), mice (*Mus*) and shrews (*Soricidae*) (discussion in Ristau, in prep.).

Many research questions will remain the same whether or not we postulate a universal consciousness. To determine the potential attributes of consciousness, we need to ascertain organisms' sensitivities and detectable electromagnetic wavelengths, sounds, odours, etc. We need to understand how that information is analysed to create the particular patterns or perceptions that give rise to the experience of an object or a colour. We still want to understand von Uexküll's "Umwelt" for an animal.

But a significant difference will be our openness to accept the possibility of consciousness and the world that an animal perceives and in which it lives. We need not emphasize a search for merely stimulus–response connections; we can be more open to researching an integrated set of perceptions held by an organism.

Neuroanatomical Considerations

Let us begin by considering the variety of neuroanatomical systems that may "partake of"/"exhibit" consciousness and what those neural connections might or might not contribute to conscious experience. We should note that any "pathway" proposed is almost always a far more complex system than a simple line drawing suggests; there are typically many inputs from other brain parts. Even at the level of the neuron, there are many connections and different kinds of connections between individual neurons, such that a neuron can pool information from many or fewer other neurons and from different levels of the system; some portions of the system can include feedback loops. A neuron may have up to 10,000 connections with others. And then there are the mysterious glial cells, originally thought to be providing merely structural support to other neurons, then a potential nutritive function was added and more recently, they are considered to be exerting field effects, such that they influence the responsiveness of neurons nearby. Although the critical aspect in complexity of brain function across species appears to be similar micro patterns of individual neural connections in addition to the broader connectivity across the brain; the specific brain region involved in a function can differ between species (Ristau 2013: 5). If consciousness is indeed universal, then evolutionary variation may represent novel solutions to the problem of engaging the outside world by organisms from different taxa. The opportunities arise for the development of model taxonomic systems for experimentation, such as the fruit fly (*Drosophila* sp.) did for classical genetics or the bacteriophage for molecular scale investigations.

The lesson: it is difficult, if not impossible, to determine what an organism is *in*capable of experiencing by considering its neural structure, though neural sensitivities can help us understand the potential sensitivities and discriminating capacities of the organism. Consider the seminal paper, "What the Frog's Eye Tells the Frog's Brain" (Lettvin et al. 1959). Frogs have a "spot detector" built through neural connections at the level of the eye, which, peripherally and rapidly, is detecting a fly, indeed a moving fly. That interpretation caused some consternation among scientists, but it remains a sound one.

Flies (*Diptera*) have a compound eye, as do other insects and many crustacea, meaning it has multiple visual sensors or ommatidia, rather than our two eyes with single lenses. Other sensors, ocelli, located elsewhere on the insect simply detect changes in light, rather than images. Many were the beautiful illustrations purporting to show the complicated, pixel-like representation of the fly's visual world. But the fly has a brain, small though it be, an integrative brain and there is no good reason to suppose that the fly zooms about with a pixelated world view. Indeed, with its compound eye, it has a far wider immediate range of vision than we humans and, with that view, very readily detects movement, all without moving its own head or eye.

We already know that complex cognitive functions need not, as in humans, be mediated by the cortex; in birds it is the nidopallium. And consider the cephalopods, particularly the octopus, whose advanced cognitive capacities we are slowly coming to better appreciate (Laschi 2009; Wells 1978), while squid and cuttlefish also keep surprising us with their capacities. Within the octopus's nervous system are three main components: a large brain of two central masses, the nervous system of each arm and optic lobes. The system contains about 500 million neurons; by comparison, rats have 100 million and dogs 600 million (Hochner 2008). The octopus and vertebrates may have undergone convergent evolution, both needing extensive memory and learning, driven perhaps by the vertebrates' sociality and the challenges faced by the octopus as a solitary hunter and a vulnerable, soft bodied animal, its ancestral protective shell having been lost earlier in evolution (Anderson et al. 2010; Ristau 2013).

To repeat, neuroanatomical considerations can help suggest potential capacities of a species, but seldom can totally rule out any abilities.

Finally, a recognition by a group of prominent scientists in cognitive neuroscience and related fields at the First Francis Crick Memorial Conference on Consciousness (7 July 2012) which signed the "Cambridge Declaration on Consciousness" stating (Low et al. 2012):

> The absence of a neocortex does not appear to preclude an organism from experiencing affective states. Convergent evidence indicates that non-human animals have the neuroanatomical, neurochemical and neurophysiological substrates of conscious states along with the capacity to exhibit intentional behaviours. Consequently, the weight of evidence indicates that humans are not unique in possessing the neurological substrates that generate consciousness. Non-human animals, including all mammals and birds and many other creatures, including octopuses, also possess these neurological substrates.

Sensitivity to the Environment

THE "UMWELT"

In adopting either the modified Copenhagen Interpretation of QM or the concept of Consciousness as a Fifth Force, we want to ask what aspects of the universal consciousness are accessible to each species and individual and what "Umwelt" does each create from that consciousness? To create an "Umwelt", not only does the potential sensing capacity matter, but also the relative emphasis placed on each by that species and in what circumstance. Capacities can differ. Many species have sensory capacities far exceeding our own, which becomes in its own right, an example of how challenging it is to consider the cognition of other animals.

ULTRAVIOLET AND POLARIZED LIGHT

Many arthropods, including both insects and some crustacea, detect ultraviolet (UV) light and also polarized light direction, both of which we cannot (von Frisch 1950; G.L. Gould and C.G. Gould 2012: 91-96). Species typically use the directional information as part of the sun compass for orientation, navigation and in spatial orientation tasks. For honeybees, the polarized light from even a small patch of blue sky provides a directional mechanism when the sun is hidden behind clouds. Ants likewise use it for navigational purposes. Some fish have evolved to detect polarized light and some open ocean fish use polarization to afford themselves better camouflage when there is no place to hide. Specifically, certain structures in their scales scatter polarized light differently in different directions, most effectively at the "chase angle" of predators. Birds are mysterious, apparently using the directional information in polarized light, but scientists cannot determine how birds detect the polarization.

What of UV light? UV sensitivity occurs via different mechanisms. Many species have visual pigments with maximum sensitivity below 400 nm, a region of the electromagnetic spectrum termed UV. Normal human vision lies between approximately 400-700 and so we do not normally detect UV. Having the specialized pigments, UV sensitivity is quite extensive among invertebrates, amphibians, reptiles, fish and birds. A very few mammals possess those pigments, only some rodents, a mole, several marsupials and some bats (references cited in Douglas and Jeffery (2014). Yet most mammals can see ultraviolet, if it is sufficiently intense, because their lenses do not block the UV transmission while humans' do. Humans without lenses due to cataract surgery or congenital defect can also see UV; the sensation is a pale violet. The seemingly mysterious phenomenon is due to the fact that the three-colour sensitive cones we and most other mammals possess actually have a broad range of sensitivity to electromagnetic waves. We label the cones blue, green and red sensitive, or, more accurately, short, medium and long wavelength detectors. In fact, those cones respond to a wide span of wavelengths, with the peak lying at the named colours. But the example serves to show how difficult the task of identifying receptive mechanisms for sensory capacities.

That mammalian sensitivity to UV also has consequences for our conservation practices, to be discussed in a later section.

Like many other insects, the familiar honeybee can detect 300 to 650 nm, thereby not seeing red, but detecting UV. During the course of evolution, presumably both the bees' capacities and the environment have co-adapted to better ensure that flowers are pollinated and that the bees find nectar and pollen. Landing zones and pathways are laid out on flowers in apparently alluring UV patterns to entice bees to reach the nectar and pollen. We humans cannot see them. Some pollen adheres to the bee's bristly body and rubs off to pollinate another flower.

And note that these and other visual processes are occurring at very minute levels, below microscopic, indeed at quantum levels. One photon is sufficient to excite a photoreceptor, specifically a rod, which is more sensitive than a colour sensitive cone and detects only presence of light (Hecht et al. 1942). Rods are our main source of vision as the light intensity fades and we perceive less saturated colour, finally no colour. Practically speaking, it takes more than one photon to make its way successfully through the cornea and absorption of the lens and the morass of neural fibres and capillaries before it reaches that rod.

Earth's Magnetic Field and Quantum Mechanics

Still tantalizing scientists is the ability of some species, most notably birds, to detect and use magnetic information (Deutschlander et al. 2019). By accessing data about the earth's magnetic field orientation and strength, the birds have cues to guide them home ("homing") and to navigate over often vast distances during their seasonal migrations (Humans, too?) (Wang et al. 2019). Once again, basic explanations derive from at least the atomic level and likely the quantum level. The underlying phenomenon of any magnetism is due to the movement of electrons creating a surrounding magnetic field. On the quantum level, some theories of animal magnetoreception involve subatomic quantum systems which rely on very specialized pigments in the retina of the eye, specifically photosensitive cryptochromes.[1] The perplexities exist in various domains: some animals seem to sense the earth's magnetic field, as revealed by "nonsense orientations", i.e. aligning at rest preferentially

---

1 Quantum mechanics enters the explanation in providing a means whereby the magnetic field can create stimuli to the neural pathways. In short, in the eye, or rather in the retina of *night*-migrating birds, *during* the migrating season certain cryptochrome proteins become more plentiful; this does not occur in non-migrating birds. When stimulated by light, those proteins are activated, in the sense of reaching a more excited state of the electrons, with impacts, as well on the electron "spin". At first glance, it would seem that the scales of energy interaction are not compatible. The energy of a chemical bond requires $10^2 - 10^3\, k_B T$ while the molecular interaction with the geomagnetic field is less than $10^{-7}\, k_B T$. But … we learn … that's for stable systems, systems in equilibrium. If, for example, a block is almost tipped over, very little effort is required to complete the push and tip it. Similarly, with the described quantum interactions, the molecules involved or the so-called "radical pairs" are in a (dim) light-induced *unstable* state, which can be impacted by the very small geomagnetic field changes the bird is experiencing (Hore and Mouritsen 2016; Mouritsen 2018b, see also Schulten et al. 1978 and Ritz et al. 2000). Thus, a stimulus is created, presumably sensed by the visual system and sent to the brain, apparently to area *N*, a cluster of forebrain regions. Here, the magnetic compass information is believed to be processed. Is there any neurophysiological evidence for such claims? Indeed. If at night, night migrating birds are exposed to magnetic fields, we find high activity in area *N*, not so in non-migratory birds. Cover the eyes of a migrating European Robin and there is no such activity in *N*, even with exposure to magnetic fields, indicating that the input to *N* is via the visual system. The proper migratory direction is disrupted if area *N* is ablated (Mouritsen 2018a).

in any of the four compass directions (Gould 2012: 100), but the adaptive use is not clear. Other animals, including honeybees and vertebrates, such as reptiles, amphibians, fish, birds and mammals, have "magnetite organs", i.e. pieces of permanent magnetic material, biologically constructed and located in highly innervated areas. Scientists, however, often do not know whether or how the potential magnetic information is used. In fact, magnetite crystal chains' important role in orientation was first discovered in some micro aerobic bacteria, where the magnetite *was* adaptive; the magnetite chain aligned the bacteria so that they were correctly oriented to swim away from surface toxic oxygen (Gould 2008, 2010). Still other species *do* use magnetic field information for navigation, but just how they detect and integrate the information remains mysterious. In particular, the quantum level cryptochrome theories are considered to provide either a 3D magnetic model for a bird (Mouritsen 2018a, b) or, more simply, just compass information (Gould 2008; described in Ristau, in prep.). Note that correct navigation requires *both* a map and a compass.

Furthermore, we must recognize that there appear to be multiple systems for sensing magnetic fields. Additionally, magnetic orientation seems to have evolved several times and then further specialized several times. Even a single species apparently can have several systems (Gould 2008). Let us consider just one case, that of migrating birds, whose path, we now know, depends on many cues; there is no "silver bullet" key stimulus. Examples include positions of the sun, of the stars, (most birds migrate in the evening or night to reduce predation risk and overheating from their strenuous flying activity), sounds (including the low-pitched sounds of waves breaking at coastlines), cognitive visual and acoustic maps of the earth and more local cues from specific visual and olfactory stimuli ... and ... for the long haul, the earth's magnetic field. For shorter journeys of homing, olfaction can also play a prominent role.

Many scientists had noticed that caged birds are restless during migrating seasons and seemed to try to move in specific directions. Provoking much controversy, some scientists suggested birds were sensing the earth's magnetic field; that tumultuous history is described elsewhere (Deutschlander et al. 2019; G.L. Gould and C.G. Gould 2012: 206-25). An ingenious experiment later provided potent evidence. In a lab in Russia, caged migrating reed warblers (*Acrocephalus scirpaceus*) were shielded from the earth's magnetic field and subjected by Mouritsen and his team to a magnetic field identical in all ways to the earth's magnetic field, except that it corresponded to a site in Scotland. The birds adjusted to their "new location" and altered their direction of travel ... from Scotland ... as shown by the recorded direction of their footprints (Chernetsov et al. 2017; Mouritsen 2018b). The team then began detailed explorations into the neuroanatomical basis of the phenomenon.

Mouritsen continued his work at another site, the University of Oldenburg. But the birds in his new lab made *no* directed movements during migration season. After six years of failed efforts, a physics grade student suggested the possibility of electromagnetic interference. To determine this, with birds in a shielded room and equipment to create magnetic fields, Mouritsen turned the "earth's magnetic field" on or off or changed its direction. Finally, the birds responded appropriately. Mouritsen had moved from bucolic surroundings to a large university with all the usual lighting, electric and telecommunication facilities ... and the associated electromagnetic interference.

This avian sensitivity to fields we humans and other creatures experience daily does give one pause; with what else are we interfering? What other extraordinary sensitivities, possessed by other species, are unbeknownst to us and unknowingly (or knowingly) disrupted by our human activities? This, too, a question for our discussion of conservation.

Other Potential Conscious Abilities of Non-human Animals

Are animals conscious? If consciousness is a given, as we have stated, we shall assume that animals, too, are conscious. Some properties likely to be characteristic of many conscious beings include communicating, problem solving, tool use, strategic behaviour sequences, self-awareness and morality. Other creatures may possess lower levels of sentience. Which animals are capable of which possible attributes of consciousness? We cannot begin to deal adequately with these issues in the space of this manuscript. For an entry into the broad literature, we suggest reviews of Cognitive Ethology (Griffin and Speck 2004; Ristau 2013), Griffin's books (1976, 1981, 1992), books of collected papers (Ristau 1991b; Bekoff et al. 2002) and recent "popular" books such as those by Bernd Heinrich (2014), Frans de Waal (2016), Charles Foster (2016) (reviewed in Ristau 2016b) and, among many other writings, particularly articles in the open-access, online journal, *Animal Sentience.*

COMMUNICATION

The possibility of communicating *with* another species is alluring, but quite what we may be communicating, if anything, is more than challenging. Yet animals communicate with each other and scientists attempt to probe their methods and meanings, while having to recognize that some species' means of communicating (e.g. odour, vocalization, etc.) may be quite beyond our abilities to detect and interpret. For some modes, instrumentation may help, e.g. for some odours, for bats' and other species' ultrasonics, etc. Usually, we surmise, but do not know, what matters they choose to communicate about.

But, assuming a universal consciousness, varied though it be, as partaken by different species, can guide us to frame our research questions more perceptively. We can examine an organism in its environment and ask what problems it needs to solve. Would sentience or a higher level of consciousness help solve them? Can we humans attempt to determine the mind state, the goals and purposes of a non-human?

Animal communication was seen by Donald Griffin as a potential "window on animal minds" (1992: ix). From that perspective, he examined research in animals' artificial and natural communication systems. In the various artificial lexicons, using hand signing, distinctive plastic chips, computer based geometric patterns, sometimes even spoken words, animals were taught to associate each lexical item with an object or simple state or action, e.g. "Koko want banana" (Koko was a gorilla). The subjects in these experiments were usually common chimpanzees (*Pan troglodytes*), but also bonobos aka "pygmy chimps" (*Pan paniscus*), a Western gorilla (*Gorilla gorilla*) and African grey parrots (*Psittacus erithacus*) among others (Ristau and Robbins 1982). Whether these individual items could be combined in meaningful, novel ways and functioned symbolically created much heated debate, for such animal capacities were seemingly destroying the uniqueness of humans, the linguistic barrier that separated humans and non-humans.

Similar issues arose in studies of animal communication. Could, for example, a monkey's vocalization function symbolically, i.e. "stand for" something in the environment such as a specific predator or type of predator? Observations in the wild by Thomas Struhsaker of specific vocalizations by vervet monkeys (*Chlorocebus pygerythrus*) in the presence of different predators as well as different responses to those signals by other monkeys led to a series of field experiments which supported his findings (Seyfarth et al. 1980; Struhsaker 1967). Using recordings of the monkeys' calls and playing them back in the field, Seyfarth, D.L. Cheney and P. Marler found evidence that the vervet monkeys had distinct signals for an aerial predator, a leopard and a snake, with different appropriate responses to each: hiding from a martial hawk, climbing a tree for a leopard and standing alert and looking about on the ground when hearing a "snake alarm" call. Other researchers have refined their results.

And vervet monkeys are by no means the only species in which there is evidence to support interpretations of alarm calls beyond that of urgency (predator's threat level). With studies that included both field observations of naturally occurring events and the use of predator models or artificial stimuli, acoustically distinctive calls for aerial and for ground predators have been found in diverse species, from chickens to monkeys (reviewed in Kaplan 2014; Ristau 2013; Slobodchikoff et al. 2012).

Some species apparently provide yet further information in their alarm calls. Among the potential categories of functionally referential information are: predator type (aerial or terrestrial, specific species), predator's spatial location, physical qualities such as size, shape and colour and predator behaviours such as movement (no movement, speed, kind of movement such as hawk perched, searching for prey or attacking (Griesser 2008)).

Two different types of animals, meerkats (*Suricata suricatta*) and prairie dogs (genus *Cynomys*) appear to have very complex vocal communication systems. Meerkats' calls apparently can convey both predator type and urgency (Manser 2001); prairie dogs respond differentially to different colours and to different geometric shapes such as triangles vs circle-square and different colours. Slobodchikoff suggests (pers. comm. to Ristau) that the geometric sensitivities may be related to the prairie dogs' predator classes: triangular for raptors, circular–rectangular for mammalian ground predators.

Other differently sensitive approaches to the study of animal communication have also been undertaken. W.J. Smith (1977, 1998) encouraged a "message–meaning analysis" of signals, noting that the same auditory production can have different meanings, depending on recipient and context (including past history, environment and other stored information). Thus, in the spring, a male bird may, with the same call, be signalling likely aggression if approached by a male and an invitation to a female. Within a message may be information about the communicator's location and identity and the likelihood and type of its behaviour. Even information about external referents such as food, predators or other items may be included. To attempt a message–meaning analysis requires detailed observations about correlations with conditions and the signaller and recipient(s)' behaviour, prior to, during and after the signal. It is difficult to do well (Ristau 2013).

Due in part to such difficulties, another type of signal analysis has been used, "functional analysis", which deals only with immediate responses and with restricted types of signals, so-called "alarm" and "food" calls. Acoustic playback experiments, though able to specify the particular vocalization produced, also have their own limitations. Playbacks entail no contextual information with which the receiver(s) can calibrate their behaviour and so are more likely to result in the "default" or "fail-safe" response (Townsend and Manser 2013). Likewise, just as we can identify an individual by the sound of her voice, so can many animal species. Thus, a researcher must consider such matters as whether the vocalizer is present when "playing back" a vocalization. By affording animals such *possible* higher levels of cognition and consciousness, biologists can design more sensitive experiments in the field and in the laboratory.

Other concerns arise from the existence of potential "order information" or simple "grammar", which has found considerable support in studies of natural animal communication. In the least "... sound and call combinations can be found across diverse (avian and mammal) species" (review article by Engesser and Townsend 2019). Zuberbühler and his team have conducted extensive analytic and stochastic studies of the combinatorial properties of primate vocalizing. They have found convincing evidence for meaningful use of the order of individual vocal units (review in Zuberbühler 2018). For Zuberbühler, the current debate is whether the animal signalers can vary the meaningful units to create utterances with novel meanings, a property many linguists have considered to be unique to human language.

Many aspects of referential meaning remain controversial. However, the simplistic "groan of pain" interpretation (Griffin 1985) that at all animal calls simply indicate a state of arousal, aggression, fear, etc. has had to be abandoned. Researchers must conduct long-term field studies, attempting to understand an animal's "Umwelt". They can then begin to design appropriate experiments, using non-intrusive audio, video and probably other techniques.

TOOL USE AND STRATEGIC BEHAVIOURS

Another supposed unique human ability, tool use, is generally defined by scientists as manipulating a movable object on a target to modify the physical characteristics of the target (Alcock 1972). Using tools provokes particular interest, because it implies a goal, requires short-term (or longer) planning and can entail flexible behaviour, in some cases modifying the tool to become more efficient (Ristau 2013). Tool use actually occurs widely in the animal kingdom. Perhaps most intriguing are experiments with corvids, particularly with captive New Caledonian crows (*Corvus moneduloides*), which exhibit much innovative behaviour. They have been observed to bend a wire to reach food otherwise unavailable. The birds had not witnessed such wire bending and the solution required the formation of a novel idea (Weir et al. 2002).

Strategic behaviours are common, especially easily observed in the field and in laboratory experiments with great apes, but in many other species as well. Among them are deceptions, whereby a chimpanzee might hide a coconut, a desirable food, but waiting until others have gone to do so (Ristau, personal observation).

Tanagers (*Lanio versicolor*) and shrikes (*Thamnomanes scistogynus*) have been observed to produce false alarm calls, thereby allowing them to access food as a conspecific immediately flew away or even dropped an insect, then captured by the vocalizer (Munn 1986). Capuchin monkeys (*Cebus apella nigritus*) have been observed in a forest environment modified with platforms for food. The capuchins uttered more alarm calls when a desirable food (banana chips) was available and the vocalizer was in a better position to access the food and was a subordinate rather than a dominant who could simply grab the banana pieces without reprisal (Wheeler 2009).

Other behaviours may be interpreted by a human observer as deceptive, but simpler, yet strategic, interpretations are probably preferable. An example arises with piping plovers (*Charadrius melodus*) a ground nesting shore bird which performs many distinctive behaviours when its eggs or young are threatened by an intruder or predator. Among them is "injury feigning" aka "broken wing display" which, in various plover species, is used to lure the intruder away from the nest or young. It is a very effective display, focusing the attention most of any observer.

The broken wing display itself is innate, as is the human smile, both of which, nevertheless, can be used strategically. In a series of field experiments, Ristau (1991a) demonstrated that the piping plover adjusts its behaviour, depending on the responses of the intruder, a human in the fieldwork. The disturbed bird does not just move randomly, as had been assumed previously. If the human follows the bird, the bird leads the person away from the nest; if not, the plover returns to re-engage the intruder, varying its behaviour with loud (for a plover) peeps and perhaps yet more intense displaying.

It does not seem necessary, from a scientific point of view to claim that a plover understands that its behaviour is a "deception"; rather, its actions "work". Further, other field experiments demonstrated that a plover could very quickly learn to react more strongly to a human who had previously closely approached its nest compared to a distinctively dressed second person who had walked by, much farther from the nest. A necessary kind of learning since a parent must decide when to stay on the nest and when to leave, because a nest without the incubating parent on it is better camouflaged, but the eggs are at greater risk from the hot sun or the cold rain.

SELF-AWARENESS: THE MIRROR SELF-RECOGNITION EXPERIMENTS

Relevant to all the research discussed is the issue of self-awareness. Is an animal, which animal, aware of itself? A long series of "mirror self-recognition" (MSR) experiments have attempted to explore that matter (Ristau 2013). Initially it was a chimpanzee which had a mirror in its cage and many opportunities to look in it (Gallup 1970). At first, like many species, including young humans, it behaved to the mirror as though it were another individual; sometimes it reacted aggressively or fearfully, sometimes not. Some chimpanzees looked behind the mirror. Again, like young toddlers, it might seem to be testing the correlation between its movements and those in the mirror, walking back and forth and regarding the mirror image. In the actual "mirror test", a mark was placed on the chimp's face where it could not be seen, except in the reflected image. Would the chimpanzee attempt to explore or remove the mark? Most chimpanzees did specifically touch the mark and so passed the test, as do some, not all, bonobos, orangutans (*Pongo abelii*), gorillas, dolphins and common magpies (*Pica pica*) (Prior et al. 2008); ... indicating ... what exactly? Certainly not a sense of self that we may imagine as a thinking, conscious entity existing today, yesterday and into the future. Perhaps a sense of self as a body? Elephants (*Elephas maximus*) did not pass the test ... initially (Povinelli 1989). Finally, using a massive, sturdy metal mirror and allowing the elephants to explore it with their trunk resulted in a successful result (Plotnik et al. 2006). A smaller mirror placed behind a barrier did not suffice, again emphasizing the salience of sensory systems and modes of interaction when purporting to examine a species' cognitive capacities. Peculiarly, African grey parrots, the impressive artificial language learners and corvids, including the intelligent crows and ravens, do not pass the test either, while the magpie, also a member of the Corvid family, did (Prior et al. 2008). Yet a tiny tropical fish, the bluestreak cleaner wrasse (*Labroides dimidiatus*), a fish which cleans dead skin and parasites off larger fish, did apparently pass the test, though some scientists do question the interpretation (Kohda et al. 2019). The fish *is* known to have complex social relations, keeping track of hundreds of other fish, as it performs its cleaning tasks and avoids being eaten by the other fish. Other animals with complex social relations, such as monkeys, do not pass the MSR, nor do chickens, our pet cats and dogs and a host of other species. Intriguing matters.

THEORY OF MIND

Underlying these and other studies is a question of whether animals have a "Theory of Mind", that is, the ability to attribute mental states to oneself and others. Significant research on this issue began almost a half century ago, when Premack and Woodruff (1978) studied captive chimpanzees. The apes were shown several videos of humans struggling with problems; some were the classic tasks, such as inaccessible bananas, used decades before by Wolfgang Köhler (1925) to study chimpanzees' insightful problem solving. Other tasks were more complex, such as a human shivering due to a malfunctioning heater. After each video, a chimp was shown several photos, one of which provided a solution to the problem, viz. a stick that could be used to reach the bananas or a lit wick that could light the heater. Consistently, the chimp chose the correct solution which the researchers interpreted as indicating that the chimpanzee "recognized the videotape as representing a problem, understood the actor's purpose and chose alternatives compatible with that purpose".

Decades of further experiments and controversy ensued. Among the most impressive research is work recently conducted using a "false-belief" paradigm with three species of great apes, chimpanzees (*Pan troglodytes*), bonobos (*Pan paniscus*) and orangutans (*Pongo abelii*) (Kano et al. 2019). Understanding "false-beliefs" requires that an individual is aware that another's behaviour is driven by the other's beliefs about reality, which may differ from one's own. Many consider false-belief as the "hallmark of a representational theory of mind". In short, an individual, in this case, a great ape, can grasp when someone else believes information that is untrue. The experiment was rather complicated and we refer the reader to the publication. Basically, the great ape either had experience with a screen that was opaque or translucent. A human then saw a reward placed in one of two identical boxes. Then the human went behind the screen and the reward was moved from one box to the other and then removed altogether. The human returned and, without the screen barrier, decided which box held the reward. Simultaneously, the ape's eye movements were recorded. Depending on the ape's past experience with the screen, the ape presumably assumed the human could either see through the screen or could not. The ape's eye movements matched the presumed expectation. The apes who had experienced an opaque screen looked more often towards the original box placement, while there was no difference in looking biases for the apes who had experienced a translucent screen. The apes had used their own past experience to infer the mind state of another being. A complicated scenario, but a convincing demonstration of understanding false-belief.

Human–Animal Relations

Perhaps the most relevant and immediate impact of a universal consciousness, and the one in which the largest number of human stakeholders will be transformed, is in the arena of the human–animal bond (HAB) (see The American Veterinary Medical Association website for accepted definition – https://www.avma.org) and in animal-assisted interventions (AAI) (see Animal Assisted Intervention International for thorough description of AAI – https://aai-int.org/what-we-do/). In these domains, people are intimately connected to their non-human partners as domestic pets, working animals, sensory surrogates and sources of nutrition. Each of these human communities relies on non-human animals – often in life-or-death situations. A general recognition that we share a conscious world together would require a wholesale reframing of the norms under which these actions take place.

The evolutionary history of animal domestication is complex and under considerable debate (e.g. farm foxes and domestication syndrome (Lord et al. 2020)). Although the cognitive capacity of domesticated animals is often implicated as a key characteristic of domesticability, the notion that consciousness may be shared universally would likely pivot the conversation considerably. For example, the origin of domestic dogs has multiple possible histories and time courses, but is grounded in a mutualism of shared diet, pathogens and socioecology (Thalmann and Perri 2019). This interspecies relationship is closely linked to our past and present shared health outcomes and to the human stewardship of the earth (Sykes et al. 2020).

In the laboratory setting, animal welfare committee review panels, such as the federally mandated Institutional Animal Care and Use Committees (IACUC), currently monitor the well-being of vertebrate animals used in research. Pain and suffering are central issues to their mandates, but what of a recognition of deeper consciousness of these animals? In light of these revelations, the social ecosystem that these animals inhabit would need to be reimagined in order to reduce the stress of anticipation and traumatic effects of the experiments themselves. The regulatory framework of IACUC's would need to be recast from a reduction in suffering model to a more nurturing environment. The end results would be added costs and complexity in housing and experimentation details of these animals, but might likely yield more reliable data and may result in fewer vertebrate animals needed for research.

Conservation Practices and Animal Well-Being

Conservation practices have been informed by recent novel paradigms in which the anthropocentric perspective is flipped on its head. Models such as *compassionate conservation* (CC) and *multispecies justice* (MJ), as articulated by Santiago-Avila and Lynn (2020), have challenged the traditions of the dismissal of individual non-human claims in conservation biology and biodiversity conflicts. These frameworks for action represent attempts to aggregate the recognition of inclusive features of non-human animals that derive, in part, from their cognitive capacities. The addition of a universal consciousness to the interpretation of animal sentience will require an even more robust engagement of an ethical component in the formation of durable conservation strategies, well beyond what we currently have in the canon.

With a deeper understanding of the likely cognitive capacities, emotional states and social relationships of our non-human animal cohabitants of the earth, we also recognize through CC and MJ our responsibility in attempting to preserve their existence and thereby their environments – both from the standpoint of traditional ecosystem services, but also from the recognition of the individual sentience of each of the animals. Some, such as poaching and habitat fragmentation are already generally recognized as destructive and can be addressed with traditional conservation frameworks using universal consciousness as an additional supporting reason. Others, although well-meaning, such as species translocation and reintroductions, may cause suffering and destabilize the ecology of the region. These practices would require a re-examination of the motivation for using these conservation tactics.

We have known, for example, that reindeer avoid areas where transmission lines occur. It was assumed that perhaps they feared being exposed to predators while in the open spaces. Now we recognize that additionally, they and most other mammals, are able to detect ultraviolet light. As electrons rush through the power lines, if the lines are not well shielded, the nearby air particles will ionize, producing a "corona discharge", or sudden burst of ultraviolet light, a fairly terrifying event for any animal (Zastrow 2014).

The plastic bags we use so wantonly, finally end up, by the tons, in the ocean. There they collect marine algae and other bio debris, which is highly attractive as potential food to many fish, sea turtles and even marine birds. In fact, the preferred food of the endangered leatherback sea turtle (*Dermochelys coriacea*) is jellyfish (class *Scyphozoa*), species whose burgeoning populations can threaten the existence of many other marine organisms. A plastic bag not only looks like a jellyfish, but smells appealing too. Once eaten, the bags can prevent digestion of food while simultaneously creating a signal that the animal is "full" (Sevoca et al. 2016).

And the ocean is a noisy place, from our motors, submarines and particularly seismic testing, sometimes for military purposes, but often in deep water oil and gas explorations. Whales utilize very low frequency sounds in their interoceanic communications. Dolphins and whales echolocate with clicks to find their way. We cannot determine specifically why so many whale and dolphin strandings have been occurring, but the human's underwater noise production looms as a distinct possibility.

Yet another endangered species, one already endearing to many humans, is the elephant. Its existence is threatened due to habitat destruction from general development, but particularly from logging and other invasive industries such as agriculture, oil and gas facilities and mining. The Indian government, pressured by animal advocacy groups, has banned the use of elephants (*Elephas maximus*) in the logging industry, where they were used to haul logs through difficult terrains. That measure, though reducing the often-cruel practices with elephants, has now left them without the use of large areas to find grasses, small trees and wild fruit to eat. As the elephants' habitat shrinks in India and elsewhere, humans and elephants interact with dire consequences for both. Without the needed wild food, the elephants find farmers' crops and devour them, terrifying the farmers who fear both the massive beasts and their destructive economic impact. Some research is being conducted to better understand the personality of the elephants, in order to determine which are the daring ones which will enter the farmers' fields and humane means to deter them. The elephants' mahouts, the longtime owners and carers of the animals, are an integral part of the measures (Baker and Winkler 2020; Gritz 2020).

Conclusion

From the biological perspective, the challenge of integrating universal consciousness into the construction of hypotheses, design of research and interpretation of results is a daunting task. Inherent in this challenge is the recognition that a common language between physicists and life scientists has yet to be fully developed. However, the complexity does not have to be interpreted as an impediment. Instead, the opportunity to work across scientific disciplines is a tremendous opportunity to invite new ways of understanding the living world. The relevance of universal consciousness is unquestionable, even if the discovery is fraught with technical difficulties. The advantage that the life sciences has is a long history of working with issues of sentience across a broad scale of taxonomic examples and temporal variations. From the trans-oceanic acoustic communication of humpback whales, with dialects that change over decades to the microfluctuations in the membranes of neurons which occur in just a few milliseconds, the opportunity exists to apply the lens of universal consciousness to nearly limitless paradigms. The requirement for a robust investigation will hinge upon the ability of interdisciplinary scientists to work together, create an agreed-upon set of scientific definitions and attract the necessary funding to conduct experiments. The outcomes are unpredictable, but the importance and potential significance cannot be overstated.

References

Alcock, J., 1972, "The Evolution of the Use of Tools by Feeding Animals. *Evolution*, 26(3): 464-73.

Anderson, R.C., J.A. Mather & J.B. Wood, 2010, *Octopus: The Ocean's Intelligent Invertebrate*, Portland, OR: Timber Press.

Baker, L. and R. Winkler, 2020, "Asian Elephant Rescue, Rehabilitation and Rewilding", *Animal Sentience*, 28(1): e 296.

Ball, P., 2019, "Neuroscience Readies for a Showdown Over Consciousness Ideas", *Quanta Magazine* (6 March), Retrieved from https://www.quantamagazine.org/neuroscience-readies-for-a-showdown-over-consciousness-ideas-20190306/#

Baluška, F. and A.S. Reber, 2019, "Sentience and Consciousness in Single Cells: How the First Minds Emerged in Unicellular Species", *Bioessays*, 41(3): e1800229.

Bekoff, M., C. Allen and G.M. Burghardt (eds), 2002, *The Cognitive Animal: Empirical and Theoretical Perspectives on Animal Cognition*, Cambridge, MA: MIT Press.

Bennett, J., 1983, "Cognitive Ethology: Theory or Poetry", *Behavioral and Brain Sciences*, 6: 356-58.

Block, N., 1995, "On a Confusion about a Function of Consciousness", *Behavioral and Brain Science*, 18(2): 227-87.

Chalmers, D.J., 1995, "Explaining Consciousness: The Hard Problem", *Journal of Consciousness Studies*, 2(3): 200-19.

———, 1996, *The Conscious Mind: In Search of a Fundamental Theory*, New York: Oxford University Press.

Chernetsov, N., A. Pakhomov, D. Kobylkov, D. Kishkinev and H. Mouritsen, 2017, "Migratory Eurasian Reed Warblers Can Use Magnetic Declination to Solve the Longitude Problem," *Current Biology*, 27(17): 2647-51.

Darwin, C., 1872, *The Expression of the Emotions in Man and Animals*, London: Murray. (Reprinted Chicago, IL: University of Chicago Press; 1965 with Preface by Konrad Lorenz.)

Dennett, D.C., 1983, "Intentional Systems in Cognitive Ethology: The 'Panglossian Paradigm' Defended", *Behavioral and Brain Sciences*, 6(3): 343-90.

Descartes, R., 1989, *Passions of the Soul* (tr. S.H. Voss), Indianapolis, IN: Hackett Press. (Original work published in 1649.)

Deutschlander, M.E., R. Muheim and F. Bairlein, 2019, "Magnetic Orientation in Migratory Songbirds", in *Encyclopedia of Animal Behavior*, ed. M.D. Breed and J. Moore, 2nd edn, vol. 2 (pp. 655-65), Oxford: Academic Press. https://doi.org/10.1016/B978-0-12-809633-8.90099-2 This is an update of Deutschlander, M.E. and R. Muheim, 2010, "Magnetic Orientation in Migratory Songbirds", in *Encyclopedia of Animal Behavior*, ed. M.D. Breed and J. Moore (vol. 2) (pp. 314-323), Oxford, England: Academic Press. http://dx.doi.org.ezproxy.cul.columbia.edu/10.1016/B978-08-045337-8.00363-6.

Douglas, R.H. and G. Jeffery, 2014, "The Spectral Transmission of Ocular Media Suggests Ultraviolet Sensitivity Is Widespread among Mammals", *Proceeding of the Royal Society B: Biological Sciences*, 281(1780), 20132995. http://doi.org/10.1098/rspb.2013.2995.

Emlen, S.T. and J.T. Emlen, Jr., 1966, "A Technique for Recording

Migratory Orientation of Captive Birds", *The Auk*, 83(3): 361-67. https://doi.org/10.2307/4083048.

Engesser, S. and S.W. Townsend, 2019, "Combinatoriality in the Vocal Systems of Nonhuman Animals", *WIREs Cognitive Science*, 10(4): e1493. https://doi.org/10.1002/wcs.1493.

Foster, C., 2016, *Being a Beast*, London: Profile Books.

von Frisch, K., 1950, "Die sonne als kompass im leben der bienen", *Experientia (Basel)*, 6(6): 210-21.

Gallup, G.G., Jr., 1970, Chimpanzees: Self-recognition", *Science*, 167(3914): 86-87.

Gould, J.L., 2008, "Animal Navigation: Evolution of Magnetic Orientation", *Current Biology*, 18(11): R482-84. https://doi.org/10.1016/j.cub.2008.03.052.

———, 2010, "Magnetoreception", *Current Biology*, 20(10): R431-R435.

Gould, J.L. and C.G. Gould, 2012, *Nature's Compass: The Mystery of Animal Navigation*, Princeton, NJ: Princeton University Press.

Griesser, M., 2008, Referential Calls Signal Predator Behaviour in a Group-living Bird Species", *Current Biology*, 18(1): 69-73.

Griffin, D.R. and G.B. Speck, 2004, "New Evidence of Animal Consciousness", *Animal Cognition*, 7(1): 5-18. https://doi.org/10.1007/s10071-003-0203-x.

Griffin, D.R., 1976, *The Question of Animal Awareness*, rev. 2nd edn, 1981, New York: Rockefeller University Press.

———, 1984, *Animal Thinking*, Cambridge, MA: Harvard University Press.

———, 1985, "Animal Consciousness", *Neuroscience and Biobehavioral Reviews*, 9(4): 615-22.

———, 1992, *Animal Minds*, Chicago, IL: University of Chicago Press.

———, 2001, *Animal Minds: Beyond Cognition to Consciousness*, Chicago, IL: University of Chicago Press.

Gritz, J.R., 2020, "Researchers Are Learning How Asian Elephants Think: In Order to Save Them", *Smithsonian Magazine* (April).

Retrieved from https://www.smithsonianmag.com/science-nature/researchers-learning-asian-elephants-think-save-them-180974366/.

Harnad, S., 2016, "Animal Sentience: The Other-minds Problem", *Animal Sentience*, 1(1): 2016.001.

Hecht, S., S. Shlaer and M.H. Pirenne, 1942, "Energy, Quanta and Vision", *Journal of General Physiology*, 25(6): 819-40. https://doi.org/10.1085/jgp.25.6.819.

Heinrich, B., 2014, *Ravens in Winter*, New York: Simon & Schuster.

Hochner, B., 2008, "Octopuses", *Current Biology*, 18(19): R897-R898.

Hockett, C.F., 1958, *A Course in Modern Linguistics*, New York: Macmillan.

Hore, P.J. and H. Mouritsen, 2016, "The Radical-pair Mechanism of Magnetoreception", *Annual Review of Biophysics*, 45: 299-344.

Kano, F., C. Krupenye, S. Hirata, M. Tomonaga and J. Call, 2019, "Great Apes Use Self-experience to Anticipate an Agent's Action in a False-belief Test", *Proceedings of the National Academy of Sciences of the United States of America*, 116(42): 20904-20909. https://doi.org/10.1073/pnas.1910095116.

Kaplan, G., 2014, "Animal Communication: Advanced Review", *WIREs Cognitive Science*, 5(6): 661-77. https://doi.org/10.1002/wcs.1321.

Kohda, M., T. Hotta, T. Takeyama, S. Awata, H. Tanaka, J.Y. Asai and A.L. Jordan, 2019, "If a Fish Can Pass the Mark Test, What Are the Implications for Consciousness and Self-awareness Testing in Animals?", *PLoS Biology*, 17(2): e3000021. https://doi.org/10.1371/journal.pbio.3000021.

Köhler, W., 1925, *The Mentality of Apes*, London: Routledge and Kegan Paul.

Larson, G. and D. Fuller, 2014, "The Evolution of Animal Domestication", *Annual Review of Ecology, Evolution and Systematics*, 45: 115-36.

Laschi, C., 2009, *Fundamentals of Inspirations from Octopus Biology to Flexible Robotics* [PDF document]. Retrieved from Embodied

Intelligence. Seventh Framework Programme: http://www.octopus-project.eu/files/OCTOPUS_IP_D3.1_300409.pdf.

Lettvin, J.Y., H.R. Maturana, W.S. McCulloch and W.H. Pitts, 1959, "What the Frog's Eye Tells the Frog's Brain", *Proceedings of the IRE*, 47(11): 1940-51.

Lord, K.A., G. Larson, R.P. Coppinger and E.K. Karlsson, 2020, "The History of Farm Foxes Undermines the Animal Domestication Syndrome", *Trends in Ecology and Evolution*, 35(2): 125-36. https://doi.org/10.1016/j.tree.2019.10.011.

Low, P., J. Panksepp, D. Reiss, D. Edelman, B. van Swinderen and C. Koch, 2012, "The Cambridge Declaration on Consciousness", in *Francis Crick Memorial Conference: Consciousness in Human and Non-human Animals*. Panel conducted at the first Francis Crick Memorial Conference in Cambridge, England.

Manser, M.B., 2001, "The Acoustic Structure of Suricates' Alarm Calls Varies with Predator Type and the Level of Response Urgency", *Proceedings of the Royal Society B: Biological Sciences*, 268(1483): 2315-24. https://doi.org/10.1098/rspb.2001.1773.

Margulis, L., 2001, "The Conscious Cell", *Annals of the New York Academy of Sciences*, 929(1): 55-70.

Millikan, R., 1984, *Language, Thought and Other Biological Categories: New Foundations for Realism*, Cambridge, MA: MIT Press.

———, 1998, "A Common Structure for Concepts of Individuals, Stuffs and Real Kinds: More Mama, More Milk and More Mouse", *Behavioral and Brain Sciences*, 21(1): 55-100. https://doi.org/10.1017/S0140525X9800040.

Mouritsen, H., 2018a, "Long-distance Navigation and Magnetoreception in Migratory Animals", *Nature*, 558: 50-59. https://doi.org/10.1038/s41586-018-0176-1.

———, 2018b, "The Magnetic Sense of Night-migratory Songbirds", in *27th International Conference on Ornithology* (August), Plenary Address conducted at the meeting of the International Ornithologists' Union, Vancouver, BC.

Munn, C., 1986, "Birds that 'Cry Wolf'", *Nature*, 319: 143-45. https://doi.org/10.1038/319143a0.

Nagel, T., 1974, "What Is It Like to Be a Bat?", *Philosophical Review*, 83(4): 435-50.

Nealson, K.H., T. Platt and J.W. Hastings, 1970, "Cellular Control of the Synthesis and Activity of the Bacterial Luminescent System", *Journal of Bacteriology*, 104(1): 313-22.

Pavlov, I.P., 1960, *Conditioned reflexes*, ed. and tr. G.V. Anrep, New York: Dover. (Original work published in 1927.)

Plotnik, J.M., F.B.M de Waal and D. Reiss, 2006, "Self-recognition in an Asian Elephant", *Proceedings of the National Academy of Sciences of the United States of America*, 103(45): 17053-57.

Povinelli, D.J., 1989, "Failure to Find Self-recognition in Asian Elephants (*Elephas maximus*) in Contrast to Their Use of Mirror Cues to Discover Hidden Food", *Journal of Comparative Psychology*, 103(2): 122-31. https://doi.org/10.1037/0735-7036.103.2.122.

Premack, D. and G. Woodruff, 1978, "Does the Chimpanzee Have a Theory of Mind?", *Behavioral and Brain Sciences*, 1(4): 515-26. https://doi.org/10.1017/S0140525X00076512.

Prior, H., A. Schwarz and O. Güntürkün, 2008, "Mirror-induced Behaviour in the Magpie (*Pica pica*): Evidence of Self-recognition", *PLoS biology*, 6(8): e202. https://doi.org/10.1371/journal.pbio.0060202.

Reber, A.S., 1996, "Caterpillars, Consciousness and All That", Invited Address conducted at the meeting of the British Psychological Society, Southampton, UK.

———, 2016, "Caterpillars, Consciousness and the Origins of Mind", *Animal Sentience*, 11(1): 1-13.

———, 2018, *The First Minds: Caterpillars, 'Karyotes and Consciousness*, Oxford: Oxford University Press. https://doi.org/10.1093/oso/9780190 854157.001.0001.

Rescorla, R.A., 1967, "Pavlovian Conditioning and Its Proper Control Procedures", *Psychological Review*, 74(1): 71-80. https://doi.org/10.1037/h0024109

———, 1988, "Pavlovian Conditioning: It's not What You Think It Is", *American Psychologist*, 43(3): 151-60. https://doi.org/10.1037/0003-066X.43.3.151.

Ristau, C.A. (in prep.) *The Scientist Who Discovered Bat Sonar and the Minds of Animals: Donald R. Griffin: A Revolutionary* (will be self published).

———, Personal observations, Drill Ranch, Pandrillus Foundation, Afi Mountain, Cross River State, Nigeria.

Ristau, C.A. and D. Robbins, 1982, "Language in the Great Apes: A Critical Review", in *Advances in the Study of Behavior*, ed. J.S. Rosenblatt, R.A. Hinde, C. Beer and M.C. Busnel, vol. 12, pp. 142-255, New York: Academic Press.

Ristau, C.A., 1991a, "Aspects of the Cognitive Ethology of an Injury Feigning Plover", in C.A. Ristau (ed.), 1991b, *Cognitive Ethology: The Minds of Other Animals: Essays in Honor of Donald R. Griffin*, pp. 91-126, Hillsdale, NJ: Lawrence Erlbaum Associates.

———, (ed.), 1991b, *Cognitive Ethology: The Minds of Other Animals: Essays in Honor of Donald R. Griffin*, Hillsdale, NJ: Lawrence Erlbaum Associates.

———, 2005, "Donald Redfield Griffin: A Biographical Memoir", *Proceedings of the American Philosophical Society*, 149(3): 399-411.

———, 2013, "Cognitive Ethology, Advanced Review", *WIREs Cognitive Science*, 4(5): 493-509. https://doi.org/10.1002/wcs.1239.

———, 2016a, "Beginnings: Physics, Sentience and LUCA: Commentary on A. Reber, Caterpillars, Consciousness and the Origins of Mind", *Animal Sentience*, 11(4): 1-4.

———, 2016b, "Wild Things", *Science*, 352(6292): 1402. https://doi.org/10.1126/science.aaf8235.

Ritz, T., S. Adem and K. Schulten, 2000, "A Model for Photoreceptor-based Magnetoreception in Birds", *Biophysical Journal*, 78(2): 707-18.

Romanes, G.J., 1884, *Mental Evolution in Animals*, with posthumous essay on instinct by Charles Darwin, repr. 1969, New York: ABS Press.

Santiago-Avila, F.J. and W.S. Lynn, 2020, "Bridging Compassion and Justice in Conservation Ethics", *Biological Conservation*, 248: 108648.

Schulten, K., C.E. Swenberg and A. Weller, 1978, "A Biomagnetic Sensory Mechanism Based on Magnetic Field Modulated Coherent Electron Spin Motion", *Zeitschrift für Physikalische Chemie*, 111(1): 1-5.

Searle, J.R., 1980, "Minds, Brains and Programs", *Behavioral and Brain Sciences*, 3(3): 417-57.

Sevoca, M.S., M.E. Wohlfeil, S.E. Ebeler and G.A. Nevitt, 2016, "Marine Plastic Debris Emits a Keystone Infochemical for Olfactory Foraging Seabirds", *Science Advances*, 2(11): e1600395. https://doi.org/10.1126/sciadv.1600395.

Seyfarth, R.M., D.L. Cheney and P. Marler, 1980, "Vervet Monkey Alarm Calls: Semantic Communication in a Free-ranging Primate", *Animal Behavior*, 28: 1070-94.

Signorelli, C.M., 2018, "Can Computers Become Conscious and Overcome Humans?", *Frontiers in Robotics and AI*, 5: 1-21. https://doi.org/10.3389/frobt.2018.00121.

Skinner, B.F., 1938, *The Behaviour of Organisms: An Experimental Analysis*, New York: Appleton-Century Crofts.

Slobodchikoff, C.N., W.R. Briggs, P.A. Dennis and A.-M.C. Hodge, 2012, "Size and Shape Information Serve as Labels in the Alarm Calls of Gunnison's Prairie Dogs *Cynomys gunnisoni*", *Current Zoology*, 58(5): 719-26.

Slobodchikoff, C.N., J. Kiriazis, C. Fischer, E. Creef, 1991, "Semantic Information Distinguishing Individual Predators in the Alarm Calls of Gunnison's Prairie Dogs", *Animal Behavior*, 42(5): 712-19.

Smith, W.J., 1977, *The Behavior of Communicating*, Cambridge, MA: Harvard University Press.

———, 1998, "Cognitive Implications of an Information-sharing Model of Animal Communication", in *Animal Cognition in Nature*, ed. R.P. Balda, I.M. Pepperberg and A.C. Kamil, pp. 227-43, New York: Academic Press.

Struhsaker, T.T., 1967, *The Red Colobus Monkey*, Chicago, IL: University of Chicago Press.

Sykes, N., P. Beirne, A. Horowitz, I. Jones, L. Kalof, E. Karlsson, T. King, H. Litwak, R.A. McDonald, L.J. Murphy, N. Pemberton, D. Promislow, A. Rowan, P.W. Stahl, J. Tehrani, E. Tourigny, C.D.L. Wynne, E. Strauss and G. Larson, 2020, "Humanity's Best Friend: A Dog-centric Approach to Addressing Global Challenges", *Animals*, 10(3): 502.

Thalmann, O. and A.R. Perri, 2019, "Paleogenomic Inferences of Dog Domestication", in *Paleogenomics: Genome-scale Analysis of Ancient DNA*, ed. C. Lindqvist and O.P. Rajora, pp. 273-306, Berlin/Heidelberg: Springer International.

Titchener, E.B., 1901-05, *Experimental Psychology*, vols 1-4, New York: Macmillan.

Titchener, Edward B., n.d., in *Encyclopaedia Britannica online*. Retrieved from www.britannica.com/biography/Edward-B-Titchener.

Tononi, G. and C. Koch, 2015, "Consciousness: Here, There and Everywhere?", *Philosophical Transactions of the Royal Society, B: Biological Sciences*, 370(1668): 20140167.

Townsend, S.W. and M.B. Manser, 2013, "Functionally Referential Communication in Mammals: The Past, Present and the Future, *Ethology*, 119(1), 1-11. https://doi.org/10.1111/eth.12015.

von Uexküll, J., 1985, *Environment (Umwelt) and the Inner World of Animals*, tr. C.J. Mellor and D. Gove (Originally published in *The Foundations of Comparative Ethology*, ed. G.M. Burghardt, pp. 222-45, New York: Van Nostrand Reinhold in 1909).

de Waal, F., 2016, *Are We Smart Enough to Know How Smart Animals Are?*, New York: W.W. Norton.

Wallace, A.R., 1858, "On the Tendencies of Varieties to Depart Indefinitely from the Original Type", *Journal of the Proceedings of the Linnean Society of London*, 30: 53-62.

Wang, C.X., I.A. Hilburn, D.A. Wu, Y. Mizuhara, C.P. Cousté, J.N.H. Abrahams, S.E. Bernstein, A. Matani, S. Shimojo and J.L. Kirschvink, 2019, "Transduction of the Geomagnetic Field as

Evidenced from Alpha-band Activity in the Human Brain", *eNeuro*, 6(2): 1-23.

Weir, A.A.S., J. Chappell and A. Kacelnik, 2002, "Shaping of Hooks in New Caledonian Crows", *Science*, 297(5583): 981.

Wells, M.J., 1978, *Octopus*, London, England: Chapman and Hall.

Wheeler, B.C., 2009, "Monkeys Crying Wolf?: Tufted Capuchin Monkeys Use Anti-Predator Calls to Usurp Resources from Conspecifics", *Proceedings of the Royal Society B: Biological Sciences*, 276(1669): 3013-18.

Wundt, W., 1873-74, *Grundzüge der physiologischen Psychologie* (2 vols (1873-74; 3 vol., 6th edn, 1908-11); (*Principles of Physiological Psychology*), Leipzig: Verlag von Wilhelm Engelmann.

Zastrow, M., 2014, "Power Lines Look Like Terrifying Bursts of Light to Animals", PBS *NOVA Series: Nature* (20 March). Retrieved from https://www.pbs.org.

Zuberbühler, K., 2018, "Combinatorial Capacities in Primates", *Current Opinion in Behavioral Sciences*, 21: 1-169.

Contributors

Debashish Banerji is the Haridas Chaudhuri Professor of Indian Philosophies and Cultures and the Doshi Professor of Asian Art at CIIS. He is also the Program Chair for the East-West Psychology department. Prior to CIIS, he served as Professor of Indian Studies and Dean of Academics at the University of Philosophical Research, Los Angeles. He has taught as adjunct faculty at the Pasadena City College, University of California, Los Angeles and University of California, Irvine. His interests lie in postmodern, postcolonial and posthuman approaches to Indian philosophy, psychology and culture. Banerji has curated close to fifteen exhibitions of Indian and Japanese art. He has authored and edited around ten books and art catalogues on major figures of "the Bengal Renaissance" such as the Indian poet Rabindranath Tagore, the artist Abanindranath Tagore and the spiritual thinker Sri Aurobindo; on Critical Posthumanism, Yoga Psychology and on a variety of creative and art-related projects. His most recent books are the monograph *Meditations on the Isha Upanishad: Tracing the Philosophical Vision of Sri Aurobindo* (2019) and *Philo-Sophia: Wisdom Goddess Traditions*, co-edited with CIIS emeritus President, Robert McDermott. More updated information on his talks, publications and other academic activities may be found at his website www.debashishbanerji.com.

Daniele Struppa, PhD, is a mathematician whose expertise is in the area of Fourier Analysis and its applications. He is the author of more than 200 refereed publications, and several monographs, including *Slice Regular Functions of a Quaternionic Variable*, now in its second edition with Springer Nature, which is the standard text on the theory of slice-regular functions of quaternionic variables, that Gentili and Struppa introduced in 2006 in a much cited article in *Advances in Mathematics*, and that has now become a very active area of research. In 1981 he received the Bartolozzi Prize from the Italian Mathematical Union for his work *The Fundamental Principle for Systems of Convolution Equations*, published in the Memoirs of the American Mathematical Society, and in 2016 his paper "Quantum Violation of the Pigeonhole Principle and the Nature of Quantum Correlation" (co-authored with Aharonov, Colombo, Popescu, Sabadini and Tollaksen) was awarded the Cozzarelli Prize from the Proceedings of the National Academy of Sciences. Dr. Struppa's recent research has resulted in several articles on the mathematical aspects of superoscillations, a phenomenon that arises in a natural way from the notion of weak values introduced by Aharonov. Dr. Struppa is also the recipient of the Ellis Island Medal of Honor, and is currently the President of Chapman University, a position he held since 2016, after having served as its Provost since 2006.

Stanley A. Klein is an American psychophysicist. He was Professor of Vision Science and Optometry at the University of California, Berkeley and a member of the Berkeley Visual Processing Laboratory. He was a consulting editor for *Attention, Perception & Psychophysics*, a publication of the Psychonomic Society which promotes the communication of scientific research in psychology and allied sciences. His major area of research has been neurotechnology, a field of science that studies the body and mind through the nervous system by electronics and mechanisms. He was the co-chair for the SPIE (an international society on the science and application of light) meetings on human vision. Klein has authored and co-authored numerous papers on visual perception in the human brain. He is currently interested in the intersection of religion and science.

Jose Acacio de Barros is a Liberal Studies faculty at San Francisco State University, specializing in the foundations of quantum physics. With a distinguished research career, he has made significant contributions and has engaged in interdisciplinary work at the intersection of physics, foundations of mathematics, psychology and philosophy of mind.

Professor de Barros received his MSc and PhD in Physics from the prestigious Brazilian Center for Physics Research (CBPF). Under the co-advisement of Francisco Doria, Newton da Costa and Antonio Teixeira, his doctoral research explored the link between the foundations of mathematics and physics.

Throughout his career, de Barros has expanded his research interests to encompass interdisciplinary studies in psychology and philosophy of mind. His investigations have delved into the philosophical implications of quantum theory for our understanding of consciousness, cognition, and the nature of reality. This interdisciplinary approach has resulted in insights and contributed to the broader scientific discourse.

Professor de Barros has published over 100 research papers, some in the most prestigious journals. Professor de Barros has written or edited four books, including his forthcoming *Distinguishing Indistinguishables: Differences between Classical and Quantum Regimes*, in co-authorship with Decio Krause and Federico Holik.

Professor de Barros's research in the foundations of quantum physics and his interdisciplinary work in psychology and philosophy of mind demonstrates his commitment to exploring the profound implications of quantum theory. His contributions to the scientific community and his membership in the Brazilian Academy of Philosophy reflect his significant impact and recognition as a scholar.

Professor de Barros can be reached at jacaciodebarros@gmail.com.

Mailing Address (for contributor copy): 808 Arbor Rd, Menlo Park, CA 94025, USA.

David Chalmers is University Professor of Philosophy and Neural Science and co-director of the Center for Mind, Brain, and Consciousness at New York University. He is the author of *The Conscious Mind* (1996), *Constructing the World* (2012), and *Reality+: Virtual Worldsand the Problems of Philosophy* (2022). He co-founded the Association for the Scientific Study of Consciousness and the PhilPapers Foundation. In 2006, he was elected a Fellow of the Australian Academy of the Humanities. In 2013, he was elected a Fellow of the American Academy of Arts & Sciences. Chalmers is best known for formulating the hard problem of consciousness. He works in the philosophy of mind and language, metaphysics and epistemology, and the foundations of cognitive science, physics, and technology.

Kelvin McQueen is an associate professor of philosophy and research affiliate of the Institute for Quantum Studies at Chapman University. He works in the philosophy of science and specializes in the foundations of quantum mechanics and the neuroscience of consciousness. His recent quantum mechanics publications have focused on Bell's theorem with M. Waregell, "Reformulating Bell's Theorem: The Search for a Truly Local Quantum Theory", *Studies in History and Philosophy of Modern Physics* (2020), 70: 39-50, the many-worlds interpretation with L. Vaidman, "In Defence of the Self-location Uncertainty Account of Probability in the Many-worlds Interpretation", *Studies in History and Philosophy of Modern Physics* (2019), 66: 14-23 and "How the Many Worlds Interpretation brings Common

Sense to Paradoxical Quantum Experiments", in *Scientific Challenges to Common Sense Philosophy* (2020), Routledge; and consciousness-collapse interpretations with D.J. Chalmers, "Consciousness and the Collapse of the Wave Function", in *Consciousness and Quantum Mechanics* (2022), Oxford University Press. His recent neuroscience of consciousness publications have focused on the integrated information theory, on testing its experimental predictions with A.R. Hopkins, "Filled/Non-filled Pairs: An Empirical Challenge to the Integrated Information Theory of Consciousness", *Consciousness and Cognition* (2022), 97: 103245; and exploring its philosophical consequences with N. Tsuchiya, "When do Parts form Wholes?: Integrated Information as the Restriction on Mereological Composition", *Neuroscience of Consciousness* (2023), (1), niad013.

Menas C. Kafatos works in quantum physics, cosmology, data information systems, remote sensing, climate change and natural hazards. Fletcher Jones Endowed Professor of Computational Physics. Director of the Institute for Earth, Computing, Human and Observing (ECHO), Chapman University, Orange, CA. Founding Dean, Schmid College Science & Technology, Vice-Chancellor Special Projects 2008-12. At George Mason University, Director, Center for Earth Observing & Space Research, 1995–2008, Founding Dean, School of Computational Sciences, 2002-06 and Acting Chair, Department of Physics, 1989-91. BA in Physics, 1967 Cornell University, PhD in Physics, 1972 M.I.T. Thesis advisor, Professor Philip Morrison. Physicist, writer and philosopher with interdisciplinary, transdisciplinary and focused international reputation. Works extensively in consciousness, the role of the mind in quantum measurements and quantum reality. Leader of one of three successful alternative EOSDIS distributed architectural studies for NASA. Established XLB download antenna at CU. IEEE Orange County Chapter - Outstanding Leadership & Professional Service Award, 2011. Recipient Spirit of Rustum Roy Award, 2011. Chapman University $1M Club. Denny Award for work in Operational Oceanography. Forty-five years Teaching & Mentorship. Expert on quantum mechanics, measurements and the role of the mind. Since 2020, Chairman of the Board, Friends of Sivananda Ashram, Inc. Discussions in science and religion with philosophers, Buddhist monks. CU team leader to UN COP-15, Copenhagen, 2009. $50M+ from 70 grants, 1990 to present.

Publications:

- 347 Peer-Reviewed

- **Books, Blogs:** https://blogs.scientificamerican.com/observations/coming-to-grips-with-the-implications-of-quantum-mechanics/
- Bernardo Kastrup, Henry P. Stapp, Menas C. Kafatos 2018.
- *You Are the Universe Harmony*, co-author D. Chopra (2017), NYT Bestseller translated into many languages.
- *Science, Reality & Everyday Life* (2020)
  email: kafatos@chapman.edu
  Research Profile: https://www.menaskafatos.com/

Goro Kato is a professor emeritus at California Polytechnic State University, San Luis Obispo, CA. He was born in 1948 in Kariya, Japan. He came to the United States as a Rotary International Foundation Fellow in June 1972. He earned his PhD at the University Rochester in Rochester, New York with advisor Saul Lubkin. He has given talks and lectures for workshops and seminars at international conferences in Italy, Belgium, the UK, Romania, Holland, Sweden, Germany, Japan and the USA. Kato has been invited to the Institute for Advanced Study in Princeton, New Jersey in 1986, 1988, 1990, 1996, 2000, 2003, 2008. His areas of study are p-adic cohomology and its zeta invariants, cohomological algebra, and temporal topos.

He has published the following books:

- *Fundamentals of Algebraic Microlocal Analysis*, co-author Daniele Struppa (1999),
- *Kohomologi no Kokoro* (in Japanese) (2003),
- *The Heart of Cohomology* (2006),
- *Elements of Temporal Topos* (2013).
- Memoir, "The Fate Changing Door Knock by a Great Mathematician" (in Japanese) (2019).
- *Categorical and Sheaf Theoretic Methods for Epistemology and Philosophy of Sciences* (forthcoming)

He may be reached at: gkato@calpoly.edu

Home mailing address: Goro C. Kato, 2766 Flora Street, San Luis Obispo, CA, 93401-4624, USA.

Ulrich Mohrhoff studied physics at the University of Göttingen, Germany, and at the Indian Institute of Science in Bengaluru, India. He has taught a philosophically oriented course of quantum mechanics to higher secondary and undergraduate students at the Sri Aurobindo International Centre of Education in Pondicherry, India. He has published numerous papers on foundations of quantum mechanics, consciousness, and the interface between physics and Indian philosophy, as well as a textbook of quantum mechanics *The World According to Quantum Mechanics: Why the Laws of Physics Make Perfect Sense After All* (2018). His most recent papers of note are "A QBist Ontology", *Foundations of Science* (2022), 27: 1253-77; Niels Bohr, Objectivity, and the Irreversibility of Measurements", *Quantum Studies: Mathematics and Foundations* (2020), 7: 373-82; "Quantum Mchanics in a New Light", *Foundations of Science* (2017), 22: 517-37.

He now publishes *Aurocafe*, a newsletter about issues in philosophy of science and the philosophy of mind/consciousness, and about whatever matters in the long run (and what matters now so that there may be a long run).

Ruth E. Kastner earned her MS in Physics and PhD in History and Philosophy of Science from the University of Maryland. Since that time, she has taught widely and conducted research in Foundations of Physics, particularly in interpretations of quantum theory. She was one of three winners of the 2021 Alumni Research Award at the University of Maryland, College Park (https://alumni.umd.edu/news/research-award-ruth-kastner-82-ms-92-phd-99) . She is the author of three books: *The Transactional Interpretation of Quantum Theory: The Reality of Possibility* (2012; 2nd edn 2022), *Understanding Our Unseen Reality: Solving Quantum Riddles* (2015); and *Adventures in Quantumland: Exploring Our Unseen Reality* (2019). She has presented talks and interviews throughout the world and in video recordings on the interpretational challenges of quantum theory. Her author page is ruthekastner.org and she has a blog at transactionalinterpretation.org. She is also a dedicated *yoga* practitioner and received her 200-Hour Yoga Alliance Instructor Certification in February, 2020.

Subhash Kak is Regents Professor at Oklahoma State University in Stillwater, USA and a Distinguished Academic Scholar at Chapman University. His research is on AI, quantum computing, archaeoastronomy, and history of science, and he has also written extensively on the social impacts of AI. He coined the term quantum neural computing which is a theory of brain processing that is partly classical and partly quantum. He has made the surprising discovery that the ancient Indians knew that the sun and the moon are approximately 108 times their respective diametres from the earth. His most recent work is a theory that physical space has a dimensionality of *e* (2.718..) and he has used this to propose solutions to the missing dark matter and dark energy problems as well as explain many peculiarities in the organization of the genetic code. His work has been showcased in the popular media including Discovery and History channels, PBS, Public TV in Europe, and in several documentaries on science and art. He is author of thirty books that include *Matter and Mind* and *The Architecture of Knowledge*. He is currently a member of Indian Prime Minister's Science, Technology and Innovation Advisory Council (PM-STIAC). E-mail: subhash.kak@gmail.com

Mailing address: Subhash Kak, 2605 W. Summerlin Ct., Stillwater, OK 74074, USA.

Neil Theise is a professor of pathology at the NYU Grossman School of Medicine. His diagnostic subspecialty is liver pathology and he is an international thought later in human liver cancer, regression of liver scarring and cirrhosis, and stem cells in human liver maintenance and repair. Through his scientific research, he has pioneered adult stem cell plasticity and the anatomy of the human interstitium. He has published over 200 papers in peer-reviewed journals, including *Science, Nature, Nature Medicine* and *Cell*, and authored more than thirty chapters and/or edited textbooks, including the standard medical references *Robbins' Pathologic Basis of Disease* and the World Health Organization's "Blue Book" *Tumors of the Digestive Tract*. Dr. Theise's studies in complexity theory have led to interdisciplinary collaborations in fields such as integrative medicine, consciousness studies, and the science-religion dialogue. For this work, he received an honorary doctorate from the University of Bordeaux in 2020. He has recently synthesized these ideas into a book for a general readership, *Notes on Complexity: A Scientific Theory of Connection, Consciousness, and Being*.

Eric Strauss is President's Professor of Biology at Loyola Marymount University and Founding Executive Director of the LMU Center for Urban Resilience (CURes). Broadly trained in biology, ecology and multi-media communication, Eric has extended the model for traditional faculty scholarship through transdisciplinary initiatives by cofounding the Urban Ecology Institute in Boston while he served as a faculty member at Boston College and CURes in Los Angeles, both of which provide interdisciplinary educational, community based research, green restoration programmes and restorative justice to underserved neighbourhoods and their residents. In addition, Dr. Strauss is the Founding Senior Editor of a web-based peer-reviewed journal, *Cities and the Environment*, which is funded in part by the USDA Forest Service. Supported by over 100 grants and contracts, his research includes collaborative studies of coyotes, crows, hummingbirds and urban forest ecology, with a specialty in understanding animal–human relationships, humane management responses to wildlife problems and urban greenspace programme development. He has co-written multi-media textbooks in biology (*Biology: The Web of Life*) and urban ecology (*Urban EcoLab*) as well as hosting multiple video series on the life sciences and ecology. In collaboration with photographer Daniel Gottlieb, Eric has authored a natural history and photography book, *Hummingbirds of Gottlieb Native Garden* (2021). Dr. Strauss received a Bachelor of Science in Mass Communication from Emerson College and a PhD in Biology from Tufts University in 1990. He has held teaching fellowships and faculty appointments at Tufts University, The University of Massachusetts Boston and Boston College.

Carolyn A. Ristau is a cognitive ethologist whose research includes field studies of cognition and communication in primates and birds. Among her writings are extensive reviews of the language and cognition studies conducted with apes and other species. Her field experiments with plovers explore the cognitive aspects of their parental and antipredator behaviours. Her work provided evidence for the plovers' strategic use of a "broken-wing display", often previously considered a randomly directed innate response.

She also investigates human ethno-political conflict and cooperation, primarily in Africa as well as New York City, post-Sept 11. Her African work includes conservation efforts, in particular for endangered forest elephants and sea turtles.

Currently, she is completing a biography of Donald R. Griffin, who founded the field of cognitive ethology, the study of animals' mental experiences as they behave in their normal lives within their natural environment. The book encompasses Griffin's and others' work in avian navigation, bat echolocation (another field that he founded) and cognitive ethology.

Dr. Ristau received her PhD in Psychology from the University of Pennsylvania and then held a Post-Doctoral Fellowship in the Animal Behavior Group at The Rockefeller University, where she continued to be affiliated for many years. Before retiring, her other professional affiliations were primarily with Barnard College of Columbia University. She is currently an Associate of the Columbia University Seminars. Her undergraduate physics studies promote her continuing interest in the subject and in the ideas presented in this volume.

Among her writings in these areas are: "Language in the Great Apes: A Critical Review" (with D. Robbins), *Advances in the Study of Behaviour* (1982), 12:141-255; "Aspects of the Cognitive Ethology of an Injury-feigning Bird, the Piping Plover", in C. A. Ristau (ed.). 1991, *Cognitive Ethology: The Minds of Other Animals, Essays in Honor of Donald R. Griffin* (pp. 92-103); "Cognitive Ethology, Advanced Review". *WIREs Cognitive Science* (2013), 4(5): 493-509. https://doi.org/10.1002/wcs.1239; *The Scientist Who Discovered Bat Sonar and the Minds of Animals. Donald R. Griffin: A Revolutionary* (forthcoming).

She also investigates human ethno-political conflict and cooperation, both in Africa and the USA. Relevant publications include: "The Aftermath and After the Aftermath of 9/11: Civility, Hostility and Increased Friendliness" (with P. Rozin), *Peace and Conflict: Journal of Peace Psychology* (2015), 22: 168-71.doi:10.1037/pac0000156; "Sustainable Development: The End Game is Good Governance" (with W.D. Knight), Paper #111804 presented by Ristau at Meeting of SPE, Nice, France, 15 April 2008, published in Conference Proceedings.

Dr. Ristau received her PhD in Psychology from the University of Pennsylvania, was next affiliated with The Rockefeller University for many years and then Barnard College of Columbia University. She is currently an Associate of the Columbia University Seminars.

Contact: CarolynARistau@aol.com

Index

a universal complementarity, concepts of 251
absorber theory 202-03, 209
abstract mathematical frameworks 115
Ackrill, J.L. 222
Active Observation 124
adjacent possibles 302
Advaita Vedānta 252
Aerts, D. 116, 130, 139, 154
African grey parrots 334, 340
Aharonov 27, 29
Albert, D.Z. 86, 97
Alcock, J. 337
Al-Khalili 286
American Institute of Physics 43
American Veterinary Medical Association 342
ānanda 188
Anderson, R.C. 326
animal
    advocacy groups 345
    communication 334-35
    consciousness 13
    cruelty 313
    domestication, evolutionary history of 342
    mind 311-12
    well-being 311, 343
Animal Assisted Intervention International 342
Annus Mirabilus 296
Anschauung 171
Anscombe 62
anti-realist approach 144
apes 341
applicable Hamiltonian 204
Arden, Paul 200
Aristotelian logic of excluded middle 115
Aristotle 169, 221-22, 313
Arndt, M. 286
Asian metaphysics 210
associativity 155
Atmanspacher, H. 301
atomic-based aspects of the dynamics 54
Aumann, Robert 136
Aumann's theorem 136
Aurobindo, Sri 186, 190, 192
avian sensitivity 332
awareness is non-dual 256

Baars, B. 239
Bacciagaluppi, G. 201
Baker, L. 345

Ball, P. 320-21
Ballentine, L.E. 87
Baluška, F. 321-22
Banerji, Debashish 1
de Barros, Jose Acacio 13, 55, 61, 64, 71-72
Basieva, I. 130-31
basis problem 54
Bauer, Edmond 63, 66, 68
Bayes rule 136
Bayesian
    formula 147
    framework 148
    probability models 154
    rational agents 136
    scheme 147-48
Bayesian updating
    formula(s) 135, 150
    procedure 128
    scheme 135
Bayesianism 149
de Beauregard 27, 29
behaviour of mind 115
behaviourist movement 314
Bekoff, M. 333
Bell, J.S. 86, 182, 230-31
    inequalities 113
Bell's theorem 16, 22, 230
Bem, D. 42
    experiments 41, 43, 45
Bennett, Jonathan 317
Berg, G. 300
Bergmann, Gustav 257
Berkeley bootstrap 18-19
Berzin, A. 255
Bickhard, M.H. 189
Big Bang 21, 229
bio-cognitive science 271
biological
    beings as self-organizing systems 298
    complementarity 298, 300
        systems theory formulation of 300
biology as hierarchies 304
Birkhoff 27, 156
Bitbol, M. 183
black box 130, 320
Block, Ned 317
bluestreak cleaner wrasse 340
Bohm, David 10-11, 27, 29, 35, 55, 86, 110, 126, 165, 220, 232
    non-local hidden variable theory of 7
Bohmian
    interpretations 54
    theory 137
Bohr, N. 5, 7-9, 11, 13, 27-28, 53, 101, 121-24, 126, 128, 136-37, 140-41, 143-44, 163-73, 175-79, 184, 218, 251, 261-62, 273, 285-87, 298, 303
    model of the atom as quantum interpretations 322
Bohr's
    complementarity 278
    principles of complementarity and contextuality 140
    view of
        contextuality 130
        Heisenberg Cut 142
Bohr–Heisenberg interpretation 140

Bohr–Kant epistemology of unanalysable wholeness 146
Bohr–Kantian
Ontologies 140
view of the cognitive state 151
Boltzmann, Ludwig 4
bonobos 339, 341
Boolean
logic 131, 149
logical set-up 150
Born, Max 5-6, 8-9, 126, 136
probabilities 91
probability 198
Born rule 83-84, 91, 110, 136-37, 146-47, 150, 152, 212
for
computing probabilities 134
probability updating 144
Born's rule 71, 135
Boscovich, R. 179-80
Boulding, Kenneth 35
Boyle, Robert 3
Brahman 260, 270
Breuer, H.P. 201, 207-08
de Broglie, Louis 5-6, 27, 126
wave mechanics 137
broken wing display 338
Brownian motion 5, 295-96
Bruniquel, D. 294
Brussels group 139
Bub, J. 201
bucket brigade 203
Budapest Interpretation 86
Buddhism 23, 252-53, 260
Buddhist 255
Bueno, Otávio 66
Busemeyer, J.R. 114-15
by-product of brain activity 58

Cai, J. 286
Cambridge Declaration on Consciousness 327
Cantor, Chris 31
Capuchin monkeys 338
Carnap, Rudolf 257
Carroll, Sean 30
Cartesian
ego 104
substance dualism 104
theory of mind and body 62
Cassidy, D. 123-24, 126
Cat Paradox 197-98
category theory 252
Caves, Carlton 164
cell doctrine 292, 295
cellular
basis of consciousness 321
determinism, death of 294
uncertainty 293, 295
central mystery of physics 181
Chalmers, David 13, 108, 318, 323
Chang, Y. 240
chaos, edge of 291
Chapman conference 12
chase angle 328
Chemero, A. 239
Cheney, D.L. 334
Chernetsov, N. 332
Chevalley, C. 165

Chew, G. 18
chimpanzee(s) 334, 339-41
Christian theology 11
Christianity 222
CHSH 154
  inequality violations 154
Church 2
clairvoyance 40-41
Claremont conference 35
Claremont School of Theology 34
classical
  and quantum entanglements 113
  Boolean logic 115, 135
  conditioning 315
  description of reality 8
  dynamics 101
  entanglement 145
  entanglement-based framework 144
  Hilbert space modelling 145
  mechanics 218
    of particles 142
  optical modelling of human cognition 145, 150-51
  physics 51
    is essentially causal 121
  probability theory 131
  realism 124
Clifford algebra 155
clockwork universe 4
Cobb, J.B. 23, 33-39, 47-48
Cochran, Christopher 13, 25-27, 41-44, 48, 51, 57
cogito, ergo sum 313, 319
cognition modelling 152
cognitive
  capacity of domesticated animals 342
  conformism 13
  experiments 134
  modelling 132, 143, 146
  neuroscience 326
  scientists 55
  system 238
  tasks 240
Cognitive Ethology 312, 333
Cohen-Tannoudji, Claude 69
collaborative creation 212
collapse
  dynamics 92
  fundamental locus of 109
  mechanisms 16
  theory 206
Collapsing Wave Function 27
Collas, P. 294
Collini, E. 286
Collins, Francis 23
combinatorial properties of primate vocalizing 336
common
  knowledge theorem 136
  magpies 339
commutativity 155
Como Lectures 261
compassionate conservation 343
compatibilist God 23
complementarity 8, 113-14, 119, 125, 141-42, 152, 252, 261-62, 267, 273, 285-86, 291, 297
  frameworks 300
complementarity–contextuality
  framework 143
  idea 143

complementary nature of I-ness and That-ness 277
complex biological systems 286
complexity 252
 theory 285-86, 289-90, 294
comprehensive
 non-Boolean decision framework 129
 theory of consciousness 127
concept of
 momentum 172
 observation 177
 One 166
 Yin and Yang 210
concepts of
 a universal complementarity 251
 quantum theory 55
 symbiosis 299
confirmation wave 204
conscious experience, nature of 126
Conscious Universe 37
consciousness 61, 164, 252
 as a Fifth Force, concept of 327
 attributes of 333
 autonomous dynamics of 106
 being the collapse mechanism 29
 causes collapse 27, 36
  hypothesis 61, 63-64, 71-72
 collapses the wave function 103
 contents of 314
 correlates of 320
 framework of 264
 hard problem of 318
 higher level of 334
 idealist model of 260
 implications of quantum mechanics 12-13
 is global 242
 nature of 125, 240, 277
 phenomenological concept of 318
 phenomenon of 241
 physical correlates of 104
 potential attributes of 324
 science of 64
 states of 106
 undifferentiated 265
consciousness-collapse interpretation(s) 90, 92
consciousnesses, variety of 312
consciousness-involving interpretations 90
conservation practices 343
constitutive panpsychism 261
contextuality 113-14, 125, 141-42
 by default 130
 original concept of 130
conversation 312
Copenhagen 28, 57
 camp 140, 142
 debates 143
 dynamics 99
 epistemic interpretation 28
 label 86
 Orthodox interpretation 123
 paradigm, central feature of 139
 revolution 34
 school 130, 136
  of physicists 137
 tradition 144
 view 143

Copenhagen Interpretation 8-10, 12-13, 32, 52, 54, 83-84, 113, 124, 126, 136-38, 163, 165, 218-20, 231, 234-35, 237, 244, 257, 287-88, 312, 320, 322, 327
    and MWI, difference between 236
    of Quantum Mechanics 7
    inside-out view of 235
Copenhagen's interpretation 76
Copenhagen-style measurement-collapse interpretations 110
Copernican revolution 6
Copernicus 222
correspondence
    and complementarity principles 9
    principle 137
Corvid family 340
Cosh and Sinh expressions 134
Cosmic Mind 12, 17, 22-23, 27, 31, 34, 36-39, 45-46, 57-58
    primary reality is 58
counterintuitive characteristics of the mind 241
Cramer 27, 29, 203, 206-08, 211
Creative Interactivity 120, 267
crows 340
current quantum theory 231
Cuthbert, G.L. 294

d'Espagnat, B. 231-32
D'Inverno, M. 289
Daley, G.Q. 292, 294
Daly, Herman E. 35-36
Daoism 11
Darwin, Charles 4, 302, 313-14, 316
Dasgupta, S. 222
Davis, R.L. 294
Davson–Danielli Model 322
decision theory 150, 155
decision-making situation 116
decoherence time 79
decoherent quantum system 108
deeper consciousness 342
deep-seated problems in the philosophy of mind 163
Degasperis, A. 87
Delbruck, Max 18, 287
Democritus of Abdera 2
Dennett, Daniel 317
density matrix 132
Descartes, René 62, 313, 318-19
destructive economic impact 345
determinism 29, 294
    definition of 30
deterministic
    behaviour 10
    hidden-variable models 213
    interpretation 29
    objective
        materialism 11
        reality 5
Deutschlander, M.E. 329, 332
development of
    model taxonomic systems 325
    quantum mechanics 125
    thermodynamics 4
    wave mechanics 224

developmental systems theory 300
DeWitt, Bryce 10
Dilemma game 129
Dimensionality of Space 228
Dirac, Paul A.M. 43, 126, 136
Direct Action Theory 198, 203-04, 207, 209
    of fields 202
dolphins 339, 344
Don, Howard 121, 144
double-slit experiment 121, 138
Douglas, R.H. 328
Dourdent, H. 275
Druhl, Kai 73
dualist consciousness-collapse interpretation 103
dualities of object–subject relationships 268
duality 252
Dutch Book argument 147-48
Dyczkowski, M.S.G. 255
dynamic collapse theories 140, 154
dynamical collapse theories 147
dynamics, fundamental physical 93
Dzhafarov, E.N. 114, 130-31, 136

early senility 316
Eastern
    philosophical views 312
    thought 23, 185
Eastman, Timothy 35
Eccles, J.C. 237
Edgar, S. 18
effective evolution 221
Ehrlich, Paul 36
Ehtibar, N. Dzhafarov 115
Eigen subspace 132-33
Einstein, Albert 5-7, 9-10, 27, 126, 137, 230, 260, 263, 287-88, 296
Einstein's general relativity 20
electromagnetic
    and gravitational interactions, laws of 118
    interference 332
    wavelengths 323
elephants 339, 345
Ellsberg 115
emanation of
    duality from Fundamental Awareness 255
    non-duality 273
empirical inquiry 90
empiricism, limitations of 257
Engesser 336
enhanced orthodox interpretation 123
enlightenment 1-3
entanglement 142, 286
entanglement-like features 154
entropy 243
environmental decoherence 77
epigenetic/genetic plasticity 295
epiphenomenon 239
epistemic interpretation of quantum mechanics 164
epistemology 6, 218
    and ontology of science 114

EPR 141
  correlations 202
  Paradox 7
essential wholeness of a quantum phenomenon 176
Everett, H. 10, 27, 30, 76, 86, 110
Everettian quantum mechanics 147
Everett-style interpretation of quantum mechanics 102
evolution 164
  presupposes involution 191
  Upaniṣadic theory of 166
evolutionary development 302
existence
  fundamental quality of 293
  Upaniṣadic theory of 189
experimental process 138
experiment-induced uncertainty 294
explanatory gap 187
extant models 128

fail-safe response 336
Falkenburg, B. 174, 176
false-belief 341
  paradigm 341
FAPP 182-84
Faraday's lines of force 179
features of
  human behaviour 115
  non-Boolean logic 155
Feynman, R.P. 18, 22, 24, 127, 180, 201-03, 209-10, 220
field oscillators 203
finite dimensional Hilbert space 134
first
  digit phenomenon 218
  person experiences 254
First Law 119
five universal and logical (mathematical) statements 266
fixation of the initial state 177
Fock space 153
folklore of decoherence 201
formal
  algorithmic systems 253
  system of FAM 278
formalism 273
  of quantum mechanics 75
formula for total probability 134-35, 146, 149-51, 153-54, 156-58
Foster, Charles 333
foundational theory 291
founding
  fathers of quantum physics 286
  generations of QM 303
FR 199-200
  paradox 198-99
  paradoxes 139
van Fraassen, B.C. 170
Francis Crick Memorial Conference on Consciousness 326
Frank, Philipp 257
Frauchiger, D. 75-76, 126, 137, 139, 197-98

Freeman, W.J. 55, 241
Fresnel, Augustin 4
von Frisch, K. 316, 327
Fuchs, C.A. 27-28, 146, 164, 166-68, 275
fulfilment of rationality 2
functional analysis 336
fundamental awareness 252, 255-56, 260, 264-65, 268, 271, 273-74, 277-78
  and an emanated physical universe, relationships between 277
  axiom of quantum mechanics 226
  framework 254, 277
  locus of collapse 109
  physical dynamics 93
  quality of existence 293
fundamental awareness model (FAM) 251-52, 254, 256, 262, 264, 278
  formal system of 278
  mathematical models 256
  to consciousness, relationship of 252
future technologies 118

Gaea hypothesis 262
Galileo 3, 222
Gallup, G.G. 339
Gamez, D. 239
Gandy, R. 87
Gauger, E.M. 286
Gautam, A. 233
Geach 62
Gebser, Jean 186
Gedankenexperiment 75-76
Gelfand, S.I. 272
Gell-Mann 18
general relativity 30, 114, 116
generalized biological uncertainty 295
geomagnetic field changes 330
geometric sensitivities 335
Ghirardi, G.C. 30, 86, 110, 199
Ghose, P. 114, 116, 145, 150
Gibson, James J. 239
Gifford Lectures 33
Gilboa, A. 240
Gisin, N. 198-99, 208
global
  sensing 290
  workspace theory 240, 320
God language 39
Gödel, K. 13, 253, 255-56, 258-59, 263-64, 273
Gödel's
  incompleteness
    result 276
    theorems 251, 253, 256, 273-75, 277-78
  theorems 251-53
Godelian incompleteness 298
Gödel-unprovable statements 253
Goldstein, R. 253, 256
gorillas 339
Gould, J.L. 302, 327, 331-32
Gould, S.J.
Graham, Neil 10

Greene, B. 261
Griesser, M. 335
Griffin, D.R. 35, 312, 316, 318, 333-34, 337
Griffiths 27
Gritz, J.R. 345
groan of pain 337
Grothendieck topology 269
Grupen, C. 182
Gurdon, John 294

Hadley, R. 253
Hahn, Hans 257
Hahn-Neurath, Olga 257
Haikonen, P. 240
Hameroff, Stuart 55, 79
Hamiltonian 268
harmonic 69
Harnad, S. 318
Harris, H. 289, 292-95
Hartshorne, Charles 33-34
Hausdorff dimensions 228
Haven, Emmanuel 114-15
Hayes, B. 226
Hecht, S. 329
Hegel 254
Heidegger, Martin 317
Heil, John 62
Heinrich, Bernd 333
Heisenberg, W. 5, 7-9, 11-12, 27-28, 43, 53, 55, 57, 101, 123, 126, 136-38, 141, 143, 165, 167, 199, 278, 285-86, 292-94, 297, 302
    algebras 150
    cut 130, 138-39, 142, 219-20
Heisenberg's uncertainty relations 140
Heisenberg–von Neumann cut 301-303
heliocentric
    cosmology 3
    theories of Copernicus 3
Henry 19
Hepp, K. 286
Heraclitus 120, 125
Hermetic philosophy 3
Hermitian operator(s) 93-94, 102, 132-33, 145, 234
Hibbs, A.R. 220
hidden-variable
    interpretation 86
    theories 10, 220
hidden-variables theory 165
Higgs 21
higher order theories 320
higher-order interference 228
Hilbert space 65, 68, 113, 128, 132, 213, 252, 254
    geometry 251
    modelling 131, 145, 155
Hiley 55
Hill, T.P. 226
Hochner, B. 326
holarchy 286
    of self-organizing systems 260
homeostatic
    feedback mechanisms 289
    zones 289

Hooker, C.A. 165
Hore, P.J. 330
Hubel, D.H. 187, 189
human
 and animal mentation, barrier between 318
 behaviour, features of 115
 cognition 136
 consciousness, neural mechanisms of 320
 knowledge and nature, dynamics between 53
 quantum system interactions 13
 subjectivity, paradox of 186-87
human cognitive
 modelling 146
 processes 144
human–animal
 bond 342
 relations 13, 341
 relationship 311-12
humanism 1, 51
humanistic attitude towards scientific knowledge 51
Husserl, Edmund 187
Husserl's paradox of human subjectivity 163, 166

idealism 165, 252
idealist/panpsychist hypotheses 277
Idel, M. 255
incipient transaction 206
incompleteness 252, 263-64
 theorems 252, 256, 259, 264
Indian philosophy 192
infinite dimensional Hilbert space 145
information transfer and energy transfer, distinction between 202
information-theoretic understanding of symbol representation 217
injury feigning 338
innate consciousness 191
Institute for Theoretical Physics 7
Institutional Animal Care and Use Committees 342-43
instrumentally conditioned 315
integrated information theory 241, 319
 model 320
Integrated Polarity 119
integrating universal consciousness into the construction of hypotheses, challenge of 345
intellectual
 intuitions 259
 life of the Western world 222
intentional behaviours 327
intentionality 164, 166
interaction between
 matter and consciousness 243
 spin and field gradient 72
interaction Lagrangian 207
interactivity 120
interdisciplinary scientists 346
interference phenomena 142

interpretation(s) of quantum
mechanics 28, 32, 52, 57, 83, 86-88, 92
physics 52
interspecies relationship 342
intervening variables 314
intrinsic non-unitarity of quantum theory 201
intuition 171
in mathematics 259
inverse quantum zeno effect 69
invocations of irreversible amplification effects 177
involution 164
irreversibility of measurements 176, 179
Isherwood, C. 255
Ishii, Y. 296
Islam 222
Ismael, J. 91
isomorphism 272
Itano, W.M. 87

Jaeger, G. 220
James, William 11, 55
Jantsch, E. 262
Jeffery, G. 328
Conditioning 148-49
jellyfish 344
Jesus 39
Johnson, G. 86
Jordan, Pascual 136
Josephson, P. 121, 144
Jung, Carl Gustav 11
Kabbalah 252
Kabbalist 255
Kafatos, Menas C. 1, 13, 16, 27-28, 31, 37-38, 46-48, 55, 57, 123-24, 126-27, 154, 219, 231, 243, 253-56, 259-62, 264-65, 267-68, 271, 273, 277-78, 289, 297-300
Kahneman, Daniel 115
Kaiser, D. 19
Kak, S. 13, 124, 126-27, 219, 221-22, 228-29, 232-33, 239-40, 243, 267
Kaṇāda 222, 224
Kano, F. 341
Kant, Immanuel 140, 164, 170-71, 174, 178, 254, 260
Kant's theory of science 173
Kantian acknowledgment of human inability to know the thing-in-itself 8
Kaplan, G. 335
Kashmir Śaivism 253, 264
Kastner, R. 13, 27, 29, 198-99, 204, 206-08, 210-11, 220
Kastrup, B. 254
Kato, G. 13, 126-27, 255, 268-69, 271-72, 275, 278
Kauffman, Stuart 290, 302
Keeton, Hank 35
Kepler 3
Khrennikov, A. 114, 129-31
Kierkegaard, Søren 11
Kim, Y.H. 268
Kirchhoff, M. 300
Klein, A.C. 255

Klein, S.A. 13, 19, 25-27, 40-44, 48, 57
knowledge as science 1
Koch, C. 239, 286, 319-20
Kochen–Specker-type contradictions 75
Koestler, A. 260, 304
Kohda, M. 340
Kohen, A. 286
Köhler, Wolfgang 340
Kolmogorov
  measure theory 131, 155
  measure-theoretic approach 157
Kolmogorovian measure theory 115
Kraft, Viktor 257
Krause, D.S. 292-93
Kremnizer, K. 109
Kremnizer–Ranchin approach 109
Kurakin, A. 294

Ladyman, James 76
Laplace, Pierre-Simon 4
Laschi, C. 326
Lave, Lester B. 128
Law of Complementarity 274
Lawrence Berkeley Lab 18-19
laws of
  electromagnetic and gravitational interactions 118
  Nature 34, 118
  physics 64, 287
  quantum mechanics 24, 118
Lee, H. 286
Lettvin, J.Y. 325
Leucippus 2
Levine, J. 187
Lewin, Roger 291
Lewontin, Richard 293
Libet, B. 235
Lie brackets 145
Liebniz, Gottfried Wilhelm 3
life on Earth, history of 31
life-or-death situations 342
light, corpuscular theory of 4
limitations of empiricism 257
linear superposition of basis states 131
Lockean empirical substances 176
Loeffler, M. 292-94
Logical Positivism 258
Logical Positivists 256, 258
logical processes 275
London, Fritz 63, 66, 68
Lord, K.A. 342
Lovelock, J. 262, 297, 301
Low, P. 327
Löwdin, P.O. 286
Lucas, J. 252-53, 277
Luder updating rule 116
Luder's rule 146
Lurianic Kabbalah 260
Lynn, W.S. 343

macroscopic state of the matter 69

magnetic
compass information 330
field 329
magnitude of three-path interference 227
Malafouris, L. 300
mammalian sensitivity to UV 329
man, quantum conception of 51
Manin, Yu. O. 272
Manser, M.B. 335-36
many
aspects of referential meaning 337
worlds interpretation 10, 71, 86, 218, 234-35
Many Worlds 31, 54
Marchildon, L. 210
Margulis, Lynn 297, 299, 301, 321
Markov blankets 300
Marler, P. 334
Marr, David 187
Martin, E. 211-12
Marxist critique 165
Masgrau, L. 286
material engagement theory 300
materialist doctrine 54
mathematical formalism(s) 251, 254-55, 264-65, 273
of FAM 278
mathematical
incompleteness theorems 13
logic 275
property of quantum mechanics 102
techniques of classical polarization optics 146
theories 231
mathematical–logical
expression of fundamental aspects of existence 275
framework of quantum-like modelling 129
matter and consciousness, interaction between 243
Maudlin, T. 210
Maxwell's demon 276
McFadden, J. 286
McKaughan, D.J. 287
McQueen, K.J. 13, 93, 108
measurement problem 84, 86, 286, 291
measurement-collapse
dynamics 110
of quantum mechanics 89
interpretation(s) 84, 86-88, 90, 92-93, 96-97, 109-10
process 99
view(s) 95, 104
meerkats 335
Meier, C.A. 288
mental causality 61
mere philosophy 52
Mermin, N.D. 10, 12, 164, 166, 168-69, 177-78
Mesle, C.R. 33-35, 38-39, 48
message–meaning analysis 335-36
metaphysical distancing 275
metaphysics 253, 257, 259
methods for assessing thought experiments 276
von Meyenn, K. 288
microbiome 299

Millikan, Ruth 317
mind being non-physical 66
mind–body dualism 100, 103-04, 106-07, 110
mindful universe 51
mind-independent external reality 168
mind-like ontic existence 116
mind–matter
- interaction 61, 75
- model 72
- problem 55-56
- QZE interaction hypothesis 74

minority interpretations 25
mirror self-recognition 339-40
mirror test 339
Misner, C.W. 181
Misra, B. 87, 236
Misra–Sudarshan paradox 87-88
mnemonic morphism 272, 275
model taxonomic systems, development of 325
modelling 125
modern quantum theory 143
Mohrhoff, Ulrich 13
Mohrhoff, V. 173
molecular motors 296
momentum, concept of 172
monadic individual ego 2
monkey's vocalization function 334
Montemayor, Carlos 61, 71-72
Moore, W. 224, 236
de Morgan Laws 131
morphism 271
Morrison, S.J. 292
Mouritsen, H. 330-32
MRI machine 293
multiple interpretations of quantum mechanics 25
multispecies justice 343
Munn, C. 338
mysteries of quantum mechanics and consciousness 15
mystical hypotheses 184
mysticism 252-53

Nadeau, R. 16, 123, 126, 219, 231, 271, 297, 299-300
Nakazato, H. 87
Namiki, M. 87
Narasimhan, A. 37, 126-27, 254, 264, 267, 268, 271, 301
Nash equilibrium 129
Nassikas, A.A. 299
natural philosophy 4, 52
naturalistic property dualism 104
nature
- as Cosmic Mind 19
- laws of 34, 118

nature of
- conscious experience 126
- consciousness 125, 240, 277
- quanta 120
- universe 126

Nazification of academic life in Austria 258
Nelson 27
neoclassical economics 128
neocortex 72

von Neumann 8-9, 13, 28-29, 44-45, 53, 57, 62, 66-68, 71, 84, 92, 123, 126, 137, 156, 199, 206, 212, 218-19, 239, 286, 299, 302
  cut 219
  updating rule 116
Neumann–Leuder type operators 150
neural
  activity, dynamics of 319
  correlate(s) of consciousness 219, 316, 320
  mechanisms of human consciousness 320
  oscillators 74
    freedom of 78
Neurath, Otto 257
neuroanatomical
  basis 332
  considerations 324
  systems, variety of 324
neurophysiological substrates of conscious states 327
neuropil oscillators 79
New Caledonian crows 337
new theory of quantum physics 33
Newcomb–Benford law 225
newer theories of physics 236
Newton, Sir Isaac 2-4, 169, 257
Newtonian 125
  framework 139
  mechanics 287
Newtonian world view 55-56, 58
  objective basis of 140
  of classical physics 56
Nielsen, Kristian Hvidtfelt 10
nine
  classes of substances 223
  columns of different aspects of QM 25
Nishimura, K. 271-72
Nobel
  lecture 180
  Prize 8, 30, 292
  prizes 294
no-go theorem 75-76
non-Boolean
  features of behaviour 145
  framework 155
  human mind 154
  logic 131-32 148, 155-56
  logical perspectives 155
non-canonical morphism 272
non-dual
  awareness 260
  consciousness 11
  fundamental awareness 251, 254, 256, 262, 264, 268, 277
  Vedānta 253
non-duality 252, 260
non-Euclidean geometries 288
non-Hermitian operators 154
non-human psyche 318
non-interfering quasi-classical alternatives 108
non-Kolmogorovian QDT 156
non-linear
  Schrödinger type equations 154
  versions of QM 154
non-local
  consciousness 46
  correlations between entangled subsystems 203

hidden variable theory of David Bohm 7
non-obligatory rules 200
non-relativistic particle mechanics 142
non-revisionary interpretation of quantum mechanics 84, 110
nonsense orientations 330
non-unilateral theory 203
non-unitarity subject 200
non-unitary reduction of the wave function 231
non-zero probability 70
Nurgalieva, N. 199, 276

Oas, Gary 61, 64, 71-72
object of sensible intuition 178
objectification 170
objective
 basis of Newtonian world view 140
 character of atomic phenomena 168
 divide between observer–observed 130
 physical processes 178
objectivity of science 178
object-oriented language of classical discourse 173
objects of
 sensible intuition 173
 sensory experience 188
object–subject relationship 120
observation
 concept of 177
 notion of 177
observer causes collapse hypothesis 13
Observer Role 27
observer-centred reality 218
occult alchemy 3
offer wave (OW) 204
Old Quantum Theory 5
One, concept of 166
ontological
 baggage 71
 indeterminacy 5
 universe 270
ontology 6
orangutans 339, 341
orchestrated reduction model 79
order
 effects 155
 information 336
origin of
 awareness 241
 non-classical aspects of reality 245
original concept of contextuality 130
orthodox interpretation 51-52, 137
 of quantum mechanics 53, 137
orthodox view of quantum mechanics 12
Other Minds 318
out of body experience 40
Oyama, Susan 300

Packard, Norman 291
Page, C.C. 286

pain, groan of 337
panpsychism 239
paradox of human subjectivity 187
paradoxes of QM 276
Parama Śiva 260
paranormal (psychic) phenomena 15
Pareto optimal 129
Parsons, C. 256
participatory quantum universe 127
particle–wave duality 6
Pascazio, S. 87
passion at a distance 202
Passive Observation 124
Patra, S. 13, 114, 145, 150, 277
Pattee, Howard 300
Pauli, Henry 11, 27-28, 55, 57, 126, 143, 285-86, 298, 303
Pauli, Wolfgang 11-12, 53, 123, 136, 288
Pavlov, Ivan 315
peaceful coexistence between quantum theory and relativity 202
Pearle, P. 109-10
Penrose, R. 27, 31, 79, 108, 220-21, 226, 239, 252-53, 277
  hypothesis 30
perpetual motion 3
Perri, A.R. 342
Petruccioni, F. 201, 207-08
phenomenological concept of consciousness 318
phenomenon of consciousness 241
philosophical foundations of quantum physics 52
philosophy
  of the Upaniṣads 163, 166, 188
  history of 187
photon superposition plus atom 66
photosensitive cryptochromes 330
physical
  correlates of consciousness 104
  interactions, unification of 115
  phenomena, interface between 301
  reasoning 221
  substrate of consciousness 241
  theories, axiomatization of 220
  theory 243
Physical Laws 118
physicalism 239
physicists and life scientists, common language between 345
physics
  central mystery of 181
  laws of 64, 287
physiological consequences 72
Pilot wave theory of de Broglie–Bohm 147
piping plovers 338
Pitowsky, I. 169

Planck, M. 5-6, 126, 139
Plato 254
Platonic idealist perspective 253
Platonic ideals 256
Platonism 252, 256
Plotnik, J.M. 340
Plotnitsky, A. 141
Podolsky, B. 7, 230
Poincare sphere 150-51
Popescu, S. 139
Popper, K. 237
positive operator value measures 116, 148, 153, 155-57
post-Enlightenment classical view 10
post-Second World War world 9
potential attributes of consciousness 324
potentialities, world of 53
Potten 292-94
Prabhavananda, S. 254
prairie dogs 335
preadaptations 302
precognition 40, 45, 48
Premack, D. 340
pre-measurement 170
 wave function 84
present physics, eighteen wavicles of 57
primary reality is Cosmic Mind 58
Primary Reality of Nature 58
primordial mathematics 274
Princess Elisabeth of Bohemia 62
principle of
 causality 184
 complementarity 7
 correspondence 8
 identity of indiscernibles 191
 least action 220
 veiled non-locality 221, 232-33
principles of QM 133
Prior, H. 339-40
prisoner's dilemma 129
probabilistic
 dynamic of measurement 67
 dynamics 68
probability of events 120
probability wave
 collapse of 9
 function 6
probing action 138
problem of
 classical physics 225
 self-energy 209
Process God 39
Process Naturalism 39
process of
 decoherence 220
 fertilization 211
Process Theism 39, 48
Projection Postulate 199-200
protoplasmic flow 321
psi
 experiments 42
 flaws of 18
 sceptic 40
psychic phenomena 16, 40, 46, 48
 and God phenomena, connection between 35

psychokinesis 40-41
psychon 21
psychophysical response 44
psychophysics 19, 34
Pure Awareness 254
pure quantum entanglement 145
Putnam, Hilary 187
pygmy chimps 334

QBist 136, 146, 148, 151
- framework 149
- propositions 147
- stance 165

QBists 152, 166, 169-70
QBIT states 131
Quach, J.A. 228
qualia/subjectivity 16
quanta, nature of 120
quantitative indeterministic law 208
quantum 286
- behaviour 8
- biology 286
- brain 116
  - hypothesis 150
- collapse 61, 206
- computation 78-79
- computing algorithms 244
- conception of man 51, 55
- decision theory 113
- effects 287
- electrodynamics 198
- eraser 124
  - experiments 37
- events, basic probabilistic nature of 137
- field theory 12, 114, 116, 120, 127, 144, 152, 261
- foam 261
- formalism 267
- foundations 129
- games 113, 136
- Gödelian hunch 275
- indeterminacy 9
- information theory 130
- integrated information 109
- interference effects 90
- interpretation 54-55
  - for physicists and philosophers 54
- interpretations of reality 13
- logic 156
- measurement 71, 198
  - theory 265
- mechanical
  - equations 120
  - formalism 175
  - outcome 41
- non-locality 267
- object(s) 7, 180
- phenomena 118, 123
- possibility 198
- potentialities 53
- principles 101
- probabilistic
  - description 205
  - framework 132
- probabilities of subatomic particles 5
- probability theory (QPT) 131, 133
  - features of 131
- probability wave 8
- processes, evolution of 245
- reality 122, 125, 217
  - symbolic logic of 13

revolution 11
rules 157
statistics 181
superposition of photons 65
superpositions 100
system 217, 269
systems, evolution of 67
tunnelling 286
uncertainty and complementarity 10
universe 152, 261
views of non-classical reality 116
zeno model 69
Quantum Age 197-98
quantum basis
consciousness 311-12
for consciousness 322
Quantum Bayesianism (QBism) of Fuchs 12-13, 76, 113, 144, 146-47, 163-66, 174, 186
FTP 149
quantum mechanics (QM) 5-7, 10-11, 16-21, 22, 25, 30-32, 34, 42-44, 46-47, 54, 59, 63-64, 75, 84, 88, 90, 93, 101, 107, 110, 114-16, 118, 120-21, 123-25, 127-29, 131, 138, 140, 142-44, 147, 151-52, 154, 163-64, 166, 169-70, 174, 179-80, 218, 238, 244, 254-55, 258, 260, 265, 276, 278, 285-86, 293, 302, 312, 327, 329
and
classical realms, boundary between 286
consciousness, links between 114
consciousness, mysteries of 15
complementarity 287
consciousness implications of 12-13
consequences of 11
development of 125
foundational 288
concepts of 10
thinkers of 291
founders 288, 303
founders of 53, 126
founding generations of 303
fundamental axiom of 226
humanistic dialogues on the implications of 52
implications of 51, 289
interpretation 58
interpretation(s) of 28, 32, 52, 57, 83, 86-88, 92
laws of 24, 118
mathematical property of 102
measurement-collapse dynamics of 89
multiple interpretations of 25
non-linear versions of 154
non-revisionary interpretation of 84, 110
occult ideas of 25
of particles 142
orthodox 44, 138, 153
interpretation of 53, 137
view of 12
paradoxes 275
paradoxes of 276
principles of 133
stochasticity of 297
unique interpretation of 36
wave/particle complementarity 263
wavicles, seven types of 20
quantum physics 5, 9-10, 12, 62, 101, 114, 136, 140, 155

founding fathers of 286
fundamental aspects of 269
interpretation of 52, 55
new theory of 33
philosophical foundations of 52
Quantum Retrocausation III Conference 43
quantum theory 7, 113, 128, 139, 154-55, 172, 174-75, 197-98, 200-202, 232, 271
alternative formulation of 203
and relativity, peaceful coexistence between 202
concepts of 55
evolution in 231
quantum wave
function 107
mechanics 6
quantum Zeno effect (QZE) 61, 64, 70, 75, 78, 83-84, 86-87, 95, 236, 241
quantum-Bayesian 148
quantum–classical
distinction 101
divide 101, 139
dualism 101, 106
quantum-like 116, 125, 128
cognitive modellings 135
descriptions 152
framework 155
modelling 114-16, 129, 135-36, 139, 145, 154
mathematical–logical framework of 129
paradigm 114
models 146, 155
paradigm 152-53
processes in biology 13
qualities in biology 285
reality 127, 153
quantum-mechanical
formalism 175, 177
systems 84
quantum-theory framework 114
quasi-classical
oscillator 69
process 107
property 93

Raatikainen, P. 253
Radacovic, Theodor 257
radical pluralization 2
radioactivity 5
Rāmānujan 264, 267
and Śaivite philosophies 277
Ranchin, A. 109
random
effects 121
number generator 41
rational
ego (cogito) 1
omniscience of material knowledge 2
science 3
ravens 340
real quantum theory 199
reality
constructions of 231
is veiled 232
Reber, A.S. 321-22
receptacles of consciousness 312
receptive mechanisms 328

recursion 119, 267, 277
reductivism 303
relationship
  between the Subject and Object 267
  of FAM to consciousness 252
relationships between
  Fundamental Awareness and an emanated physical universe 277
  variables find laws and make predictions 238
Relativistic Transactional Interpretation 212
relativity and complexity theory 254
Renaissance 3, 120
Renner, R. 75-76, 126, 137, 139, 197-98, 276
representational theory of mind 341
res cogitans 62
res extensa 62
Rescorla, Robert 315
retrocausal phenomena 42
retrocausation 43
  mystery of 44
Return of Realism 9
Richie, D.M. 189
Ridley, M. 302
Rimini, A. 30, 199
del Rio, L. 199
Ristau, C.A. 13, 312, 316, 321, 324-26, 333-39
Ritz, T. 286, 330
Robb, David 62
Robbins, D. 334
Roll-Hansen, N. 287
Romanes, G.J. 314
Rosen, N. 7, 230
Rovelli 27-28, 143
Russell, B. 33, 257-58

Sagan, D. 299
Śaivism 252, 260, 267
Śaivist 255
Śaivite intuitions 264
Sambridge, M. 226
Santiago-Avila, F.J. 343
scalar wave function property 109
Schack, R. 12, 164
Schatten, G. 212
Schlick, Moritz 257-58
Schlosshauer, Maximilian 71-73, 77
Scholem, G. 255
Schopenhauer 254, 260
Schrödinger, E. 5-6, 11, 13, 67, 126, 137, 163-64, 166, 181-83, 185-86, 197-99, 224, 242, 278, 285-87, 298, 303
  dynamics 97
  equation 6, 83-84, 87, 110, 204, 244, 268
  evolution 87, 95-96, 98, 101-03
Schrödinger's
  cat 76, 206, 301
  equation 68, 71
  evolution, linearity of 68
  quantum evolution 69
  wave function evolution 143

Schrödinger-like equation 68
Schrödinger-type equation 65
Schubert, Horst 272
Schulten, K. 330
Schwartz, R.H. 55, 294
science
    and spirituality, bridge between 56
    as Cubism 164
    history and philosophy of 55
    of consciousness 64
science–religion dialogue 25
scientific
    knowledge, historical revolutions of 52
    materialism 259
scope of formal logic 251
Scully, Marlan O. 73
sea turtle 344
Searle, John 317
Second Law of Thermodynamics 4, 119-20
self-awareness 319, 339
self-determining force 191
self-organization 286, 297
    levels of 261
    novel modes of 290
self-organizing
    biological systems 286
    biomolecules 296
self-perpetuating 289
self-referential paradoxes 130
sensitivity to electromagnetic waves, broad range of 328
sentience, lower levels of 333
seven types of QM wavicles 20
Sevoca, M.S. 344
Seyfarth, R.M. 334
Shamanic and monotheistic mystical cultures 253
Shanahan, M. 240
Shear, J. 253
Shi, Y. 294
Shimony 202
shrikes 338
Shwartz, B. 182
sigma algebra 155
Signorelli, C.M. 320
Simon, J.C. 301
Sims, N. 253
Sinha, A. 227
Sinha, V. 226
Sivasundaram, Sujeevan 10
Skinner, B.F. 314-15
Slobodchikoff, C.N. 335
slow-moving offer wave 210
Smith, W.J. 335
Smolin, Lee 140
snake alarm call 335
Socratic statements 116
solipsistic philosophical attitude 313
some quantum-like approaches to human cognition, contrast between 147
Sorkin parameter 227-28
Sornette, D. 114-15
Sorokin, A. 121, 144
space–time 37, 261, 268, 270
    description of electron 143

66
-matter, categories
emporal structure of
ian sensory experience
175, 188
special relativity 139
Speck, G.B. 318, 333
speech recognition 320
van Speybroeck, L. 288
spin and field gradient, interaction between 72
Spinoza 254, 260
spontaneous-collapse interpretations 86
Squire, L.R. 242
Stadler, F. 257
standard
formulation of quantum theory 197
measurement-collapse dynamics 84, 94
model 261, 323
of atomic physics 322
set theoretic formulation 128
standard quantum field theory 202
consistency problems of 210
standard quantum
framework 154
mechanics 23
physical set-ups 134
Stapp, H. 11-13, 15-18, 22-23, 27-29, 31-33, 35-38, 40-44, 46-48, 51-57, 61, 64, 66, 69, 71-74, 76, 104, 106, 124, 136-37, 233, 299, 301
Stapp's
hypothesis 74
model 77-79
consequences of 72
states of consciousness 106
Stern-Gerlach
apparatus 72
experiments 172
stimulus–response connections 324
stochasticity of QM 297
Stöltzner, M. 220
strategic behaviours 337
Strauss, Eric 13
string theory 261
strong continuous measurement 95
structural organization and complexity of neural networks 319
structures of consciousness 163
Struhsaker, Thomas 334
Struppa, Daniele C. 1, 271, 282
study of animal behaviour and animal mind 322
Styer, D.F. 164
subject and object
cognizance 185
cut between 219
dichotomy between 186
relationship between 267
subjective
aspects of consciousness 15, 28, 38
interpretation of probability 146
self 274

subjective–objective relationship 266
subjectivity, mystery of 47
subject–object
 duality 264
 identity 268
 relationship 252
 separation, evolution of 264
substance, dust of 2
subtleties of quantum physics 57
Sudarshan, E.C.G. 87, 236
Sudbery, A. 199
superposition 108, 291
 of space–time structure 108
 principle 131
superposition-resistant observables 109
 property 109
superpositions of the quantum variables 231
sure thing principle 128
Sutherland 27, 29
Sykes, N. 342
symbiosis, concepts of 299
symbolic logic of quantum reality 13
systems theory formulation of biological complementarity 300

Tait, W. 253
tanagers 338
Taoism 253
Tausk, D.V. 199
Tegmark, Max 79, 121, 140, 286
telepathy 40
Templeton Prize 23
temporal topos 252, 268
tensor calculus 288
Thalmann, O. 342
Thalos, M. 95
Theise, N.D. 13, 55, 126-27, 252-56, 259, 260-62, 265, 278
theological foundation(s) of
 Church 3
 modernity as a mode of knowing 1
theories of
 animal magnetoreception 329
 everything 115
theory of
 a microbial mind 321
 consciousness 105, 259
 decoherence 54
 evolution 4
 mind 125, 340
 Umwelt 317
 uncertainty 7
 wave mechanics 5
thermodynamics, development of 4
Third Law 120, 125
three fundamental Laws 120
three-body problem 225
three-dimensionality 228
three-slit variant 225
three-way
 behaviour 228
 representation 228
time-symmetric aspect 29
Titchener, Edward 314
Tonomura, A. 232

Tononi, G. 89, 241, 319-20
totalitarian regimes 290
Townsend, S.W. 336
tradition of the hermetic philosophers 119
 ecosystem services 343
 quantum theory 200
transactional interpretation 199, 204-05, 220
 of John G. Cramer and Ruth Krartner 12
transcendental
 agency 4
 clockmaker 2
transition from the quantum to the classical world 233
transmogrification of calculational tools 179
trans-oceanic acoustic communication of humpback whales 346
triadic Śaivism 253
triggered-collapse interpretations 92
Trismegistus, Hermes 119
Tsirelson bound 139
Turin, L. 286
Turing, Alan 87
 machine 239
two-body problem 225
two-dimensional Hilbert space 67
two-slit experiment of quantum theory 225

Uebel, T. 257-58
von Uexküll, Jakob 317
Ulfbeck, O. 184
Ultimate Object 185, 191
Ultimate Subject 185, 191
ultrasonic acoustic frequencies 324
Umerez, J. 300
Umwelt 324, 327, 337
uncertainty 285-86, 291
 principle 5, 7-8, 137, 269
unconventional aspects of quantum mechanics 22
understanding consciousness, framework for 277
unification of physical interactions 115
unified microbiome 301
unique
 causal agent 183
 interpretation of QM 36
unitary
 and deterministic evolution 71
 evolution of Schrödinger's equation 66
unitary-only 200
 dynamics 200
 quantum paradigm 199
universal
 awareness 256
 complementarity 252, 278
 consciousness 37, 255, 271, 311-12, 322-23, 333
 knowledge 1
 totality 2
universality 119
universality of

quantum
mechanics 76
theory 130
universe
evolution of 229
nature of 126
Upaniṣadic theory of
evolution 166
existence 189
Upaniṣads 164, 185, 191-92
philosophy of 163, 166, 188
vacuum-to-vacuum transition 207

Vaiśeṣikasūtra 222
variables find laws and make predictions, relationships between 238
variety of
consciousnesses 312
neuroanatomical systems 324
Vaxjo 136
approach 150
FTP 149
interpretation of FTP 156
Vedānta 224, 260, 264
Vedāntic thought 11
veiled non-locality 234
versatility of animal communication 318
vertebrates' sociality 326
vervet monkeys 334
Vienna Circle 256-58
Vitiello, Giuseppe 55
Vrba, E.S. 302
de Waal, Frans 333
Wallace, A.R. 313
Wang, Y. 294
Wangyal, T. 255
Watanabe 27, 29
wave
functions 302
mechanics, development of 224
theory 4
of matter 5
wave function 95, 121, 219, 233, 236, 286
collapse of 12, 65-66, 69, 78, 138, 302-03
collapse(s) 70-71, 84
dynamics 97
ontology 143
property 100, 107-08
Weber, T. 30, 199
Weir, A.A.S. 337
Weisskopf, Victor S. 9
Weissman, I.L. 292
von Weizsäcker, Carl Friedrich 167
Wells, M.J. 326
Wesley, D. 209
Western
gorilla 334
philosophy 254, 277
science, history of 222
thought 210
world, intellectual life of 222
whales 344
Wheeler, B.C. 55, 57, 126, 138, 202-03, 209-10, 221, 275, 338

Wheeler, John A. 12, 43, 121, 127
Wheeler–Feynman
  DAT model 208
  theory 208, 209
which-path information 73
Whitehead, A.N. 32-35, 47, 55, 254, 257-59
Wiesel 187
Wigner, E.P. 9, 13, 29, 61, 63-64, 66, 71, 75-79, 86, 90, 126, 130, 136, 197, 232-33, 276, 299
Wigner's friend 61, 198
  paradoxes 206
  Redux 74
  thought experiment 75
  type paradoxes 139
Wigner's thought experiment 76
Wigner-friend-type argument 65
window on animal minds 334
Winkler, R. 345
Wittgenstein, L. 258
Woodruff, G. 340
Wundt, Wilhelm 314

Xie, H. 294

Yamanaka, Shinya 294
Yanagida, Toshio 296
Yang 211-12
Yin 211
Yin and Yang
  concept of 210
  duality of 210
Yin/Yang direct action model of fields 212
Yin–Yang diagram of Daoism 11
Young, Thomas 4
Yukalov, V. 114-15

Zalta, Edward N. 201
Zastrow, M. 344
Zeh, H.D. 27, 30, 55, 231-32
Zeki, S. 219
Zeno 86
  dilemma 84, 93-94, 98, 102, 104-05, 107, 110
  effect 87-88, 99-103, 106
  phenomenon 87
  problem 96, 104-07, 109-10
Zeno's paradox for quantum theory 87
zero prior trap 135
Zuberbühler, K. 336-37
Zurek, W.H. 218, 220-21, 236, 238